Clear Blogging

How People Blogging Are Changing the World and How You Can Join Them

■ ■ ■

Bob Walsh

Apress®

Clear Blogging: How People Blogging Are Changing the World and How You Can Join Them

Copyright © 2007 by Bob Walsh

ISBN-13 (pbk): 978-1-59059-691-3

ISBN-10 (pbk): 1-59059-691-9

Printed and bound in the United States of America 9 8 7 6 5 4 3 2 1

Lead Editor: Jonathan Hassell
Technical Reviewer: Thomas Rushton
Editorial Board: Steve Anglin, Ewan Buckingham, Gary Cornell, Jason Gilmore, Jonathan Gennick, Jonathan Hassell, James Huddleston, Chris Mills, Matthew Moodie, Dominic Shakeshaft, Jim Sumser, Matt Wade
Project Manager: Tracy Brown Collins
Copy Edit Manager: Nicole Flores
Copy Editor: Marilyn Smith
Assistant Production Director: Kari Brooks-Copony
Production Editor: Laura Esterman
Compositor: Susan Glinert
Proofreader: Elizabeth Berry
Indexer: John Collin
Cover Designer: Kurt Krames
Manufacturing Director: Tom Debolski

Distributed to the book trade worldwide by Springer-Verlag New York, Inc., 233 Spring Street, 6th Floor, New York, NY 10013. Phone 1-800-SPRINGER, fax 201-348-4505, e-mail orders-ny@springer-sbm.com, or visit http://www.springeronline.com.

For information on translations, please contact Apress directly at 2560 Ninth Street, Suite 219, Berkeley, CA 94710. Phone 510-549-5930, fax 510-549-5939, e-mail info@apress.com, or visit http://www.apress.com.

This book is for John and June Rossi for their support and love these many years, and for Linda Sinclair—you are greatly missed by all who knew you.

Contents at a Glance

PART 4 ■■■ Blogging Toward the Future

Contents

PART 1 ■■■ Revolution in Progress: Please Make Noise!

PART 2 ■■■ Building Your Blog

PART 3 ■■■ Secrets of Influential Bloggers

PART 4 ■■■ Blogging Toward the Future

Foreword

The moment comes at different times for a new blogger, but it is unforgettable. After posting a fleeting thought, curious insight, personal theory, or random rant on your blog, you go off to attend to regular business for a few hours. Then, returning to your email box, you start to see tens, sometimes hundreds, of messages. Your heart starts to pound as you see your daily reader statistics shoot through the roof, and read comments about your post from bloggers around the world.

In this quiet, exhilarating, and scary moment, you realize that people are listening to you, and they care about what you have to say. Whether blogging for personal or professional reasons, discovering your voice is a liberating and revolutionary feeling. For so many people who feel stifled, not heard, taken for granted, or disrespected, the feeling of creative outlet is invigorating. Finally, there is a vehicle for saying the things that need to be said.

Most people are changed by this experience and become thoroughly immersed in the world of blogging. The pursuit of new ideas, creative partners, and reader contact consumes many hours of the day. Most bloggers care profoundly about what their readers think, and always strive to create fresh, useful, and insightful information. Doing so can be a big challenge and can take up more time than is healthy or reasonable, if you are not careful.

For wannabe or new bloggers, *Clear Blogging* offers an efficient, easy-to-understand, and compelling overview of what blogging is and how you can quickly jump in and participate. For more seasoned bloggers, it offers multiple ways to more efficiently plan, research, write, connect, and promote the ideas contained in your blog. When I started Escape from Cubicle Nation a little over a year ago, I had never even read another blog, and I set up most of it in a wildly inefficient way. As I read Bob's multiple technical tips and tricks for blogging more efficiently and effectively, I only wished that I had this information a year ago! It would have saved me a lot of grief. The multiple case studies and interviews highlight what I have found by tripping all over the blogosphere: There is much wisdom in the everyday insights of men and women around the world. You just have to know the right places to find them.

The act of blogging changes your status from passive observer to active participant and expert witness. While the medium is still relatively new, the potential for your personal and professional growth through writing about what you deeply care about is without limits.

Those like Bob who we deem "experts" on blogging hold that distinction because they have dove in, contributed the best of their minds to developing the medium, and actively participated in shaping conversations.

You, too, have something important to contribute and people eager to hear what you have to say.

What are you waiting for?

Pamela Slim
Author, Escape from Cubicle Nation Blog and Podcast
www.escapefromcubiclenation.com

About the Author

■BOB WALSH has been a contract software developer in the San Francisco Bay Area for the past 23 years, specializing in desktop information systems. His company, Safari Software, Inc., has for the past decade amazingly focused on the same thing, albeit at a higher hourly rate.

In 2005, Safari Software, Inc., joined the ranks of micro self-funded software companies, with the release of MasterList Professional. Bob quickly discovered he knew squat about all the nonprogramming aspects of being a micro-ISV. He did interviews and research, and then wrote *Micro-ISV: From Vision to Reality* (Apress, 2006), so he would know what to do right with his next software product, ActionTasks (http://actiontasks.com).

Bob started his first blog, ToDoOrElse (http://ToDoOrElse.com), in October 2004 and was quickly hooked by the sheer fun, ease, and reach of blogging. His second blog, My Micro-ISV (www.mymicroisv.com), is a must-read for programmers who want to strike out on their own. His third blog, Clear Blogging (http://clearblogging.com) continues where this book leaves off, and focuses on ways to improve blogging and ways blogging is improving this world.

Before joining the ranks of the computer industry, Bob was a reporter for several news organizations, most worth bragging about being United Press International (UPI).

About the Technical Reviewer

THOMAS RUSHTON has been programming since his first computer, a Sinclair ZX80. He has since progressed through creating complex workflow and document management systems for financial and legal organizations, and now works as IT Technical Development Manager for a UK-based law firm. He has a BSc in Computer Science from Durham University, and spent some research time in the field of software quality, before moving into the more financially rewarding IT career roles of programmer, DBA, and consultant.

When not slaving away over a hot keyboard, he enjoys spending time with his wife, Sarah, their young son, William, and his double bass.

Acknowledgments

A lot of people gave freely of their time to answer nosy questions from this author, including, but certainly not limited to: Alvin Toffler, Seth Godin, Darren Rowse, Andy Wibbels, Cameron Reilly, David Copperfield, Dharmesh Shah, Eric Mack, Eric Marcoullier, Fabrice Florin, Gary Walten, Guy Kawasaki, Hiten Shah, Jane Anderson, Julie Vieira, Maeve Salla, Marshall Kirkpatrick, Meg Hourihan, Mike Magee, Pamela Slim, Patrick Galvin, Rajesh Setty, Neil Scheibe, Steve Rubel, Toby Bloomberg, Tom Foremski, Tom Reynolds, David Sifry, Ian Landsman, Kurt Opsahl, Nick Wilson, Josh McAdams, Amber MacArthur, Brina Kinser, Chad Coleman, George Westby, Andrew Anker, Lori Anderson, Mary Anne Walker, Michelle Tampoya, Christopher Parr, Don Dodge, Aniruddha Malpani, Eric Stutzman, Gretchen Ledgard, Zoe Goldring, Itzy Sabo, Kevin Pho, Michael E. Duffy, Nicholas Genes, Zane Safrit, Brian and Cambria Rollo, Richard Edelman, Nicola Hewitt, Sharla Oliveri, B.L. Ochman, Elan Nahari, Steve Olechowski, Shuna Fish Lydon, David Lebovitz, Alder Yarrow, and Blake Rhodes.

Next, the Apress people are first-rate all the way. Thanks again to Apress editorial director Dominic Shakeshaft, my editor Jonathan Hassell, and project manager Tracy Brown Collins for your help, support, and ever-professional guidance.

Hats off, too, to Marilyn Smith, copy editor extraordinaire, who kept her cool as she unmangled my manuscript, and Laura Esterman, who managed the alchemy of turning Word docs into correctly formatted PDF files and kept the compositor happy.

And a big, big thanks to Thomas Rushton, my technical reviewer, who made sure of each and every URL and whose comments in the margins would crack me up when things got too dull.

One last person to mention at Apress: Tina Nielsen, who was ever so nice as I pestered her for Apress books to keep the programming part of my brain from wasting away.

And, of course and always, my partner in life Tina Marie Rossi, for putting up with the missed family stuff and a lot more.

Introduction

A funny thing started happening right around the start of this century: A few programmers and geeky people in general started putting on their websites a running weblog of what was happening with them, what cool thing they had just stumbled over on the Internet, and even a few pictures of their family and cats. Nothing too important, nothing too disruptive, nothing to pay attention to, right? Wrong.

Seven years later, there are nearly 60 million blogs, and something like 30 million active bloggers, with the number of blogs steadily doubling every six months or so. You see, the people formally known as the audience, consumers, and likely voters have started hearing, reading, reacting, and conversing via blogs.

Today, blogging profoundly shapes:

- What products, fashion, and music are hot and not

- Public opinion, policy, and politics

- What news is—from the evening news and the *New York Times* right down to your local newspaper

- Who knows what about the company you work for, the industry or profession you strive in, and the occupations and avocations out there

More than a few of the old rules about how people find out about what's going on in their world have gotten a massive upgrade called blogging. It's my hope and intention that this book will help you learn and master blogging for your own benefit.

Given the title of this book, I ought to make a few things clear about what this book is not. If you're wondering how your corporation can implement and deploy blogging as an efficient marketing tool, best to look elsewhere—this book is not for you. It doesn't cover how to start the next Engadget.com or Gizmoto.com tech-toy blog, or how to become the next Arianna Huffington or Michelle Malkin. And this is not your usual Apress technical, code-on-every-page book. In fact, there's exactly one line of actual code in this book for a simple reason: As millions have already found out, you don't need to be a programmer to blog, and that's good.

What I think you will get from this book is how and why you should start your own personal, business, professional, or occupational blog (or all of the above), and if you're already blogging, some of the ways you can make your blog more successful.

Who This Book Is For

Whether you are someone looking to connect in an increasingly disconnected world, you're wondering how to get ahead in your profession or in the online world, or you just want to tear up your passive-audience ticket stub and start participating in the conversations around you, this book is for you.

I had two types of readers in mind in this endeavor to nail down how to blog successfully. First, I wanted to help people who have never blogged, and because blogs have now come to their attention, they wonder if blogging has something in it for them. The short answer is yes! The long answer is in this book. You'll find out about blogging if you run a business, are building a career, do hazardous work, would like to report the news, or just want to join the online conversation about your interests.

The second audience for this book is bloggers who, for one reason or another, just haven't gotten the results they expected when they started blogging weeks or months ago. Here, you'll find a ton of advice, tips, and help from bloggers who've found their road to blogging success.

How This Book Is Structured

Here's a quick rundown of what you'll find in *Clear Blogging*. If you're absolutely new to blogging, by all means read it sequentially. If you've already started blogging, you might want to have a look at specific chapters that catch your eye, then circle back to see what other kinds of blogging are going on.

Part 1, "Revolution in Progress: Please Make Noise!" details what blogging is, why you should care, and how to get started.

Chapter 1, Why Blog?: If you think blogs don't matter, this chapter is for you. We'll talk with one of those "A-List" bloggers, Steve Rubel, about how blogging is changing, and how buzz and influence now work.

Chapter 2, Hooking into the Blogosphere: So what exactly is a blog, and how do you find blogs that you want to read and comment on? You'll find out in this chapter. We'll walk through going from what matters and interests you to finding blogs worth your time to read. You'll discover how to turn the blogosphere into your own personal information wire.

Chapter 3, Getting Started: We'll cover how to start a blog with three typical blogging services: Blogger, TypePad, and Windows Live Spaces. You'll get some idea of how to size up which of these three, or any other blogging service or software, is right for you.

Part 2, "Building Your Blog," is where we have a good, hard look at the different types of blogs out there: personal, professional, and business.

Chapter 4, What Do Good Blogs Share?: Whatever kind of blog you decide to create, good blogs have certain practices and traits in common. This chapter takes a look at these and shows you potentially career-ending mistakes to avoid. We'll also talk about your legal rights as a blogger with the man who literally wrote the book on it, at least for Americans.

Chapter 5, Building Your Personal Blog: There are blogs for the whole world, and there are blogs for just you, your family, and perhaps your friends. We'll look at two popular personal blogging systems, LiveJournal and Vox, and talk with several bloggers about the whys and wherefores of having a personal blog.

Chapter 6, Professionally Blogging, Blogging Professionally: Professional people of all sorts are finding blogging can build their reputation online and off. In this chapter, we'll talk with legal, medical, and other professionals about why they blog, what they've learned, and what they've gotten from blogging. We'll also see how one company, Microsoft, has embraced blogging. Finally, we'll take a look at an emerging new kind of job: the professional blogger.

Chapter 7, Building Your Company Blog: The smaller your company the bigger the impact can be of starting a blog. We'll talk with a variety of small business people who are using their blogs to not just even out the playing field, but to tilt it in their favor. And we'll talk with the CEO of the largest privately owned public relations firm, Richard Edelman, about why he's telling some of the most powerful corporate leaders out there that they had better start blogging.

In Part 3, "Secrets of Influential Bloggers," we'll dig down deep into the technologies, techniques, and wisdom of some extremely successful bloggers. If you are now blogging, this is the part of the book you're going to want to read page for page.

Chapter 8, Power Tools for Bloggers: Two tools bloggers want to take full advantage of are Technorati and FeedBurner. In this chapter, we'll talk with David Sifry, CEO of Technorati, and Steve Olechowski, cofounder of FeedBurner. We'll also look at how to get the most value from these two services.

Chapter 9, Successful Blogging: So how do you blog successfully? This chapter covers the mechanics of continuously finding topics for new posts, writing well, and how to make it easier for your readers to find you. We'll get some advice from people whose blogs are highly influential (Rajesh Setty, B.L. Ochman, and Seth Godin) about what makes a good post and what makes a good post great.

Chapter 10, The New Fourth Estate: Blogging is changing mainstream media in ways reporters, editors, and politicians would not have imagined a few short years ago. In this chapter, we'll talk with several reporters who have fired their newspapers and gone the blog route, and some people who are redefining just who is a reporter. We'll also look at how you can become a "citizen journalist."

Chapter 11, Adding Podcasting to Your Blog: In the same way blogs made written posts easy to do, find, and discover, blogs make it simple to create and distribute audio blogs, or podcasts. In this chapter, we'll look into what it takes to create and post a podcast, and talk with two leading podcasters about the subject.

Chapter 12, Monetizing Your Blog for Fun and Profit: While blogging, like the Internet itself, may have started out as noncommercial, that was then and this is now. If you fall somewhere between not minding a little more pocket money and wanting to make your livelihood blogging, this chapter is for you. Besides covering the ins and outs of dozens of ways of successfully monetizing your blog, we'll talk with Darren Rowse, who is making over $100,000 a year with his blogs, about how he does it.

Chapter 13, Building Readership: For public blogs, the bottom line is building readership. In this chapter, we'll cover how you measure, build, and create readership. We'll also look at a couple of ways outside the blogging box to further the reach of your blog and introduce it to even more potential readers.

In Part 4, "Blogging Toward the Future," we change direction.

Chapter 14, Blogging from the New Front Lines: Whether you're a copper in the UK, a lawman in the American Southwest, the wife of a cop in Los Angeles, a scientist in Antarctica, or a soldier in Iraq, your blog is your way of communing and communicating. Welcome to the new front lines.

Chapter 15, Welcome to Your Future: Finally, in this chapter, I haul out my crystal ball and make eight predictions about where blogging is going.

Getting Updates

This is one of the very few Apress books out there with no code, honest! But, if you're looking for updates on the ever-changing blogosphere or posts on the never-ending stream of new tools to help personal, company, and professional bloggers, please click right over to http://clearblogging.com.

Contacting the Author

Got a question or want to learn more? Please visit one (or more!) of my blogs at http://clearblogging.com, www.ToDoOrElse.com, and www.mymicroisv.com. Or you can stop by my micro-ISV website at http://safarisoftware.com. Also, feel free to drop me an email at bobw@safarisoftware.com.

PART 1

■ ■ ■

Revolution in Progress: Please Make Noise!

This part covers what you can get out of blogging, how to hook into and discover what the blogosphere is, and the basics of getting your blog up and running.

Answering the first question—what you can get out of blogging—is the fuel for the rest of this book. In the Future-Shocked world of multiple, insistent demands for your time, I want to put to you the case for spending some of your valuable time and attention on blogging. In Chapter 2, we'll take a closer look at what blogging is, and in Chapter 3 we'll zip through just how easy it is to start blogging using three popular blogging platforms.

■■■

CHAPTER 1

Why Blog?

You were probably expecting the first chapter of a book on blogging to lead with how much fun blogging can be, how easy it is to blog, a whole bunch of tips and techniques to improve your blogging, and so on. I'll get to all that and more in this book, but first I would like to deal with the issue of why blogging matters, before you decide to put this book back on the shelf.

Blogging is about power, and shifting it from them to you.

When you start tossing around words like *power,* you better get your definition right. In my big, fat, red hardcover *Merriam-Webster's Collegiate Dictionary* (*Eleventh Edition*, no less), *power* is defined right there on page 973 as "ability to act or produce an effect."

Yep, that's blogging all right.

The reason the number of people blogging keeps doubling every five months—and companies, organizations, media, churches, and, at last count, somewhere between 50 and 100 million people have started wildly blogging in less than a few years—is that blogging gives us a new way to communicate, to share, to influence, to connect, to outrage, to matter.

Blogging Now

Back in the twentieth century, the media defined the news, companies marketed their products, publishers produced books, record companies published CDs, and your job was to go along to get along and be a happy little endpoint in everyone else's power chain. If you didn't like the evening news, you could switch to a different channel with another talking head. Maybe something you paid 200 bucks for yesterday broke today—so you buy some other product. Didn't like what your "public servants" were serving you? Write a letter to the editor.

That was then. This is now.

Now, bloggers are breaking news, and reporters and editors are chasing their dust as they cover stories in politics, business, science, and entertainment. Now, if you get suckered into buying a crappy product that breaks in a week, you blog about it, and the whole world can take note. Now, if you want to know what's new in your occupation, you don't have to wait for a book to explain it—you can go directly to the people making what's new and read their blogs.

Now, blogging becomes for many the way to define, maintain, and grow their circle of (online) friends, customers, colleagues, and acquaintances. Your personal, professional, or business blog connects you to people who care about the same things you do—have the same interests, worries, and hopes—zipping right around all those twentieth century institutions, relationships, and conventions.

Back in the twentieth century, when the Internet escaped from academia and went ballistic, there was a period when people pooh-poohed search engine companies like Google as quick-passing fads, flash-in-the-pan sorts of things. Now that Google has a value five times plus that of General Motors, the model of the industrial economy success, no one is talking about search engines going away.

Now, the days of asking if blogs are going to go out of fashion and fade away are long gone. Just like search engines and the rest of the Internet, blogs are not going away. They are the new normal.

Talk, Talk

One of the easiest and truest criticisms of blogging is that it is like a broken fire hydrant of talk, talk, talk. With 57 million self-contained blogs[1] and another 80 million blogs in online communities like MySpace, Vox, and LiveJournal, it's more like 10 thousand broken fire hydrants, a hundred Niagara Falls, and a small inland sea or two. You can read yourself blind or listen yourself deaf trying to absorb a thousandth of the daily outflow of the blogosphere.

So a constant theme in this book will be ways to zero in on the one part per million of the blogosphere that you will find interesting and useful, and let the rest of the info stream go by. This is not a trivial task. Drinking from a fire hose going full bore needs to be done with some delicacy or not at all.

And, since this book is about the whys and wherefores of starting or building your own blog, you can bet I'll be covering techniques and approaches so you can be interesting, useful, and valuable to other people you care about, too.

Welcome to the Attention Economy

Another criticism of blogging is that it's just a bunch of people showing off to get attention. True! You'll find people shouting, screaming, and writing the most absurd nonsense you've ever read to get your attention. In fact, add in audio blogging (podcasts) and now video blogging, and you can wander into various corners of the blogosphere where the inmates not only rule the asylum, they positively revel in it.

Of course, for every nutcase out to save the world from aliens through the power of positive tinfoil hats, and every blog about all the utterly unexciting (to you) things that Fluffy the Cat did, you're a click away from hundreds of bloggers who can teach you more than a few tricks of your trade, entertain you with their great prose, and help you learn things you really want to know.

There are some very substantial, very serious people blogging, from Ray Ozzie, Chief Technical Officer at Microsoft and heir apparent to Bill Gates, to the Honorable Judge Richard Posner, United States Court of Appeals, to Donald Trump (see Figure 1-1).

---

1. This statistic is as of October 1, 2006, according to David Sifry, CEO of Technorati, a company that, among other things, tracks the number of blogs started and active (www.sifry.com/alerts). A general note about the "how big is the blogosphere" numbers in this book: These statistics may seem to vary because different chapters were written at different times. One key number to consider: 55 percent of the people who start a blog are blogging three months later.

Figure 1-1. *Even The Donald is blogging.*

Why are the rich and famous, the powerful and influential, blogging? Because they, like all bloggers, want your attention. Blogging is all about attention, and attention is the coin of the blogging realm.

In a world with 6.5 billion people, and something like 1 billion people online, attention is a very valuable resource. Through blogs, these things are possible:

- You can find out what people you respect are paying attention to (and maybe you're not).

- You can pay attention to people through commenting on what they post and by linking to their posts.

- You can gain attention for your favorite products, passions, politicians, causes, and beliefs.

- You can define who you are online, making it easy for other people with the same interests, passions, and concerns to connect to you.

- You can bring attention to the things that make up your world—whether they are good, bad, or truly heartbreaking.

For instance, Renee, the wife of a Los Angeles Police Department officer, started her blog, LAPD Wife (www.lapdwife.com/) as a way of reaching out to help and be helped by the spouses of cops who must endure that life (see Figure 1-2). In an email message, Renee wrote:

The singularities of life married to a veteran LAPD narcotics police officer are very unique—and I was craving community and friendship with others who understood and could empathize.

What stood out to me is how amazing it is that wives of officers from around the nation—and even in other countries—have so many similar issues that concern us in our lives. Guns in the house, keeping our children protected from idiotic police stereotypes, worrying about our husbands when they are overdue from work, feelings of being left out from their "world" at work, etc. I started out writing this mainly for LAPD wives. Turns out I'm writing for all law enforcement wives out there.

Ed Davis Memorial

The family of Ed Davis, the legendary former Chief of the Los Angeles Police Department and maverick three-term Republican State Senator who died Saturday, after a brief bout with pneumonia have announced a public memorial service to celebrate his life.

The celebration of life will take place on Thursday, May 4th at 2:30 pm at the Los Angeles Police Academy in Elysian Park, 1880 N, Academy Road, Los Angeles.

In lieu of flowers, the family requests that donations be made to The Los Angeles Police Memorial Foundation, which was established to provide assistance to families of police officers who were killed in the line of duty. Checks should be made payable out to the Los Angeles Police Memorial Foundation, 1880 N. Academy Dr., Los Angeles, CA 90012

April 26, 2006 in L.A. Insight | Permalink | Comments (1) | TrackBack (0)

Ring of Fire

RECENT POSTS

Ed Davis Memorial

Ring of Fire

Married to The Badge: Police Wives Unite!

Former LAPD Chief Ed Davis, 89

Married to The Badge: Viewer Statistics

Married to the Badge: Fantasy vs. Reality

Former Chief Ed Davis Update

Married to the Badge: Family Concerns

Married to the Badge: High Priority Issues

National Dispatchers' Week

RECENT COMMENTS

ME & MY BLOG

Who Am I?

Want to be a guest writer here?

Email Me

BOOKS I'D RECOMMEND

Click here to purchase these books at Amazon.com. Select "Book Reviews" in the categories section on the left to read all about them.

How to Be the Funniest Kid in the Whole Wide World (or Just in Your Class)

Everyday Italian: 125 Simple and Delicious Recipes

I Love a Cop: What Police Families Need to Know

Figure 1-2. *LAPD Wife*

Renee has more to say in Chapter 14, but now, a word from our sponsors! Or, I should say, the legends of advertising, marketing, and public opinion who sell you everything from the shoes you wear to the candidates you vote for. Marketing has found blogging.

The Hidden Persuaders

"This book is an attempt to explore a strange and rather exotic new area of American life. It is about the large-scale efforts being made, often with impressive success, to channel our unthinking habits, our purchasing decisions, and our thought processes . . ." is how Vance Packard's classic *The Hidden Persuaders* began 50 years ago.

Today, Vance would be writing about how everyone from tiny one-person companies to continent-spanning corporations have taken to blogging as a way of persuading, building brand awareness, and claiming your attention for their goods and services.

A funny thing is that while some advertisers want to treat the blogosphere as a series of billboards along the side of the information superhighway, blogging is changing advertising, marketing, and public relations more than the other way around. All of the sudden, companies large and small are finding out—sometimes to their delight, often to their dismay—that the consumers are acting up and not going with the program. Blogs have become the top dog in the persuasion food chain, a very uncomfortable fact for many businesses, but not all of them.

Steve Rubel is now Senior Vice President of a division of Edelman, the largest independent global PR firm and one of the most-read bloggers in the world. Steve was kind enough to be interviewed for this book, and his thoughts on why blogs matter are definitely worth reading.

AN INTERVIEW WITH STEVE RUBEL, MICRO PERSUASION

Steve Rubel (http://www.micropersuasion.com) is one of Technorati's top 100 bloggers and a passionate believer that the Internet is fundamentally changing the role of PR professionals. As Steve puts it, conventional marketing has seen its heyday of using mass media to pound messages into the buying minds of millions. Smart companies, large and small, are hitching their wagons to *conversational marketing*—the idea that through the Internet, and especially blogging, manufacturers and producers can talk with their markets, instead of at them.

The idea that the Internet makes—indeed, requires—a new form of marketing is not new. Back in 1999, the Cluetrain Manifesto (http://en.wikipedia.org/wiki/Cluetrain_Manifesto) was published online and offline. Its central ideas have become the unofficial rallying cry for many of the most influential business bloggers.

Q. *Maybe the place to start here is focusing on the stuff that you work with so much, which is marketing, advertising, and PR. My first question would be for those not on the clue train, how would you summarize conversational marketing versus conventional marketing?*

A. Well, conventional marketing, it tends to be one way. It's communicating a message to an audience group, while conversational marketing is really engaging in a dialog with an audience, and having that be a form of marketing.

Q. *What is the big advantage of conversational marketing?*

A. The big advantage of conversational marketing is that the consumers reach their own decision under their own power. It is helping them reach their own conclusions.

Q. *Does this mean that you see that traditional, conventional marketing and advertising are sort of dying?*

A. I don't think they are necessarily dying. I think it's changing. I think that consumers now have a higher, stronger filter put on what comes their way through the media and different channels. I think that it is almost like you need to go ahead and continue to do the carpet-bombing type approach while you go in and guerrilla warfare.

Q. *Okay, but do you think conversational marketing is going to be as big a percentage of marketing, or will it always be the little one percent icing on the cake?*

A. No, I think it's big, because what is happening is that the consumers are going to trust most of what they hear from each other. Your job, as a brand, is to stimulate that conversation, so it takes place. But you can't control it.

Q. *If you are a press relations professional, either that is your title or one of the things you have to do to keep your business going, what should you be doing as far as conversational marketing?*

A. Well, I think it is four steps. One: you need to find where your audience lives, where they convene. Two: you have to find ways to listen to that audience actively and hear what they are saying. Three: you need to engage the audience directly in dialog, not just media. You can do that through a number of ways, one is by having your own blog. Another way is just by getting in with the people who write the blogs. The last thing you should do is empowering them to achieve things they might not be able to do on their own.

Q. *What does that mean?*

A. It's thinking about what the audience wants to do, what are their desires, and figuring out how to help them meet that. For example, the Tourism Board of Amsterdam recently took a bunch of bloggers around Amsterdam for free, for them to see the country and obviously, the goal was for them to write about it. They probably had this hidden desire to go to Amsterdam, so they empowered them to do something they might not be able to do on their own.

Q. *Time for the crystal ball. What do you think you're going to see, when you look at the Fortune 500s and blogging in three years?*

A. I think we will see half of them blogging.

Q. *Up from about two percent right now?*

A. That's right.

Q. *What's going to drive that? That's a fairly major change in behavior there.*

A. I think what is going to drive that is that the consumers are going to want them to come down from the mountaintop and have a conversation with them. Not all of them are going to be willing to do it.

Q. *The ones that do will benefit, do you think?*

A. I definitely think so, if they do it right.

Q. *How about the rest of the pyramid, economically, in other words, all those small companies out there? Do you think it's going to be a mandatory thing, to have a blog, if you're going to have web presence?*

A. No, I don't think it's going to be a mandatory thing, but I think it's going to be something that will help them if they do it. They have to have somebody who is going to invest time in it and do it right.

Q. *Let's say three, four, five years from now, do you think you will see the job title of blogger at all sorts of different companies, or do you really see that as what people are doing right now?*

A. No, I think this is going to evolve into something else, which I don't have the answers for right now. But, as it does, that's what it will be. I try not to focus just on blogging. There is a bigger trend here and that is that consumers want to share. They want to find each other online and communicate. Then they are going to use whatever tools that are available to them to do that.

Q. *Including blogging, but also the other social networking things?*

A. Including blogging. Podcasting is another one, social tagging—all of that is just going to evolve.

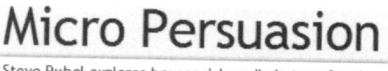

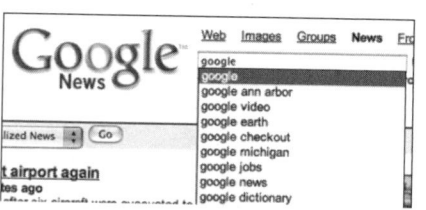

Steve Rubel explores how social media is transforming marketing, media and public relations.

« Fortune 500s Adopt Blogs Faster than Small Growing Companies | Main | The Digg Effect Analyzed »

FRIDAY, JULY 14, 2006

Trendspotting with Google Suggest for Google News

One of my favorite marketing/PR tools is one that really wasn't created for this purpose. It's Google Suggest for Google News. This special version of Google News, which launched earlier this year, brings back the most common search queries related to yours. You can really learn a lot about how people think about news by seeing how they search. Consider the following examples...

Figure 1 - Google's move into Ann Arbor is attracting more visit than the newly launched Google Checkout

Blogs and Businesses

By the way, if you're thinking that blogs and your business or company have zero in common, you might want to take a look at what mainline corporate pillar General Motors is up to with its blogs, starting at `http://fastlane.gmblogs.com`. There, you'll find Serious People like GM's number 2 Bob Lunz blogging. And he is not channeling marketing hype or well-crafted corporate messages,[2] but blogging about what he thinks and feels, and his reaction to the blogs he reads.

Now, it's no surprise that Bob has a lot of favorable things to say about GM and its cars. What is surprising is that he is actually listening and responding to real people who have posted negative comments about their experiences with some aspect of GM. People who run multinational corporations do not have public conversations with the public, or at least they didn't used to.

Maybe Bob Lunz and GM are too large and remote for you to relate to. And GM is the exception to the corporate rule. As of October 5, 2006, only 8.0 percent of the Fortune 500 had blogs,[3] for a total of about 40. Who else is blogging?

Well, there's Ian Landsman for one. Ian's software company UserScape is what I call a micro-ISV (independent software vendor), a one-to-five person, self-funded software company. For every large company out there, there are thousands and thousands of these tiny companies that have discovered that blogging is the way to connect to prospective customers.

---

2. See "How GM's Fastlane blog was born," on Debbie Weil's BlogWrite for CEOs blog (`http://blogwrite.blogs.com/blogwrite/2005/06/how_gms_fastlan.html`).
3. This statistic is from Fortune 500 Business Blogging Wiki (`www.socialtext.net/bizblogs/index.cgi`).

According to Ian:

The most unexpected aspect has been the success in blogging about the process. From the start, blogging the process to share my experience starting a company with others was part of my plan, but I had no idea it would be such a huge asset to UserScape, and the HelpSpot product.

The direct dialog with my readers has, very often, resulted in a perspective on specific features or overall design I wouldn't have considered without them. Of course, the sheer reach of the blogging community has allowed HelpSpot to capture the attention of over 200 companies, which are currently on our mailing list, as well as the over 80 organizations participating in the beta.

That was back in 2005, before Ian started selling HelpSpot. Ian is using his blog to connect with his market, to get feedback on his product, and to talk about how he sees the world and his company's place in it. As you can see from Ian's blog (Figure 1-3), blogging has been good for business!

« Larkware Contest — Free HelpSpot License
HelpSpot in the Wild: Rails Machine »

9 Month Revenue Update

So it's been 9 months since HelpSpot went on sale, I can't believe it's been that long already! Totally amazing.

Below are a few charts on HelpSpot revenue, transactions, and trials. HelpSpot is far exceeding my expectations for this point. In fact in my planning budgets before I started I had right around now as the point where HelpSpot would start selling more than a few licenses a month. I'm very happy to have been so wrong!

HelpSpot

The Smarter, Easier, Web-based Helpdesk Tool.

Simply **Better** Customer Service.

Ian at UserScape.com

`XML`

`+ MY YAHOO!`

`+ newsgator`

`SUB BLOGLINES`

[   ] `Go!`

Articles - Business
 » Creating a Business Logo
 » Starting a MicroISV
 » Don't be Afraid of Contract Work
 » 4 Rules for the Practical

Figure 1-3. *Blogging is good for small businesses.*

I will be getting into much more detail about blogging for your business in Chapter 7 (and the business of blogging in Chapter 12). But make no mistake, blogging done right is very good for business.

Blogs and You

I've touched on the value blogs can bring in the business world, so what about in your personal world? One fascinating viewport into how blogging has changed people is the site Blogger Stories (www.bloggerstories.com/), as shown in Figure 1-4.

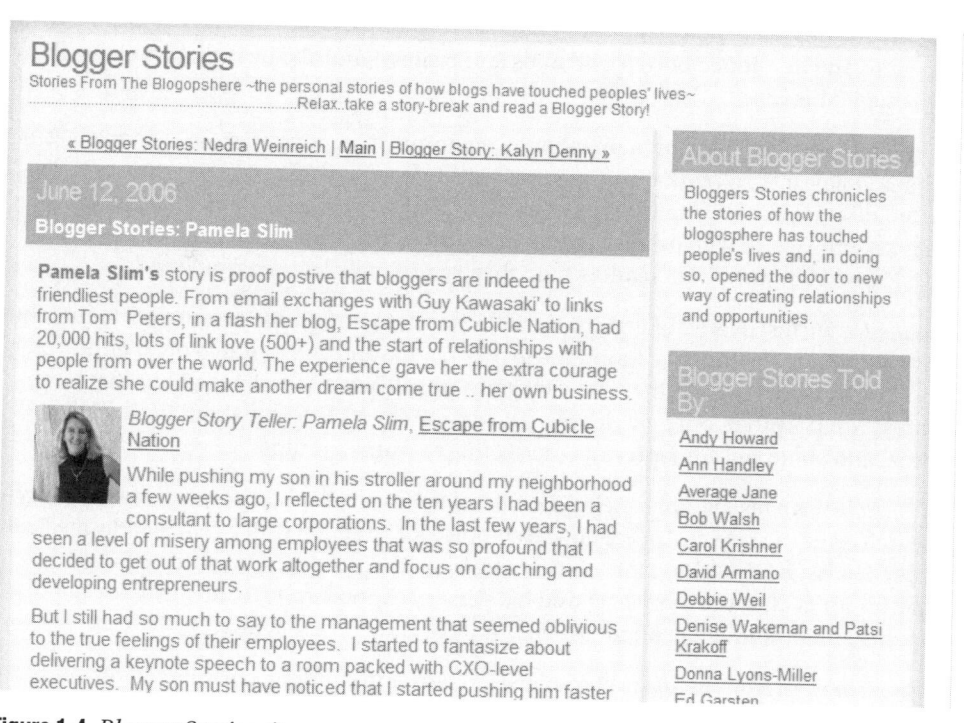

Figure 1-4. *Blogger Stories site*

As you read through these stories of how blogging has changed the lives and professions of all sorts of people in all sorts of ways, the one common theme is that blogging has the power to change how people work and live:

Pamela Slim, a corporate trainer, posted "An Open Letter to CEOs, COOs, CIOs and CFOs Across the Corporate World" on her blog Escape from Cubicle Nation (www.escapefromcubiclenation.com/) and hit a major nerve, with more than 500 fellow bloggers linking to it. "This experience has opened my eyes to the power and reach of blogs. When we speak our truth and it finds the right people, the level of exposure can be amazing," Pamela said in her Blogger Story.

Dave Armano describes himself before starting his blog, Logic + Emotion (`http://darmano.typepad.com/logic_emotion`), as "just another interactive professional minding my own business. I've got a portfolio site and blah, blah, blah. Then I launch a blog, and all of the sudden, people read my words and thoughts—and I have this new set of friends who I connect with digitally on a near daily basis. I had no idea! No idea."

Nedra Weinreich, a year ago, never expected to become a blogger. She didn't have the time, didn't want to bare her thoughts with strangers, didn't know if anyone would be interested in what she had to say about how nonprofits could and should use social marketing. After doing a guest post at a fellow professional's site, she got the bug and started her blog, Spare Change (`www.social-marketing.com/blog/`). She says, "I have found that blogging is a fantastic way to reach new people and build connections. I have met people from all over the world and developed both friendships and professional alliances that would not have happened otherwise."

Holly Buchanan has strong opinions about women and marketing at her blog, Marketing to Women Online (`http://marketingtowomenonline.typepad.com/blog/`). According to Holly, "I started this blog for two main reasons: to share my knowledge, insight, and experience in the marketing world with others, and to, in return, learn from them. I can honestly say I have learned far more from readers than they've probably learned from me."

Yvonne DiVita discovered blogging as an alternative to traditional newsletters to promote her book, and in the process, found the love of her life and collaborated on Yvonne's blog, Lip-Sticking (`www.lipsticking.com`). "By golly, people were actually reading what I was writing! Not only that, but I was learning so much about blogging, about networking online, and about my core interest—marketing to women online."

Nick Jacobs has a real day job—being the CEO of both a small urban hospital and a nonprofit research center—and a real need: how to compete for attention with a giant nearby medical center. His blog, Nick's Blog (`http://windberblog.typepad.com/nicksblog/`) is both his organizational attention equalizer and his personal opportunity to advocate his view of what healthcare should be about. As Nick puts it, "I'm having a ball."

Ed Garsten went from being a veteran news reporter to running a private for-reporters-only blog for DaimlerChrysler. His Blogger Story is one of how traditional journalism's 20-year game of diminishing musical chairs became a chance to once again get in on something new, exciting, and alive. "It took about a second to take the job. It was just like those early days at CNN when the thought of sustaining a 24-hour television news network seemed both a folly and an unmistakable opportunity. You just had to take the chance, and I've never regretted it."

What's It All About?

Blogging changes bloggers to be sure, but what about the world outside the blogosphere? Let me tell you a little story about how blogging is changing things as a way of summing up this chapter on why you should blog.

Say you want to buy a new car. Decades ago, you would have gone to your local auto row of dealerships, kicked a few tires, dodged a few salespeople, and been, as Vance Packard pointed out, unconsciously persuaded that this or that vehicle was the right one for you.

Five years ago, you would turn to the Internet, researching what the *Consumer Reports* website had to say about safety and maybe what the *Kelley Blue Book* online showed your old heap was worth in trade-in value.

Now? Well, when my partner Tina went shopping for a new car last month, she spent hours reading blog postings she had Googled, written by happy owners of Mini Coopers,[4] talking about the hundreds of things they loved and the few quibbles they had. Tina is a very practical person; normal advertising messages just bounce off her. But as you can see in Figure 1-5, blogs persuaded her in a way that twentieth century advertising never could.

Figure 1-5. *This car brought to us by blogging*

Your Action Tasks

As with each chapter of this book, the final bits of this chapter are a few steps you can take to either get your feet wet or dive right into the themes and practices presented here.

Here are your next steps in getting started:

Who do I know that's blogging? Who do you respect in your profession, your community, your world? Are they blogging and are people blogging about them? An easy way to find out is to visit `http://blogsearch.google.com/`, Google's blog-only search portal.

Join in by commenting. After you've found a blog posting you're interested in and have an opinion about, add a comment to it. Congratulations! You've joined the blogosphere, and it didn't hurt a bit.

---

4. Buying a Mini Cooper is more like joining a club than purchasing transportation. Owners wave at each other as they drive, while the rest of us sit in our SUVs and sedans, wondering what's going on.

Expand your view. Now that you've found one interesting blog worth your time to partic-ipate in, are there more? You bet. And an easy way to find other good blogs is to look at the first blog's blogroll. Most bloggers have a list off to the side of their blog of the blogs they read. This most basic form of social networking is often a good next step to take for inter-ested readers.

And you can continue your journey with these next steps:

Read Micro Persuasion. If you have anything to do with marketing, PR, or selling a product online or offline, or you want to find the best return for your attention on these matters, point your browser or RSS reader to `www.micropersuasion.com`. Steve Rubel's blog is well worth reading.

What's the biggest lie about blogging? This is the question Ann Handley at Marketing Profs (`www.mpdailyfix.com/2006/06/whats_the_biggest_lie_about_bl.html`) asked several dozen fellow marketing bloggers. She got back some interesting answers.

■ ■ ■

CHAPTER 2

Hooking into the Blogosphere

Have you ever see the old Steve McQueen science-fiction flick, *The Blob?* For the uninitiated, the blogosphere can be a lot like *The Blob*.[1] At first, people don't believe it's out there. Then a few victims—also known as early adopters—encounter it. Seemingly overnight, it's everywhere, coming through your browser when you are looking for things to buy, invading your email in the form of messages sent from people you know, absorbing all of your free and unfree time.

Okay, that was a bit of a stretch.

What this chapter is really about is profiting from the blogosphere *on your terms*. It's not that it's evil, devouring, or malevolent—quite the contrary. The problem is the blogosphere is a growing, engaging whirlwind of information and opinion, and it is much too easy to find yourself sucked in, spun around, and overwhelmed.

Whether you've never intentionally read a blog in your life or you spend five hours a day doing nothing else, this chapter will help you better manage the unmanageable, find the right blogs for you, and start being part of nifty conversations.

In this chapter, I'm going to suggest ways of exploring the world of blogs without succumbing to terminal information overload, finding bloggers you want to interact with without being rude, and gently and comfortably getting into the shallow end of the pool.

Getting Started: You Are Here

First off, there's a myth I would like to dispel. The myth is that only the top 100 blogs, the so-called A List, are worth reading. This is nonsense. Certain blogs—thanks to getting into blogging early, the diligent work of the blogger, and luck—have gained ongoing readership that rivals traditional newspapers and magazines. While one or more of the Technorati 100 most popular blogs (www.technorati.com/pop/blogs/), as shown in Figure 2-1, might interest you, they are by no means the extent of the blogosphere.

So if the blogosphere isn't the top 100 most famous blogs, what is it? I submit that the blogosphere is actually more like hundreds of thousands of online communities differentiated by interest. Some of these interests are shared by millions, but many are of interest to relatively few people scattered across the globe.

When I say hundreds of thousands of different interests, I mean just that. Name just about anything you can think of, imagine, or want to know more about, and someone (perhaps a lot of someones) is blogging about it right now.

---

1. Great movie! Check out www.imdb.com/title/tt0051418/.

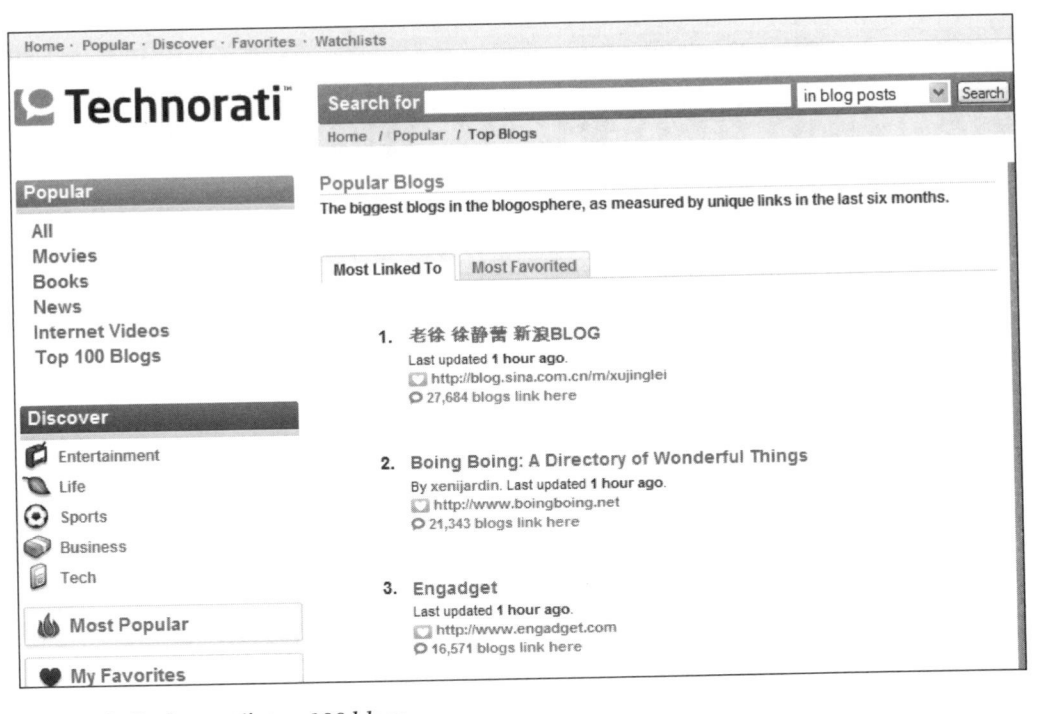

Figure 2-1. *Technorati's top 100 blogs*

Getting Ready

So before we cover all the whiz-bang ways of finding exactly what you're interested in, you need to take a moment to write down what you want to find in the blogosphere, say the top five things. Seriously, taking a moment to write these down will make all the difference between this chapter bouncing off you like a ping-pong ball and this chapter repaying the time you spend reading it many times over.

To give you an idea, here are five things that, at this particular moment, have my attention.

Interest	Why Interested	Want to Find
Dave Brubeck	A favorite jazz musician/composer	I like his music. Where do I find more of it?
iPods	I've mastered the basics, now what?	Cool things to do with my iPod. Mistakes to avoid.
Pilates	Have never tried a class at my gym on this	What would I get out of this? Is it too "soft"?
Getting Things Done	Ongoing major interest	Any new ideas out there I can use to be more productive?
Global warming	Just saw a special on this on television; how real is it and how does it affect me?	What *practical* things can I do about this?

Okay, that was my starter list of things to find in the blogosphere. You can see that I've included three fairly trivial (at least to me) topics and two more substantially (again, to me) important ones.

Now it's your turn. List anything at all you're interested in—large or small, work-related or not—whatever works for you.

Interest	Why Interested	Want to Find
1.		
2.		
3.		
4.		
5.		

Now that you have your List of Five, it's almost time to sit in front of your PC or Mac and start to find out what the blogosphere has of value for you. Try the examples in this chapter using the topics from your list of interests.

I say that you're "almost" ready because, just as keeping a travel journal is a great way of getting more enjoyment from a vacation before, during, and after you go, you could use a little something to keep track of where you visit in the blogosphere. Fortunately, the good people at Google have a tool you can use, regardless of whether you use Firefox or Internet Explorer to access the Internet. It's called Google Notebook.[2] To get this free tool, visit www.google.com/notebook, as shown in Figure 2-2.

While I will be covering other tools for cataloging and managing your relations with the blogosphere, notably Really Simple Syndication (RSS) readers, later in the chapter, Google Notebook is a free, easy, and painless way of keeping track of your blog wanderings. It surely beats adding even more bookmarks and/or favorites to your browser!

Once you've installed it, you'll see the Google Notebook icon in the bottom-right corner of your browser. Click it to open Google Notebook, as shown in Figure 2-3.

---

2. Want more information on Google Notebook before deciding if it's right for you? See www.google.com/googlenotebook/faq.html. For that matter, you might want to check out two alternatives: Surfulater at www.surfulater.com (Firefox and Internet Explorer, Windows Only, $35.00) and for just Firefox, the free ScrapBook extension at https://addons.mozilla.org/firefox/427/.

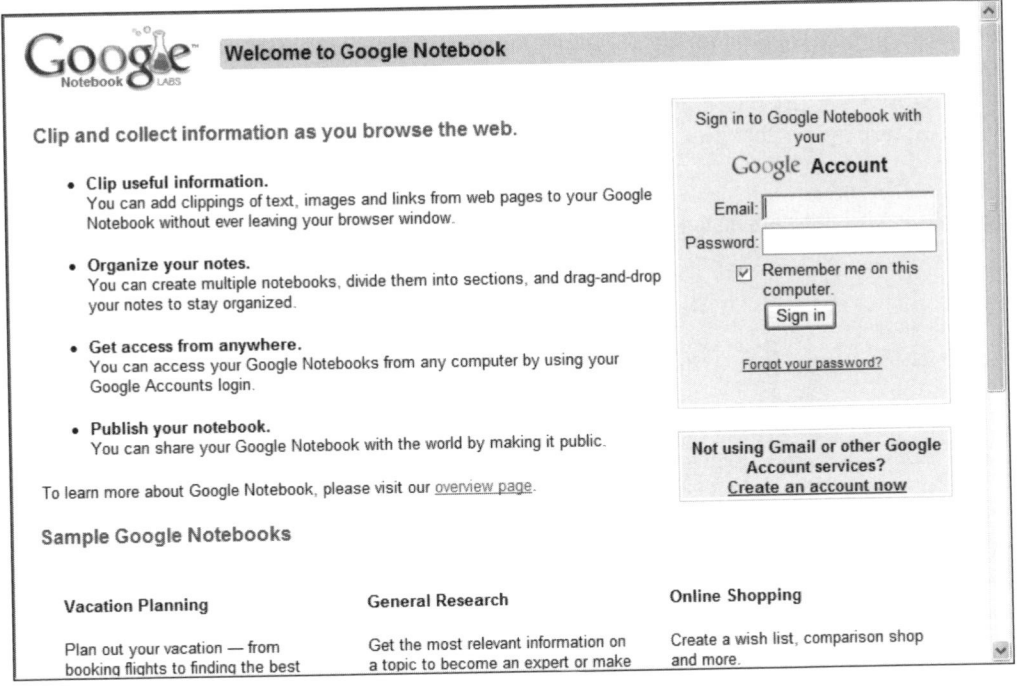

Figure 2-2. *Google Notebook signup*

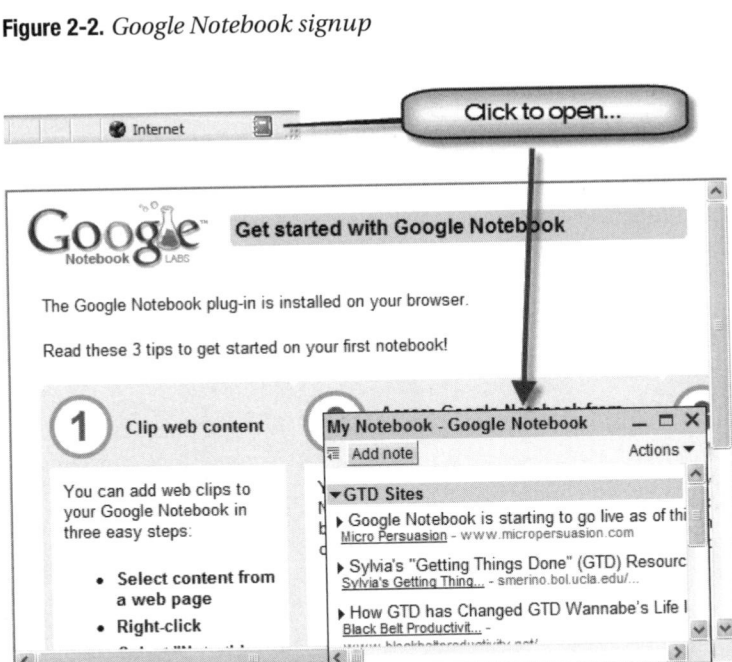

Figure 2-3. *Google Notebook lives in your browser*

As you work through the rest of this chapter using your interests from your List of Five, you can just select text and images you find, right-click, and choose Note This (Google Notebook) from your browser's pop-up menu. You can also add directly from the results of a Google search to your Google Notebook by clicking the Note This link in each found item.

All set? Let's get started connecting to the blogosphere.

Finding Your Interests in the Blogosphere

The first tool you'll use to find what interests you is the part of Google dedicated to just searching blogs. It's called Google Blog Search (Beta)[3] and located at `http://blogsearch.google.com`, as shown in Figure 2-4.

Figure 2-4. *Google Blog Search*

I'll start, for the hell of it, with **Pilates,** and since I know I don't know anything about it, I add **+beginning** to my search. Figure 2-5 shows the results.[4] Some major differences between Blog Search and Search in Google are worth noting:

- You get a lot fewer results. In this example, I got just under 20,000 results. The same search in regular Google yielded 937,000 results. *This is a good thing.* Fewer results mean a less daunting task.

- You can easily set Google's Blog Search to filter your results to see what people are saying about this as recently as within the last hour. This is also good if you decide you want to join an ongoing conversation at someone's blog, rather than just mine information.

- You can subscribe to this search somehow. We'll be covering the love fest between blogs and RSS later in this chapter, but with a click or two, you can get a constant feed of blog posts on something you're interested in, without repeatedly running the same search.

---

3. As of November 2006, Google Blog Search was still officially in beta, which in Google's case means absolutely nothing.

4. Keen observers will notice that Google Blog Search results don't have a Note This flag you can use to add them to your Google Notebook. I guess beta in this case does mean something!

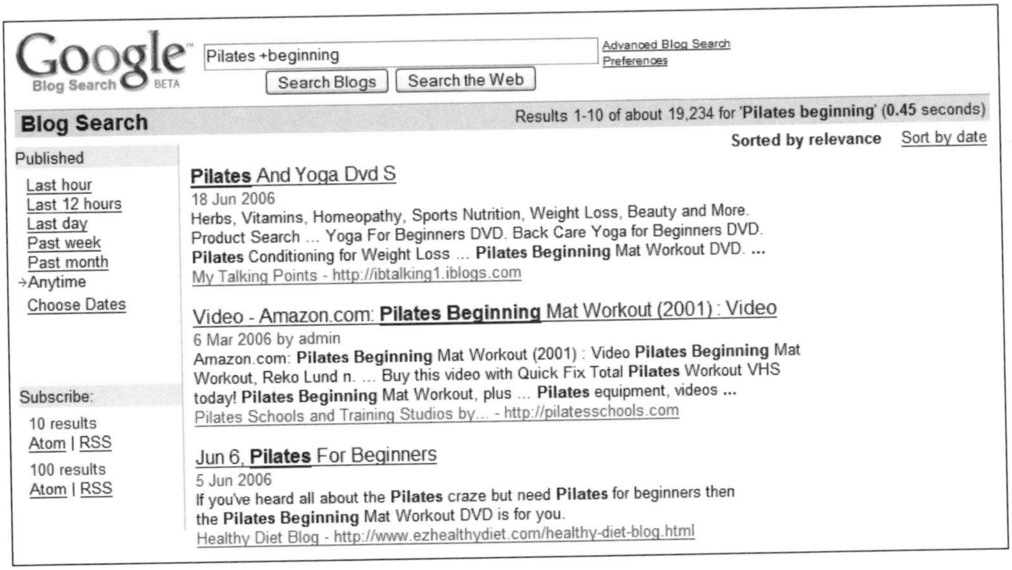

Figure 2-5. *Google Blog Search results*

Six items down, I found a blog posting entitled, "What to Expect from Pilates Method" (`http://blog.stephenholtfitness.com/274/what-to-expect-from-the-pilates-method/`), which is exactly what I wanted to know. There, I learned Pilates strengthens the abs, back, and stabilizer muscles, and improves posture and alignment. I should start feeling the difference in about ten classes. Now, how do I know any of this is true?

I don't. Neither do you.

The point I'm trying to make here is that the adage "Don't believe everything you read on the Internet" applies in spades when it comes to blogs. There's a white label warning with big, black type stuck on the side of the blogosphere:

Caution This blogosphere contains lies, falsehoods, misstatements, and utter nonsense, along with great ideas, thoughtful commentary, life-changing conversations, and insights. Use of common sense, skepticism, critical thinking, and multiple sources is strongly advised at all times.

After a few more clicks, I learn the blogger in question, Stephen Holt (`http://blog.stephenholtfitness.com/`), is a professional personal trainer in Maryland. He has made it on to the local television news, is gearing up to do a fitness book, and probably knows more than a few things about fitness. That's good enough for now.

EIGHT MORE WAYS TO FIND BLOGS

Of course, there are many more ways of finding blogs. Here are eight of my favorites:

- **The Blog Catalog** (`www.blogcatalog.com/`): One of the earliest blog directories, the Blog Catalog of submitted blogs has "only" about 30,000 blogs organized into familiar categories.

- **StumbleUpon** (`http://buzz.stumbleupon.com/blogs/`): This is the anti-search engine. StumbleUpon tosses up random web pages (including just blogs). It's often quirky and sometimes startling. You may click into an utterly cool, incredibly crappy, or just plain weird blog.

- **Sphere** (`www.sphere.com/`): Sphere has two nice features that recommend it: a clean and attractive layout and an average posts-per-blog site.

- **Blogs by Women** (`http://blogsbywomen.org`): Blogs by Women currently lists 1,657 blogs on a wide variety of subjects. Its random blog thumbnail images are an easy way to get a sense of the featured blog.

- **IceRocket** (`www.icerocket.com`): IceRocket is much like Google Blog Search, but tends to find a different variety of blogs for different terms.

- **Globe of Blogs** (`www.globeofblogs.com`): This blog directory strives to take a global rather than US-centric view toward the blogosphere.

- **BritBlog** (`www.britblog.com/directory/`): Speaking of non-US blogs, this directory for British bloggers worldwide offers about 5,500 blogs arranged in various categories.

- **The Guardian Unlimited** (`www.guardian.co.uk/weblog/special/0,10627,744914,00.html`): While search engines rule, there's still a place in this world for the discerning eye of an editor, and these blog picks tend to combine creativity with passion.

Having Your Say with Comments

Once you start finding blogs you're interested in, what's the next step? Joining the conversation with comments. Comments are what make blogs, well, blogs. All too often, would-be bloggers rush by this important idea: If you want to be a successful blogger, you need to be a successful commenter as well.

Let's take one of the other topics from my List of Five: Getting Things Done.[5] I do a search to find who has been blogging about this topic recently, hoping to pick up a pointer or two or a useful idea. I see some guy by the name of Dave Cheong has posted an entry on his blog with the title, "Time Boxing is an Effective Getting Things Done Strategy" (`www.davecheong.com/2006/07/26/time-boxing-is-an-effective-getting-things-done-strategy/`).

Now I don't know Dave, but he has gotten my attention. He is a Java programmer with an easy-to-read writing style. His post on approaching some tasks by limiting up-front how long you are going to spend on them, no matter what, sounds like a useful alternative to the more usual approach of working a task until you've finished, no matter what. Dave writes:

---

5. Getting Things Done is a productivity methodology championed by David Allen (`http://davidco.com`) in his best-selling book by the same title. It's very popular among geek/programmer types I know.

Time boxing is particularly useful as a reality check when working on open ended tasks. By limiting the time we spend on a given task, as long as it is complete though not perfect, we can objectively decide when something is done. This frees us up to work on the next task.

But how do you know which tasks should get "time boxed"? Dave mentions complex tasks and uninteresting tasks, but that's kind of vague. If we were at a party where we were talking and somehow got on this topic, I would ask him for a couple of examples, or if he had a check-list he uses to decide which tasks to time box. Instead, I add a comment to his post, as shown in Figure 2-6.[6]

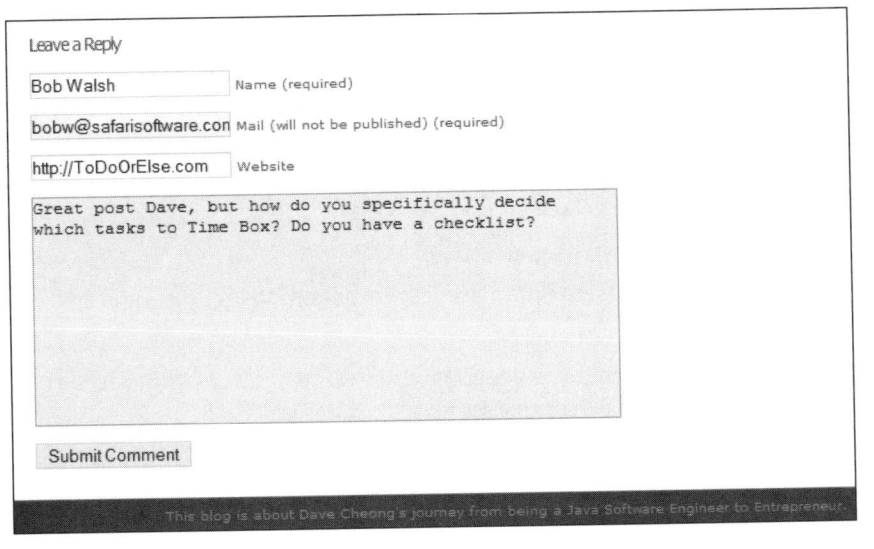

Figure 2-6. *Posting a comment on a blog*

Effectively Commenting: Do's and Don'ts

A post to a popular blog can ignite dozens, even hundreds of comments that go off in all sorts of directions and subconversations. Sometimes, they're just a way for you to say thank you to the blogger or to point out where he went completely wrong in his post. In any case, here are some common sense and best practices for adding comments:

Never spam: The difference between spam and not spam is context. If you comment about something that has nothing to do with the post, you're spamming. At the very least, you will be ignored, if not outright banned.

Be polite: Do you scream in people's faces? Do you call people names when you want to talk with them? Of course not. You may strongly disagree with someone, but if you want to post your comment on their blog, be civil.

---

6. Update: Dave did not respond to my comment directly, but that is not surprising. There were 22 comments and trackbacks to this post. Several made excellent points and added much to the conversation.

Add to, don't hijack, the conversation: Have you ever been talking to someone when a third person walks up and completely takes over the conversation? Remember how annoyed you were? Don't do that!

Include relevant links: If you've seen another blog that it makes sense to bring into the conversation, include a link in your comment by all means. This also applies to web pages or anything else you can provide a URL to reach.

Be a real person: Most blogging software these days requires a valid email address and your name. By all means, supply a real address. If you are already dealing with too much spam, get a Google or Hotmail email account and use it just for comments.

Keeping Track of Your Comments

The most frustrating part of adding comments to other people's blogs is the need to come back periodically to see if the blogger has replied to you, or for that matter, if other people have subsequently posted comments that are worth reading. It's simple enough to bookmark one blog and track it, but what about ten or a hundred?

One of the nice things about the Web is that as new problems evolve, so do solutions. More and more blogs come equipped with the ability to subscribe to an individual post's comments via RSS. This is workable, but cumbersome. Fortunately, at least three different Web 2.0 sites are designed to centralize the job of tracking your comments for you: Commentful, co.mments, and coComment. Let's take a quick look at each of these.

Commentful

Commentful (`www.commentful.com`) has the fewest features, but it's the easiest to use. You can build a watch list of up to 50 different blogs, social networking sites, or other pages. Each watched item expires in 30 days unless renewed, and gets checked for new content every ten minutes.[7]

Commentful works with the Mozilla Firefox browser via a Firefox extension you download and install. Once installed, when you get to a blog comment page you want to follow, you can right-click and choose Add to Commentful from the pop-up menu.

Commentful's claim to ease-of-use fame is a Firefox extension that shows a blinking icon when new comments have been added to a post on your watch list, saving you the bother of either checking Commentful manually or subscribing via RSS to your watch list.

Co.mments

The newest of the comment-watching web applications, co.mments is the brainchild of Assef Arkin, who created this handy free way of tracking conversations for himself in 2006. Assef wrote:

I created co.mments because I needed a better way to track comments, and no one else was doing it. I developed it for myself without any plans to charge for it.

And I plan to keep it that way. No hidden agenda.

---

7. This describes the site features as of when this chapter was written, when Commentful was still in beta.

I recently opened the co.mments API, so I no longer own your data. You can take it out and use it in other services if you want.

I'm even releasing pieces of the co.mments code as open source (check out my personal blog). I'd like other people to build more services like co.mments.

The service is free, and the data is free. And it will stay that way.

After you register for free at co.mments (`http://co.mments.com`), you can load what's known as a bookmarklet (see the "Getting More Value from Your RSS Feeds" section later in this chapter) into Microsoft Internet Explorer, Apple Safari, or Mozilla Firefox, and can track conversations in Blogger, TypePad, WordPress, Movable Type, LiveJournal, and the new kid on the block, Vox. The next time you want to track the comments to a particular post, just click co.mments bookmarklet, and you'll start tracking the conversation, as shown in Figures 2-7 and 2-8, and get email notifications or daily email digests if you like.

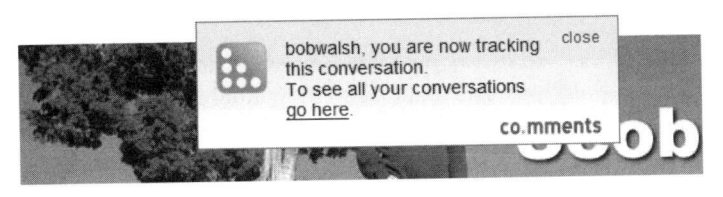

Figure 2-7. *Adding a conversation with co.mments*

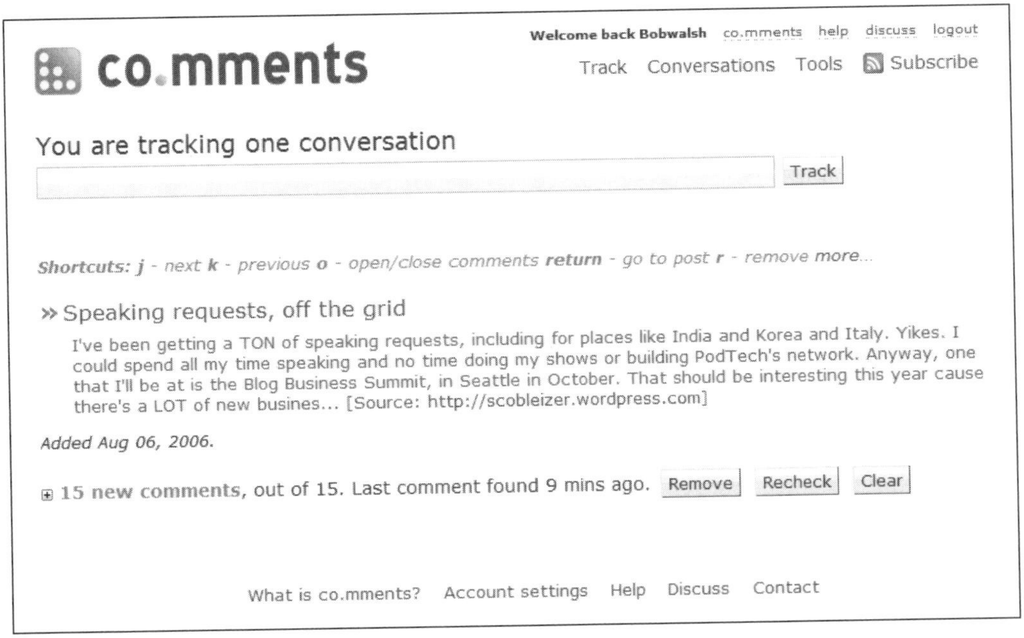

![co.mments interface screenshot]

co.mments

Welcome back Bobwalsh   co.mments   help   discuss   logout

Track   Conversations   Tools   🔊 Subscribe

You are tracking one conversation

[   ] [Track]

*Shortcuts: **j** - next **k** - previous **o** - open/close comments **return** - go to post **r** - remove more...*

» Speaking requests, off the grid

I've been getting a TON of speaking requests, including for places like India and Korea and Italy. Yikes. I could spend all my time speaking and no time doing my shows or building PodTech's network. Anyway, one that I'll be at is the Blog Business Summit, in Seattle in October. That should be interesting this year cause there's a LOT of new busines... [Source: http://scobleizer.wordpress.com]

Added Aug 06, 2006.

⊞ **15 new comments**, out of 15. Last comment found 9 mins ago. [Remove] [Recheck] [Clear]

What is co.mments?   Account settings   Help   Discuss   Contact

Figure 2-8. *Your conversations in co.mments*

One thing to note about co.mments: What you track is public and appears as you add it in the Conversations web page. This is another good way of finding conversations you want to join and track with co.mments. Just keep in mind that what you're tracking (but not who you are) appears there.

coComment

If you are looking for the absolute least amount of effort to track your blogging conversations, coComment (`www.cocomment.com`) is the Web 2.0 tool for you. Once you create a free account and download a Firefox extension, coComment has the ability to automatically watch as you comment on almost any blog or site and track that conversation for you. The beauty of this is the "automatically" part. You just post your comments, and coComment takes care of the rest.

What's more, coComment automatically adds a toolbar to most blogs you visit, letting you tag your comments, as shown in Figure 2-9. Tagging is an extremely useful way of finding and categorizing things on the Web, as you'll learn next.

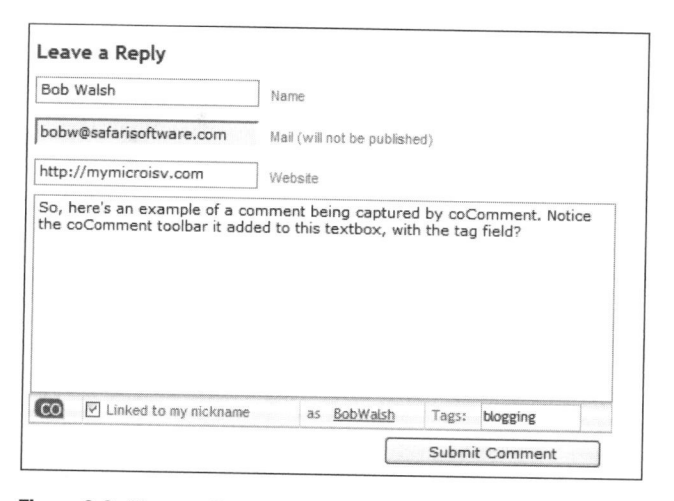

Figure 2-9. *Your coComment toolbar on their blog*

Welcome to Tagland

Once upon a time when the Web was just beginning to emerge from the halls of academia, web directories were all the rage. If you wanted to find out if anyone had created a website on, say freshwater fishing, odds were good you would be able to find it in one of the half-dozen directories out there, like AltaVista, Yahoo, or Excite.

Then the Web grew. Directories, which had morphed into portals, weren't cutting it anymore. The Web was too big, and 1,500 listings are almost as useless as none. So, about a decade ago, a couple of very bright Stanford University students figured out a cool way to better search the Web, and Google was born.

Then the Web grew some more, and web logs became blogs, and almost overnight, millions of people were blogging. Blogging is all about self expression, so why rely on some search engine to control what the world thinks your blog is about? A search function alone wasn't cutting it.

Welcome to tagland.

What Are Tags?

Tags are just that: one or a few words that bloggers use to categorize each post. You'll find them at the end or start of each post of just about every serious blogger. They may be flagged with text saying `Filed under:`, `Categories:`, `Tagged:`, or `Technorati Tags:`, but each tag will be a link, and that's where the magic lives.

Let's say you came across Steve Rubel's excellent Micro Persuasion blog at `www.micropersuasion.com` and noticed at the bottom of his latest post what you see in Figure 2-10.

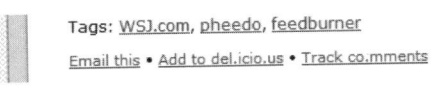

Figure 2-10. *Tags in action*

This example has six links in all. The ones along the bottom let you email the post to someone (a handy feature), add it to del.icio.us (discussed in Chapter 9), and follow comments using coComment (as described in the previous section). Above these are three tags: `WSJ.com` (*Wall Street Journal*), `pheedo` (an RSS advertising network), and `feedburner` (an indispensable service for your blog, covered in the next section). Each of these tags leads to a page at Technorati where other posts with the same tag are listed, from newest to oldest, as shown in Figure 2-11.

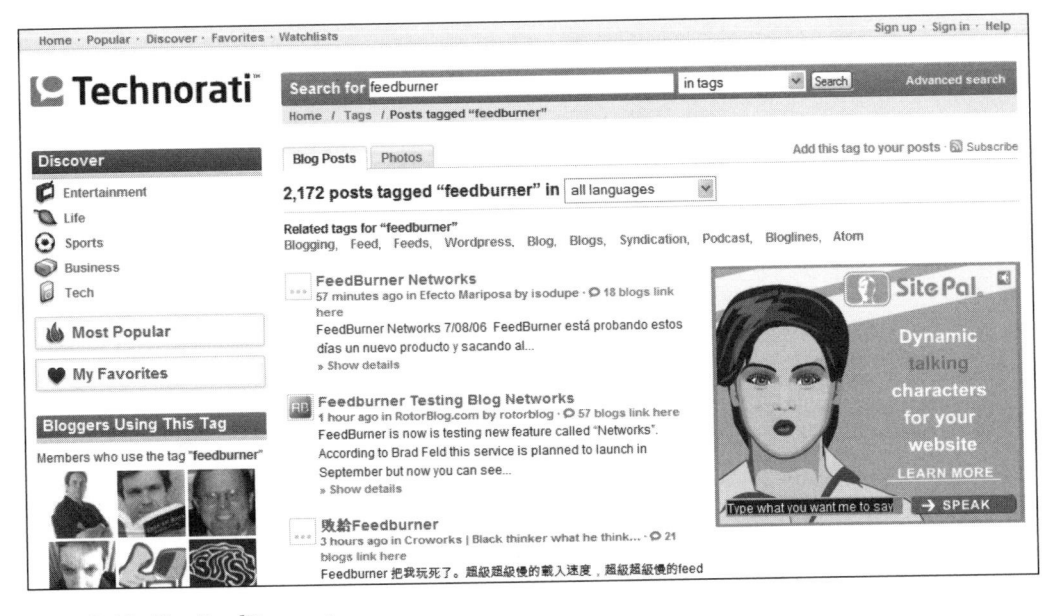

Figure 2-11. *The FeedBurner tag*

Tags are the magnets that pull together posts from all over the blogosphere that, in the opinion of the bloggers involved, should be together. Whether Technorati, WordPress, or some other tag center does the work, tags are the high road to finding what you want. Tags work not just in blogs, but also in more and more online media organizations of all sizes and stripes. In fact, tagging is such a good way of organizing information on the Web, the use of tags is spreading far and wide:

- Every single item Amazon sells or facilitates selling has a place where you and other shoppers can decide how to tag that particular product.

- Social networks, like del.icio.us, Yahoo Flickr, Facebook, and MySpace, are powered by tags. (See http://en.wikipedia.org/wiki/List_of_social_networking_websites for one list of tagging networks.)

- First adopted by tech-oriented media organizations like CNET (www.cnet.com), tagging is becoming more common as a way of organizing news.

Where Do You Find Tags?

Tags are fast becoming the glue that binds together blogging communities large and small, and coming across them as you peruse blogs is extremely helpful. But where do you find what tags have been applied? Many places keep track of tags, but the leading contender for Tag Central at this point is Technorati.

Technorati tracks, indexes, and provides search capabilities for blogs, with tagging being one of its most powerful tools for finding the blog postings you want. Technorati has been popularizing and evangelizing tagging in the blogosphere for several years now. With its recent deal with the popular blogging platform TypePad, the relatively tiny company has cemented its lead in the tag race.

Technorati currently tracks no less than 8.8 million tags. A visit to www.technorati.com/tag at any given time will show you the current hottest subjects in the blogosphere and let you search for tags of interest to you.

Going Pro with RSS

So far, you've sampled various ways to dip a toe into the blogosphere, but what happens when you start amassing more blogs than you can keep up with? You start subscribing to blogs and stop visiting them.

One of the features of blogs from nearly the first day has been their use of RSS to make it easy to subscribe to a blog. Instead of visiting the blogs you follow one by one, you subscribe to them, and postings to that blog appear in your RSS reader, whether online or on your desktop. From the latest news in a blog you and four other people read to all the news, sports, and info-tainment CNN, large and medium newspapers, and media properties now make available, RSS has become the other Big Tool for dealing with web overload.[8]

RSS is one of those "messy" computer standards, like WiFi. Several different versions exist. Some work for everything; others won't handle things like podcasts. GYM (Google, Yahoo, and Microsoft) are busy expanding, bear hugging, and innovating this protocol. But you don't need to worry about any of this.

Subscribing to an RSS Feed

Today, you can get a free RSS reader from Google (www.google.com/reader) or MyYahoo (http://my.yahoo.com/). Firefox, Internet Explorer 7, and Microsoft Outlook 2007 have built-in

---

8. The other Big Tool being search engines like Google and, umm, Google.

support for subscribing to and presenting RSS. Or you can use one of the estimated 1,900 other desktop and web-based RSS readers. All of them can handle RSS properly.

To use RSS, follow these simple steps:

1. Pick an RSS reader to try online or download (see the next section).

2. Find out how your new RSS reader adds a blog, newsfeed, or other site you want to follow.

3. Look for the orange icon shown in Figure 2-12 that is now the almost universal[9] RSS available symbol, and subscribe. (Also keep an eye out for other, older orange icons that say RSS or XML, the format of RSS and other related feed mechanisms.)

Figure 2-12. *The subscribe icon*

Picking an RSS Reader

With all of the RSS readers out there—for your PC, Mac, Linux box, or entirely on the Web, which RSS reader is right to for you? That is entirely a matter of taste. However, whichever RSS reader you decide to use should have at least these five critical features:

Clean interface: Reading your RSS reader will soon replace reading your daily newspaper. You want a clean layout that makes sense, is easy on the eyes, and makes it easy for you to get in and get out with the information you want.

Sync me up: Even if you use only one computer, you'll still find it very handy if your RSS reader has both a Web and desktop presence that automatically synchronize. If you travel, or use two or more computers, this is a must-have feature.

Command and control: Even with a good RSS reader, you can still easily find yourself overloaded with information. Your RSS feeder should have tools like filtering by keyword or tag; multiple sort options; support for headlines, extracts, or full items; and the ability to put a given subscription on hold temporarily.

Hold that thought: RSS readers are great for delivering the latest and greatest, but what if you want to hold on to an item after you've read it? Or maybe you want to pull together items from different feeds into one collection. Look for these features.

---

9. In December 2005, the Microsoft Internet Explorer team and Outlook team announced in their blogs that they were adopting the cool feed icons created by Canadian freelance designer Matt Brett (`http://mattbrett.com/archives/2005/12/the-new-standard-feed-icon/`) and first adopted by the Mozilla open source project for Firefox. This is a great example of the power one blogger can have.

The old in and out: We are still in the very early days of all this RSS stuff, and the odds are good your first tool for managing your feeds won't be your last. The Outline Processor Markup Language (OPML) format has become the format of choice for this, and your RSS reader should support it.

Being a Windows person and still doing almost all of my computing on my PC, I strongly recommend NewsGator's FeedDemon 2.0 (www.newsgator.com), as shown in Figure 2-13.

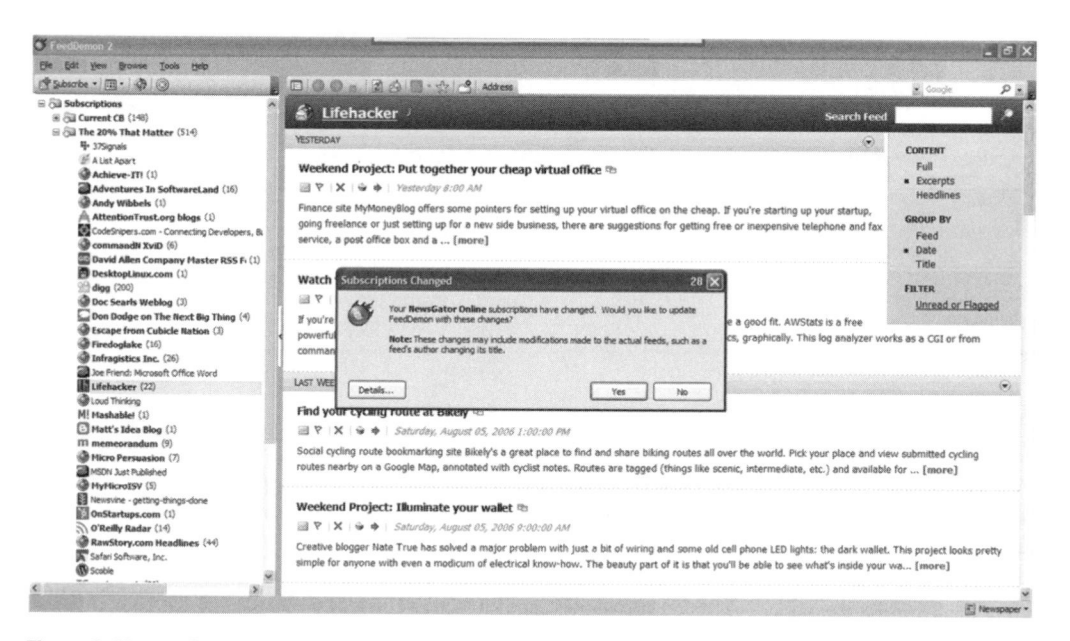

Figure 2-13. *FeedDemon 2*

Table 2-1 lists some popular RSS readers you may want to investigate.

Table 2-1. *Popular RSS Readers*

Name	Website	Type	Comments
FeedDemon	www.newsgator.com	Windows	My personal favorite because it synchronizes with NewsGator Online, which means I can add feeds with one simple command (see the next section). It has powerful filtering capabilities. And because programmer heavyweight Nick Bradbury wrote it, it absolutely refuses to crash. (Currently $29.95)
Google	www.google.com/reader	Web	If you use Gmail, you're going to really like Google free reader's interface for reading RSS feeds. It's a bit more basic than some web-based readers, but still good.

Table 2-1. *Popular RSS Readers (Continued)*

Name	Website	Type	Comments
Shrook	`www.utsire.com/shrook/`	Mac	With an interface that's a cross between Mac OS X mail and iTunes, Shrook is powerful, attractive, and free. With a free Shrook.com account, you can synchronize your feeds across several Macs.
PulpFiction	`http://freshsqueeze.com/products/pulpfiction/`	Mac	With its mail-like interface and fast search capabilities, PulpFiction is another very nice RSS reader. (Currently $25)
Pluck	`www.pluck.com`	Windows	Another popular RSS reader for PCs running Windows, Pluck has a clean and easy-to-use interface, and it's free.
Bloglines	`www.bloglines.com`	Web	Bloglines was one of the first web RSS readers, and while it has not seen much in the way of new features for a while, it still has its supporters.

Getting More Value from Your RSS Feeds

I recommend three simple ways to spend less time getting more value out of your RSS feeds: 80/20 your feeds, shortcut your bookmarklets, and track your interests with a Google Blog Search RSS feed.

80/20 Your RSS Feeds

The 80/20 idea has been around for a while: 80 percent of your sales come from 20 percent of your customers, 80 percent of your leads come from 20 percent of marketing activities, and so on. The same principle works for information: 80 percent of the value of all the RSS feeds you've accumulated comes from about 20 percent of the feeds.

Organize your feeds into two main folders or groups: the 20 percent that are really worth following, and the rest that you might sporadically scan. Figure 2-14 shows a close-up of what this looks like in FeedDemon.

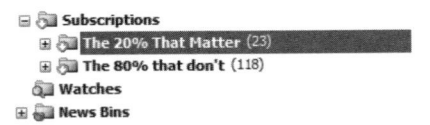

Figure 2-14. *80/20 organization: 20 percent of your feeds yield 80 percent of the good stuff*

Shortcut Your Bookmarklets (Firefox)

A poorly documented trick in Firefox will save you several steps when you come across a blog to which you want to subscribe. First, you need to be using Firefox (of course) and you need to be using an RSS service like say NewsGator that offers a *bookmarklet*, which is a tiny JavaScript program that looks like a bookmark.

Most online RSS readers and social bookmarking sites offer bookmarklets as a quickie bookmark that you add to your browser and punch whenever you want to subscribe to a blog. This billboard-sized bookmark needs to go on a diet: In Firefox, in the Properties dialog box for the bookmarklet, change the Keyword setting to a nice, short, easy-to-remember code, as shown in Figure 2-15 (I use rsn, for RSS into NewsGator).

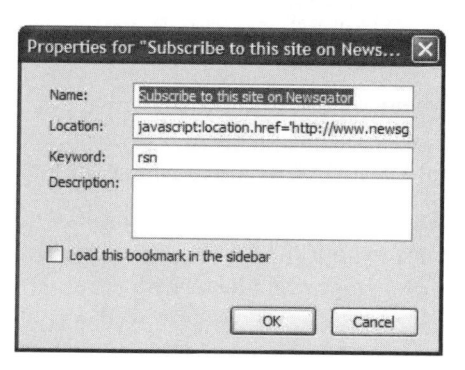

Figure 2-15. *Supercharging a bookmarklet in Firefox*

When I get to a blog I want to subscribe to, I enter rsn in the Firefox address field where I would usually type a URL, and the feed is pulled right into NewsGator, where I can organize it. The next time I start FeedDemon on my PC, the feed is there. And you can group all your bookmarklets into a folder and move it off your Bookmarks toolbar. Nice!

Track Interests with a Google Blog Search RSS Feed

One nice feature of Google Blog Search is you can turn any search into an RSS feed. Just do the search (limiting it to, say, today), then subscribe using your RSS reader of choice. This is a great way of tracking ongoing interests. Figure 2-16 shows an example where I'm subscribing after a Getting Things Done search.

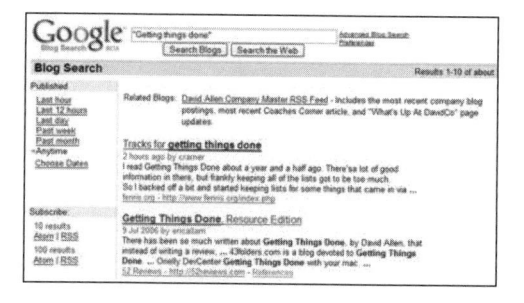

Figure 2-16. *Subscribe to a Google Blog Search*

Your Action Tasks

By now, you should be just about ready to start blogging yourself. In this chapter, you've learned about finding blogs to read, commenting on them, using tagging to find your online commonalities, and using the power of RSS.

Here are a few steps for getting started in the blogosphere:

Pick five things you're interested in. Think of five things in your life you're interested in—anything from how to get a job to great grill recipes—and punch them into Google Blog Search at `http://blogsearch.google.com`.

Accessorize. You're going to want to keep track of the blogs you find that are especially well written, so pick up Google's Notebook for Internet Explorer or Firefox at `www.google.com/notebook`, or invest some time in trying out any one of the free or trial RSS readers.

Start commenting. Every blog is an open-ended invitation to a conversation. When you read a post that's worth your time, drop the blogger at least a quick "attaboy" to encourage the blogger. Got something to say about the subject of a post? That's what comments are for!

What's your tag? As you find, read, and surf blogs, you'll start to notice certain tags get your attention time and again. To improve your ability to hone in on what you want out of blogs, visit `www.technorati.com/tag/` and see what other tags might be related.

And then you can continue with these steps:

Spring-clean your feeds. Take a good hard look at your feeds in your RSS reader of choice. How many are still pulling their weight, and how many are old, tired, and faded? Feed-weeding is a fact of online life. Make it easier on yourself by pruning your feeds at least once a month.

Collect your comments. Whether you use one of the services mentioned in this chapter or some other tool, being able to track, manage, and respond wherever you comment is a powerful tool for building a reputation as someone who matters in the blogosphere.

Work your tags. Find the handful of tags that matter most to you. These are centers of attention online. Spend the time and energy learning at Technorati and elsewhere who is paying attention to these tags on an ongoing basis, and pay attention to them.

CHAPTER 3

■ ■ ■

Getting Started

So far, we've covered why you should blog and how to plug in to the blogosphere so you can find interesting blogs. The time has come to dive right in and see what it's like to start a blog yourself.

The three blogging services I'll talk about in this chapter—Google's Blogger, Microsoft's Windows Live Spaces, and Six Apart's TypePad—currently host the bulk of the blogs out there that are not running on individually controlled servers, and definitely get the job done. Each has advantages and disadvantages that you should know about before you start investing your time and perhaps your money.

Creating a Blogger Blog

Google's Blogger does a good job of making it easy to select a good working layout for your particular blog, and a great job at letting you customize that layout to enhance, support, and brand your blog as a unique and valuable part of the blogosphere.

Blogger Blog Startup

Starting a blog at Blogger is as simple as it gets: Go to `http://blogger.com`, and, as shown in Figures 3-1 and 3-2, create an account and name your blog.

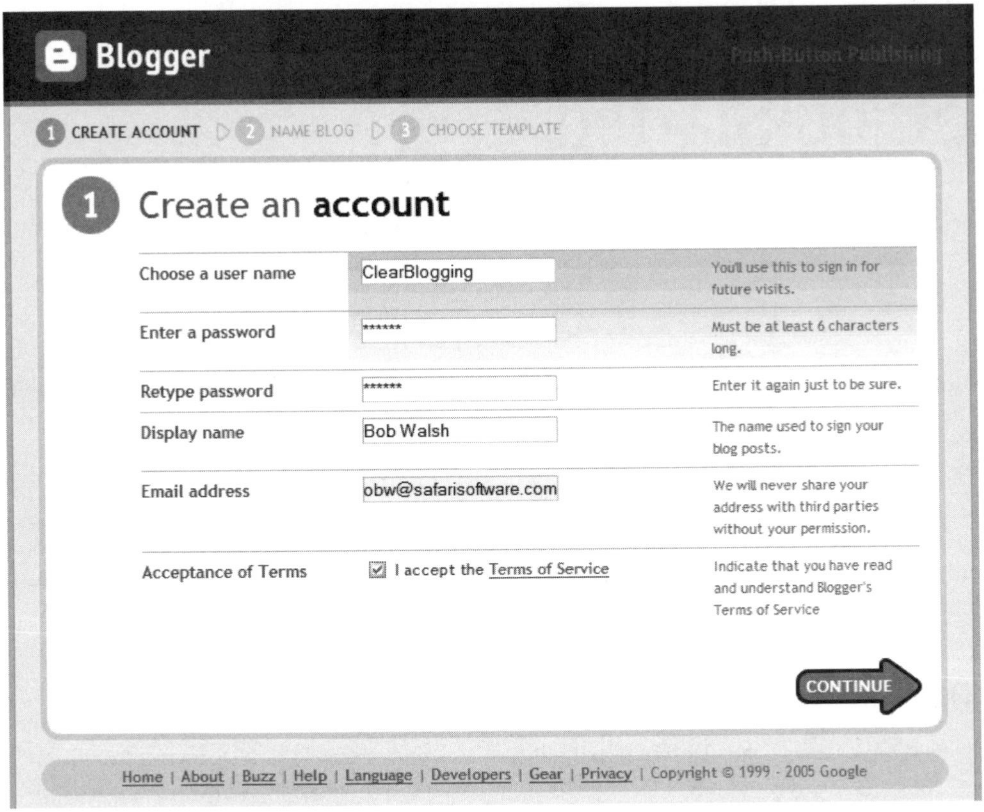

Figure 3-1. *Starting a Blogger blog*

Figure 3-2. *Setting your blog's title*

Next, pick a template for your blog, as shown in Figure 3-3. Templates are an easy way to make your blog more readable, usable, and interesting. We'll look at them in more detail in a moment.

A moment or so after you pick your initial Blogger template, you'll get a happy bit of news, as shown in Figure 3-4.

Before we get into all the other settings or start customizing your blog's template, let's take a look at some of Blogger's strengths.

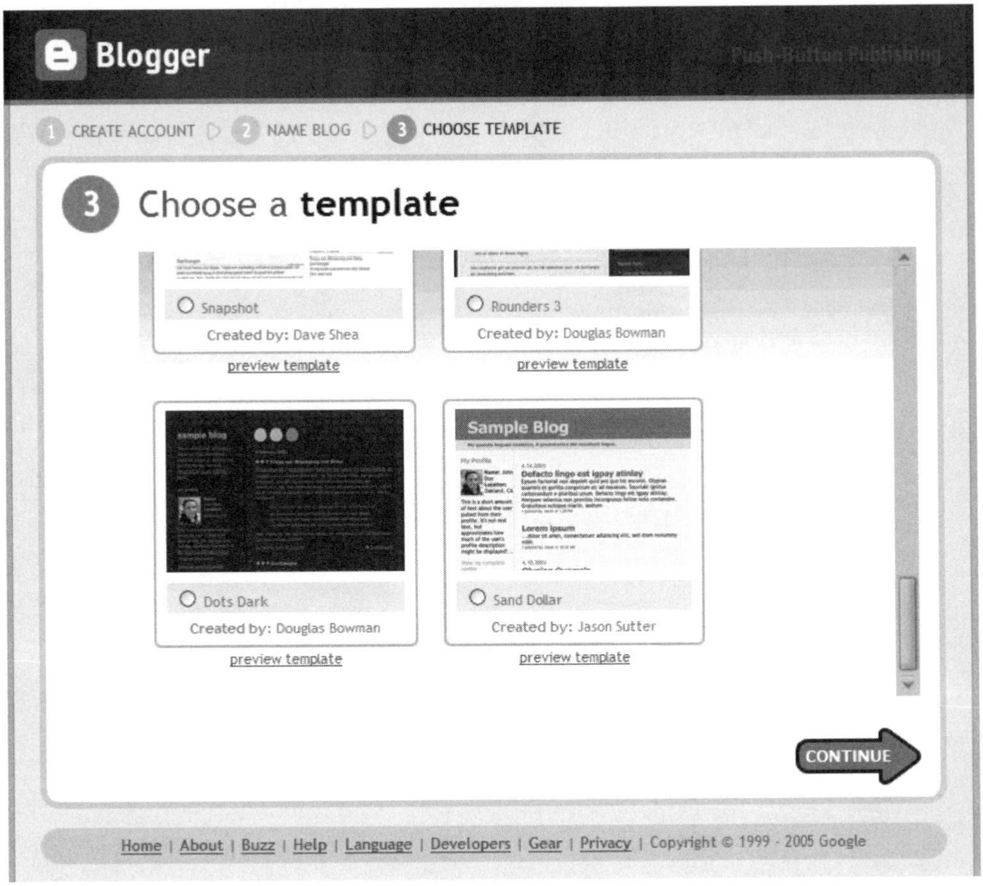

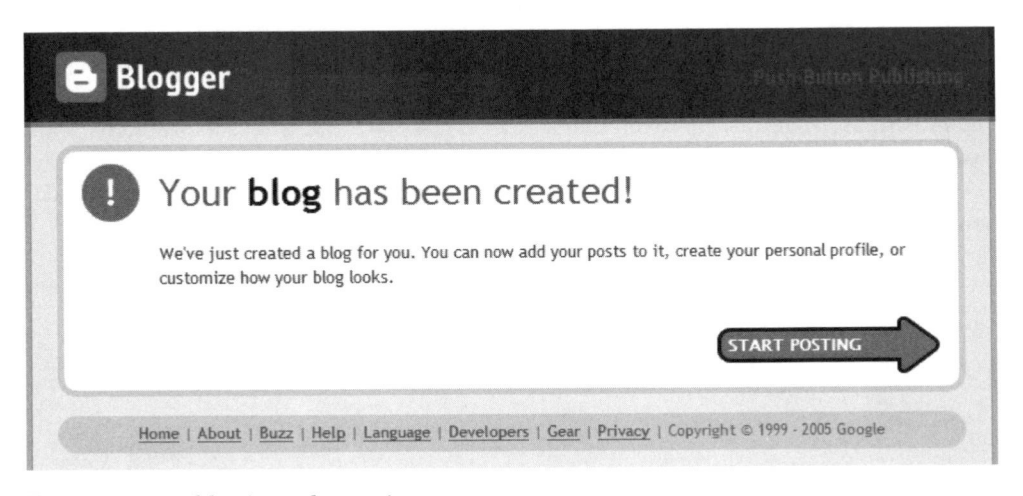

Figure 3-3. *Picking an initial blog template*

Figure 3-4. *Your blog is ready to go!*

Blogger Features

One of Blogger's strengths is its Create Posting page, as shown in Figure 3-5. If you've ever written something on a PC, you will feel utterly at ease working with this clean, friendly interface.[1]

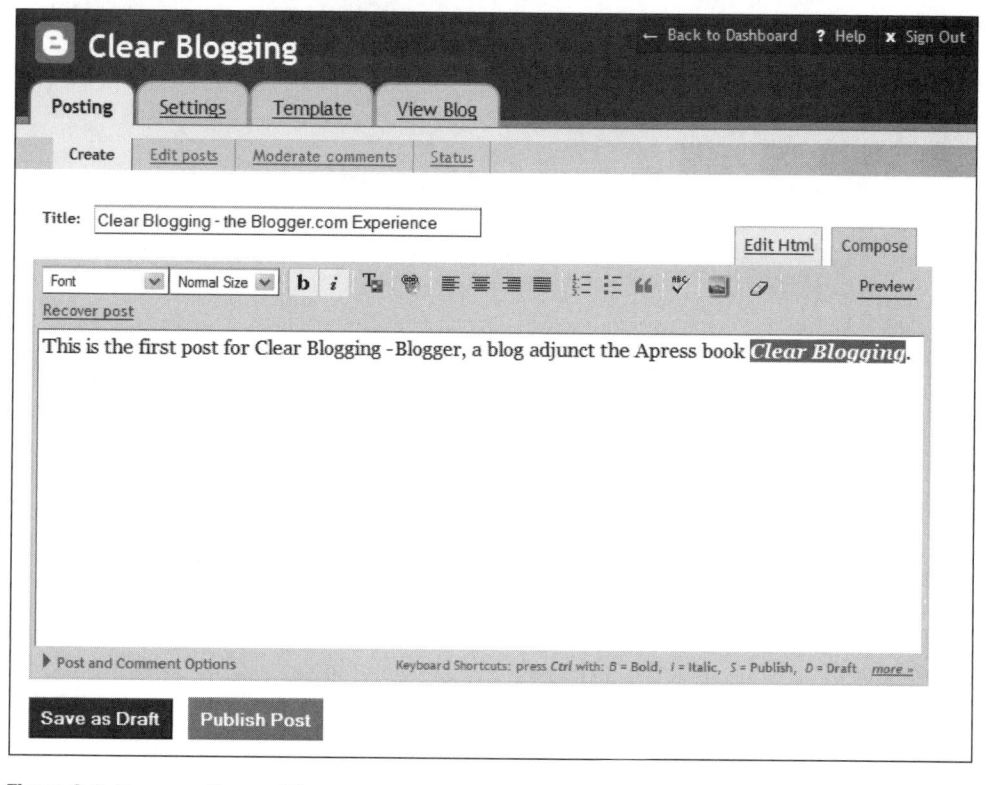

Figure 3-5. *Easy posting at Blogger*

Clicking Publish Post on the Create Posting page does just that. Then, if you went to http://clearblogging.blogspot.com, or found that blog on Google Blog Search, you would see the page shown in Figure 3-6.

---

1. If you don't like this interface, you can create posts directly in Microsoft Word (for Windows) instead using the free Blogger for Word add-in utility. For more information on this tool, see http://help.blogger.com/bin/answer.py?answer=1180&query=Microsoft%20Word&topic=0&type=f, or, more easily, click Help and search for Microsoft Word. You can also use third-party tools like BlogJet (http://blogjet.com) or Windows Live Writer from Microsoft (http://windowslivewriter.spaces.live.com).

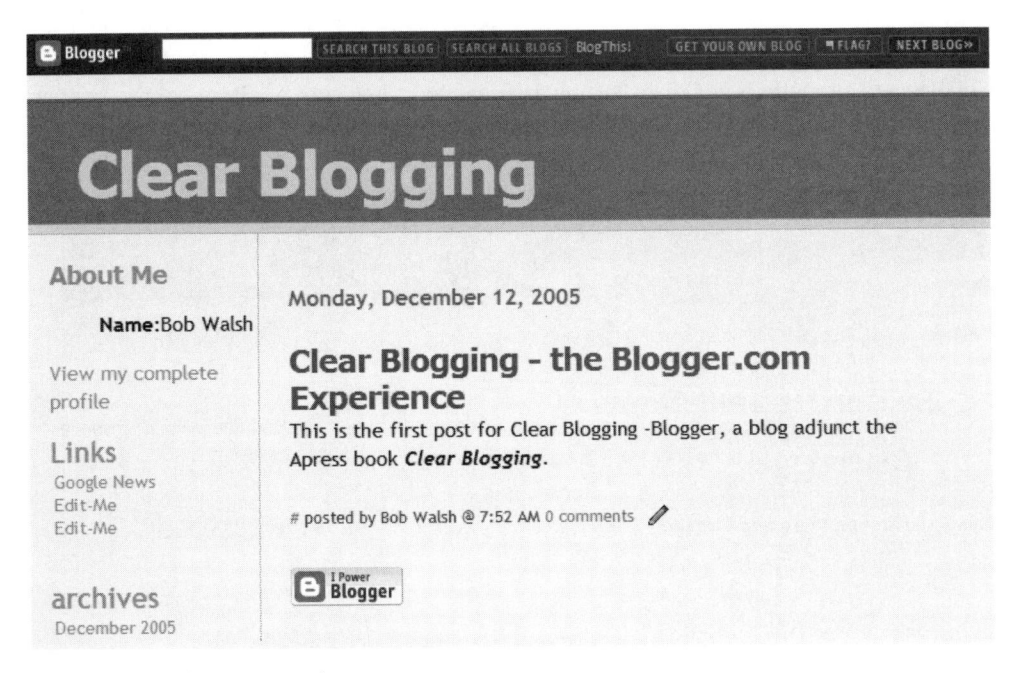

Figure 3-6. *My first post at Blogger*

Two more strengths of Blogger are its anti-spam word verification feature and how easy it is to start making money with your blog.

Spam—those utterly worthless, obnoxious crap messages from despicable craven scum who should be boiled alive in barbed-wire soup—is not something you want stuck on your blog.[2] At Blogger, automated comment spam is thwarted by requiring commenters to read and type a computer-unreadable word in order to add a comment to one of your posts. It's not perfect, since an alleged human can still manually post a spam comment, but it does filter out most of the automated evildoers.

As for making money, Blogger is tightly integrated with Google AdSense, which we will look at in detail in Chapter 12.

---

2. Never, ever, ever spam or tolerate spam comments on your blog. Nearly all blog readers, upon sighting a spam blog or a spam comment on a blog, will leave and never return. It is not true that all spammers go immediately to hell when they die. Even hell has standards.

AN OVERVIEW OF ADSENSE AND BLOG ADVERTISING

Google (and others; see Chapter 12) can feed your blog site with advertisements automatically. If someone reading your blog clicks an ad, you make money—anywhere from 5 cents to 5 dollars, depending on what the advertiser set as its budget. No click, no money.

The keys to successful blog advertising for both the blog owner (that's you) and advertisers are relevancy, readership, and respect.

- In the same way Google finds the right sites for you when you search, it finds the right websites and blogs for advertisers. If your blog is about the tips and travails of being a professional and a parent, Google will know to serve ads to your blog that are relevant to that topic.

- Advertising is a numbers game, and the greater your readership, the more ad clicks and the more revenue. But blog advertising (especially how Google does it) is even more about relevancy than readership.

- Respect is the foundation of a good blog, and a good blog's advertising. Respect your readers by not loading up your blog with advertising, or you won't have readers.

Templates and Your Blog

One of the keys to the growth of blogging is that layouts are automated by the use of templates. Templates are the mold into which your content gets poured. As a blogger, you don't have to worry about where your content goes or how it's formatted, because the template takes care of that.

Blogger comes with more than 30 standard templates, and these are fine to start with. But this is your blog, and its template should arrange and format your content the way you want it. With Blogger, it's easy to make changes.

Backing Up Your Template

If you've decided to create a Blogger blog, there's one step you should take before you start changing your templates: Back up your current template. Here are the steps:

1. Navigate from the Blogger dashboard to your blog, and then from there, go to the Template page, as shown in Figure 3-7.

2. Copy all of the text in the box, and paste your current Blogger template into a word processing or text editor document.

3. Save that document to your computer.

Now, if your edits don't work out, you can replace your changes with your original template.

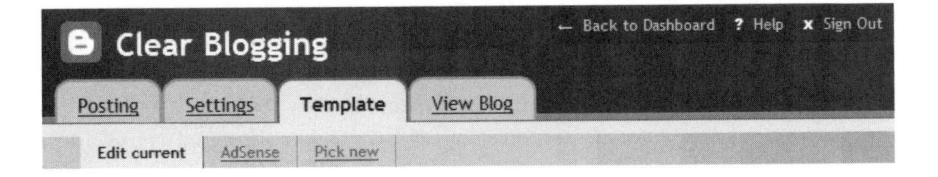

Make Money! Use AdSense to earn money with your blog. New easy signup.

Change the Blogger NavBar

Blue ▾

The Blogger NavBar is a navigation bar and toolbar with a form that allows people to search *just your weblog* using Google's SiteSearch and gives you the ability to check out what's happening on other recently published blogs with one click. This bar replaces the advertisements that used to be displayed at the top of some blogs.

```
<html>
    <head>
        <title><$BlogPageTitle$></title>
        <style type="text/css">
            body{margin:0px;padding:0px;background:#f6f6f6;color:#000000;font
            a{color:#DE7008;}
            a:hover{color:#E0AD12;}
            #logo{padding:0px;margin:0px;}
            div#mainClm{float:right;width:66%;padding:30px 7% 10px 3%;border-
            div#sideBar{margin:20px 0px 0px 1em;padding:0px;text-align:left;}
            #header{padding:0px 0px 0px;margin:0px 0px 0px;border-top
            h1,h2,h3,h4,h5,h6{padding:0px;margin:0px;}
            h1 a:link {text-decoration:none;color:#F5DEB3}
            h1 a:visited {text-decoration:none;color:#F5DEB3}
            h1{padding:25px 0px 10px 5%;border-top:double 3px #BF5C00;border-
            h2{color:#9E5205;font-weight:bold;font-family:Verdana,Sans-Serif;
            h3{margin:10px 0px 0px 0px;color:#777777;font-size:105%;}
            h4{color:#aa0033;}
```

Save Template Changes   **Preview**   **Clear Edits**

Figure 3-7. *Your current Blogger template*

Modifying the Template

You have a choice here of whether you want to tweak and nudge the basic template or replace it with a custom template. Let's make just two changes to get a feeling for how this works. Throughout Part 2, we will be looking at the whys and wherefores of blog formatting in much more detail.

First off, let's change the Blogger NavBar (at the top of every Blogger blog) from standard blue to something slightly less standard. Just pick Black from the Blogger NavBar drop-down menu at the top of the Template page (see Figure 3-7).

Next, change the blog headline ("Clear Blogging" in my blog) to be a little smaller than it is now. After perusing Blogger's excellent Help feature,[3] I know that the following line in my template:

---

3. For help with templates, see http://help.blogger.com/bin/topic.py?topic=22, then http://help.blogger.com/bin/answer.py?answer=114&topic=22, and especially http://help.blogger.com/bin/answer.py?answer=637&topic=22.

```
h1{padding:25px 0px 10px 5%;border-top:double 3px #BF5C00;border-bottom:solid 1px ➡
#E89E47; color:#F5DEB3;background:#DE7008;font:bold 300% Verdana,Sans-Serif; ➡
letter-spacing:-2px;}
```

defines the format for an h1 heading. Since the headline for my blog is the first and largest, it seems logical that changing it would change what I want. So I'll change that font:bold 300% to font:bold 200%. Figures 3-8 and 3-9 show the before and after.

Figure 3-8. *"Clear Blogging" at 300 percent of the base size*

Figure 3-9. *"Clear Blogging" at 200 percent of the base size*

Now, I can go on tweaking this format, clicking the Preview button, and then saving template changes for as long as I want. It's easy, and I can learn just enough Cascading Style Sheets (CSS)—the stuff that defines how to format different parts of a web page—by trying some of the examples in Blogger's Help. I can even dig into the whole CSS thing by searching the blogosphere or Web, or by getting my hands on a good CSS tutorial.[4] But, I really don't want to do that right now.

Don't get me wrong. I'm a programmer, and I love this stuff. But as much fun as it is, it's a tangent left best for another time, if you are so inclined. So, let's look at the other way of changing your Blogger template to something new and different, which I call, ahem, copy and paste.

Replacing the Template

First, do a search for **Blogger Templates +free** online. When this was written, these were three of the best sites for free Blogger templates:

---

4. I recommend *Head First HTML with CSS & XHTML* (O'Reilly Media, 2005) or Simon Collison's *Beginning CSS Web Development: From Novice to Professional* (Apress, 2006). You can read more about the former and get a sample chapter at http://headrush.typepad.com/creating_passionate_users/2005/12/ head_first_html.html. For more on the latter and a sample chapter, visit http://apress.com/book/ bookDisplay.html?bID=10148.

- The Open Directory Project (http://dmoz.org/Computers/Internet/On_the_Web/Weblogs/Templates/)

- Angie McKaig's great list of blogger templates sites (www.angiemckaig.com/misc/blogtemplates.html)

- NOIPO.org (http://blogtemplates.noipo.org/)

Let's take the "Subdued Lily" template from NOIPO.org as the new template, without the lilies in the background. First, go to NOIPO.org and download the template, as shown in Figure 3-10.

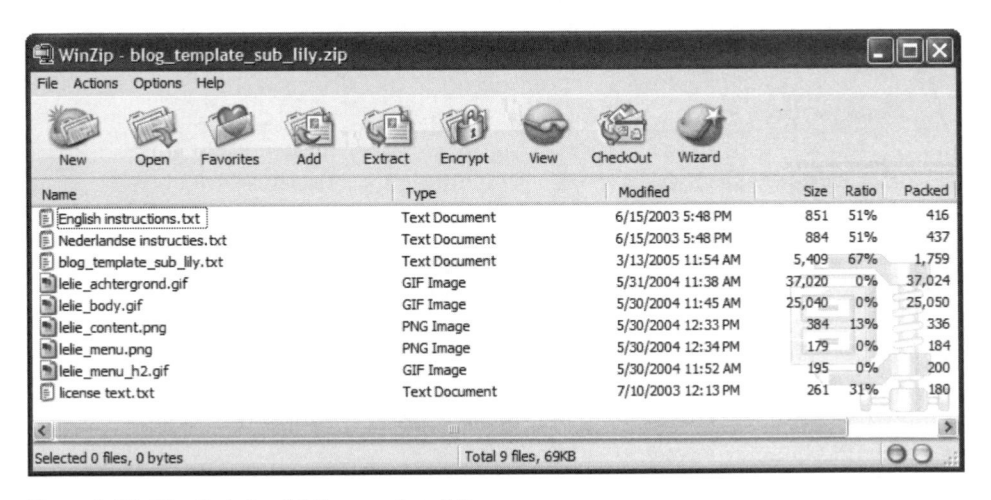

Figure 3-10. *The Subdued Lily template bits*

After unzipping the file, open and *copy* the contents of blog_template_sub_lily.txt. Then go to Blogger's Edit Current Template Page and *paste*. Then preview the effects of the new template, as shown in Figure 3-11. From here, you can do more tweaking if you like.

If you had wanted those faded lilies in the background of your blog, or any other images in the background, you would have to put those lilies on a server somewhere in the vastness of the Internet[5]—either yours or someone else's—and change the CSS to point to them. The benefit of services like Blogger is that you don't have to delve into all those code bits as you would if you ran your blog from your own server. The disadvantage is that there are limitations you have to work around if you want special features for your blog.

Well, enough of this visual template tweaking stuff. It's time to move on to an alternative to Blogger in our survey of easy ways to start a blog. Next up is Windows Live Spaces.

---

5. If you are comfortable with the HTML, here's a list of places you can park images for your blog: http://blogger-templates.blogspot.com/2005/01/host-your-images.html. Also check with the company you use to connect to the Internet—often even basic accounts get some storage you can use for this purpose.

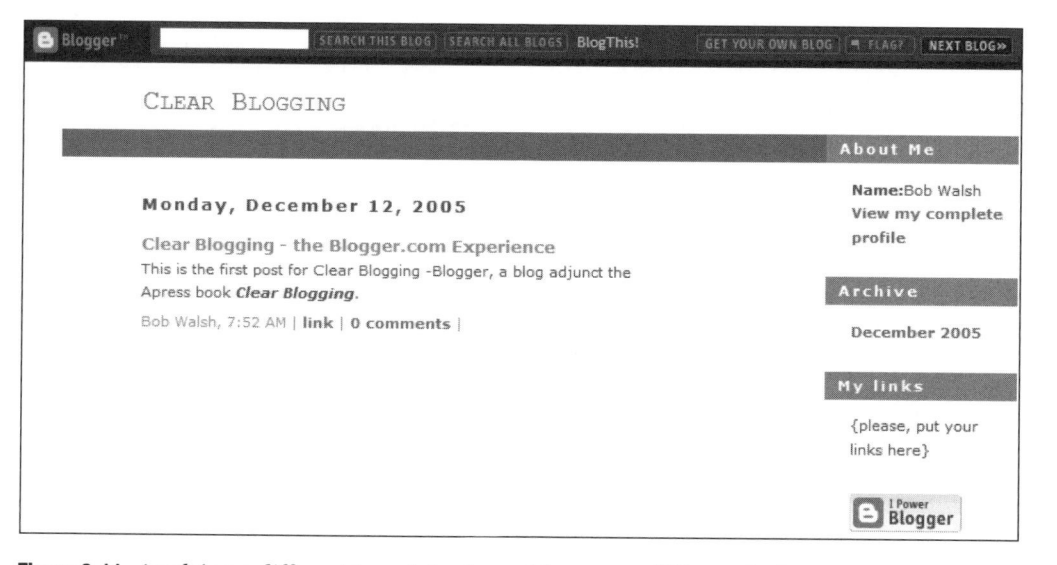

Figure 3-11. *Applying a different template gives a blog a very different look.*

Creating a Windows Live Spaces Blog

Like a lot of things Internet, Microsoft was late to the blog party, and it is working hard to catch up by leveraging its existing operating systems, websites, and software. But while Microsoft tends to be very businesslike, Windows Live Spaces, Microsoft's free blogging service at `http://spaces.live.com`, definitely tends toward the personal end of blogging, and if that's the type—or one of the types—of blogging you want to do, this is a good place to do it.

Windows Live Spaces Blog Startup

Signing up and creating your own Windows Live Spaces blog is relatively easy. If you have a Microsoft Passport, Hotmail account, or Microsoft Messenger account, you're already signed in. If not, fill in one screen, and you're off to the races, as shown in Figure 3-12.

At Microsoft, more integration with other Microsoft products and services is always better, so once you create your blog (or *space*, as Microsoft calls it), your first choice is whether you want a by-invitation-only blog, a public blog, or a blog limited to your MSN Messenger contacts, as shown in Figure 3-13.

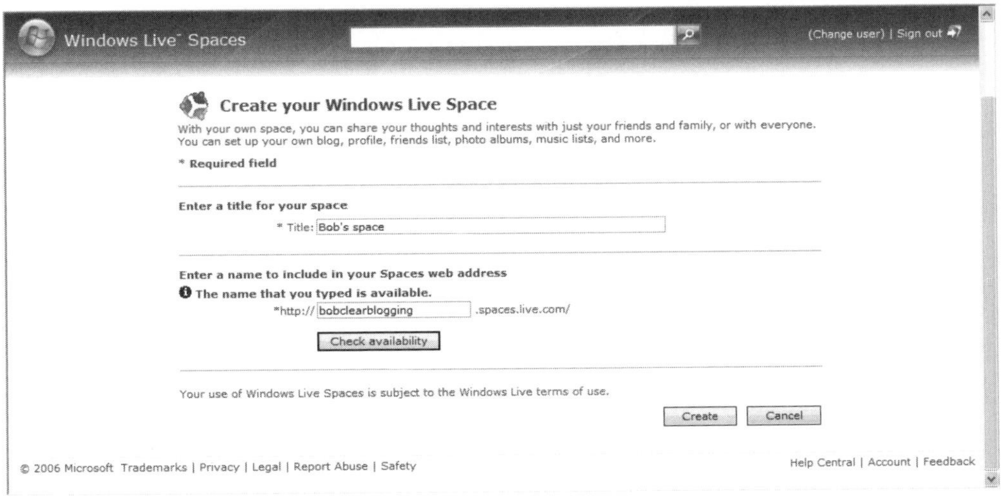

Figure 3-12. *Defining your Windows Live Spaces blog*

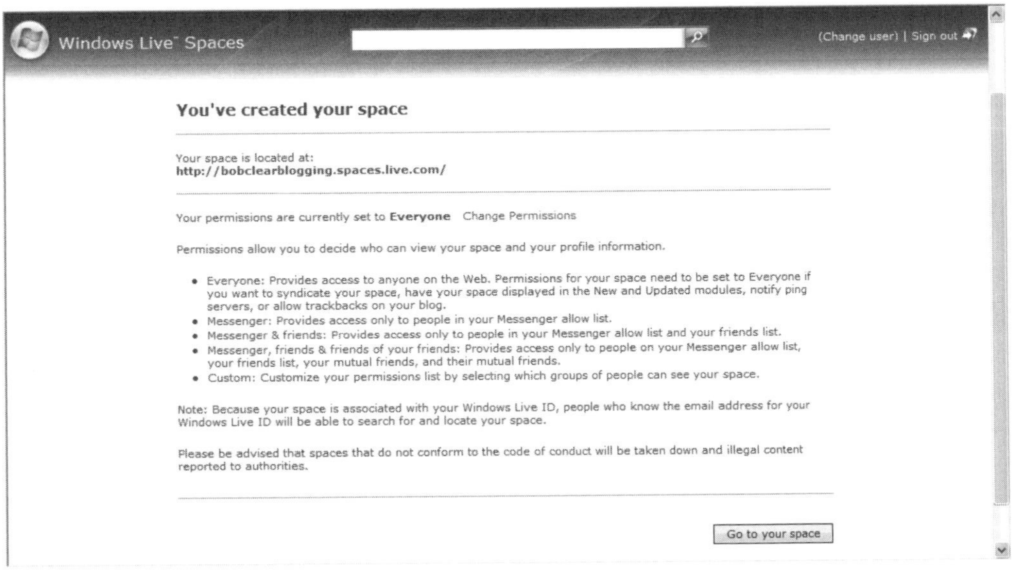

Figure 3-13. *Defining who gets into your Windows Live Space*

Customizing your space is a matter of picking which of 81 graphic themes you want to use, 12 "modules" (such as Photo Album and Blog List) you want to include, and which of the six available layouts you want to use. Figure 3-14 shows what a default Windows Live Spaces blog looks like while editing it, and Figure 3-15 shows what you can do in just eight mouse clicks.

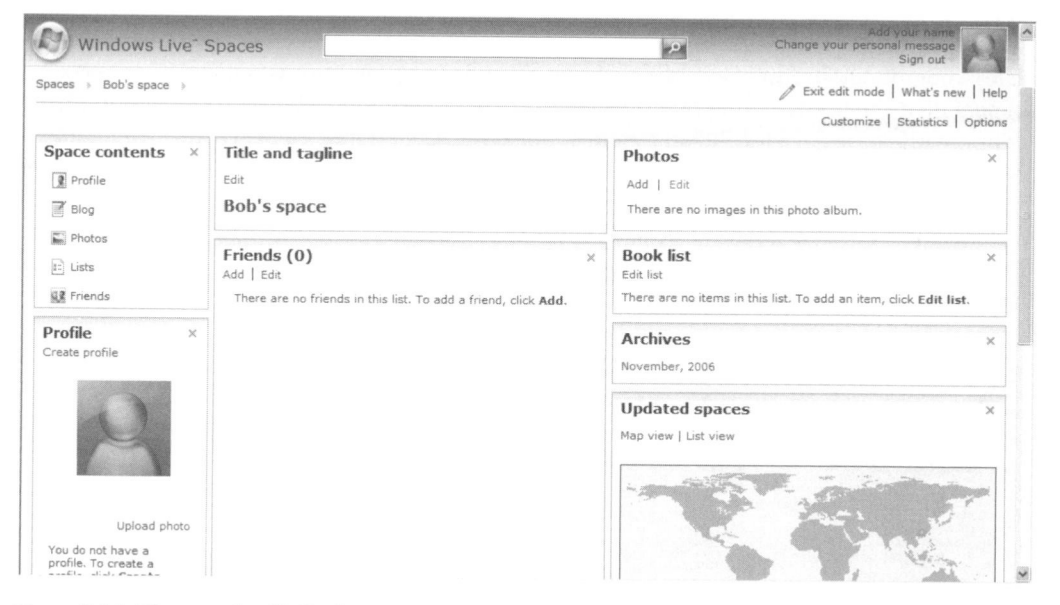

Figure 3-14. *The standard Windows Live Spaces blog*

Figure 3-15. *A nicer Windows Live Spaces blog*

Windows Live Spaces Features

The strengths of Windows Live Spaces are music and photos, as long as you're a Windows kind of person. If you use Windows Media Player to organize your music, you can pull in a playlist of your favorite tunes in a few seconds, and people visiting your blog can click those tunes and buy them for themselves, at Windows Live Music, naturally.[6]

It's easy to display, organize, and manage photos for your Windows Live Spaces blog. You can assemble photo slide shows by picking photos off your PC, as shown in Figure 3-16, or from existing Windows Live Spaces photo albums, and the presentation at your blog is nicely handled, as shown in Figures 3-17 and 3-18.

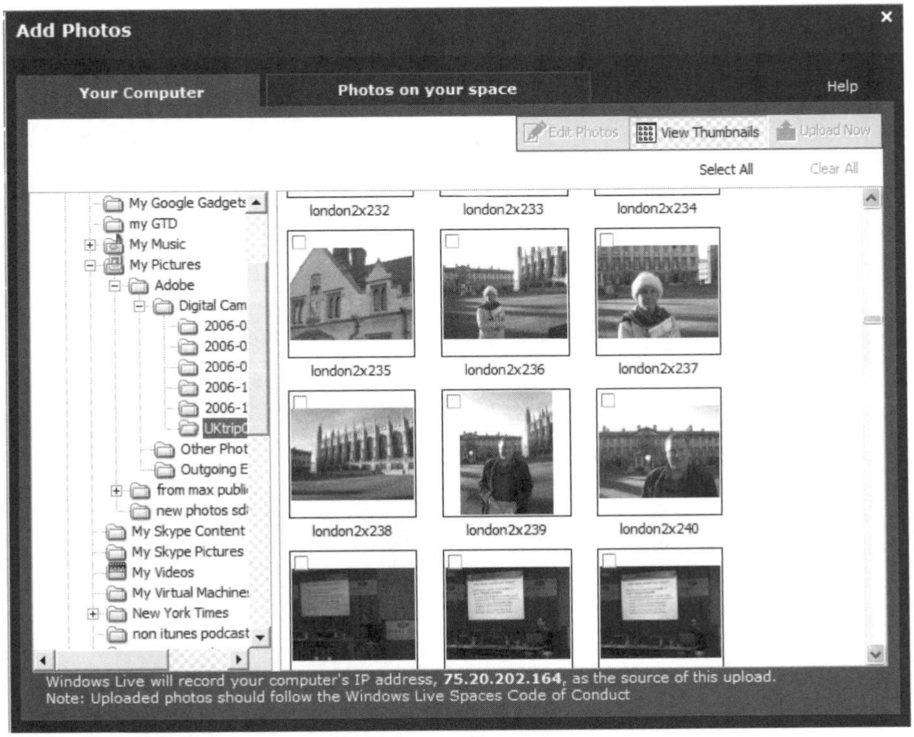

Figure 3-16. *Adding photos to your Windows Live Spaces blog*

---

6. When you click a song and go to MSN Music, you'll notice that the URL ends in `affid=100001`, as in `http://music.msn.com/album/?song=33260510&album=32405490&affid=100001`. That `affid=100001` looks like a hook into an affiliate program that might just might mean a way of making money someday with your Windows Live Spaces blog, and there's a bit more information here: `http://entertainment.msn.com/music/partners`.

Figure 3-17. *A slide show sidebar panel at my Windows Live Spaces blog*

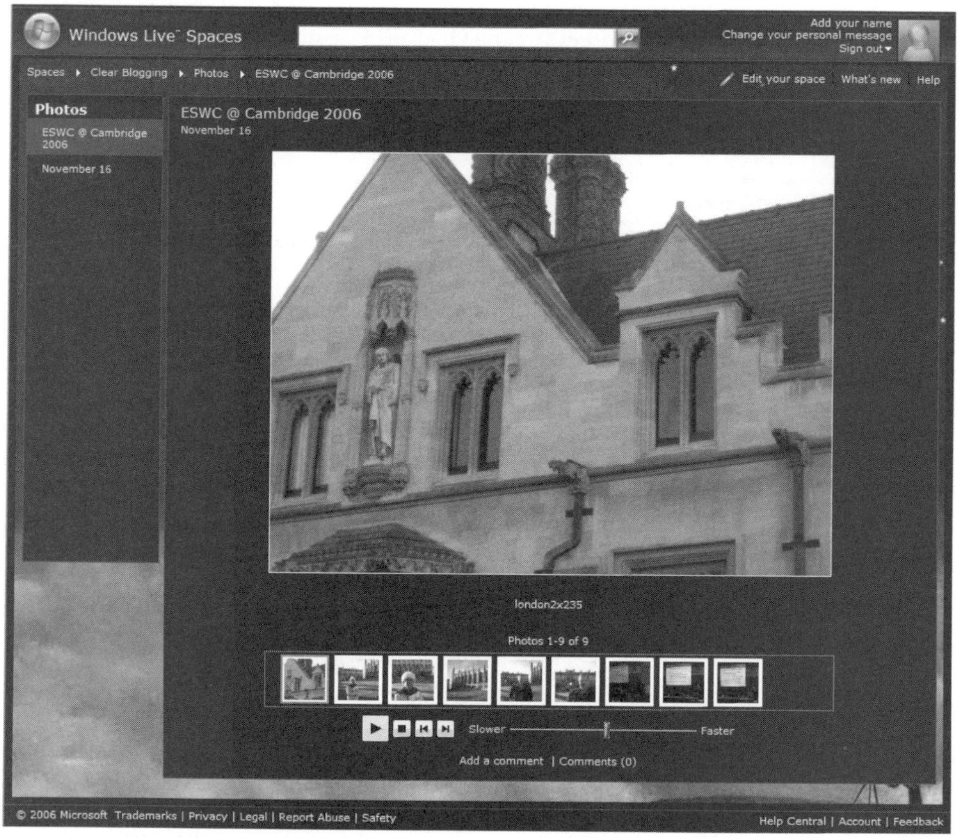

Figure 3-18. *Going to the Photos section of a Windows Live Spaces blog*

All in all, if you want an easy-to-manage, free blog—a blog that's an extension of your Windows world—Windows Live Spaces is an excellent choice.

While there are many, many other free blogging host services, Google's Blogger and Microsoft's Windows Live Spaces are the clear leaders. But, like a lot of things free on the Internet, you get what you pay for, and whoever is providing the free service is making money off your efforts, usually with advertising.

If you've decided you want to blog for results, and one of those results is revenue, it's time to get acquainted with another blog hosting service, TypePad.

Creating a TypePad Blog

I'm a big fan of TypePad (`www.typepad.com`). My main blog, `http://ToDoOrElse.com`,[7] has been hosted by Six Apart, the company that provides the TypePad service, since October 2004. Six Apart[8] has been making and selling Movable Type, one of the leading blog software packages, since blogging began.

With TypePad, you get much of the functionality of Movable Type without the messy complexity and programming, and even programmers occasionally like not having to code just to get something done. Apparently, so do a lot of people. As of the end of 2006, more than 30 million bloggers were using Six Apart's products and services.

Unlike Blogger and Windows Live Spaces, TypePad is not free, but its rates are pretty reasonable for the benefits and functionality you get, as shown in Table 3-1. Also, you can try the service free for 30 days.

Table 3-1. *TypePad Pricing*

Monthly Cost*	Service
$4.95	Basic, for one person with one blog, and a choice of predefined templates to use.
$8.95	Plus, for one person with up to three blogs or photo albums, with some customization possible. Also, you can map your domain (for example, ToDoOrElse.com) to your blog, so that is what people enter to get to it.
$14.95	Pro, for multiple authors, unlimited blogs, complete customization, and domain mapping.

* As of November 2006

TypePad Blog Startup

Starting your blog at TypePad once you've created an account means giving it a name and deciding if TypePad should include it in its directory, as shown in Figure 3-19.

---

7. Yes, you can capitalize inside a web address. That way, people don't think I have a blog about doors. But, come to think of it, a blog about doors would probably monetize well! See Chapter 12.
8. The company is named for the number of days between the birthdays of its founders, Mena and Ben Trott.

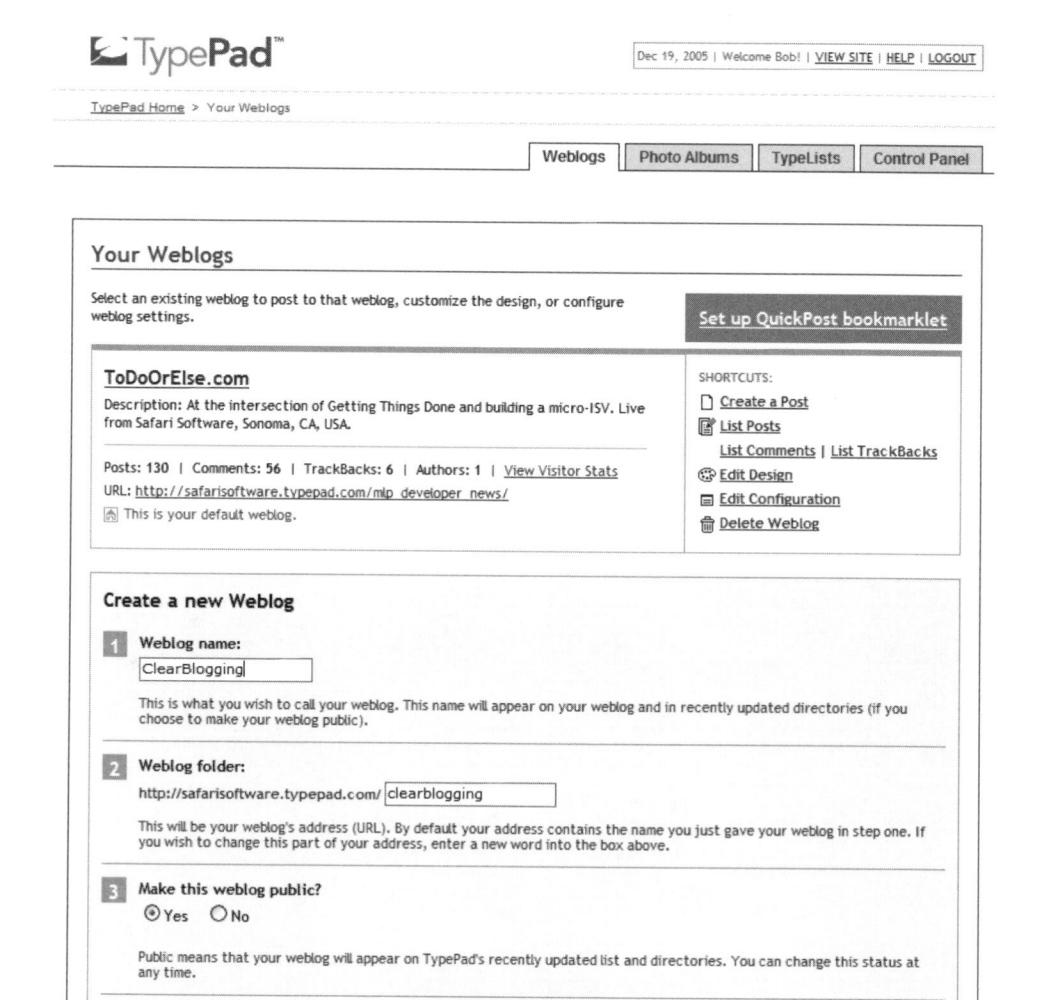

Figure 3-19. *Creating a new blog at TypePad*

To customize your TypePad blog, your first decision is the kind of layout you want. As you can see in Figure 3-20, you have a good selection.

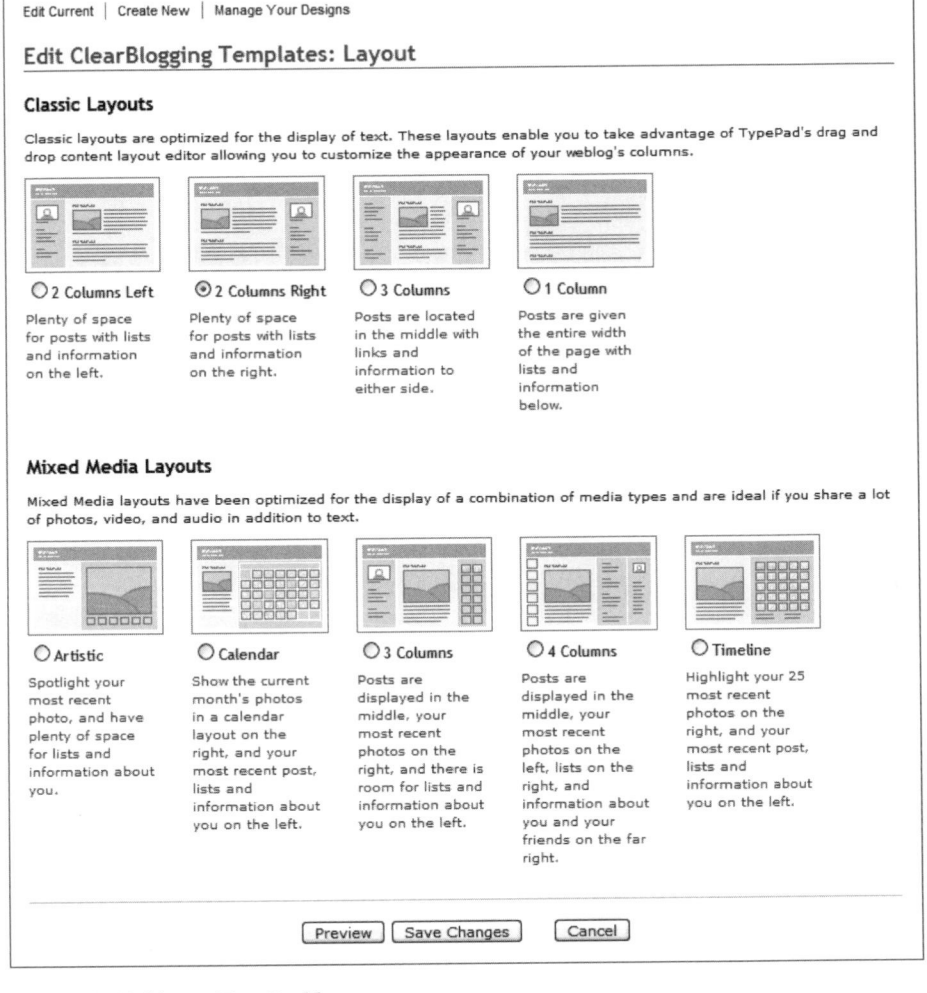

Figure 3-20. *Picking a TypePad layout*

Once you've decided on a layout, you can either pick from one of the dozens of predefined themes, as shown in Figure 3-21, or design your own, as shown in Figure 3-22. In Figure 3-22, I'm changing the page banner via its own edit window.

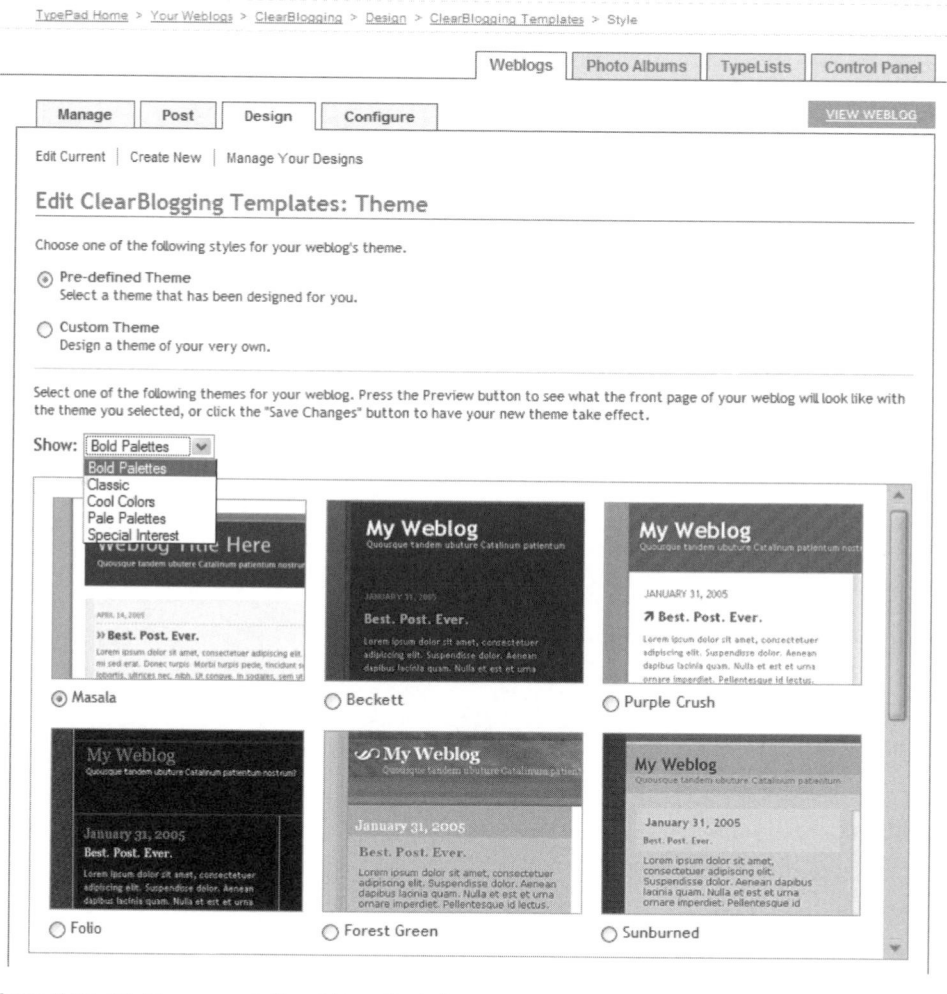

Figure 3-21. *Picking a predefined TypePad theme*

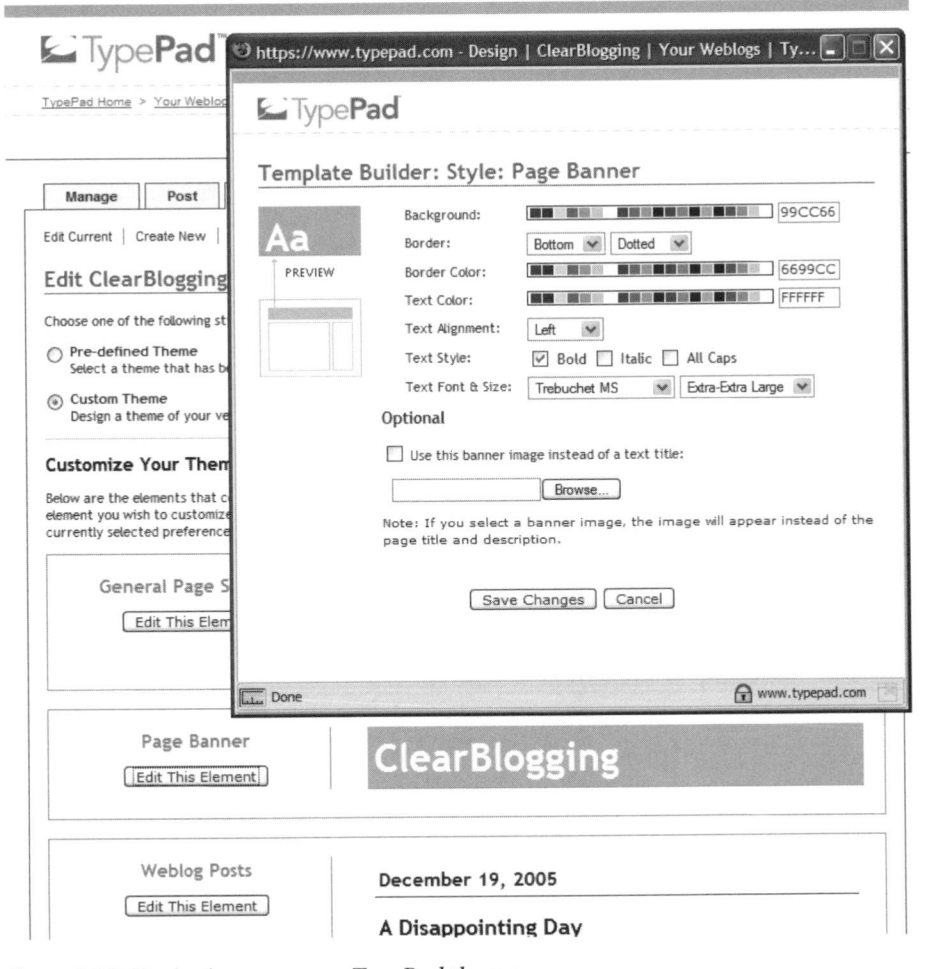

Figure 3-22. *Designing your own TypePad theme*

TypePad Features

You can post to your TypePad blog from within TypePad, or use the TypePad QuickPost book-marklet. QuickPost looks like a typical bookmark in Internet Explorer or Mozilla Firefox, but when you find something on the Web you want to blog about, you click it, and it becomes a blog posting window with a link already entered to the web page you were viewing. In Figure 3-23, I'm looking at one of my favorite sites for new programmer stuff, Larkware (www.larkware.com), and I've decided to do a QuickPost to my TypePad Clear Blogging blog.

Now, bookmarklets are not unique to TypePad. Blogger has one built into the Google Toolbar for Internet Explorer and Mozilla Firefox, for example. But TypePad's bookmarklet feature has far more options.

The big advantage TypePad has over Blogger and Windows Live Spaces is how easy and how deep you can customize your blog to make it your own. While you can take advantage of TypePad's many predefined themes and layouts, and choose from a substantial list of predefined content blocks (some of which make you money, as you'll learn in Chapter 12), you can also add your own code snippets to enhance your blog.

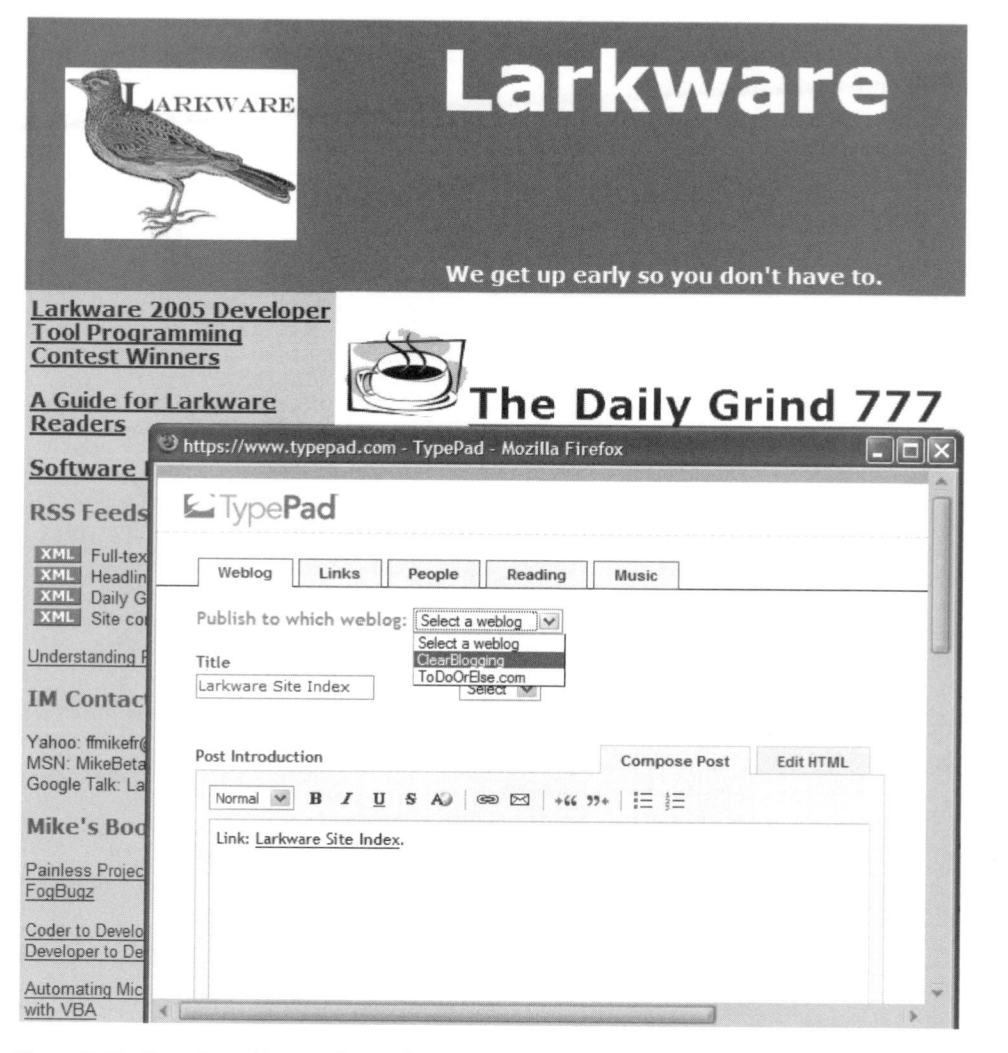

Figure 3-23. *Creating a TypePad QuickPost*

Which Is the Right Blogging Service?

The main point of this chapter is that starting a blog is one of the easiest things you've ever done on your PC or Mac. If it were hard and technically painful, 37.3 million[9] blogs would not already exist.

---

9. This data is according to Technorati.com as of May 1, 2006. While the number of blogs Technorati indexes continues to climb, the chapters in this book were written out of order, so don't be upset if the numbers I cite vary!

As easy as it is to start a blog, it's worth some consideration before committing, because the longer you blog and the more people read it, the harder it gets to change to a different blogging service or to host it yourself.

There are plenty of blog hosting services out there. See `www.google.com/Top/Computers/Internet/On_the_Web/Weblogs/Hosts/` for an idea of what is available.[10] In Table 3-2, I summarize what I see as your six choices.

Table 3-2. *Pros and Cons of Blogging Services*

Who	Pros	Cons
Blogger	Free, easy to set up, and easy to use.	Limited customization. Limited moneymaking potential (mainly Google AdSense). Spam blog haven you might not want to associate with.
Windows Live Spaces	Free. Integrates very well with all things Microsoft. Very good with photos and music.	Very limited customization. There are advertisements—Microsoft's.
TypePad	The most customization. You can have your own domain name. Offers plenty of ways of monetizing or can be ad-free.	Costs between $4.95 and $14.95 a month. More customization options means more time invested in applying them.
Vox	A new, free Six Apart blogging service, with great features, a strong community-building infrastructure, and more (see Chapter 5).	As of this writing, Six Apart controlled all advertising on Vox.
Others	May have features more prominent hosts don't. Possible stronger sense of community.	Costs and ads vary. May be too small to survive, so might disappear overnight.
Self-host	Total customization and total control.	Requires at the least the ability to set up and maintain a web server; blogging software* does most of the work, but HTML/XML skills are necessary. Costs vary widely, depending on your choices.

* *Six Apart's Movable Type (*`www.sixapart.com/movabletype`*) and the open source WordPress* (`http://wordpress.org`) *are the best-known blogging publishers.*

Now, you might happen to know of a small blogging host that does everything better than the three profiled here, or perhaps you're the type of person who can configure a server as easily as most people can order a book from Amazon, and you are wondering why I haven't covered those options. Good question!

---

10. As of November 2006, I recommend a look at BlogHarbor (`www.blogharbor.com`), Weblogger (`www.weblogger.com`), and Rotten Tomatoes (`/www.rottentomatoes.com`).

I think the answer is that as of the end of 2006, blogging has matured to the point where it's a three-horse race: Six Apart, who in many ways started the blogging movement; Google, who bought Blogger.com and, in its drive to be the core of all things Internet, is strongly supporting blogging; and Microsoft, who has a long record of coming late to the high-tech party, but walking away the clear leader.

Which is the right blogging service? For personal blogs or to experiment with blogging, Google's Blogger or Windows Live Spaces makes sense. For your professional, small business, company, or advocacy blog, my choice is TypePad, but your mileage may vary. While there's no right answer for everyone, there are some things all good blogs have in common, and that's the focus of the next chapter.

Your Action Tasks

Here are a few steps for getting started with your own blog:

Decide what kind of blog you are interested in creating. You have to start somewhere, and the first key decision is what kind of blog you want. You might want a personal blog for yourself, family, and friends (see Chapter 5); a blog about your profession (see Chapter 6); something about your business or the company you work for (see Chapter 7); or something entirely different. Once you decide on the type of blog, you can decide which blogging service fits best.

Start thinking about a name. "John Smith's Blog" works, but it's kind of boring. Have some fun here. Catchy blog names are almost a tradition in the blogosphere.

Go visiting. Have a look at the blogging services mentioned in this chapter and any others you've heard about. How do they look and feel to you as a prospective customer?

And then you can continue with these steps:

Taglines matter. Besides a name, invest some time in coming up with a tagline for your blog. Taglines are a must for most standard blog templates and helpful to let first-time visitors to your blog know what they're in for.

Name that rose. If you are going to have a TypePad, Movable Type, or WordPress blog, start shopping now for a domain name at a domain registrar. I recommend `www.godaddy.com` because of the years of excellent service I've gotten from this company. How you affix your new domain name to your new blog differs with each service, but you're going to want to do this from the get-go.

■ ■ ■

PART 2

Building Your Blog

This part's four chapters cover the building blocks of all good blogs, and the specific things you should think about if you're building an individual, professional, company, or whatever blog. While all good blogs have certain things in common, which we'll cover in Chapter 4, a blog for yourself and your friends is very different from a blog about your professional interests, which is very different from a blog primarily meant to converse with the world at large about what your company or business has to offer.

■ ■ ■

CHAPTER 4

What Do Good Blogs Share?

When you first start surfing the component atoms of the blogosphere, its like walking into a three-ring circus in the middle of Grand Central Station transplanted to Las Vegas during a movie filming. Everyone is doing something, going somewhere, saying something. If you can imagine it, it's somewhere in here.

But after a while, you start making choices about what part of the bedlam you want to read. This blog over there is easy to read and stays; that one has spelling mistakes and goes. This blog makes its easy to learn about a product; that one is a hodgepodge of stuff you're interested in and things you don't care about.

In this chapter, we're going to cover a framework of guidelines to make your blog one that stays in your readers' minds, hearts, bookmarks, and RSS readers. Some of these guidelines are so basic they really are the rules of this particular road; others are more open to wildly different interpretations.

Before pontificating rules for other people to follow, it's a good idea to cite your authority. You won't find a D.B. (Doctor of Blogging) on my business card or a Wizard of Oz–like certificate hanging on my wall, stating I have fulfilled all of the requirements necessary to pontificate. But I have applied these guidelines and seen them work at my two main blogs over the past two years, and you'll be hard-pressed to find a successful blog that ignores them.

Be Credible

If you are going to be successful, you must be credible. If you go find a good dictionary and look up *credible*, you'll find it means "offering reasonable grounds for being believed" (from my good dictionary, *Merriam-Webster's Collegiate Dictionary, Eleventh Edition*). Your blog, like other successful blogs, needs big hulking heaps of credibility to be successful. Since no one has found a way to bottle and sell trust and believability,[1] you're going to have to do it the old-fashioned, mainstream media journalistic way: owning your words, writing for your readers, and citing your sources.

---

1. Or maybe someone has! See "Trust-building Hormone Short-circuits Fear in Humans" at `www.sciencedaily.com/releases/2005/12/051207180159.htm`.

Owning Your Words

Never say anything on your blog you don't want people to know that you said. While you may decide to dance on the edge of the cliff by blogging anonymously and saying whatever you please, by and large, anything you post had better pass this particular test.

Every so often, you'll see a post or a news story about bloggers getting fired, being sued, or being subpoenaed for what they said. Figure 4-1 shows one example (from `http://news.bbc.co.uk/2/hi/technology/3974081.stm`).[2] The bottom line is you can be held responsible for what you say and how you say it in the blogosphere, just as you can in the real world.

Figure 4-1. *A cautionary tale*

---

2. Other examples are "Dinner with the fired Google blogger" (`http://redcouch.typepad.com/weblog/2005/02/dinner_with_the.html`) and "Is Atrios Responsible for Libel?" (`http://balkin.blogspot.com/2003_10_26_balkin_archive.html#106752909158205263`).

Please don't think I'm trying to scare you into being bland or getting out of the blogosphere entirely. Somehow, millions of people blog every day without a legal care in the world. And, in fact, as a blogger, you already have some well-respected legal talent in your corner: the Electronic Frontier Foundation (EFF, www.eff.org). As shown in Figure 4-2, the EFF is dedicated to defending freedom in the digital world, including the freedom to blog.

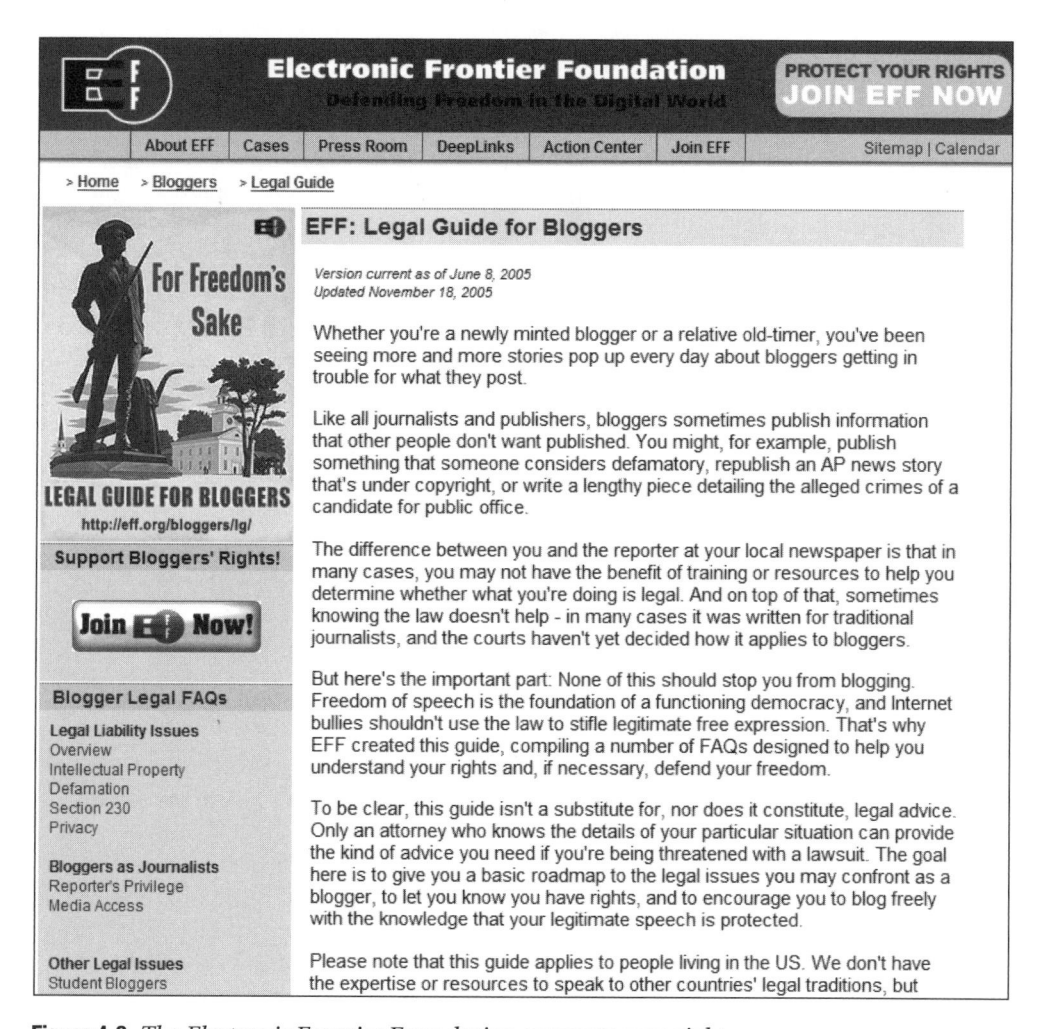

Figure 4-2. *The Electronic Frontier Foundation supports your rights.*

I strongly recommend that you read EFF's "Legal Guide for Bloggers," at www.eff.org/bloggers/lg/. This guide does a great job of spelling out the realities and the law (not always the same thing) of blogging in the United States.

AN INTERVIEW WITH KURT OPSAHL, STAFF ATTORNEY, EFF

So what are the legal considerations of blogging? Kurt Opsahl, the staff attorney at EFF who wrote EFF's "Legal Guide for Bloggers," had this to say when I interviewed him.

Q. *What's the mission of the Electronic Frontier Foundation when it comes to bloggers?*

A. We're dedicated to defending their rights. To inform bloggers about their rights, and help promote those rights, both through appropriate litigation and advocacy work.

Q. *Are there people trying to take away those rights of bloggers?*

A. Let me give you an overview. First of all, on the Additional Resources page of the [EFF] Legal Guide, there's a link to the Media Law Resource Center's list of cases involving bloggers.[3] Those are the cases. In addition, one of the things we are trying to address in the Legal Guide for Bloggers is situations that don't actually lead to litigation; rather, the blogger gets a cease and desist claim, or some correspondence by someone who has been offended and makes a legal threat. This [the guide] is to help the bloggers understand what their rights are, lest inappropriate legal threats chill their speech, and that's far more common.

Q. *This "chilling effect" you talk about—is this about various dingbats out there, or are you seeing a concerted effort out there?*

A. Take a look at a site called `http://chillingeffects.org`. That's a site that keeps a list of cease and desist letters people have submitted.

Q. *Let's go back to the EFF's Legal Guide for Bloggers for a moment. Why did you create this?*

A. Well, we wanted to create a guide to help bloggers understand their rights, and if necessary, defend them.

Q. *I'm recommending to my readers that they read that guide, but can you boil it down to the bottom line? What should bloggers do and not do?*

A. I would direct them to the guide and to the first part of the guide, Overview of Legal Liability Issues FAQ [`www.eff.org/bloggers/lg/faq-overview.php`]. I understand the notion of "don't put it in legalese—how would you explain it to your friends," but the truth is that actually this guide is my attempt at explaining these issues as clearly as possible without putting it into too much legalese.

Q. *Forgive me if I'm sounding like a reporter here, but on one hand, anybody can sue anyone for anything.*

A. Indeed.

Q. *On the other hand, there are millions of bloggers out there saying whatever they want about anything they want. What's the problem EFF is trying to address? What should I do? Or maybe another way to ask it is if I wanted to get sued as a blogger, what should I do?*

A. If you *wanted* to get sued? Defame somebody who's very litigious. Or you can violate somebody's copyright if you want to get sued. The Church of Scientology is very litigious, so you can always look to them. I wouldn't recommend it though.

Q. *There are certain protections, at least at the state level, for reporters. Do bloggers enjoy those freedoms, or has that not been litigated out?*

A. As you may or may not know, we're doing the *Apple v. Does* case,[4] where we've asserted the reporter's privilege against subpoenas by Apple to reveal the confidential sources of some online journalists reporting about Apple products. What should determine if someone is protected by this is whether they are functioning as a journalist.

---

3. You can find the Media Law Resource Center's (MLRC's) list at `www.medialaw.org/Template.cfm?Section=Home&Template=/ContentManagement/ContentDisplay.cfm&ContentID=3457`, or, more easily, click the link to MLRC's List of Legal Cases Against Bloggers at `www.eff.org/bloggers/lg/additional.php`.

4. In May 2006, EFF won the case when a California state appeals court ruled in EFF's favor, holding that online journalists have the same right to protect the confidentiality of their sources as offline reporters do.

Q. *So it's not for someone else to give you your "Journalist License," but whether you act like a journalist that makes you a journalist?*

A. What makes a journalist a journalist is whether you are gathering news for dissemination to the public. It shouldn't be the medium you use.

Writing for Your Readers

The second leg your credibility as a blogger stands on is remembering why you are blogging in the first place: to communicate with your community of readers. While writing blogs does not and should not sound like your local newspaper or television news show, you need to show respect for your readers by writing in a way that makes it as easy as possible for them to understand what you are saying.

After spending 30 years writing as a reporter, software designer, and a businessman, I'm still amazed when I encounter people who say, "Oh, I can't write well!" or "I was never any good at writing." Bull! Writing is a whole lot more like talking than it is like singing, and you don't need to have the gifts of Celine Dion or Frank Sinatra to be able to write well. In fact, writing is sometimes even easier than talking, because you can edit what you write—something usually impossible to do when you're talking.

In fact, when you're writing for your blog's readers, you get the best of both worlds: You can say whatever you want, however you want, *and* you have the opportunity to look over your posts to clean them up, straighten them out, and punch them up.[5]

Here are a few practical rules of thumb to keep in mind when writing for your readers:

Spell-check, grammar-check, and read your posts before publishing. Nothing turns off a reader faster than too many spelling mistakes and punctuation mistakes. Nearly every blogging service has a spell-checker built into it, as does Mozilla Firefox 2.0 and later. And if all else fails, you can always copy and paste your post into your word processor and spell-check there. Unfortunately, no one has written a brain-checker yet, so besides spell-checking, you need to read and sometimes reread what you write. A dropped word here, the wrong word there, and similar errors can completely mess up what might have been a great post.

Write the way you speak. Your writing shouldn't sound like a college professor unless you happen to be a college professor. If what you write in your blog doesn't sound like you, it's not.

Write first, then edit. It's amazing how much you can mess yourself up if you worry about what you are writing instead of just writing it. First, get the words out, get your meaning across, and get your thoughts on the screen. Then, and only then, swap your jaunty writer's cap for your nitpicky editor's cap and edit. No amount of second-guessing and nitpicking yourself is going to make your writing good if you don't first get some writing done.

---

5. If you're looking for a quick way to improve your blog postings, and don't have a lot of time to spare, pick up just two great, short books on writing. *Random House Webster's Handy Grammar, Usage, and Punctuation, Second Edition* (Random House, 2003) is especially good for sorting out commonly confused words like *among/between* and *amount/number*. The *Elements of Style, Fourth Edition*, by William Strunk Jr. and E.B. White (Allyn & Bacon/Longman, 2000) has been making writers out of scribblers for 70 years. It is *the* writing book.

Good writing comes from rewriting. After you've written your first draft—even if it's a one-sentence post—take a second look at what you've written. Is it clear? Are you getting your meaning across? Is what you are trying to say there, but all tied up in too many words and twisty punctuation? Don't hesitate to show some respect for your time and your readers by rewriting what needs to be rewritten.

Short is good, especially when writing blogs. Cut the fluff, get to the point, and remember that your readers have other things to do.

Citing Your Sources

On one level, blogging is all about clicking. Say you read a post about a free and easy way to stick images on the Internet so you can use them in your blog. Where's the link?[6] You hear a biased news story that leaves you steaming mad. How do your readers email that television or radio station, and better yet, read, hear, or see the story themselves?

If a post you publish on your blog doesn't have a link, there had better be a very good and self-evident reason. Blogging, like the Internet, is all about the linkages. In fact, if you take a look through the 100 most read blogs (according to Technorati), it's clear that links are good and more links are better.

On another level, blogging is like reporting, and for every news story relying on "unnamed sources," there are a few hundred thousand articles that spell out exactly who said what, where, and when. This is for good reason: That one unnamed source's story is cashing out all the credibility built up with readers or viewers by all those named sources' stories.

Whether you're blogging about someone or something, or you're writing about what you think, feel, or want to say, making it clear which ideas and words belong to whom is a hallmark of a good, believable blog.

Get the Mechanics Right

Whether you go with TypePad, Windows Live Spaces, Blogger, Vox, or any other way to blog, there are some mechanics you need to get right. Fortunately, nearly all blog publishing hosts and software packages make doing the right thing easy, but it never hurts to follow the lead of successful people.

Good blogs, or at least blogs a lot of people read and follow, nearly always cover the same four bases: let people comment, trackbacks are important, no tolerance for spam, and enable RSS for your readers' sake.

Letting People Comment

The one single thing that sets blogs apart from mere websites is comments. Comments make it possible to converse with and include your readers in what you have to say. Sometimes, comments are more interesting and entertaining than the original posts.

---

6. The link for this image hosting service is TinyPic Free Image Hosting (http://tinypic.com), by way of Steve Rubel's excellent blog, Micro Persuasion (www.micropersuasion.com).

Again, if you look at the most popular blogs—whether they are blogs about politics, products, people, or what have you—you'll find very, very few that don't allow people to comment on their posts.

For instance, take the popular `http://BigPictureSmallOffice.com` blog about office politics by a nameless senior vice president at an undisclosed company. Right after the list of recent posts is the list of recent comments, as shown in Figure 4-3.

Figure 4-3. *Comments count*

Whether you highlight comments, show them right after each post, or just have a link to them at the end of each post (as in Figure 4-4) is between you and your blogging software.

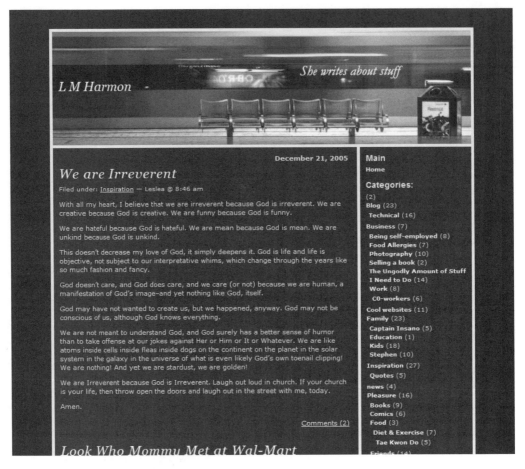

Figure 4-4. *LM Harmon at www.lmharmon.com*

Turning on Trackbacks

The flip side of comments is trackbacks. Say you read a post you think is really hot and some-thing your readers would or should know about. Many blogs have a trackback URL, which, if you copy and paste into your posting editor, will handle the plumbing so your post gets a mention at the post you're blogging about.

Trackbacks are one of those things easier to see than to explain. For example, in Figure 4-5, you see a posting by marketing guru and Squidoo.com CEO, Seth Godin at his blog (http://sethgodin.typepad.com). It has two trackbacks. If you clicked the first trackback, you would see what Brad Fallon has to say about this sort of instant AdSense, as shown in Figure 4-6.[7]

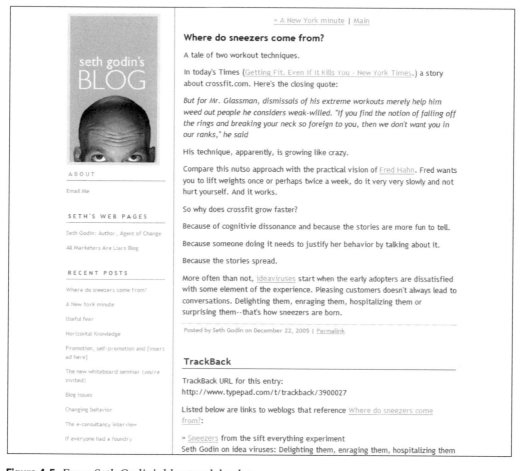

Figure 4-5. *From Seth Godin's blog track back to . . .*

---

7. Seth's specific post is at http://sethgodin.typepad.com/seths_blog/2005/12/a_new_york_minu.html, but his blog is so good, I wanted you to have a look at it now. Brad Fallon's post where he talks about Seth's post is at www.bradfallon.com/2005/12/discuss-think-fast.html. If you're interested in online marketing, add Brad's blog at www.bradfallon.com to your list of blogs to follow.

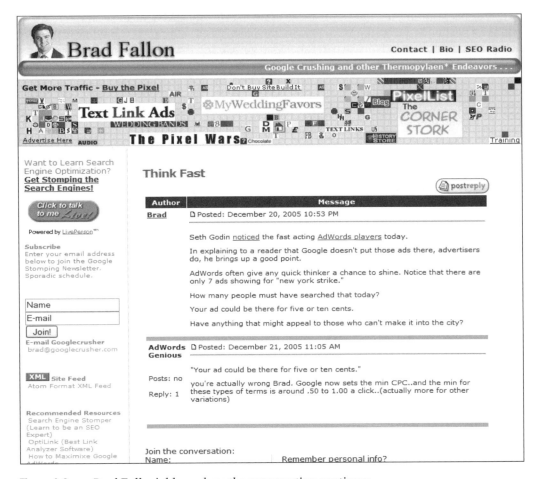

Figure 4-6. . . . *Brad Fallon's blog, where the conversation continues.*

Trackbacks are by no means universal. Many bloggers feel they are losing control of the conversation if they allow trackbacks, and more and more popular blogs are turning off trackbacks. Why? Like a lot of good ideas on the Internet, trackbacks still have a few bugs to work out, chiefly the digital cockroaches also known as spammers. My advice is to turn on trackbacks for your blog, but only after reading the next section about what good blogs have in common: zero spam.

Eradicating Spam

Just when you give up one-mail, because most of it is spam, and embrace the blogosphere, what do you find? You got it: spam. For the one person out there who has somehow avoided it, *spam* is all those wonderful fake notices from not your bank, free trips to nowhere, instant fame and fortune in just three hours a week, and all the other crap Internet users are bombarded with each and every day. And you thought telemarketers and direct-mail advertisers were bad!

Never, ever, for a second tolerate spam on your blog. Delete it, ban the poster, stick a big fat pin in the eye of your spammer voodoo doll, and move on. Fortunately, the blogging industry as a whole has been quick to adopt anti-spamming measures, but like their brethren cockroaches, spammers evolve and grow resistant. Even if you don't post every day, spending a minute looking at your most recent comments and trackbacks is a good way to stay spam-free.

Speaking of insects, you need to watch out for another couple of species out there: spam blogs and fake blogs. Spam blogs, such as the one shown in Figure 4-7, are nothing more than brainless attempts to influence the rankings of equally crappy websites in search engines. I say brainless because search engines now harshly punish charlatans who try this "keyword-stuffing" technique.

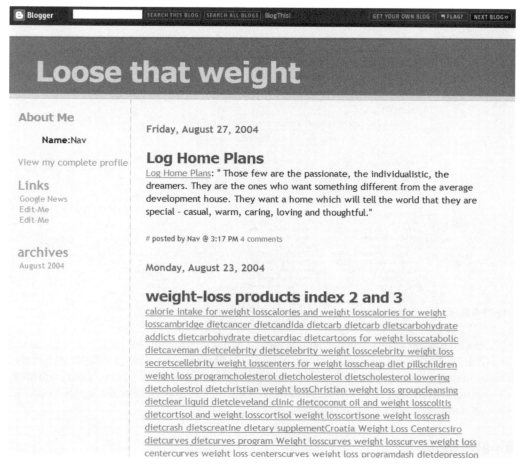

Figure 4-7. *A typical spam blog, aka a sblog*

If spam blogs are the empty beer cans on the Internet beach, fake blogs are the poisonous stinging jellyfish. These are sites built by ripping off legitimate content, as in the example shown in Figure 4-8. They are wrapped in highly targeted Google AdSense ads to further click fraud, or wrapped in some "make money fast" scam.

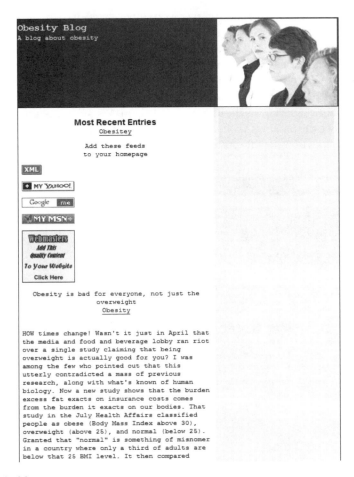

Figure 4-8. *A fake blog*

Avoiding spam blogs and fake blogs is just good digital hygiene along the lines of washing your hands after a trip to the toilet. While it's easy to recognize spam blogs, fake blogs come in shades of gray—is it a fake blog created by a scumbag armed with a renegade piece of software, a clueless effort by some lackwit, or a real blog? It can be tough to tell, but dodgy URLs that misspell legitimate sites are a dead giveaway.

Enabling RSS

I only mention RSS here on the off chance that your blogging host or software somehow might have this turned off. Turn it back on! RSS gives your readers control of how and when and where they read your content. It's what fuels the RSS readers we discussed in Chapter 2.

Like most things in the blogosphere, there's nothing like agreement on what to call RSS or what its button should look like. But in November 2005, the developers of Microsoft Internet Explorer 7, John Lilly and Chris Beard of Mozilla Corporation and the Microsoft Outlook team, agreed that it's in the common interest of bloggers to standardize (see `http://blogs.msdn.com/rssteam/archive/2005/12/14/503778.aspx`). Expect to see the button shown in Figure 4-9 become the standard.

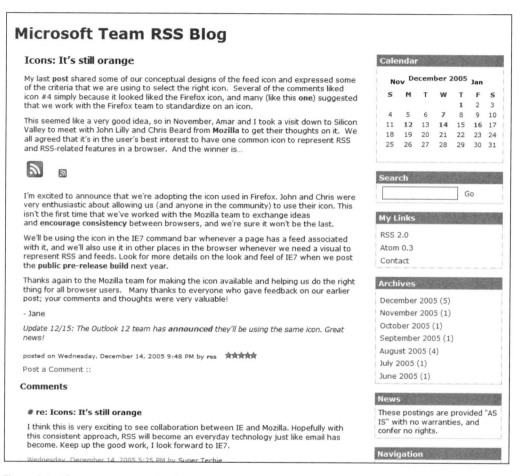

Figure 4-9. *The new RSS standard button*

Pay Attention to Usability

Regardless of what type of blog you want to run, paying attention to making it easy to use pays off. Large software companies like Microsoft spend millions of dollars each year studying how people actually use their software and websites. In fact, much of the impetus for substantially changing Microsoft Office, a product that made $11.5 billion for Microsoft in 2005,[8] came from usability testing.

---

8. I got this figure from the Microsoft 2005 Annual Report (`www.microsoft.com/msft/ar.mspx`).

Jakob Nielsen's Alertbox (`www.useit.com/alertbox/`) has been preaching the importance of usability on the Web for over a decade, and his observations about blog usability are the lowdown on this important topic.

Here are some selected basic usability points Jakob makes that you should take to heart:

Include your biography. If your blog is going to be read, your readers have to trust you. How can they do that if you don't tell them about yourself?

Include your photo. Having at least one photo of yourself gives readers a chance to put a face to the name, improves your credibility, and puts your blog on a more personal level.

Posting titles matter. A posting title is a first and most important bit of information your readers use to decide if your post is worth their time. If they are reading your post via their RSS reader, it may be the only piece of information. Make it short, to the point, and active.

Categorize your posts. If you're posting about water skiing, antique cars, and Jimmy Buffet songs, make it easier for your readers by creating and using those subjects as categories, and let your blogging software or service handle organizing your content for you.

Stick to a schedule. Whether you plan to blog four times a day or four times a month, set a schedule and stick to it, so your readers have some idea of when your content will change. If you won't be blogging (for instance, because you're going on vacation), post on that so you're readers know what to expect.

Focus. A blog about anything and everything is a blog no one will read. Define and stick to the focus of your blog, and thereby build readership and value for your readers. This is an important point we will be coming back to elsewhere in this book, especially Chapter 9, but here's a little test for you now: Can you tell a friend in ten words or fewer what your blog is about? Yes? That's focus.

Describe your links. When creating links in your posts, make it very clear what you are linking to. Links like click here and here and here mean nothing, make more work for your readers, and lower the value of your posting in search engines.

Show your "best of." Give new readers a break and a reason to read your blog. In your blog's sidebar, list your five best posts. And don't forget to link to prior posts you've authored, because they expand the conversation and value of your current post.

This summarizes Jakob's findings, but hardly does them justice. I strongly recommend you read Jakob's article on blog usability at `www.useit.com/alertbox/weblogs.html`, shown in Figure 4-10.

Search

Jakob Nielsen's Alertbox, October 17, 2005:

Weblog Usability: The Top Ten Design Mistakes

Summary:
Weblogs are often too internally focused and ignore key usability issues, making it hard for new readers to understand the site and trust the author.

Weblogs are a form of website. The thousands of normal website usability guidelines therefore apply to them, as do this year's top ten design mistakes. But weblogs are also a special genre of website; they have unique characteristics and thus distinct usability problems.

One of a weblog's great benefits is that it essentially **frees you from "Web design."** You write a paragraph, click a button, and it's posted on the Internet. No need for visual design, page design, interaction design, information architecture, or any programming or server maintenance.

Weblogs make having a simple website much easier, and as a result, the number of people who write for the Web has exploded. This is a striking confirmation of the importance of ease of use.

Weblogs' second benefit is that they're a **Web-native content genre**: they rely on links, and short postings prevail. You don't have to write a full article or conduct original research or reporting. You can simply find something interesting on another site and link to it, possibly with commentary or additional examples. Obviously, this is much easier than running a conventional site, and again indicates the benefits of lowering the barriers to computer use.

As a third benefit, weblogs are **part of an ecosystem** (often called the Blogosphere) that serves as a positive feedback loop: Whatever good postings exist are promoted through links from other sites. More reader/writers see this good stuff, and the very best then get linked to even more. As a result, link frequency follows a Zipf distribution, with disproportionally more links to the best postings.

Some weblogs are really just private diaries intended only for a handful of family members and close friends. Usability guidelines generally don't apply to such sites, because the readers' prior knowledge and motivation are incomparably greater than those of third-party users. When you want to reach new readers who aren't your mother, however, usability becomes important.

Also, while readers of your **intranet** weblog might know you, usability is important because your readers are on company time.

Usability Issues

Figure 4-10. *Alertbox on blog usability issues*

First Steps to Building Your Blog

If this chapter were a PowerPoint presentation, the last slide would have just two bullet points as a conclusion:

- Own your words.

- Write for your readers.

Owning your own words means being credible. It also means that you should blog responsibly or suffer the consequences, but never be afraid to speak the truth as you see it.

Writing for your readers is easy. Just imagine yourself as one of them. Is this post too long and meandering? Have you made it easy for your readers to turn your monologue into a dialog with comments and trackbacks enabled? Have you done what you could to prevent spam, and are you taking the time to delete spam when it shows up?

Whatever kind of blog you decide to create, owning your words and writing for your readers are your basic guidelines to follow.

Your Action Tasks

Here are a few steps for strengthening your blog-writing muscles:

Know your rights! Go to EFF's Legal Guide at `www.eff.org/bloggers/lg/` and bookmark it. Plan to spend some time perusing this very readable guide, especially if you plan to link your business to your blog.

Who are you? Every good blog has an About page, and after reading a post or two on your blog, you can bet your readers will be looking for it. Start thinking about what you want to say about yourself on your About page. Consider how you want people to email you if they are so inclined, and what personal or professional information you want to include.

Find that picture! Every blog needs an About page, and that About page needs a photo of you! So start reviewing your digital pictures for something suitable. Think close-up head shots, since most services will limit the size of the image you can use.

And then you can continue with these steps:

Create a disclosure policy. If you're going to be talking about or reviewing products or services at your blog, it's a great idea to have a disclosure policy. Your readers will want to know if your glowing review of Acme TurboWidgets comes from your heart or from Acme's marketing budget. You'll find a simple-to-use disclosure policy maker at `www.disclosurepolicy.org` (funded by PayPerPost, which is discussed in Chapter 6).

Start your "my bad" list. Start noticing which words you tend to misspell or mistype. With attention comes correction.

Buy a current dictionary and thesaurus. Yes, I know, your word processor has both of these built in, and you can look up a word online in a moment, but just remember you're dealing with the training-wheels version of your language of choice that way. Nothing beats a good dictionary for understanding what a word really means or a thesaurus for finding a more punchy way of saying something. Visit a bookseller, browse the reference section, and take home a few new friends.

CHAPTER 5

Building Your Personal Blog

I think the hallmark of our age is great loneness.

—Futurist Alvin Toffler, in an interview with the author

What's driving the blogosphere? How does the practice of a few geeky programmers seem to suddenly become something important to 50 million people? What is it about blogging—posting your political rants, work rages, personal interests, and even your cats' best pictures—that matters to so many other people? That we can isn't the answer. The answer for many, many bloggers is that they need to do this.

If you can read blogs, odds are very good you live in a world profoundly different than it was when you were growing up or the world your parents knew. Nothing is the way it used to be. As futurist Alvin Toffler writes, we're rapidly being demassified, desynchronized, and disconnected from each other, and at the same time, we have ever more choices and decisions and ever more work to be done.

Our feeling of being more and more apart from everyone is borne out in the numbers. In a major study published in the *American Sociological Review*, entitled "Social Isolation in America" (`www.asanet.org/galleries/default-file/June06ASRFeature.pdf`), fully one-quarter of those surveyed reported that they had no one they could confide in, up from 10 percent 20 years ago. On average, our number of close personal friends has dropped from three to two.

And yet, while the number of people we know and share with offline diminishes, because we have too much to do and too little in common with the people who share some physical space with us, the number of people we know online, especially if we blog, soars. Blogging is the new campfire, office water cooler, town meeting, pub, and place of worship—the place where you can connect with people who understand you and who you can understand.

In this chapter, we're going to look at blogging from the personal angle, walking through how you can start connecting with others using a blog. We'll cover three ways to blog: Blogger, where personal blogging began; LiveJournal, the blogging service that puts personal into blogs; and Vox, the new service on the block. Along the way, you'll see a few "man-in-the-street" type mini-interviews with people in the blogosphere. Welcome to your personal blogosphere; come right in.

Blogger.com: Where It Started

If you're looking for the place where personal blogging started, look no further than Meg Hourihan's blog. She and her partner Evan Williams started a little project management

Internet startup in 1999 called Pyra Labs. While the application was still in beta, they realized they had a much more interesting weblog management program than a project management program. So, they repurposed it to make it easier for the hundred or so webloggers out there to use.

Blogger.com was born. Acquired by Google in 2003, Blogger.com is now called Blogger, with millions of active blogs today. And it's still the easiest and quickest way of starting a blog, especially a personal blog.

Blogs As Evolution

If you go to Meg Hourihan's blog (`http://megnut.com`) today, you won't find post after post about her days at Pyra Labs, or what it was like during the dot-com days. Meg has moved on, and now her blog focuses on what she is focused on: food and cooking, as you can see in Figure 5-1.

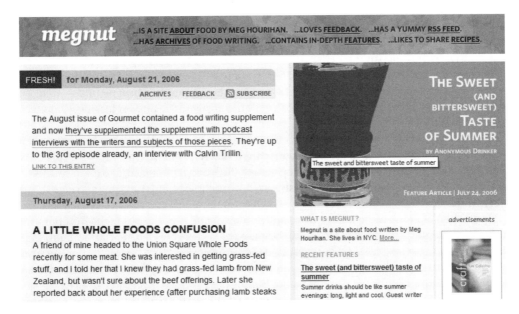

Figure 5-1. *Meg Hourihan's blog*

As one of the first bloggers in the world, Meg has been at it longer than just about anyone else. Her insights about personal blogging (and food blogging in particular) are definitely worth noting. Here's what Meg had to say in an email interview:

Q. *Since the very early days of blogging, you've had a blog. How has what blogging is changed for you?*

A. Blogging for me hasn't changed much over time. My site has changed focus over time and become less personal, but in general, I don't view blogging any differently than I did in 1999. How other people view blogging has changed quite a bit, and the word *blog* is now applied to a broader style of site than it was originally. But in my mind, it's still a site with links in reverse-chronological order about whatever is interesting to write about.

Q. *For people doing personal (as opposed to business/political/product) blogs, do you have any advice based on your blogging experience?*

A. Don't write anything you wouldn't want your grandmother or boss to read. Remember your audience is/can be bigger than you think, and with sites like Google indexing everything, what you write now can be found five years from now. And you might not feel the same way about things then. Unwise blog posts can come back to haunt you.

Q. *Your blog has changed over the years, and some of your earlier readers might have been disappointed. What should bloggers say to readers when their blogs change direction?*

A. I think it depends how the site changes direction. With Megnut, the transformation from entrepreneurial activities to cooking and food happened gradually, over the course of several years. Since the site never purported to be about anything except what I was interested in, it seemed logical that over time its focus would change. I think it's harder to get away with changing your blog's topic if it has one to begin with—e.g., you have a travel blog and then one day decide to change it to a gadget blog.

But in terms of my readers, I feel like they saw the change coming—many before I even did! There wasn't much to say to them until I finally decided to go food full time, and then most were happy. I imagine the ones who were interested in the tech stuff had stopped reading long ago.

Bloggers should always strive to be honest with their readers, so if/when the blog changes direction, they should just explain why. Is it a business reason? Personal interest? If your readers are interested in you, they'll understand and probably continue to read.

Q. *Megnut.com now focuses on food. How is blogging about food different from blogging about tech?*

A. It's a lot more fun! Actually, it's not all that different, although I do a lot more linking than I used to. When it was more about tech (and whatever caught my eye), I had a lot of anecdotes about business or startup life.

Once I was no longer in that environment, I didn't have as much to write about. Mostly the food blogging is different because it's new for me, and there's so much I don't know. Every day I read so much and learn so many new things. What I link to is a result of that process and is the best stuff I've learned that day that I think is worthy of sharing.

Q. *As a food blogger, what catches your eye?*

A. It really depends. Something that's well written usually will, especially if it's informative. I'm not too into the basically journal accounts of what another food blogger has eaten or cooked. But if there's something new there, I might link to it. Articles about whatever topic I'm currently interested in are common. So it was the Chicago foie gras ban for awhile, and then high-fructose corn syrup and corn-fed beef. Now it's soy and whether soy is as healthy as people claim. Plus I like great food photos, and weird recipes, and whatever else just strikes me as neat.

Q. *How does food blogging fit in with your life now? How does blogging in general fit in?*

A. Well, now food blogging is blogging in general for me. I spend about four to five hours a day doing Megnut, from reading food-related links and articles to researching longer pieces or doing some cooking on my own that I want to write about. It takes up a good chunk of my day, every weekday.

As an example of another type of personal blog, consider Michelle Tampoya's Blogger blog (www.mishsplayground.com), shown in Figure 5-2.

Figure 5-2. *Michelle Tampoya's blog*

Here's what Michelle, a marketing professional from Toronto, had to say in a brief interview:

Q. *What do you use your blog for?*

A. As a way to communicate with others—whether they are my family, friends, or strangers—about what is happening in my life and my passions.

Q. *Is your blog a major or minor way of connecting with people?*

A. It has become a major way. For my close friends and family, they can see what I have been up to through my blog. For strangers and others, it has been a way for me to connect with people. Many have contacted me outside my blog to ask for advice, talk about my passions, or give me advice. It is brilliant!

Blogging at Blogger

If you're thinking about starting a personal blog, and want to try out the concept with the absolute least amount of effort and cost, Blogger is an excellent platform to use. As an additional service, as of August 2006, Google allows bloggers to create private blogs, visible only to the people you invite.

This ability to decide who sees your blog, as opposed to just blogging to the entire online world, is a powerful and important concept. There are things you want to talk about, but don't necessarily want to share with certain people, such as strangers, coworkers, or potential employers. The more you can control who you share with, the more inclined you are to share, and the more important your online community is to you.

LiveJournal: The Community of Bloggers

If you're looking for the center of gravity when it comes to personal blogging, look no further than LiveJournal (`www.livejournal.com`), shown in Figure 5-3. Begun in 1999 by computer science college major Brad Fitzpatrick as a means to keep in touch with his high school friends, LiveJournal has become an online mega-community, with some 1.1 million actively involved and connected.[1]

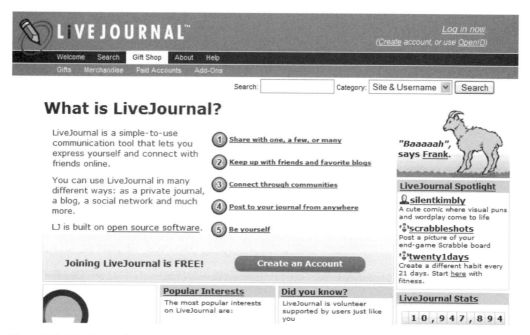

Figure 5-3. *LiveJournal*

---

1. This statistic comes from `www.livejournal.com/stats.bml`, where you can find other interesting LiveJournal statistics, such as the blogger population's gender and demographics.

I say "mega-community," because unlike other services such as Blogger, where each blog stands alone, LiveJournal strongly supports creating, finding, and building online communities of people who share or want to share something in common.

LiveJournal has more than a half million active communities. Table 5-1 lists a sampling summarized from a listing by Jane Anderson at Six Apart. Six Apart acquired LiveJournal in 2005.

Table 5-1. *Some LiveJournal Blog Communities*

Community	URL	Description
Fashion/Beauty/Do It Yourself (DIY)/Shopping		
Fruits	www.livejournal.com/ community/fruits/	For fans of Japanese street fashion (think Gwen Stefani's Harajuku Girls).
MadRadHair	www.livejournal.com/ community/madradhair/	Users post photos of their haircuts for feedback/advice (young and hip).
ThriftWhore	www.livejournal.com/ community/thriftwhore/	Users post photos of their thrift store finds.
Hot_Fashion	www.livejournal.com/ community/hot_fashion/	For fashion lovers to share photos, advice, questions, and so on about fashion.
CraftGrrl	www.livejournal.com/ community/craftgrrl/	For DIY designers.
Sew Hip	www.livejournal.com/ community/sew_hip/	For hip people who sew.
DIY Marketplace	www.livejournal.com/ community/diymarketplace/	Where DIY designers can sell their creations.
A Community for The Sampler	www.livejournal.com/ community/samplersampler/	For The Sampler (www. homeofthesampler.com), with tons of photos.
Gossip/Celebrity		
Elyse Sewell	www.livejournal.com/ users/elysesewell/	Journal of a contestant on the first season of "America's Next Top Model" TV show.
Oh No They Didn't	www.livejournal.com/ community/ohnotheydidnt/	About celebrity gossip.
Movies		
M15m = Movies in 15 minutes	www.livejournal.com/ community/m15m/	Based around a user who writes commentaries/summaries of movies via 15-minute-long scripts. (She has a book deal now. Perhaps she was "discovered" via her LiveJournal site?)

Table 5-1. *Some LiveJournal Blog Communities*

Community	URL	Description
Literature/Book Clubs/Writers		
Dispatches from Tanganyika	www.livejournal.com/ users/docbrite/	Journal by Poppy Z. Brite (author).
Fiction Writers' Community	www.livejournal.com/ community/fictionwriters/	Users can post fiction and get comments.
The Reading Room	www.livejournal.com/ community/thereadingroom/	Users answer the question "What are you reading?"
Little Details	www.livejournal.com/ community/little_details/	Writers ask other writers about little details that they want to get right.
Harry Potter	www.livejournal.com/community/ harry_potter/	For Harry Potter fans.
Photography		
Jumping Pictures	www.livejournal.com/ community/jumpingpictures/	People post photos of other people jumping.
Picturing Food	www.livejournal.com/ community/picturing_food/	People post photos of food.
Photography	www.livejournal.com/ community/photography/	Members can post photos for feedback and comments.
Domestic/Wedding		
Hip Domestics	www.livejournal.com/ community/hip_domestics/	For the discussion of all things hip and domestic.
Wedding Plans	www.livejournal.com/ community/weddingplans/	About wedding plans.

On LiveJournal, you can find other people who share the same interest, or (if you up your membership from free to paid, $3 USD/month) country or region, age, or online friends.

LiveJournal Users

LiveJournal entries tend to be exactly that: online journal entries shared with others. For example, take Lori Anderson, 17, a student at Concord University in West Virginia, whose LiveJournal blog lives at http://head-xplody.livejournal.com, as shown in Figure 5-4.

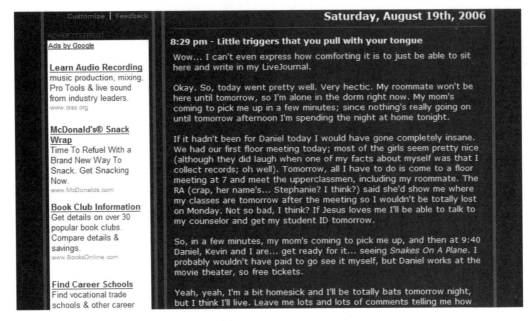

Figure 5-4. *Lori Anderson's LiveJournal blog*

Here's what Lori had to say:

Q. *What do you like about blogging?*

A. I like the fact that I can keep a record of what I've been doing or thinking, and then go back and see it later. I also like meeting other people through their blogs and keeping up with friends.

I use my blog as a journal. I write about what has been going on in my life, and my thoughts and opinions on things. I also frequently post photos.

Q. *How important is your LiveJournal blog to you?*

A. Blogging is a major way of connecting with other people for me. I have met many friends from different parts of the world through LiveJournal, and I can keep in touch with old friends by reading their LiveJournals and letting them read mine.

Or consider Ron DesGroseilliers of Spring Lake, North Carolina, who has been in the high-tech industry for 30 years. Figure 5-5 shows his LiveJournal blog at sprezzaturaron.livejournal.com (he also has a blog at sprezzaturarrd.blogspot.com).

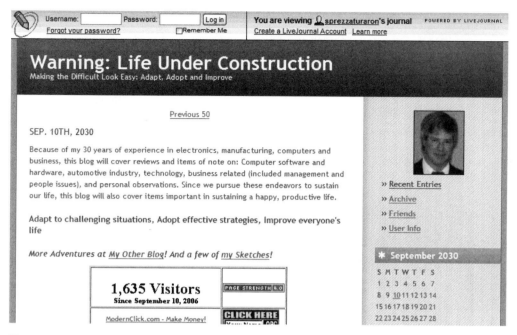

Figure 5-5. *Ron DesGroseilliers's LiveJournal blog*

Ron replied to my questions about his blog as follows:

Q. *What do you like about blogging?*

A. It gives me the chance to record events that I transition through, happenings in the worlds of technology and science, silly jokes that occur to me, accomplishments and worries, and posts that get me paid (via PayPerPost).

Q. *What do you use your blog for?*

A. In the days when dinosaurs roamed the earth and silicon was still sand, I used to write in a journal. Now I blog to mark events for future review and I write because of the thera-peutic release I get in doing so. However, until a couple of months ago, I wasn't as vigilant a blogger as I wanted to be. I've since found that some of my postings could generate money as long as I made the effort to blog as often as possible. So you can add "helping to pay the bills" to my reasons for writing.

Q. *Is blogging a major or minor way of connecting to other people for you?*

A. Very minor. When I write, it still feels like I'm transcribing into my journal—that there is no one behind my screen looking at these black letters on a white glow. Of course, you can lock up a journal from prying eyes. Not so with blogging. Yet, the idea of strangers reading my ramblings doesn't worry me. Every so often, someone will send a very insightful comment and give me a better perspective on my thoughts. While I look forward to such connections with people, I'd rather not seek them out as the main focus of my postings. That would be rather selfish and egotistical, wouldn't it?

Q. *Any advice on getting the most out of LJ?*

A. That is a good question! I'm still learning what LJ has available. As an open source appli-cation, it is still changing. Recently, they added certain styles to the way your blog is orga-nized. I would say that, as with any application or website, read the FAQs, visit the forums, and ask questions, even in your blog.

Then there's Mary Anne Walker of Maryland, who lists 51 interests in her LiveJournal user profile (among them Ayn Rand, cats, and indie rock). Mary Anne's LiveJournal blog at `pers1stence.livejournal.com`, shown in Figure 5-6, is a place for her to share with family and friends, but she keeps other entries to herself as a form of therapy.

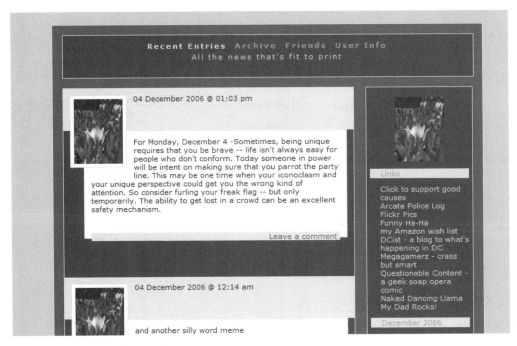

Figure 5-6. *Mary Anne Walker's LiveJournal blog*

Mary Anne also answered a series of questions about her blog.

Q. *What do you like about blogging?*

A. Blogging has three functions in my life: a) time wasting (reading other folks' blogs, taking silly quizzes, etc.); b) staying in touch with family and "real-life" friends; and c) locked, private entries that I use for "therapy" in much the manner of a traditional, paper-based diary.

Q. *Is blogging a major or minor way of connecting to other people for you?*

A. Blogging for me is not so much about connecting with new, online-only friends as it is a way to stay in touch with family and friends scattered across the country, especially college friends.

Q. *What do you especially like about LJ?*

A. I like that LJ allows for levels of privacy of entries—"private" entries that are only readable by me, "friends" postings that any of my friends with LJ accounts can read, and "custom filters" that allow me to set postings to only be read by specific friends with LJ accounts (with groupings like "family only" or "anyone but family," or even a filter to allow just one person to read like "mom only").

Getting the Most Out of LiveJournal

Here are some tips for LiveJournal blogging:

Go with the paid service. While you can certainly get a lot from LiveJournal's free service, $3 a month buys you access to more user pictures, a gallery, more customization options, better search features, and other goodies. Plus, you can say good-bye to advertising on your blog.

Get connected. Blogging at LiveJournal is about communities—either people you already know offline or connecting with people who have the same interests and concerns as you do. Use either the basic or advanced search function to find and try different communities.

Shop around. Not all communities are the same. Don't just pick the first community returned alphabetically by LiveJournal's search. Check out more than one, with an eye toward how recent the last post was, how interesting the journalers are to you, and how comfortable you feel with those particular people.

Download a client. You can find a wide variety of clients with features beyond what you can do in Internet Explorer or Firefox (for PCs, Macs, and other operating systems, as well as cell phones). Download one from LiveJournal's Download page at `www.livejournal.com/download/` and give it a try.

Make friends. All LiveJournal users can have up to 750 friends, and if you have a paid account, these friends don't have to also be LiveJournal users for you to keep track of their latest posts and photos.

WHAT ABOUT MYSPACE?

If you're looking for information in this book about MySpace, I'm sorry to disappoint you.

MySpace is a huge and growing social networking site. It is now owned by NewsCorp, with some 100 million user accounts. According to Alexa Web Information Service (`www.alexa.com`), in August 2006, MySpace was the world's fourth most popular English-language website and the seventh most popular in any language.

Social networks like MySpace, Bebo, FaceBook, Flickr, Cyworld, and many more (see `http://en.wikipedia.org/wiki/List_of_social_networking_websites`) often support blogging and blog-like activities, but primarily are about networking with others who share the same interests, age, or desires. For many, MySpace and other social networks provide a purer form of connection than personal blogs or journals.

As interesting as social networking is, it's not the same as blogging. So, it is a topic for a whole other book.

Vox: Second-Generation Blogging

Most LiveJournal's users are 25 or younger, and their journals, posts, and interests reflect this. But no one gets to stay that age forever, and LiveJournal's corporate owners are keenly aware of both the pressure from below of sites catering to even younger people who grew up on and with the Net (like MySpace) and older people who, for better or worse, no longer have the concerns and challenges they did when they were in their twenties.

Enter Six Apart's Vox (http://vox.com), shown in Figure 5-7, the first true second-generation blogging system.

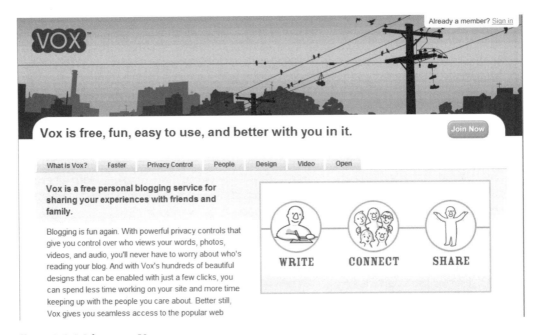

Figure 5-7. *Welcome to Vox*

I have not discussed very much of the history of blogging in this book, since what happened five years ago, in the early days of blogging, is not much help to someone who is interested in blogging today. But like trying to understand why something happens in the analog world, sometimes the backstory of an online product or website really can explain if it's right for you.

Vox's Backstory

Web designers Mena and Ben Trott started Six Apart in September 2001 after the web design firm they worked for went belly up just as Mena's weblog, Dollarshort, was in need of new and better software. A month later, the Trotts released Movable Type 1.0, which quickly became one of the most popular blogging platforms people could install on their server.

Mena and Ben's micro-ISV[2] was in the right place, with the right product, and in just a few years, it graduated to being a full-blown, venture capital–funded company. The Trotts were quick to realize that for every geek with a server willing to license Movable Type, there were a hundred, a thousand, ten thousand people who just wanted to have a weblog (now called a blog). By October 2003, Six Apart launched TypePad.

Now you might be asking yourself, so what? TypePad may be a great blogging platform (in my opinion), but there's WordPress, Blogger, Community Server, LiveJournal, and a whole slew of other blogging tools. Here are three reasons why Mena and Ben's endeavors are of interest:

- Mena and Ben's Six Apart bought LiveJournal in January 2005 from Brad Fitzpatrick's company, and made him Six Apart's chief architect.

- Mena and Ben have been living, breathing, and thinking about blogging and all of its implications for as long or longer than anyone else in the world.

- Six Apart put a major portion of its revenue into the design, creation, and provisioning of Vox.

Back in mid-2005, I interviewed Mena Trott for another book I wrote,[3] and toward the end of the interview, she had this to say:

Q. *Do you think there will be as many people blogging as emailing?*

A. I think it's very possible. I should explain that more. In terms of blogging, I don't think blogging always has to be necessarily public. There's personal blogging, there's private blogging, and then there's public. More people are going to want to have private weblogs, where they're chronicling events, sharing things with small groups. And so we see this with LiveJournal, which we purchased this year. These are small groups of people kind of having a conversation.

My mom, when she starts to blog, she isn't going to want anyone but me and my aunt reading it—and that's an important form. That's why I think blogging is going to be as important as emailing—it's a form of communication that takes the form of archiving, of photo management, of comments, and RSS, and it allows people to communicate better. There's that group and then the other group who want to reach larger groups. That will be a lot of businesses, people who have stories to tell, or politics, or just larger communities. Blogging can be used for any purpose.

What Mena was talking about was Vox, Latin for voice, Six Apart's new blogging platform and deeper interpretation of what personal blogging could and would become.

---

2. By micro-ISV, I mean a self-funded, under-five-person software company.
3. The book is *Micro-ISV: From Vision to Reality* (Apress, 2006). This is a book for programmers who want to start their own micro-ISVs and are looking for guidance on the dozens of different marketing, planning, technical support, payment systems, and like topics you need to master to be successful. The whole interview with Mena, and about 60 others, appears in that book.

What Makes Vox Different?

The most obvious difference about Vox compared to, say, TypePad or Blogger is just how easy and painless it is to actually write posts and incorporate all sorts of other things into your content—from video on YouTube and IFILM, to books on Amazon, to photos on Flickr, as shown in Figure 5-8.

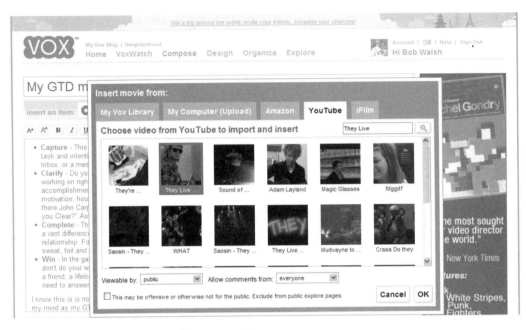

Figure 5-8. *Adding a YouTube video to your Vox post*

Vox's fast, built-in, Ajax-powered spell-checking (see Figure 5-9), easy tagging, and great looks you can change in an instant, all backed up with automatic saving and recovery,[4] put the other blogging services to shame.

---

4. If you've ever lost a posting at a blogger service because of a server or browser error, you'll know just how cool Vox's recovery feature is. If not, imagine using Microsoft Word without being able to save your document until you finished it.

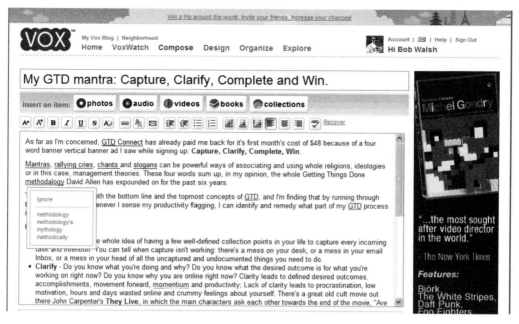

Figure 5-9. *Vox spell-checking in action*

The next thing you'll notice about Vox isn't the ads that pay for the free version of the service; it's that you can decide whether anyone, just your friends and family, just your family, just your friends, or just you can see that post.

Being able to control who sees your post makes a world of difference in what and how you post in Vox. There are parts of your life you want to share with anyone, parts that are more personal and appropriate for just your friends, and some things that matter only to your family. With Vox, you don't have to constantly be your own censor, editing out posts you may not want your current or next employer to see.

Vox uses the concept of Neighborhood, which can consist of your family, friends, and other people whom you're interested in including. Unlike with LiveJournal communities, you are the center of your Vox Neighborhood. Each time you log in to Vox, you start at your blog and see the most recent posts and comments from whatever portion of your Neighborhood you want to track. It's like having an up-to-date display of the people you know online and what they are doing.

For example, take Andrew Anker, Vox's General Manager. Andrew has 225 people visible in his Neighborhood, as shown in Figure 5-10. Now a lot of these people are Six Apart employees, but a lot are not. Andrew's Neighborhood includes people he wants to keep in touch with and keep up on, despite the crazy, busy world in which we now live.

Figure 5-10. *Andrew Anker's Vox Neighborhood*

As General Manager of Vox, Andrew pretty much has the destiny of this blogging service in his hands. Here is what he had to say about Vox in a recent interview.

Q. *There's TypePad out there. There's LiveJournal out there. Why does the world need Vox?*

A. It really gets down to a different market segment than what we see a lot of the other properties, including LiveJournal, going after.

As far as we're concerned, the under, let's call it 30, market is very well served by a number of great properties, certainly LiveJournal, MySpace, FaceBook, Zanga—we can go on and on—but a number of people are going after the community aspects of blogging for a younger audience.

Whether you're trying to meet people like LiveJournal, meet people to date like a Friendster or MySpace, meet people in school like a FaceBook, there are lots of different reasons to be blogging in that age group. But we really feel like it's a very well-served market. When we looked at the overall market though, and certainly the big part of the market being people over 25, we really felt that there was no tool available that hit the types of personal blogging that we think is really the most important future way people will blog. And if you're familiar with the functionality, in particular, it's having the ability to create privacy groups and post only to the people who you want to see something.

So, again, when you're trying to collect friends in the MySpace parlance, you want to be very public, and that's great. When you're trying to show pictures of your newborn to the rest of your family and to your very close friends, you want that to be in a private space. And there really isn't a place right now to do that. And that's what Vox is going after.

So we don't think it replaces TypePad. We don't think it replaces any of the other great platforms for publishing in a big public way. We think it sits nicely to the side of those.

When we're talking from a business standpoint on a one-to-many kind of context, TypePad is still the best tool out there by far. But when we want to talk among our friends, when we want to bring videos of our kids—well, I've got some older kids now who are doing music videos, and it's wonderful, but I don't want to share that with my 10,000 closest friends. I want to share that with my 10 closest friends and family. And so Vox is really going after that exact market.

Q. *I'm hearing that you're not looking at this as being a blog for businesses. You're looking at it as being a first-person blog for people. Am I correct in thinking that?*

A. Yes.

Q. *What about things like churches, organizations, political parties? How do you see Vox getting used in those areas?*

A. That's a great question. Again, we should talk about use cases.

So if I'm a church—we'll pick that—and I run a community-outreach portion of that church trying to get people involved in events, trying to talk about the sermon last week or what's coming up this week, I might actually not want to use Vox. I may be much better positioned to use TypePad, which again is this idea of one-to-many. It still lets you have feedback. It still lets you have comments. It still lets you do all the things that blogs do. But it's much more designed around the idea of one person, or two or three people, writing something that then will be read by hundreds or even thousands.

If you're talking about the other aspect of a church or a community group, which is actually to get a very interactive rich dialog among a lot of people—not just a linear "I write something and you want to comment on it," but actually have multiple people talking, have multiple people sharing pictures of events that have just happened—then you want to talk about Vox.

I want to talk about a feature in Vox that we're going to add this year which is a community model. Again this is one of those things we don't have yet [as of early December 2006]. So caveat.

Right now in Vox, the only way to be a member of Vox is to have a blog yourself and talk about things that you are interested in. Later this year, we're going to release a community feature where you, or any other user, can actually create either a closed or an open community that's going to have much more of a group discussion, group feel.

We're going to keep all the same things that you know and love about Vox. So there'll still be things like privacy, and tags, and ability to bring in photos and audio files and videos, and all the other good stuff about Vox. But you will have much more of a group feel, as opposed to an individual feel.

So the community leader in that particular instance might set up for the local church or baseball team an open community, where the 100 or 200 people in the community group want to come in and participate. That way, anybody in that group, if they're given the permission by the owner of the group, could then post to that community.

So it becomes much more of a many-to-many experience as opposed to one-to-many, which is what TypePad is really good at.

Q. *How do you avoid becoming yet another forum software package, if you go that route?*

A. I'm not sure you want to avoid being forum software.

I think how you avoid being "yet another" is really by doing the stuff that I think we've done pretty well with Vox, which is make it look great. That is something that most forum software that I've seen doesn't do. That's one.

Two is allowing people to bring in all of the rich media stuff, including via web services things like YouTube and Photobucket and Flickr photos and videos. Which again, I have not seen forum software do.

But I think probably the most important thing, and this is key to why blogs matter and certainly key to to Six Apart's brand,, is that in each case in a Vox community, it's still about a person and an identity. So in most forum software, the reason conversations tend to break down is because you have anonymity. You have this sense of whoever speaks the loudest gets heard the most.

And without having a forced identity, without having to sort of state who you are, you really do very quickly get to the lowest common denominator. Which pushes out, if they even came in the first place, the people who you want to have in that dialog.

So with Vox, again the community model is not fully built, so I'm talking a little bit speculatively now.

But we will still have to keep that sense of identity. Or to have the ability to say "only certain people can participate in this community."

So we really think that the big breakdown in forums, and for that matter in unmoderated open commenting in blogs, is a lack of the sense of ownership of your personality, your user presence, and your identity. When you don't have that, you have this very quick dash for the bottom.

Q. *Here's a high-level question for you: Is one of the things that you're trying to get done with Vox sort of being your online digital dashboard of relationships?*

A. That's a big goal. You said it's a high-level question, and it certainly is. If you ask the ten-year goal, the five-year goal, absolutely.

And I think I'd say that it's the Six Apart goal; it's not just the Vox goal. With my audience, which is the over-25 crowd, Vox is going after that. LiveJournal would say the exact same thing for its audience.

Mena Trott talks about life reporting and this idea of tracking all the things that are important to you. And that's really very critical to Vox. Whether those things that are important to you are pictures or videos or audio files, they're your friends, or they're just the random thoughts that you have, we really wanted to make Vox the place that you want to put it all.

And this is where the privacy is so important, and this is true even of my TypePad blogging. When I blog on TypePad, I have one model which is "to the world."

There are times that you start to write and you sort of go, "Hmm, I don't know that I want everybody to see this," and you just stop. With Vox, I find I don't do that anymore because I know that once I'm done writing it, I can then decide who sees it, including the extreme, which is only me. And that's just as important a mode as friends, family, and the others.

And so the idea is you just start typing. When you're done, you say, "No, this is just a random thought. I'm not ready to show this to anybody, so I'll keep it as only visible to me." Or, "This is something that I feel so good about that I'll make it available to everybody." We've all found this personally. By knowing you go in with the control, you really then are much more comfortable to just start talking. And then later on, once you've seen what it looks like, decide exactly how you want to deal with that.

In fact, it's funny, I was talking yesterday to a good friend of ours who runs a company and has a corporate blog. And he said that he has been on Vox now for about two months, probably three months. He said that he's now using his public blog, his corporate blog, much more often, because he was taught by using his Vox blog to just blog and to feel comfortable about the whole process. Even though the vast bulk of what he does on Vox is private, it has now encouraged him to go do much more public blogging on his TypePad blog, his corporate blog.

And so getting back to your high-level question, we think this tool is built to encourage people to report, to bring all of their assets in. And not just bring into Vox. If you bring them into Flickr, that's great. We work with that. Or bring it into YouTube; bring it into Photobucket.

We don't want to say we're the best photo tool. So if we encourage you to take more pictures and you think Flickr is better, great. Use Flickr, and when you want to bring that into your blog, we'll help you with that, very easily.

Q. *I notice you pretty severely limit formatting options in Vox.*

A. My internal design goal is "no angle brackets." People should not have to deal with HTML. If you want to deal with HTML, there are a lot of great platforms, including LiveJournal and TypePad, that let you get into the real hacking of HTML. In the case of Vox, we want to keep you away from that, because we want to get you back to talking about things, not hacking code.

And so, assuming you do what we just talked about, and then you hit publish, now you're users and you, yourself, can see that YouTube video. They can play it directly from your blog. And the fact that there's some JavaScript and HTML that we've taken from YouTube and inserted into your blog and formatted nicely is sort of beside the point. You just care about the fact that you put a nice video into your blog.

Q. *What are collections?*

A. Collections is on the list of features that are sort of starting. I would say probably 20 percent done, not even 35 or 40 percent done.

Collections is really the idea of a photo album where you can take a number of photos and put them into one group and say "these are my vacation shots," or "these are my big party shots," or "pictures of my dog."

Collections is something that we're really going to spend a lot of time with over the next couple months, and really bring out much more of an ability to collect any random set of assets and turn them into something that you want to present. Again, we're talking more hypothetical book time frame as opposed to podcast time frame.

But if you wanted to do something like, "Here's all my stuff from San Francisco. Here are the videos I shot. Here are some podcasts. Here are some photos." Maybe, "Here's a YouTube video." Maybe, "Here's a couple of posts about my vacation to San Francisco." You can wrap that all up and say, "Here is my San Francisco collection."

And over time, we'd like to give you a lot of control over that and almost to turn it into its own blog, if you think about it that way.

Q. *Regarding comment spam, now with a TypePad key, that type of authentication works well. But it seems like as soon as there's a new thing on the Net, the spammers find a way to spam. What will you be doing about that as far as Vox goes? How do you keep them out?*

A. The easy answer is that there's no easy answer.

This is an arms race. As you mentioned yourself, as soon as we come up with a tool, they come up with a way around the tool, and there's a back and forth.

I think really what we do is a couple of different things. We leverage the knowledge that we already have at Six Apart. We have tens of millions of people visiting our blogs every month. We've been doing this now for upwards of seven years. We have a lot of knowledge internally about what has worked and what hasn't worked in Movable Type, TypePad, and LiveJournal.

We're certainly not starting from scratch here. We're going to take all of the learning and make sure to apply it. And a lot of that is lots of little things. There's no one big thing, because one big thing is really easy to get around. So it's lots of little things, which is much harder to get around. So that's one answer.

The second answer is, by keeping a much more closed community, you actually naturally avoid some of that. If you're talking about a very popular TypePad blog, that reaches 100,000 people, the value of spam is actually pretty high. A lot of people might see the comment. You get a lot of link juice, Google juice. And there's a whole set of reasons why there's value to spamming that blog. If you're talking about a personal blog, which is mostly private friends and family, only for five other people, there's obviously not a lot of value to that. Yeah, you [the spammer] are getting in front of those five people, but you don't know who they are. There's no link juice because it's all private anyway, or mostly private. The other thing, the sort of easy answer, is the nature of Vox automatically makes it much less valuable. And you see that already on LiveJournal. So that's two.

Three is we do have features already, and we're going [to] continue to expand those to actually control your comments. So right now on Vox, you can do something like say "let anybody read this, but only let my friends and family comment on it." And then you control it. That's fully moderated, because you control who are your friends and who are your family. And so you can do things like say, "I want everyone to read it. I think this is something that's world-ready. But I really don't care what anybody but my family thinks." And so, again, you can do that.

Connecting with Your Online World

Your wealth is where your friends are.

—Titus Maccius Plautus, Roman playwright

Recent surveys show that a full 9 percent of American adults and 11 percent of Britons have started blogging.[5] These are amazing statistics and a good indication that blogging is more than just endless talk about tech, politics, and sports.

Blogging is a powerful way of connecting to other people on a personal level, in an increasingly impersonal world. Your personal blog is more than a soapbox to rant from or a virtual soft shoulder to cry on. It's a way of sharing who you are and what matters to you with other people who look for connections online with kindred souls.

The idea of having more than one persona we share with the world is older than Rome. We all have our "game face" for work, our way of interacting with personal friends, and that part of ourselves only family and the closest of friends can and should ever get to see. Online identity is a tricky thing. A lot of people want to share, but not necessarily with the whole wide world, including their current or next boss.

As you can probably tell, I'm a big fan of Vox. I think Six Apart, building on all its experience with blogging and with blogging communities like LiveJournal, has a winner out of the gate.

Your Action Tasks

Whether you go with Blogger, LiveJournal, Vox, or another way of blogging, here are a few next steps to finding your personal connection in the blogosphere:

Share, but anonymously. With the notable exception of Vox, if you are going to bare your soul in a blog, keep your real identity something you share only with family and friends you trust. Remember that Google never forgets, and few employers, ex-lovers, or ex-anythings are likely to forgive you.

Blog for yourself, then others. Personal blogs, like traditional diaries and journals, are a way of having a meaningful conversation with yourself first and foremost. If you don't feel better for posting to your blog, why bother?

Respond to comments. If you're blogging in a public way, talk with the people who have taken the time to read and comment about your posts. This is the quickest way of making the type of online connections and actual friendships every blogger values.

A picture is worth a 1,000-word post. Blogs with pictures tell a far more interesting story than those without. You don't need an expensive digital camera and extensive photography skills—a camera-enabled cell phone and Yahoo Flickr are good enough.

---

5. This usage data is reported by Steve Rubel, Jupiter Research, www.micropersuasion.com/2006/08/adage_takes_a_r.html and *The Guardian* newspaper, http://technology.guardian.co.uk/news/story/0,,1824769,00.html, respectively.

And then you can continue with these steps:

Go Vox. Unless Six Apart seriously stumbles, I predict Vox is going to be the place for personal blogs. Get a free account, learn your way around, feed your friends' email addresses into Vox's search function, and build your Vox Neighborhood.

Share your interests. Whether at Vox or LiveJournal, interests make communities. Start with a few things you have an abiding interest in, then branch out from there.

Play in your class. As young at heart as you may be, people in their teens have different interests, concerns, and issues than people in their twenties, or ahem, in their post-twenties. Whether you pick a big site like LiveJournal or the quasi-blog MySpace, or any of the hundreds of other smaller blogging sites springing up, you're going to get more out of your personal blog if it's in the right place.

Don't be a stranger. The best way to build connections to your personal blog is to reach out to other personal blogs, those of people you know or people who are interested in the same things you are. Be active!

CHAPTER 6

Professionally Blogging, Blogging Professionally

So you've paid your dues, toiled for years, learned the ropes, and done all the things you need to do to establish your standing as a professional. Maybe you're a professional in the old meaning of the word: a doctor, a lawyer, an engineer, an accountant, or the like. Or perhaps you're a professional in one of the thousands of areas our complex, modern society has developed: graphic artist, investment banker, speech therapist, online marketing consultant, and so on.

No matter what type of professional you are, here are four things I think you know are true:

- You've worked long and hard developing expertise and experience in your chosen field.

- Most people don't really understand what you do.

- You have a million competitors all over the world just one click away on the Internet.

- You should start a professional blog to build your online global identity.

Okay, this last point may not yet be obvious to you, but after you read this chapter, I hope you will agree.

In this chapter, we're going to look at people—commonly called *professionals*—who are leveraging their hard-earned expertise, know-how, and point of view to build positive, powerful, and, above all else, professional online reputations. The bloggers you'll meet in this chapter are drawn from the "traditional" professions: law, medicine, and the ministry. The one factor they have in common is that they are influencing prospective clients via their blogs.

We'll also take a quick drive-by look at the intersection of Your Career and Blogging. I think you'll find some rather interesting things happening in the world of career building and professional recruitment, and some very useful things you need to know about how blogging can help, or hurt, you career prospects.

Finally for dessert, we'll take a look at the just-emerging field of blogging as an occupation.

Traditional Professionals Blogging

Professional has become a very slippery concept in the modern world. Wikipedia has a good definition of *profession* (http://en.wikipedia.org/wiki/Profession):

A profession is an occupation that requires extensive training and the study and mastery of specialized knowledge, and usually has a professional association, ethical code and process of certification or licensing.

For the nineteenth and much of the twentieth century, the three most recognized occupations as professions were law, medicine, and the clergy. Lawyers, doctors, and ministers are afforded special deference, standing, and legal status in most places around the world. We'll look at these three professions, with a by no means random sampling of what lawyers, doctors, and nuns are doing in and with the blogosphere.

FEAR NOT THE INTERNET PRICE

It used to be enough for a professional to spend years in college, and then some time learning what college could not teach. Plus, you did a bit of networking in your community via local charity work or business groups, to be assured of a steady supply of patients, clients, or customers.

Not any more.

Today, your services—just like everything else in the global economy, from all the goods manufactured in China to US tax returns now being prepared in India—has an Internet price. Just as the Internet became every insular retailer's worst nightmare—cheaper prices available to their customers instantly—now it's your turn.

Or not. It doesn't have to be that way if you embrace what the Internet, especially the blogosphere, can do for you.

Now you may think the Internet price won't come knocking at your door. After all, you're not an American programmer, an accountant, a radiologist, a financial analyst, a graphic artist, an architect, or a member of a few hundred other "knowledge" professions whose jobs were and can be offshored. Nope, you do real things with real people face to face: You feed people, heal them, train them, or sue them. So you're in the clear, right? Wrong.

Even if you're in a profession that is "offshore-safe," you need to face the reality that your clients, patients, or customers are going to make their purchasing decisions based on what they learn about you online. You, or your competitors, are only a Google search away.

Lawyers and Blogs

Generalizations can often get you in trouble, but the consistent message is that the jury is in when it comes to blogging for small or solo practitioners, and it's no contest: blogs are a powerful way of attracting clients, building referral networks, and gaining standing in your legal community.

Blogging for the Public or for Other Attorneys

The two main approaches attorneys seem to take are blogging for the general (and prospective) public or blogging for other attorneys and legal professionals.

Let's start with Ron Miller, who writes the Maryland Injury Lawyer Blog (www.marylandinjurylawyerblog.com/), shown in Figure 6-1.

Figure 6-1. *The Maryland Injury Lawyer Blog*

Here is what Ron had to say to a set of questions I emailed him regarding his blog:

Q. *Has your blog led to increased referrals and/or new clients?*

A. Our blog has lead to increased attorney referrals from attorneys in other jurisdictions that have a case in Maryland or from Maryland lawyers who either do not handle the type of cases we handle (personal injury) or who have a case that is of such a size that, financially and in terms of expertise, they are better off referring the case to our firm.

Q. *What do your current and old clients think of your blog?*

A. Our blog is focused directly to other lawyers. This might not be the best strategy from a marketing perspective, but it makes the blog a lot more interesting to write. There are really only so many things you can say to personal injury victims without actually discussing their case with them. Still, more sophisticated clients do read our blog and learn more about how we handle personal injury cases from the blog.

Q. *How do you find things to blog about?*

A. I read a lot. I read new Maryland cases and legal news, and read a lot of really great blogs. These things give me good ideas for interesting blog topics.

Q. *Any advice that you give to other attorneys who are considering blogging?*

A. If you like to write and you like to learn, try it. And if you are going to do it, write about what aspect of the law really interests you, not what you think you should write about. But if you are thinking of doing it solely as a marketing vehicle, forget about it. If that is your only purpose, you will never stay with it, and your time could be just as well served elsewhere.

Other advice: Don't pressure yourself to blog. No one is paying you to do it. So blog when you want. When I started, I got a few very well-intended "where have you been?" emails from regular readers. It can create pressure that the blogger really should not have.

Q. *What's been the most surprising thing about blogging?*

A. The most surprising thing is just how much I learn from the process of (1) picking a topic and (2) researching the topic I have selected. Good legal blogging gives you the chance to learn and a chance to educate.

Still not convinced? Well, consider Ben Stevens, an attorney practicing family law in South Carolina. He has not one, but two blogs going: the Family Law Blog (www.SCFamilyLaw.com), shown in Figure 6-2, and a blog for lawyers who use Macs (www.TheMacLawyer.com).

Figure 6-2. *The South Carolina Family Law Blog*

Here is how Ben responded in an email interview:

Q. *Why did you start your blog?*

A. I began my blog (www.SCFamilyLaw.com) as a service to fill what I saw as a need. When I started it back in June of 2005, it was the second legal blog in South Carolina and the first one devoted to family law issues. At that time, there simply were not many blogs devoted to family law topics, so there were not many sources from which the public (and other attorneys) could easily obtain helpful information about family law issues.

Q. *What are the positive effects of your blog as far as your practice?*

A. Writing the blog has helped keep me abreast of developing issues in family law and helped me critically analyze them before writing about them. It has also enabled me to meet great lawyers in other parts of the country through their blogs. A side and somewhat unexpected benefit is that the blog has given me notoriety and led to me being interviewed by several media outlets on various family law issues.

Q. *Has your blog lead to new referrals or clients?*

A. I have had a great many clients contact me through the blog. I find that they find my blog when researching a particular issue online, and after reading the articles on the blog, they can determine whether I am the right attorney for them. I did not start the blog as a means of getting clients, but it certainly is a nice benefit.

Q. *Are you enjoying blogging?*

A. Publishing the blog has become something that I very much enjoy. It takes a great deal of work to monitor the many blogs, research relevant issues, and write the articles, but I find it to be quite rewarding. I was very active in a service fraternity in college, and I have always enjoyed helping others. However, between my busy law practice and my wife and kids, "free" time is very scarce for me, but publishing the blog enables me to provide a valuable service in a manageable amount of time and to do so as my schedule permits.

Q. *Any advice for other attorneys considering blogging?*

A. If you are interested in blogging, first read legal blogs to make sure that it is for you, because it is not for everyone. The next step would be to find a niche that is not being addressed and take the steps to set up your blog. The options range from going with a great blogging service (like LexBlog) to a "do-it-yourself" solution (like TypePad). I have used both, using LexBlog for www.SCFamilyLaw.com and TypePad for www.TheMacLawyer.com, and there are definite pros and cons to each. Either way, I hope that any interested attorneys make sure that they can make the time commitment to maintain the blog and keep it fresh and relevant. There are too many blogs out there that got off to a promising start, only to falter or end after a few months.

Dave Swanner, another attorney in South Carolina, writes the South Carolina Trial Law Blog (www.SCTrialLaw.com), shown in Figure 6-3.

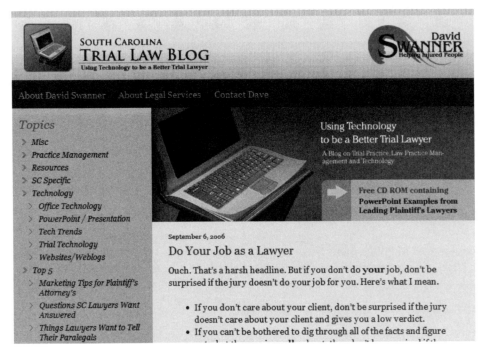

Figure 6-3. *The South Carolina Trial Law Blog*

Dave also answered a series of email questions regarding his blog.

Q. *Why did you start* SCTrialLaw.com*?*

A. The tagline of my blog is "Using Technology to Be a Better Trial Lawyer." I address trial techniques, practice management, and using computers to try cases better and run an office better.

Since I'm on the Internet on a regular basis anyway, a blog was a natural for me. I worked my way through law school as a custom programmer and am rather tech-savvy. It is a simple way to keep in touch with people.

Q. *What can you do at your blog that you can't do at your law practice's website,* www.DavidvsGoliath.com*?*

A. To me, a firm website is basically an extension of the traditional brochure. Yes, it can include more information. Yes, you can do things in a more multimedia format that hooks people in. Yes, you can provide more information than in a brochure.

A weblog allows you to write about whatever you want. On a number of the listservs, I write detailed responses, only to have the same question pop up again three to six months later. With the weblog, I can write the post, and when the question is asked again, just link to the original post.

Q. *You mention in one recent post that having a blog got you more visibility, referrals, and clients. Can you go into a little more detail about each?*

A. I have been writing the blog since January 2005. In 2005, I was well recognized in the South Carolina trial lawyer community for having technical knowledge that was valuable to trial lawyers. I had given presentations at our convention five years in a row, but I wanted to move more towards being a regional and/or national level speaker. There are two reasons for this. Education is very important to me, and I practice in Myrtle Beach. Myrtle Beach is a resort town with a lot of visitors. In 2006, I will have given presentations in seven different states, including being invited as the opening speaker for another state's trial lawyer convention. That's a solid year of speaking engagements for a sole practitioner.

I also get referrals from lawyers who I have never even met. A few weeks ago, I received a new case from an out-of-state client who was injured in Myrtle Beach, and asked where he had found out about me. Apparently the client was referred by a North Carolina criminal defense attorney who I had not heard of, but who was familiar with my blog. This has happened on a number of occasions.

I also think that the weblog increases my visibility within the South Carolina trial lawyer community. I don't think it makes a difference about whether someone will refer me a case, but I do think it makes a difference in helping them remember my name when they have a Myrtle Beach case to refer. Within the South Carolina trial lawyer community, it has also helped me make more friends and given people something to talk to me about (and vice versa).

When someone writes a weblog over an extended period of time, it's impossible for their personality *not* to come out. When people read your blog, they feel like they know you.

I have had a few clients call directly from the blog. One comment was, "I figured that if you cared enough to share this information with other trial lawyers, that you would care enough to take care of my family." You don't get that from a brochure, a website, or an advertisement.

Q. *You're a busy guy. How do you find time to blog and things to blog about?*

A. I read and am on the computer a lot. In the evening, when we watch a movie or TV, I have a laptop with a wireless Internet connection and read and blog. One of the hard things is that sometimes I *don't* have time to blog. So, I don't. The blog is fun and a good business tool, but not a be all, end all. Life is more important. Life first, blog second.

I blog about what interests me. I take notes at seminars and conventions, and post the notes. I blog about good stuff other lawyers have written about. I blog about books that I've read. With permission, I blog about good conversations or posts that are on the listservs. I blog about things that happen to me. I blog about good things that I've found on the Internet.

We're in the middle of a knowledge revolution. If you're paying attention, it's nearly impossible to *not* have topics to blog about.

Q. *There seems to be a good number of legal bloggers in South Carolina for some reason. Why is that?*

A. I think the primary bloggers in South Carolina are myself and Ben Stevens of www.SCFamilyLaw.com. Ben is a friend of mine and said I encouraged or inspired him to write the blog. Ben is pretty tech-savvy himself, and regardless of how he got started, has done a fabulous job with his family law blog. In fact, he has done such a great job with it that it makes me want to get divorced, just so I can read it more.

Dave has a lot of advice for other attorneys blogging at www.sctriallaw.com/cat-things-to-know-about-writing-a-weblog.html.

Blogging Resources for Attorneys

The following are some useful blogging resources for attorneys:

What blogs can do for you: For solo and small law firms considering plunging into the blogosphere, an excellent multipart resource is "What Blogs Can Do for Solo & Small Firm Lawyers" (http://solosmallfirmblog.typepad.com/mdbartalk/2003/11/so_what_can_web.html), written by Carolyn Elefant with Jerry Lawson in 2003. Both these practicing attorneys have blogs to this day.

American Bar Association (ABA): The ABA has several useful resources, including a Continuing Legal Education course covering blogging. You can find more information at www.abanet.org/cle/programs/t06ere1.html. Another good ABA resource is its "Blawgs" page at www.abanet.org/genpractice/resources/blawgs.html. And you can read the transcript of a roundtable discussion by legal bloggers, sponsored by the ABA, at www.abanet.org/lpm/magazine/articles/v31is5an4.html.

LexBlog: LexBlog bills itself as the leading provider of marketing blogs to lawyers and other professional service firms, and has a blog at http://kevin.lexblog.com/. Kevin wants to sell you his company's services, but does a good job of explaining the advantages and pitfalls of legal blogging along the way.

Victor Medina: Victor Medina's Small Business and Solo Law Practice Blog at http://victormedina.typepad.com covers just that, but with a decidedly high-tech focus, including blogging.

Is There a Doctor in the House?

Now, in case you're wondering, lawyers are by no means the only "traditional" professionals blogging. Doctors and medical professionals of all types have joined the blogosphere in numbers, but with a difference.

Doctors, at least when it comes to the front lines of healthcare in the US and the UK, are not very happy campers. Either flogged by HMOs who want the maximum number of patients serviced in the least amount of time or suffering the death of a thousand insurance-form cuts, few MDs have the time and opportunity offline to educate, counsel, or commiserate with their patients. For some of these clinicians, blogging has become an outlet for that part of their professional lives.

A case in point is the Cheerful Oncologist at `http://scienceblogs.com/thecheerfuloncologist/`, also known as Dr. Craig Hildreth of St. Louis, Missouri. Figure 6-4 shows his blog.

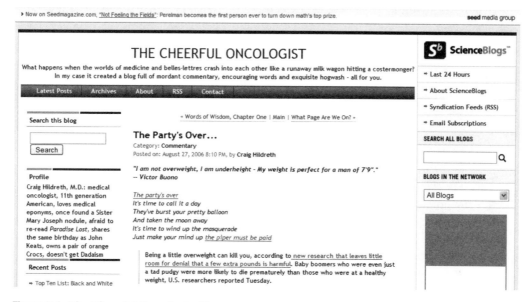

Figure 6-4. *The Cheerful Oncologist blog*

Dr. Hildreth is a fairly prolific blogger. I emailed him some questions about his blog.

Q. *How did you start blogging and why do you blog today?*

A. I started September 2004 after caring for both the father and mother of a dear friend of mine, who both died that year. The experience was not just emotional—it was devastating for the family and affected me deeply. By coincidence, I ran across a medical blog and wanted to leave a comment on it. According to the rules of this site, I couldn't unless I had my own blog. So I started "The Cheerful Oncologist" and realized that I had 20 years of catharsis and pretty darn good material locked up inside of me. It was time to release them both upon my readers. Two years later, I write to entertain both myself and (hopefully) my audience.

Q. *Are you blogging for the general public or for other medical professionals?*

A. I write for anyone and everyone, and get responses from all walks of life and all over the world.

Q. *I noticed your blog is part of the ScienceBlogs Network. How is that working out for you?*

A. I am thrilled to have been invited to join ScienceBlogs in May of this year. The experience has been great for me and has given me much more exposure than before.

Q. *What do you get out of blogging?*

A. Blogging for me is a chance to decipher esoteric aspects of cancer care with patients and families, to share new treatments and information about medicine and health, to make people laugh, and most importantly, to force the old brain to observe the world and its happenings—to synthesize these data and then write something worthwhile about it.

Q. *Would you recommend blogging to other medical professionals?*

A. Blogging is a great hobby for me, but I can only recommend it to those medical professionals who truly enjoy writing, month after month. Like most blogs in America, I suspect the owners get burned out after the initial rush is gone. I find it takes a unique passion to keep it up.

Q. *Any advice for other medical professionals considering blogging?*

A. Well, of course, they should read lots of medical blogs. Some are now classics of the blogosphere, and many new blogs are created each month. In my opinion, blogging is successful only if the writer has something of value to say. This implies that his or her life is packed with either drama, work, study, human interaction, excitement, searching, pondering, emotional trauma, or a combination of the above. My motto is: First live a fulfilled, passionate life, then write about it, or even better write about what and whom you encounter every day. The best writing is never purely autobiographical, but an amalgam of the writer and his or her unique universe.

Global Medical Blogging

Professionals in the US and UK are by no means the only professionals blogging. Consider Aniruddha Malpani, MD, of Bombay, India, whose blog at `http://doctorandpatient. blogspot.com` is read by people worldwide. Figure 6-5 shows Dr. Malpani's blog.

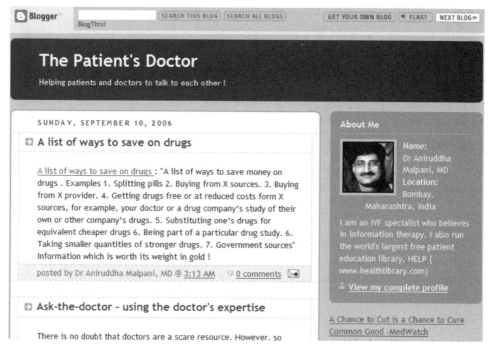

Figure 6-5. *The Patient's Doctor blog*

Here is what Dr. Malpani had to say:

Q. *Why did you decide to start blogging?*

A. I was persuaded to do this by my friend, Mr. Rajesh Jain, who is an entrepreneur, and has his own blog at www.emergic.org. I enjoyed blogging and have continued doing this.

Q. *What has been the reaction of your patients to your blog?*

A. Many of them find it interesting to read what's on their doctor's mind! The ones who do comment are very positive about it.

Q. *You run one of the most highly regarded infertility clinics in India. Many of your patients are from overseas. Is your blog helping you in this regard?*

A. Not really. Our website at www.drmalpani.com is designed for our patients. My blog is much more general, and focuses on patient education, using information technology in healthcare, and improving the doctor-patient relationship.

Q. *How do you find subjects to blog about?*

A. Usually by surfing the Net. I also get ideas from consultations (when my patients ask questions which I feel are of general interest) and by reading books.

Q. *Are you enjoying blogging?*

A. It keeps me on my toes and allows me to expand my horizons, since I need to surf and read other people's blogs to keep mine current and interesting.

Q. *How do you find the time to blog?*

A. I usually spend about an hour or two on my computer daily (answering email), and I use some of this time to blog as well.

Medicine and Controversy

While Dr. Kevin Pho may live and practice in the relatively small city of Nashua, New Hampshire, his blog, Kevin, M.D (`www.kevinmd.com/blog`), shown in Figure 6-6, has a big following on the blogosphere: 72,000 unique visitors, 170,000 visits per month, and plenty of heated comments for each post.

Friday, September 08, 2006

Informed consent doesn't shield this neurosurgeon

A physician loses a malpractice case due to a known complication:

> At trial, Wagner, OHSU's lawyer, told the jury that Ackerman's injury was a known risk of the surgery, and Ackerman had signed the consent form acknowledging that his doctor had educated him on complications.

But of course, "money was never the issue."

Posted by Kevin @ 11:22 AM | Comments (18)

Comments:
Kevin, per usual, is being deliberately misleading.

A practicing primary-care physician tells it like it is.

About
Contact
Press / Sponsor
Feeds

Patient Medical Information at
Med Help International

Premium Blogad
Advertise via Blogads

Figure 6-6. *Kevin, M.D. Medical Weblog*

Here is how Dr. Pho answered my emailed questions:

Q. *Who is your blog for?*

A. I don't have a specific group that I target. The blog can be appreciated by patients, physicians, health professionals, and lawyers.

I typically blog to express my opinions on current medical issues, or I bring controversial issues to the forefront for debate. The public, at times, is unaware of the details behind challenges facing medicine today, such as primary care access, ED overuse, the uninsured. I bring a physician's perspective to the topics at hand.

Q. *What do you think of the comments that some of your posts get?*

A. I made a conscious decision not to moderate the comments (except spam). This is controversial, as many of the anonymous comments can be vicious in nature. However, to encourage open and honest debate, I believe that these controversial comments should not be censored. Allowing comments to be anonymous can show what is really going on "behind the scenes" in medicine.

Q. *Does blogging influence your standing in the medical community, and if so how?*

A. Although there have been mainstream media mentions of blogging (in the *WSJ* and *LA Times*), it is a relatively niche phenomenon. The local medical community here applauds the blog being a tool to encourage debate or educate patients. Patients have found me via the blog, and it promotes me as an "Internet-savvy" physician who is increasingly appealing to patients today.

Q. *Has blogging influenced how you practice medicine, and if so how?*

A. Blogging has kept me up-to-date on current medical news and studies. It allows instant feedback and opinion on breaking medical news and studies, which allows me to put this information into proper context in my practice.

Q. *I notice your medical blog has a fair number of advertisements. Why?*

A. I allow sponsors on the blog to cover the cost of hosting and bandwidth. I do not use a free hosting service (i.e., BlogSpot), thus paying to maintain the blog comes via the advertising revenue.

Q. *What has been the most surprising part of blogging?*

A. The debate that it brings out. Allowing instantaneous, anonymous feedback can allow people to "let loose" with their opinions, and at times, I am taken aback by the passion (and viciousness) of people's positions and opinions.

Q. *What do your patients think of you blogging?*

A. They have been positive in general. I have been written about in local papers, and it has promoted me as somewhat tech-savvy. Unlike other blogs, I make it a clear point that I do not blog about patients, so privacy issues are not an issue.

Q. *Has blogging increased, decreased, or not affected the size of your practice?*

A. As mentioned above, it has had a positive influence on the size of my practice.

The Medical Blogosphere

Like a lot of sections of the blogosphere, medicine is developing its own versions of A-List blogs. Most bloggers have heard of Engadget (www.engadget.com/), but how about Medgadget (www.medgadget.com/), with its collection of medical gadgets to fascinate professionals and terrify patients? See Figure 6-7 for an example of what Medgadget has to offer.

Figure 6-7. *A typical Medgadget post*

One of the key writers at Medgadget and a blogger in his own right is Nicholas Genes, MD, a second-year emergency medicine resident at the Mount Sinai Hospital in New York City. Besides finding new medical technology to cover at Medgadget, Nicholas brought to medical blogs another blogging tradition, the blog carnival.[1]

Nicholas started Grand Rounds (at http://blogborygmi.blogspot.com/2004/09/grand-rounds-archive-upcoming-schedule.html) in September 2004, making it one of the longest running blog carnivals around. Figure 6-8 shows his blogborygmi blog.

---

1. The idea of a blog carnival is simple and powerful. It's a weekly or so roundup of posts edited by a different blogger each time. Think of it as a rotating editorship. We'll look at blog carnivals in more detail in Chapter 13.

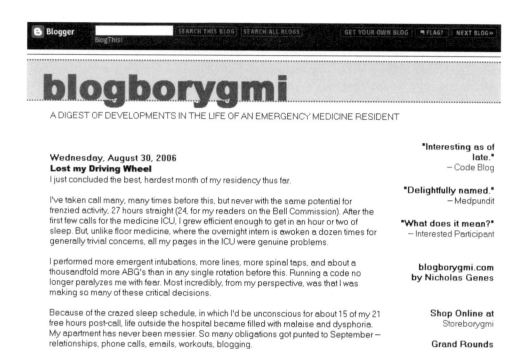

Figure 6-8. *blogborygmi*

Here's what Nicholas had to say to my emailed questions:

Q. *How did you get started in blogging?*

A. I thought a blog might be a better way to keep track of interesting links. The Google toolbar had a "blog this" button that was convenient, and my impressions of the various stories would be accessible from any web-enabled computer. Originally, blogborygmi was meant to be just for me and a few friends, to bat ideas around and hopefully develop some articles (the name was a take on "borborygmi," the medical term for gut rumblings). But the blog took on a life of its own—getting comments and traffic from the online community, sometimes just minutes after dashing off a post. It was more engaging than crafting a longer article that may never see the light of day.

Q. *I thought residents never had time to do anything. How do you find the time to blog?*

A. Well, some months are better than others. Last month (August 2006), I was rotating through the ICU [and] had very little time to do anything besides eat and sleep. But, in general, making time for blogging hasn't been too hard. The team at Medgadget.com is constantly sharing links and tips, so we can generate new posts fairly quickly. And I know my words will be edited and spell-checked before they make it to the front page, which helps.

As for blogborygmi.com, well, I update it when the mood strikes.

There are so many remarkable encounters in the hospital, in the emergency department in particular. Memorable patients, bizarre diseases, funny interactions with the staff. I swap stories with friends and colleagues, and sometimes it occurs to me, "This would make a great post." Not everything can make it online, of course, but it's good to have an outlet like this, to reflect on your job, its perks and demands.

Q. *Any advice for other medical professionals considering blogging?*

A. It depends on what kind of job you have, and what purpose your blog will serve. But if there's any reasonable chance of being discovered (i.e., if you intend to write specifically about your town or hospital), I'd recommend you be forthcoming with your employers and colleagues from the beginning. It's better to bring it up and involve others before you begin, rather than have them discover the archives later and assume the worst. Maybe the hospital or program or school will embrace your efforts; maybe they'll give some guidelines or tips on anonymity . . . But no matter how wrapped up you get in your site, it's probably not worth losing your job, alienating your boss or coworkers, or having your blog unceremoniously deleted.

As for patients, the HIPAA laws are pretty far-reaching, and bloggers must be diligent in how they obscure the details of a case. I sometimes think this is an unfortunate hassle, but then again, I can't imagine how angry it would make me to read about a family member on someone's blog, especially on those posts where someone is "blowing off steam."

My attendings [attending physicians] often instruct us about "worst-case" scenarios when we're stuck with a difficult intervention in the ER. How will it look to reviewers if you *don't* order intubate, if you *don't* order the CT scan, and something bad happens? I try to keep [this] in mind with blogging, as well. What if this post is read by the patient? Their family? What if a prosecutor reads this out loud in court? It has a chilling effect on what I choose to publish, but it's worth remembering.

FINDING GOOD MEDICAL INFO IN THE BLOGOSPHERE

How good is the medical information you read in blogs? Yes, you might be influenced by an inaccurate review when buying your next high-tech toy, but it's quite another thing to base what you do about a medical condition on what you read in a blog. Among all the charlatans, snake-oil salesmen, and scam artists, it's extremely easy to get a dose of bad information.

That's where the Health On the Net (HON) Foundation comes in. Created in 1995, HON is a nonprofit, nongovernmental organization, accredited to the Economic and Social Council of the United Nations dedicated to promoting and guiding the deployment of useful and reliable online medical and health information, and its appropriate and efficient use.

For the blogosphere, HON provides a "HON Code badge" as shown here, much like various e-commerce badges. This demonstrates that the medical blog in question has been accredited by HON and is adhering to the eight principles of online medical ethics.

Here's a brief summary of the HON Code:

- **Authoritative:** Indicate the qualifications of the authors. Any medical or health advice provided and hosted on this site will only be given by medically trained and qualified professionals unless a clear statement is made that a piece of advice offered is from a nonmedically qualified individual or organization.

- **Complementary:** Information should support, not replace, the doctor-patient relationship. The information provided on the site is designed to support, not replace, the relationship that exists between a patient/site visitor and his/her existing physician.

- **Privacy:** Respect the privacy and confidentiality of personal data submitted to the site by the visitor. The website owners undertake to honor or exceed the legal requirements of medical/health information privacy that apply in the country and state where the website and mirror sites are located.

- **Attribution:** Cite the source(s) of published information, date, and medical and health pages. Where appropriate, information contained on this site will be supported by clear references to source data and, where possible, have specific HTML links to that data. The date when a clinical page was last modified will be clearly displayed (e.g., at the bottom of the page).

- **Justifiability:** The site must back up claims relating to benefits and performance. Any claims relating to the benefits/performance of a specific treatment, commercial product, or service will be supported by appropriate, balanced evidence in the manner outlined in principle 4 (Attribution).

- **Transparency:** The site must have accessible presentation, identities of the editor and webmaster, and accurate email contact information.

- **Financial disclosure:** Support for the website will be clearly identified, including the identities of commercial and noncommercial organizations that have contributed funding, services, or material for the site.

- **Sponsorship:** Clearly distinguish advertising from editorial content. If advertising is a source of funding, it will be clearly stated. A brief description of the advertising policy adopted by the website owners will be displayed on the site. Advertising and other promotional material will be presented to viewers in a manner and context that facilitates differentiation between it and the original material created by the institution operating the site.

To date, more than 5,000 medical blogs and websites have been reviewed by HON, which provides verification via its website at www.hon.ch/ and a free toolbar for Internet Explorer and Firefox.

If you are considering starting a medical blog, or taking the advice you read in one seriously, you should know about the HON Code.

Spreading the Word, Online

The oldest profession, the ministry, has embraced blogging with open arms. A quick visit to Google will link you to blogs by priests, nuns, ministers, rabbis, and spiritual leaders from across the whole spectrum of religion and spirituality.[2]

From the Cloisters

One such blogger is Sister Julie Vieira of the Sisters, Servants of the Immaculate Heart of Mary, a Roman Catholic religious community based in Monroe, Michigan. Her blog, A Nun's Life, shown in Figure 6-9, is one of a network of "Sister Bloggers" who are blogging about their cloistered lives away from everyday society. Sister Julie and her brethren bloggers are another example of people who are making their way of life, their challenges, and their humanity accessible to the rest of us, and in doing so, opening our eyes and gaining our respect.

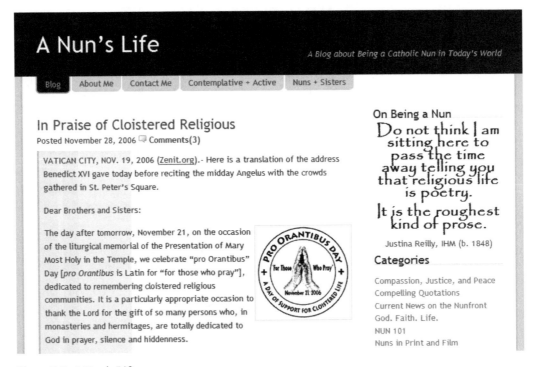

Figure 6-9. *A Nun's Life*

Sister Julie, whose blog and life have recently made it into both the pages of *Time* magazine (www.time.com/time/magazine/article/0,9171,1558292-1,00.html) and *The Times* newspaper (www.timesonline.co.uk/article/0,,2089-2471917,00.html), graciously took the time to reply to my emailed questions:

---

2. Here are two other good places to start: Beliefnet's Blog Heaven of continuously updated blog excerpts from a wide variety of religions and faiths at www.beliefnet.com/blogheaven, and the Blog Flux directory at http//dir.blogflux.com/cat/religion.html.

Q. *How did you come to start your blog?*

A. There are a few reasons why I started my blog. (1) I'm a writer and I was looking for a way to get myself back into the discipline of writing everyday. A blog is definitely something that requires regular attention by the writer but also has the benefit of receiving almost instant feedback. (2) My employer, Loyola Press, was exploring the use of online forms of communication at the time, which got me interested in seriously considering a blog. (3) I have given a lot of thought to and acted upon the principle that the Gospel message must always be proclaimed in a way that people are able to hear it.

So, if I want the Gospel message to be relevant to kids, I have to know the images, magazines, games, language, etc. that are familiar to them. So, if more and more people are on the Internet and using it as a source of information and communication, then it behooves me to learn about, understand, and use the Internet. Having a blog is one small way to open a door to people who are searching (in more ways than one) and to have a forum in which I can openly, honestly, and faithfully dialogue with people about my and their questions, concerns, or thoughts. My own faith and understanding deepen in this dialogue as well.

Q. *Who are your readers?*

A. As far as I can tell, I have a pretty varied group of readers. The blog is not aimed at any group in particular, though it would seem to attract more people with an interest in religious life or who are curious about nuns. I often write about things that are meaningful not just to nuns or religious people, but to anyone who is seeking meaning in life or who wants to dialogue about important issues in life.

So, for readers I have people who are spiritually inclined but not necessarily Catholic or Christian, people in discernment or formation (process of entering a religious community), sisters from my community and other communities, people who love the Church and people who have reservations about the Church, people who are fascinated by nuns and their way of life. I seem to have a balance of men and women who comment on the blog.

Q. *What has been the reaction by other sisters in your order, and other nuns, to your blog?*

A. The reaction has been overwhelmingly positive. There are a number of comments that sisters have left on my blog indicating that they like it. My sisters are very supportive and happy that I am engaged in this type of ministry. It's another way that we can reach out to people and meet them where they are. I've also had good reactions from other sisters and nuns. There are a small but growing number of sisters and nuns who have blogs. I'm privileged to be able to learn from their blogs and to check in with them from time to time when I have questions.

Q. *What do you see as the role of blogging for those in religious orders?*

A. I think that blogging can have multiple roles for those in religious life, just as for those in any other lifestyle. I think it is a wonderful way for religious to get in touch with where people are at. Spiritual seekers and people in need do not always show up at our churches or our front doors. So, it is important that we go where they are and experience what they experience.

I've got a few readers whose blogs are, shall we say, colorful. I visit their blogs, offer comments, and simply have a "presence." It doesn't mean I agree with or condone everything they publish, but I am there. That alone says a lot to people. So blogging for religious can have a real ministry dimension about it. Too often, ministry is understood ONLY as doing something obviously religious or preaching. But ministry is much more than that . . . it's how you are with people, and just being there and open to addressing a need when you see it.

I think blogging can also be a good way for religious to relate with one another and with other similarly minded people. Being a nun or sister or brother or monk in today's world can be a challenging experience (for many, many reasons). For one thing, there aren't many of us, and we often minister in diverse places, sometimes with no other religious around. So blogging can help to keep religious connected, maintain a support system and friendships, and encourage one another on the journey.

Blogging can also be a great way to float ideas, stimulate one's own thinking, and engage in real dialogue.

Q. *How do you find things to blog about?*

A. Most days, I worry that I'll run out of things to say. I'm not a very chatty person in general. However, I always find things to blog about. Since my blog is about what it's like to be a Catholic nun in today's world, I think that anything that I encounter is a potential topic for discussion. Some people find it very interesting that a sister can also be a mountain bike rider or like good beer or watch *The Simpsons*.

I share these things on my blog because I want people to know that nuns are real, ordinary people, not caricatures. So many stereotypes of nuns abound, so part of the goal of my blog is to dispel those stereotypes at the same time that I want to give an authentic picture of religious life. Whenever I come across a stereotype (in a movie, TV show, conversation, etc.), I write about it.

I also write about current news on nuns or religious life, so I frequent the major news websites.

Sometimes my readers will send me an article or idea that they'd like me to address.

Sometimes I'll be thinking through an issue myself—like how to respond to people who are homeless—and write about that because I'm hoping to get some new light to shed on the issue for myself and because dialoguing about such major justice issues raises awareness for anyone who happens upon my blog.

I also do a lot of commenting on the comments of other people. In this way, I think that blogging can be truly a dialogue or conversation. Every person's comment is important.

There really is no end to finding things to write about . . . it's just a matter of finding the time and finding a way to be real and relate it to people's lives in a meaningful way.

Q. *What do you like most, and least, about blogging?*

A. What I like the most about blogging is meeting all kinds of people and learning from them. I've met such different people. Sometimes they are regular readers; other times, it's just a quick hit to make a comment. People challenge me and help me to expand my universe when they address a topic from a totally different perspective or disagree with something I write or ask a question that truly boggles me. It's a privilege and a responsibility to maintain an open door because you never know who is going to show up; you just know that God calls you to welcome them and make them feel at home—it's about being hospitable.

What I like least about blogging is that it is often challenging to get a read on someone when all you have before you are some typed words, a picture, or a video. It's challenging to know how to respond to someone when they ask a serious question or share about something with which they are struggling.

Learning all the newest bells and whistles for blogs is also something I am not particularly fond of. I know the basics, but don't always have time to delve into HTML code or search through online documentation or discussion groups. So, I hope for the best and carry on!

Q. *Any advice to others in religious orders or ministries about blogging?*

A. I would highly encourage those in religious life or ministries to seriously consider establishing a blog. It's actually quite easy to get up and running—and it's free. It is imperative that we get out there and understand and use the Internet and the types of communication and networking that it offers. It may be no substitute for good old face-to-face encounters, but for some people, the Internet is the marketplace. It's the place they go for information and communication. We need to be part of that marketplace. I would encourage religious to be real about their own experiences, to talk about how they relate with God, what they struggle with or rejoice in, how they live their faith in their ordinary, everyday lives.

Religion, Everyday Life, and Blogs

Religious blogs are not only the work of "professional" religious people. There are blogs aplenty by people of all faiths who use blogging to find their way in the world they inhabit. One humorous and useful example is the Kosher Blog (www.kosherblog.net), shown in Figure 6-10. Since 2003, the Kosher Blog has been whipping up modern gourmet kosher recipes and reviewing kosher products.

Figure 6-10. *The Kosher Blog*

Jonathan Abbett, the creator of the Kosher Blog, explains why he started this site in his blog's About section:

> *In the summer of 2003, I went cold-turkey, whole-hog kosher, which meant no more eating vegetarian at treyfe restaurants, as I had been doing for about seven years, in my pre-Orthodox days. The particular milestone was my marriage to a lovely and talented woman who had been progressing, like me, toward a more observant lifestyle, so I immediately found myself with a wedding-gift-equipped kosher kitchen (and a wife who couldn't cook, save her excellent apple pies). Suffice it to say, I was cooking a lot more.*
>
> *Luckily, I had a penchant for the culinary passed to me from my mother, live-in grand-mother, and a healthy dose of PBS cooking shows. (It probably also helped that my father made occasional appearances in the kitchen—potato latkes were always his department—and would often cook for his assorted fraternal organizations.) As I sought to recapture the not-so-kosher tastes of my past, I experimented with new recipes and products, and began encountering more and more obscure hekshers the further I looked for exotic goods. Keeping it all straight grew challenging, so, in December 2003, I started the Kosher Blog, a website where I could catalog my experiences and occasional frustrations, and reach out to other kosher "foodies" who were also "trying to find the finer side of everyday kosher living."*

Blogging and Your Career

Now that we've looked at how established professionals are using blogging, it's time to look at blogging when you're just starting out in the Real World. There are plenty of horror stories about people whose MySpace or Blogger posts have torpedoed their job prospects or their actual jobs, and we covered some of the common sense do's and don'ts in the previous chapter.

But can blogs and blogging help your career?

At Microsoft, the answer is rapidly becoming a definite yes. As of today, at least 3,200 of Microsoft's 70,000 plus[3] employees have active blogs. While the most famous of those bloggers, Robert Scoble at `http://scobleizer.com/`, has left Microsoft to pursue other interests, blogging is fast becoming a core part of Microsoft's corporate culture.

In Chapter 7, we will look at how companies are blogging. Here, we will explore two other aspects: how blogs can help your career and help you find a job.

Building Your Rep, One Post at a Time

Consider what Don Dodge of the Microsoft Emerging Business Team does at his blog, Don Dodge on The Next Big Thing (`http://dondodge.typepad.com/the_next_big_thing/`), each and every blogging day: He tells the entire world what technologies and companies Microsoft is interested in, what Microsoft looks for, how it categorizes acquisitions, which Microsoft competitors are screwing up or besting Microsoft, and so on. See Figure 6-11 for an example.

Figure 6-11. *Don Dodge on The Next Big Thing*

---

3. This statistic is per `http://en.wikipedia.org/wiki/Microsoft`, up from the 2,044 Microsoft bloggers I counted in 2005 for *Micro-ISV: From Vision to Reality* (Apress, 2006).

Unless you happen to have spent the last 20 years or so in the computer industry in one way or another, it's hard to appreciate just how heretical it is to have so many employees like Don openly criticizing, discussing, and discoursing on what Microsoft does.

According to Site Meter[4] in November 2006, 1,423 people on average a day read Don's blog. That may not sound like a lot, but combined with roughly six comments per post, it's clear that a good number of people inside and outside Microsoft are listening to what Don has to say.

I asked Don one question:

Q. *What is your take on what blogging has come to mean with Microsoft?*

A. Executives at Microsoft have been very supportive, and even impressed with my blog. There are over 3,000 bloggers at Microsoft focusing on many different subjects and audiences. My blog is focused on startups and VCs [venture capitalists], and covers all product lines for Microsoft.

Blogs are the easiest way to gain a company-wide reputation at Microsoft. Of course, there are more than 3,000 employees blogging, so it takes a lot to get noticed. My blog has been picked up by *BusinessWeek, CNN/Money, Business 2.0, Seattle Post Intelligencer, Fortune, Barron's*, and many others, so my blog has definitely built a reputation inside Microsoft and outside as well. There is no way I could have gained as much visibility in the normal course of my job. Blogging is a great platform to express your views and influence public perception.

Blogging is now part of my performance metrics as a technical evangelist and business development executive. It is a critical part of my job.

Blogs are one of the best ways to find out what is going on within the product groups, and specifically who is responsible for certain features. Blogs are more up-to-date than any other repository that is available to all employees. Again, blogs are a great communication tool.

Job Blogs

In many ways, a lot of us live in the world Microsoft has created over the past 20 years or so. From a fairly secretive company last century, Microsoft has embraced openness through blogging like no other. That openness extends to the hows and whys of getting hired at Microsoft at the company's JobsBlog (`http://blogs.msdn.com/jobsblog`), a blog all about the hiring process at Microsoft.

JobsBlog, shown in Figure 6-12, may just be the future of how companies find and retain professionals. It's a blog loaded with juicy details about how a major international corporation goes about recruiting, what impresses interviewers and what doesn't, and many juicy bits about what it's like to work at Microsoft. It's very different from the standard bland drool put out by every HR department.

---

4. Site Meter (`www.sitemeter.com`) is a site-traffic service. See Chapter 13 for more information about these types of services.

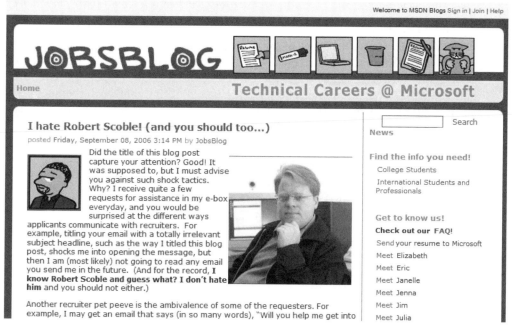

Figure 6-12. *Microsoft's JobsBlog*

JobsBlog racked up some impressive statistics[5] in 2005 in the US:

- Nearly 3,000 people applied for jobs at Microsoft via JobsBlog postings.

- Of that total, 137 JobsBlog applicants accepted an offer with Microsoft.

- For 31 of those 137 hires, JobsBlog was the main point of contact/influencer for them accepting a job at Microsoft.

I interviewed (via email) Gretchen Ledgard and Zoe Goldring, who started JobsBlog in March 2004.

Q. *Why was JobsBlog launched?*

A. Blogging was a way to reach our target audience of software developers where they lived and worked: on the Internet. At that time, blogging was very popular with technical professionals such as software developers, but it was not yet the mainstream medium it is today.

---

5. These facts are from http://blogs.msdn.com/jobsblog/archive/2005/12/20/506159.aspx/.

Q. *Were hiring managers and executives at Microsoft worried you would share too much of the hiring process with prospective candidates? If they were, how did you allay their fears?*

A. We did not hear any feedback that hiring managers and executives were worried we would share too much information. Microsoft's general hiring process, which we discussed on JobsBlog, was not a secret. If recruiters met candidates at career fairs or hiring events, they would share the same information and tips. However, blogging allowed the company to share this information more widely than ever before. Nothing we wrote was confidential, and we found that the more we educated the company's potential applicants, the more prepared and confident they were during the application and interview process. JobsBlog essentially put all applicants on equal footing to understand the company's hiring process, no matter if they had met a recruiter in person or not.

Q. *What have you heard from hiring managers about what they like and dislike about JobsBlog?*

A. When we were with the company, hiring managers were extremely supportive of JobsBlog. We received much positive feedback. Many were frequent readers who also contributed content and feedback and linked to the site from their own blogs. We also know several hiring managers and employees regularly directed potential applicants to the resource.

Q. *Do you think that hiring managers and employers should blog about job openings?*

A. It depends on the recruiting issues a company is trying to solve and how their goals and resources align with solving those problems. For Microsoft, JobsBlog and other employee blogs acted as strong employment branding tools. We educated applicants on the company's hiring process and helped them self-select for appropriate positions. This effort not only increased applicants' interest in the company, but it also eased the burden on the recruiters and hiring managers by enabling the applicants to proactively prepare for their Microsoft interview process. This education and more personal touch enhanced the overall candidate experience of the applicants.

Q. *What do prospective employees get out of JobsBlog?*

A. When we were with Microsoft, prospective employees leveraged JobsBlog to learn more about Microsoft's corporate culture and career opportunities and how best to prepare for their application and interview processes. The site also enabled them to connect with actual recruiters and employees as well as other potential applicants. In essence, it was a community resource to prepare for a career at Microsoft.

Q. *Have you heard personally from people who've gotten jobs at Microsoft who had positive, or for that matter, negative things to say about JobsBlog?*

A. JobsBlog was created to start a dialogue between technical job seekers and Microsoft's recruiting efforts. We often solicited our readers for feedback, both positive and negative, in order to improve the overall candidate experience. We received many comments from people who went through the process and felt that JobsBlog was a huge benefit to them in preparing for and surviving the interviews. At the same time, we got a lot of helpful feedback that determined what content people wanted to read about and questions that would help them better prepare.

Gretchen and Zoe are no longer at Microsoft. They've started their own business at JobSyntax.com, teaching HR departments how to blog and job seekers the same.

Occupation: Blogger

When the going gets tough, the tough turn pro.

—Hunter S. Thompson

To wrap up this chapter on professionals who blog, let's take a look at a new profession that started to coalesce in 2006: the professional blogger. These are people who blog for a living—they get a regular paycheck or at least a payment for their services. In Chapter 12, I'll talk about people who are making a living from their blogs. Here, we will look at how professional blogger jobs are being advertised.

Blogger Job Boards

In the summer of 2006, two well-respected blogging resource sites started job boards listing positions—some temporary, some salaried—for bloggers: ProBlogger and Performancing.

ProBlogger, a site with the tagline, "helping bloggers make money" started its job board at `http://jobs.problogger.net/`, shown in Figure 6-13.

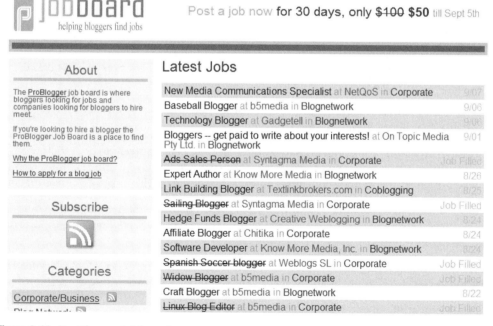

Figure 6-13. *ProBlogger job board*

Darren Rowse, the founder of ProBlogger, and a driving force behind the b5media network of more than 100 blogs, explained why the time was right to create an online marketplace for blogging jobs:

Q. *How is blogger jobs' job board doing in the, I guess, about what two, three months it has been up?*

A. Yeah, it's been up two or three months. It's a little bit out-of-date actually. I meant to change some of the coding around it. I've still got a special up there that [laugh] was going to run out on the 15th of September.

There are other job boards around that have done a lot better in that they have 10 or 15 ads go up everyday. We are probably getting two or three ads up a week at the moment, so it's not massive. But I guess I positioned this job board more for the future than for the present. I see that there is going to be an increase in people blogging or wanting to blog for money, and so yeah, it's more of a futuristic little business.

Q. *So I am assuming here that you think that it's going to become a very common job title in the business world to be corporate blogger, company blogger.*

A. I think where the people are [in ProBlogger's job board], that's their full role. Whether it is part of a wider role, I think it will definitely be something that's bigger. At the moment on that site, there is mainly blogging network advertising. But increasingly, I am having people ring up and email saying they've got corporate jobs, and they want to advertise those as well. So, yeah, I think it is definitely something there's more and more interest in. I know here in Australia, I have talked to a few businesses recently who are looking to put on bloggers, and they are sort of feeling their way on it a little bit. They are a little bit scared of the process. Blogging puts your company's name out there to be commented on positively but also negatively.

Darren has a great post at www.problogger.net/archives/2006/08/30/how-to-apply-for-a-blog-job/ on getting a job blogging. Here's my summary of his advice on what it takes to get a job blogging through a blogger job board.

Act fast. If you thought jobs at the big job boards filled fast, you haven't seen anything yet. Twenty-four hours is a *long* time in the blogosphere, so be ready and act fast.

Follow directions. The companies looking to hire bloggers want you to do it their way. They're going to specify how to apply, what they want in terms of writing samples (links, PDFs, or Word documents), and other matters. Not doing so will nix your chances for sure.

Sell yourself. Just as when you apply for any type of position, you need to assert your strengths, experience, and general enthusiasm for the job. This is not the time to be timid or share self-doubts.

Write well. When does the job interview start? With your first sentence. While you need to act fast, you also need to demonstrate in your submission that you can write well.

Show your stuff. All potential employers are going to want to see your work. Be prepared with a list of your best posts, which show off a range of writing styles, approaches, and lengths. If you have posts relevant to the job at hand, by all means, lead with them. If you're new to blogging, consider creating a post and including it in your submission.

Short is good. It can be hard to know how long to go on about why you're qualified, but if in doubt, go short. For example, a lead paragraph about who you are and bullet points of why you're right for the job will get you further than two pages covering the same thing.

Know how to blog. Your blog or blogs are going to be the strongest, or weakest, proof you're right for the job. Before running off to get a job blogging, spend the time to make your blog attractive, interesting, and professional.

Know your subject. You and your blog need to show prospective employers that you have a good grasp of at least the general topic they are going to want you blogging about. If you don't know the subject, see the next suggestion.

Don't shotgun. Apply only for blog jobs where a reasonable person could at least see that your experience and interests are related. There's no point in wasting your time and the time of employers shooting at everything that moves.

Find a way to stand out. Like most jobs, there are more people than positions in the world of blogging. Find a way to stand out from the crowd. For example, get media attention (even if it's just your local newspaper) for your blog or cite complimentary words by a Major Player in your part of the world of work.

The other major blogging job board, Performancing (`http://performancing.com/`), shown in Figure 6-14, is best known for its Firefox blogging plug-in and its free blogging metrics service. The blogger job board runs as an extension of Performancing's very active blogging forums. Forum members are free to post positions.

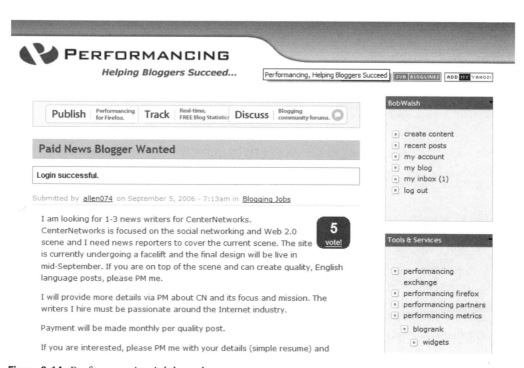

Figure 6-14. *Performancing job board*

Pay for Posts

Of course, just as in the nonblogging world, there are jobs you might not want your friends, family, or fellow bloggers to know about. When people and companies start paying bloggers to post on their own blogs about specific goods and services, they start walking very close to the payola line as far as most bloggers are concerned.

PayPerPost (`http://payperpost.com/`), shown in Figure 6-15, is one such blog job board. There, advertisers can post requests with specific dollar payments for bloggers. PayPerPost has two saving graces in the eyes of most bloggers: Advertisers determine whether the post must be positive in tone or can be either positive or negative, and the paid blogger must disclose that they were paid.

Figure 6-15. *PayPerPost*

Ted Murphy, the founder of PayPerPost, had this to say about his service in an email reply:

Q. *What is the PayPerPost value proposition?*

A. PayPerPost connects advertisers to bloggers in a way that has never been done before. Our marketplace provides a conduit for advertisers to get exposure for their products, services, and websites through our network of bloggers. At the same time, we provide a way for bloggers to monetize their blog and earn more than they could through other advertising networks.

Q. *More than a few bloggers have been severely critical of the idea of paying for posts. How would you answer them?*

A. We are a marketplace. Our role is to provide choice for advertisers and bloggers. If a blogger chooses not to take an advertiser's opportunity or not use the system as a whole, that is their prerogative. I don't have a problem with those that don't like the idea of using PayPerPost for themselves. I just wish they could be more open-minded when it comes to others who use the platform.

Q. *What's the difference between advertisers who surreptitiously pay for posts and recording labels who in the past have paid for airplay?*

A. First off, let me say that we live in a capitalist society, and I have no problem with recording labels who pay for airtime; that is how record labels market their product. If you spent millions of dollars to produce a record, would you just cross your fingers and hope that a bunch of DJs play your songs? I wouldn't.

However, there is a difference between PayPerPost and radio content. Our bloggers have the ability to disclose any payment in whatever way they see fit. Advertisers cannot force our bloggers not to disclose. Have you ever heard a DJ say "Sony paid us to play that last song"? I don't think so. Under our model, bloggers can choose to disclose the relationship between the advertiser and blogger if they see fit.

Q. *Can you give me some idea of how many bloggers and advertisers are using PayPerPost?*

A. Tens of thousands of bloggers and thousands of advertisers.

Q. *How can the average reader protect themselves from disinterested reviews on blogger sites that aren't actually disinterested?*

A. I think the best approach to reading any content on the Internet is to know your source. Who is the person or organization creating the content? Do they have a disclosure policy? If not, why?

Q. *What do bloggers like about PayPerPost?*

A. Bloggers love the freedom we provide them to choose their own advertisements. We provide a way for bloggers to make a significant supplemental income on their own time in their own way.

Q. *I notice that PayPerPost sponsors* `DisclosurePolicy.org`. *Why?*

A. We believe in the concept of disclosure policies. This site is designed to provide bloggers with the tools they need to provide transparency to their readers about the content on their blogs. By including a disclosure policy, bloggers are protecting the integrity of their blog and providing a service to the advertisers, sponsors, and organizations that support them. Disclosure encourages trust among readers and promotes an ethical blogosphere.

Blogging and the Professions: The Bottom Line

After interviewing the professionals you've met in this chapter, and others space did not permit me to include, I think there are three main points to what blogging has to offer professionals:

Blogging is the professional's antidote to the Internet price. In a world where the Internet makes nearly everything and everyone accessible and replaceable, legal and medical practitioners are using blogging to define themselves and their unique value. They are doing this not just for prospective clients and patients, but often for fellow professionals. Blogging has become a new way of building your professional network of contacts, peers, and referrals. And, in the months and years to come, this "network effect" is going to grow more powerful.

Blogging is not being bland. Whether you are a New England family doctor or an attorney in a small Southern town, no one is going to read what you post if concerns about propriety and professional restraint tone your posts down to a bland porridge. The first and foremost prerequisite to blogging as a professional is the same as it is for all blogging: passion.

Blogging is changing how people find jobs, and in some cases, what jobs they do. Microsoft—love it or hate it—is the bearer of the future in many areas, including how people learn about jobs. While there will always be a place in this world for the Monster.com-like sites and even traditional newspaper classified job postings, Microsoft's JobsBlog is a harbinger of what other companies will be doing to attract top talent. And this is the type of blog that people who want to be considered top talent in their chosen area of expertise will seek out. As blogging continues to go mainstream, jobs for bloggers will go from the oddity, to regular occurrences on various job boards, to perhaps even one day being considered a profession.

Your Action Tasks

Here are a few steps for getting started with your professional blog:

Know your ethical obligations. Nearly every profession has a code of conduct, and that code of conduct applies to the blogosphere. For some professions, such as medicine and law, breaking patient or client confidentiality is professional suicide. Even if your profession doesn't have strict canons, it is never a good idea to blog the personal details of the people who come to you for services.

Pick what interests you. Blogging is hard work. If you are going to blog week after week, month after month, you need to pick topics, themes, and subjects that interest you and that you would want to spend time learning, researching, and writing about, even if you were not blogging.

Be yourself. Blogging is not an exercise in the impersonal, third-person voice. It's about what gets you excited, engaged, and yes, angry and even enraged. Few things read as badly as a blog posting where the author has tried to be impersonal about what he is blogging about.

Keep up the good work. The number one novice mistake of bloggers, including professionals who are blogging, is to post a half a dozen times, get no comments, and call it quits. Blogs take time to be found, and it takes a good post indeed to get most blog readers to comment. Stick to it.

And then you can continue with these steps:

Talk about other professional blogs. One of the surest ways to build a blog is to post about what other bloggers have posted, both good and bad. Don't be afraid to share kudos and criticisms about other bloggers, but as the saying goes, keep it professional, not personal.

Comment, comment, comment. Commenting is the other, sometimes forgotten, part of blogging. Make a point of spending approximately half your "blogging time" reading and commenting on other blogs, and don't neglect listing your blog in the comment author information. Remember, Google is watching!

Google never forgets and doesn't forgive. It's one thing to rant about a crappy product that's utterly worthless for, say, 300 words and quite another to one day be sweating a job interview when that product's manager walks in. If venting your spleen is your thing, by all means, do it anonymously.

Team up to go up. We will be talking about this in depth in Chapter 13, but seek out opportunities to do guest posts at other, better-known blogs and to join blog carnivals like the Grand Rounds whenever possible. Who knows, it may be the start of a whole new profession for you!

CHAPTER 7

■■■

Building Your Company Blog

In the movie, *The Matrix*, Neo is given a choice by Morpheus: the Red pill, which will shatter his world but show him the truth about it, or the Blue pill, which will let him go on in his happy cocoon of a life.

Today, companies of all types, from tiny one-man operations to large, transnational corporations, are staring at their executive conference tables and kitchen countertops: Red pill or Blue pill?

Blogging—specifically, company endorsed, sponsored, and promoted blogging—is the Red pill for corporations at the beginning of the twenty-first century. It's not an easy choice. Do they do what they've been doing and risk being passed by competitors in the race for attention in an attention-deficit world, or do they start letting human faces and human beings peek from under the corporate mask?

The danger is twofold. One risk is that employees and employee-owners might develop a taste for the free life of blogging and find fitting back into their corporate slots is like putting on shoes two sizes too small. The other is that customers may decide your company blog is just the spot to erect a public whipping post for you, your company, your products, and your ancestors, and flay you alive for all your sins, real and imagined.

In this chapter, we're going to take a look at several companies, from very large to downright micro, who've decided to blog.[1] We'll start with the world's largest firm in its industry and work our way down to a company of one. You'll see what these various firms are getting from blogging, and perhaps like them, decide to take the Red pill.

Redefining Public Relations

With 40 offices worldwide, 1,800 employees, and about $100 million in sales,[2] Edelman is the largest independent PR company in the industry. Edelman, which was the first PR agency to go online in 1995, sees itself as a thought leader in its industry.

---

1. Others cover business blogging from a business point of view. Notable are Debbie Weil in *The Corporate Blogging Book: Absolutely Everything You Need to Know to Get It Right* (Portfolio, 2006), and Robert Scoble and Shel Israel in *Naked Conversations: How Blogs are Changing the Way Businesses Talk with Customers* (Wiley, 2006). These books are excellent guides for CEOs, corporations, and companies struggling with implementing blogging in the enterprise.
2. These statistics are from `http://salesworks.factiva.com` and Edelman's website at `http://edelman.com`.

Richard Edelman was one of the first CEOs to start blogging in September 2004. Now there are more than a few CEOs out there blogging.[3] What makes Edelman as a company interesting is just how seriously it takes blogging:

- The company hired Steve Rubel in February 2006 as a senior vice president. Steve Rubel is best known for his A-List blog, Micro Persuasion (www.micropersuasion.com). As Edelman said in a post announcing the hire, "What do we hope to achieve together? In short, we want to persuade our corporate clients to commit to the blogosphere."

- Edelman hired Michael Wiley in August 2006 as a senior vice president. Michael Wiley was the driving force behind the well-received General Motors corporate blog, FastLane.

- The company brought together its 16 bloggers and 2 podcasts into a single blog portal in September 2006, as shown in Figure 7-1.

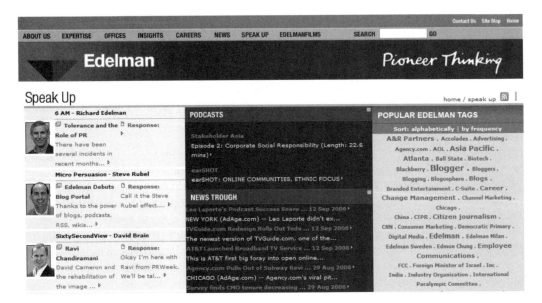

Figure 7-1. *Edelman blog portal*

Richard Edelman, CEO of Edelman, is a "real" blogger, as shown in Figure 7-2. He writes his own posts, responds to comments,[4] picks his own topics, and doesn't necessarily stick to "safe" topics.

---

3. More than a few, but not that many. According to *Wired* magazine, 30 (6 percent) of the Fortune 500 were blogging as of September 7, 2006 (www.socialtext.net/bizblogs/index.cgi).

4. For example, he responded to a comment I posted in February 2006.

6 A.M.

speak up / 6 A.M. RSS

ABOUT RICHARD EDELMAN

Biography

ARCHIVE

September 2006
August 2006
July 2006
June 2006
May 2006
April 2006
March 2006
February 2006
January 2006

September 12, 2006

Tolerance and the Role of PR

There have been several incidents in recent months that call into question our society's ability to maintain a tolerant attitude at a time of geopolitical upheaval. We should not simply excuse the perpetrators on the grounds of momentary lapses of judgment. Words matter, often as precursors to action or indicators of future behavior. We need to hold our public figures, whether actors, government officials or businesspeople, responsible for their statements. We should not be so quick to forgive or forget.

Here are a few examples of misbehavior by those in important positions:

1) Reverend Andrew Young's statement regarding the closure of smaller, mom and pop stores due to competition with Wal-Mart. "But you see, those are the people who have been overcharging us-selling us stale bread and bad meat...I think they've ripped off our communities.

Figure 7-2. *Richard Edelman's blog*

Richard Edelman is a man on a mission: Get major corporations blogging. He has an uphill battle. In an interview, he explained why he sees blogging as a major change in how a business does business.

Q. *In February 2006, when you hired Steve Rubel, you said in your blog that, in short, the goal was to get your corporate clients to commit to the blogosphere. How has that worked out?*

A. I'd say it's a work in progress. I think our decision to be so aggressive in this area is simply that we should do it by example. And my blog, as an instance, believe it or not, is up to 9,000 unique visitors a month. Steve gets 90,000 a month. For us, it's a bully pulpit about the industry and issues—whether it's pay for play, any of the other controversial things, or my little post this morning about what constitutes adequate response by a PR firm in a crisis situation.

It's a way to educate and a way to reach the next generation of PR practitioners. It's a way to recruit and retain talent. My people are always stopping me in the elevator and mentioning my blog. We have little chats about it wherever I am in the world. It's also a very good means of listening. If you're not just looking at only the comments to your blog, but also what the Technorati chatter is—what people are saying—you can actually learn and improve your product and service.

For me, it's all about this move from top-down to a peer-to-peer—to a horizontal way of communicating. That's why it's urgent that PR people not think of PR only as making media pitches. That's important, but it's not sufficient.

Q. *Corporations tend to be known for their hierarchies more than anything else. How does the idea of people just saying what they want on the company's dime at their blog go over when you talk to the various CEOs?*

A. I think there's a real trade-off between control and credibility. If you are too much of a command-and-control kind of person, blogging is probably not for you, but you're also probably not in tune with what it takes to be credible in this world. I like the spontaneity of Jonathan Schwartz's [CEO, Sun Microsystems] blog. It's a very interesting virtuous circle.

Q. *For instance, right now on the Fortune 500, only 6 percent have what you would call executive-level blogs.*

A. Right, I'm not surprised by that.

Q. *Why aren't you surprised and do you think it will all change?*

A. I do think it will change. The very fact of success stories, like FastLane for GM, Schwartz, or my own. It's critical to have these be documented over a period of time, and then show the success story. Then smart companies will all get on the bandwagon—you know, early adopters and then the guys who hop on later. We're still in the early adopters phase.

What does Microsoft have, 5,000 bloggers?

Q. *It depends on who you talked to—3, 200 is a pretty firm number. Then there are people like Mini Microsoft, who isn't a Microsoft blogger, but is some anonymous employee blogging about Microsoft. Do CEOs that you talk to raise that issue of negative blogs?*

A. Sure, and I tell them that there's such a thing in the world as a vacuum and nature hates it, and if you don't fill it, then somebody else will. That's another reason to blog: You've got to tell your story. Every company is a media company, as far as I'm concerned—some more, and some less. If you're in tech or media, of course, you're right in the center of it. Why do we want to sit there and get clobbered without telling our side? It's classic PR.

Q. *By my account, there are 16 different bloggers at the Edelman portal. What has blogging changed about the corporate culture at Edelman?*

A. I think that people—I'm talking about people in the PR industry—regard us as very much open to be in the debate. It has proved our reputation as a great place to work, and it has helped us in actually getting clients.

Q. *Besides a general recognition within the PR community and online, have there ever been any cases where people or companies have said because of your blog, they'll go with you rather than somebody else?*

A. It's not quite that explicit, but I think that they recognize us. In surveys regularly—*PR Week* does these surveys—people definitely see us as way ahead on intellectual capital and thinking ahead as to what the PR industry will evolve to.

Q. *Let's say that you were talking to one of these CEOs who has been on the fence regarding blogging. What would be the bottom line of how they should go about doing it? Should they have a portal?*

A. I'll give you an example to answer your question. We made this recommendation to Nissan about Carlos Ghosn. The way they do it for Ghosn is that they walk around with him with a tape recorder. He's going from meeting to meeting, and they just basically record his remarks and put them up.

Q. *Now, Carlos Ghosn is the . . . ?*

A. He's the boss. He's the CEO of Nissan and Renault, and he's always flying back and forth between Tokyo, Paris, New York, LA, and just everywhere. This is a guy who is one of the four or five best-known CEOs in the world. Anyway, that's their strategy. Basically, a corporate communications guy just goes around and follows him as a scribe.

Q. *Which makes sense. Is that blog up now? Or are they in the process of doing that?*

A. They're in the process of doing it. That's the way we talked about doing it this summer. That's the only way. He's not going to sit at his PC, like I do, and write.

Q. *Any problem with disclosing this? I don't want to step on anything.*

A. Go ahead, you can.

Q. *Great. That's pretty impressive. Nissan is . . .*

A. A pretty big company.

Q. *What has sold them on the idea of doing this? Why did they decide they wanted to do this?*

A. They wanted to do it because they recognized that they've got their star-power talent, Ghosn. They've got a category that is very much an interest on the Web, their cars. And their PR guy is a good guy; he gets it. He's not, "I'm just going to talk to the *Wall Street Journal.*"

Q. *Is blogging just another tool in the PR arsenal, or is it something more—deeper and fundamental?*

A. I think it's much more fundamental. I think it's very fundamental for PR people to understand this change in mentality. It is really a kind of major mind shift or mental approach to our business.

It's not a shift from defense to offense, as much as it's a change from keeping everything to yourself until you're ready to let it go to the idea of co-creating a narrative. In a way, you're sharing authorship, but you're going to have a hell of a lot better novel.

Q. *On a couple of the more controversial parts of company blogging and companies using blogging, let's be more precise. What do you think of the idea of companies basically paying for positive blogs?*

A. It's horrendous. It's unacceptable. In my mind, anything to do with buying off journalists, bloggers, or any others is pay for play. I don't accept it, because if you want to pay, then do advertising. Make it explicit. Don't do this kind of subterfuge, because once you're outed, it has twice the bad implications for you and for the industry.[5]

Q. *Anything else that we should cover?*

A. I just want everyone to understand that this is a tremendous chance for the PR business. It will only happen well and succeed if PR people improve themselves, meaning that they actually are participating in the blogosphere—reading, writing comments, doing something. Also, that they stop this mentality of having to pitch. In fact, they're not salespeople; they're in a discussion. We have to be accurate, absolutely, 100 percent accurate in what we put out, because it's going directly to the end user of information potentially. It's no longer mediated, necessarily. We have to have journalist-level content.

Blogging About Products

Now maybe you're thinking its okay for a PR firm to dive off the blogging deep end. But it will be a cold day in hell before you trust the Internet with the reputation of your product![6] Consider someone who knows a great deal about freezing temperatures, brand marketing, and brand identification: Sub-Zero.

Sub-Zero, for those of you who don't have a foodie in the house, is arguably the most prestigious kitchen refrigerator brand worldwide, commanding premium prices even in the age of the Internet price. You may wonder why Sub-Zero would decide to start a wine blog, as shown in Figure 7-3.

---

5. About a month after this interview in September 2006, a supposedly genuine blog for one of Edelman's major clients, Wal-Mart, was exposed by another blogger as a fake created by the PR firm. Faced with severe criticism over the practice, Edelman revealed that two other Wal-Mart–related blogs were fake. He said that all three blogs would be shut down, that all of the company's employees would be taking a mandatory class in "ethics in social media," and all social media programs would from now on get an internal ethics review before being launched.

6. A study done at Micro Persuasion (www.micropersuasion.com/2006/09/study_wikipedia.html) of the hundred biggest US advertisers according to *Advertising Age* found that Wikipedia articles are consistently among the most highly ranked pages in Google on direct searches. Today's Hades weather: chilly.

Figure 7-3. *SubZero Wine Blog*

I put the question to Christopher Parr, Sub-Zero/Wolf Consumer Marketing Manager.

Q. *Why did Sub-Zero decide to start a wine blog?*

A. The idea behind the Sub-Zero Wine Blog was to provide real content, interesting content, to our consumers and perspective owners. As I was developing a new Sub-Zero wine campaign, with print, brochures, web, retail and so on, it made sense to implement a blog as an extension of the campaign.

Our owners have discerning tastes. They expect a certain level of quality, so we wanted to overdeliver on their expectations. It was a fantastic challenge. So we brought in the top names in the wine industry and personalities from *Gourmet* magazine and Food Network. And I specifically directed them, "Please, don't write about our products."

Readers can see an advertorial a mile away. In focusing on wine tips, advice, recommended vineyards, it allows consumers to interact with our brands. Hopefully, it inspires them to return frequently, read more, and perhaps learn more about our wine-storage products.

Q. *What has been the reaction to the wine blog by Sub-Zero current and prospective customers?*

A. We've received fantastic feedback from our existing Sub-Zero customers. It adds value to their decision to select Sub-Zero. It's an extension of our brand, and the Sub-Zero Experience goes beyond just a purchase. It's about the good life and keepings things fresh—be it wine, food, conversation, kitchen design, or art.

To announce the site, we sent an e-blast out to 500,000 existing customers. In a two-day period, we received an 85 percent click-through to the blog and 750 wine brochure requests. They're engaged.

For prospective customers, it's a very nonobtrusive way for them to learn about our brands. We're not doing a hard sell, not at all—quite the contrary. But I feel consumers want that. Corporate blogs normally talk about themselves, their products, and service. Who cares about that? No one, except your PR group. I wanted to create a blog that I would actually want to read on a daily basis. And our readers do that, as shown by the regular comments from frequent visitors.

Q. *How do you come up with things to post day after day?*

A. For posting day after day, we opened it up to our contributors. Write what you love. Write what you know. And that's the only requirement.

Anthony Dias Blue, for example, is a James Beard Foundation award winner. As a true expert, his posts tend to be scholarly—discussing a certain vineyard in Italy. Food Network's Andrea Immer, on the other hand, is more of a wine generalist—recommending certain wines to go with salmon. That mix of content, having different voices, makes it more accessible to readers and reaches a wider audience.

Q. *Have you gathered any metrics on how effective the blog is in reaching potential Sub-Zero customers?*

A. The blog has been highly successful with traffic, repeat readers, and leads from wine brochure requests. In our first month, the blog has received a little over 1,000 leads. Most importantly, however, these potential customers are quality leads. We analyze all leads with Prizm.[7] Sixty percent of our wine brochure leads rank as high leads. Makes me think of *Field of Dreams*: "Build it and they will come."

Q. *Any surprises along the way in setting up a company blog?*

A. With other companies, depending on the content and theme, it might be more of a chore. Talking about wine, however, is quite the opposite.

It has been a delight to interact with our wine experts and readers. I find it very engaging to read comments to the articles, especially the lively opinions. Managing it is certainly more demanding than expected.

I was most surprised by hosted blog solutions. Instead of purchasing software and having it managed by our internal IT department, we turned outward and looked at possible blog vendors. We ended up selecting a very reliable company that charged $20 a month. Quite painless implementation, and you can't disagree with the cost.

---

7. Prizm is a high-end marketing research tool. Visit (www.claritas.com) for more information.

Beating the Internet Price

I've talked elsewhere about using a blog to establish value above and beyond the commoditization of most things via the Internet price. Conference Calls Unlimited is a company that has taken the Internet price out behind the blogging woodshed and given it a sound thrashing. How would you or your CEO like to have these numbers:

- Forced to cut average retail prices more than 65 percent in the past 5.5 years, but during that time, revenues rose over 55 percent.

- Customer churn is less than 1 percent. That compares to an industry average of at least 5 percent.

- An 11 percent growth in revenues for the second quarter of 2006 as compared to that same quarter of 2005. That's on top of an 8 percent growth in revenues experienced for the first quarter of 2006 over that quarter in 2005. The company's first quarter 2006 net income reflected an 18 percent growth as compared to results for 2005. And the second quarter 2006 net income reflected an increase of 40 percent over the first quarter of 2006.

Conference Calls Unlimited (`http://conferencecallsunlimited.com/index.html`) provides telephony and web-based conference calls. This is a decidedly tough business to be in against the likes of WebEx and Microsoft. Two years ago, Conference Calls Unlimited decided to stop most advertising in favor of a customer, social networking, blog-centric strategy, with seven blogs, like the one shown in Figure 7-4, and one podcast.

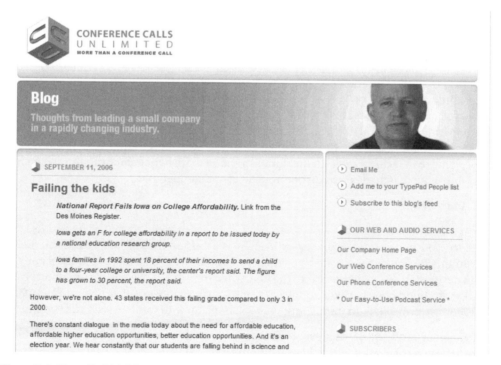

Figure 7-4. *Zane Safrit's blog*

I asked Conference Calls Unlimited's CEO, Zane Safrit, about his firm's unconventional approach.

Q. *I wondered if you could tell me a little bit about what made you decide to turn off traditional advertising and go towards word-of-mouth/blogging/teleseminar and the other things you're doing?*

A. The straight, honest answer is that traditional advertising no longer worked for us. We're in a commodity business. Conference calling, audio conference calling, web conferencing are being commoditized as quickly as our competitors can do it. I thank them for it—not really, but they seem to be driving down the prices, and driving it into a commodity status as quickly as they can.

For a long time, we were very successful using pay-per-click, even the bid-for-placement programs for Google and, at the time, Overture. I think Overture has been acquired by Yahoo since then. And we were happy as could be with that approach. It was very simple. We put money in the accounts. We would bid for the appropriate placement. I tracked, more importantly, the number of calls that came, the amount of monies that were paid to Google and Overture for this, and we were just happy.

As time went on, we moved from being lowest cost provider, to offering one of our services at 25 cents a minute, to within a few years, we were no longer the lowest cost provider, with prices for the same service now at 9 cents a minute. And that's the kind of advertising that works on pay-per-click, especially in a commodities market, and that no longer worked for us. So we had to find something that worked for us, and if anything else, we had to stop donating money to Google and Overture, which is what our budget became: a donation to those two companies.

Along the way, we came across a couple of key mentors who really showed up at about the right time. One [set] was Ben and Jackie over at Customer Evangelists Blog [http://customerevangelists.typepad.com]. Their domain is Church of the Customer, and they have introduced us to the fact of customer evangelism and word-of-mouth marketing—how you create a remarkable experience and your customers turn into your loyal and evangelistic sales force. At the same time, we ran across Seth Godin [http://sethgodin.typepad.com]. I spent a day with him at his upstate New York warehouse, and he introduced me to blogging. I realized that for us to succeed, we had to put forth the one factor, the one thing that made us stand out from all of our competitors.

Q. *And that thing is?*

A. And that was our people—everyone here. You expect to hear this, but if you ever use our service, you will experience that everyone here is a little on the anal side, a little on the neurotic side. And we've created a company where they can take that personality habit and devote it to the customer. From the first, when they call us, we answer our phone calls live, to the interactions, when they began to talk to us about teleconferencing and all of the support we provide them throughout their relationship with Conference Calls Unlimited.

Most importantly, we do whatever it takes to make a customer happy. And it sounds like the dullest, most overhyped cliché you ever imagine. The difference is that it is true for us, and has to be true, because we've got nothing else to make us stand out.

We are a little company with a funky name in a funky little town in Iowa, trying to compete against name brands like WebEx, Microsoft, and all of these people with huge advertising budgets. We are actually doing it quite well, even while prices have continued to drop. It sounds like a cliché, but in reality, it's how we make our business.

Q. *I understand. How big is your company? How many employees?*

A. We have eight people.

Q. *Like you said, it is a commodity business because you're selling data transport, basically.*

A. Basically, that's exactly it. We're selling one step above bandwidth.

Q. *So tell me, how do the blogs figure into this? How does your blog figure into it? I see that other people in your company are blogging.*

A. There are other people in my company blogging. Blogs factor into it in a lot of different ways. We have a customer newsletter blog, where the feed for that is carried on a couple of other blogs. One is the Word-of-Mouth Marketing Association's blog. It also allows our customers to find out information—from tips, to press releases about our other customers, to profiles about our customers and how they use our services, to profiles even about Conference Calls Unlimited.

The biggest way we use it is through my main blog, which is at http://zane.typepad.com. It's a blog where I talk about issues related to running a small business. And that's anything from developing a business in a rural economy, to healthcare or the lack thereof for small business employees, to HR, to advertising, to creating employee evangelists as the basis for creating customer evangelists, to Hewlett-Packard's decision to spy on its board of directors.

Q. *Let's get specific for a moment about blogs and advertising. Can you state unequivocally that there are people out there who are now your customers because they read your blog?*

A. I cannot state that. I take that back. I can, and I'm pretty sure I can go back and provide specific examples.

Q. *Is it more about getting recognition on the Internet? Are you trying to build a community out of your customers, or is it more just going to extraordinary lengths compared to traditional business and using the Internet to do that?*

A. It's a little bit of both. We're definitely trying to build a community with our customers, because we don't see ourselves as a conference call service provider. We see ourselves as a small business solutions provider. To the extent we can create a community of other companies who have solutions for small businesses, who will help our existing customers grow, we will continue to grow by expanding our revenues with our existing customers.

With our main blog, the purpose wasn't to go out and talk about Conference Calls Unlimited per se, because to a certain extent, we don't have a lot of interesting things to say about our services. They are the same services that everybody else uses fundamentally: the same technology, the same bridges, the same web conferencing solutions.

What we do is use the blog to interact with some influentials, or, as Seth [Godin] calls them, *sneezers*, to expand our conversation outside the reach of just people who are interested in finding a cheap conference call solution. We try to find other like-minded businesses out there competing in commodities, competing in a tough competitive environment regardless—companies who are looking for the innovative ways to compete, to grow through word of mouth, to build an evangelistic customer base, to create a unique type of company where they treasure their employees and see them as a resource to develop, and who are interested in maybe taking a stand on some social issues as they relate to creating quality of life for their communities.

Q. *I notice that there are not a lot of comments or trackbacks on your blog. I wonder why that is?*

A. I've always wondered that as well. I suppose if I really wanted to generate a lot of comments, I could be more striking and confrontational. I could write more posts with inflammatory language. My point isn't to inflame just for the sake of comments. It's more to nudge the discussion and open people's ideas to maybe a different perspective or to jump in and say, "You know, I think there's a little bit of information lost." I walk a fine line between speaking bluntly and encouraging participation, but at the same time not wanting to inflame the masses just for the sake of writing something inflammatory and hyperbolic.

Q. *Do you have a company blogging policy? In other words, are there things that your employees understand you should not blog about?*

A. Our employees can blog about anything they want, as long as it's not confidential information within the company.

Q. *So basically, the same rules apply as if they were talking at a bar.*

A. Exactly. And to drive the point home a little further with everyone in the company, I use the example of I really don't want to be sitting in the one or two little coffee places here in town and hear strangers discussing our financial results, or our commission structure, or our bonus base, or our most recent revenue in specific dollar amounts. And I don't want a discussion internally about what people's salaries and commissions are. Other than that, you can disagree with what we're doing. Just let me know. I hate being blindsided. You can shout out about it. You can rant about anything you want. It makes no difference. It's your blog. We'll support it.

We think the resource of blogging is so valuable because it helps. One of the reasons I blog regularly is it helps me clarify so many ideas and plans for the future in two ways. It's sort of a creative, dreaming room for me each day, where I can go out and scan the news headlines on particular topics, and begin to think about how they apply to us, and then begin to think about how I can make sure we're not like that, or how we incorporate that. Or sort of blue-sky a conversation, an issue I'm not particularly clear on, and I'll put that out on the blog, and other people will either contact me by email or maybe they might post a comment to it.

The other thing is just that regularly writing every day in a blog is such a terrific exercise for clarifying your thinking and communication resources. It's worth it just for that.

Q. *And as a CEO, that's one of, I think, sort of your primary job duties.*

A: Absolutely. And there's nothing better than to turn people loose and say, write about anything you want. Write about what you're passionate about. Just do it.

Q. *I assume that you talk and converse with other CEOs of other companies, small, large, and medium. What do your peers think of you blogging away the company secrets, if you will?*

A. You know honestly, I think they're confused by what we do here. What we do here is so organic, and I give completely away to everyone in the company to do whatever it takes to make each other happy and to make our customers happy. And I have zero desire to know everything they do. I'll see it eventually. It will show up in a report, or I'll come across it in an email. In the rare instance it has created a problem, I'll hear about it, and they know it, and they know the guidelines. The only error is to not do something to make the customer happy, and they have a complete green light to do whatever it takes.

Coming back to your question about the CEOs, I think a lot of them are curious. I think they're perplexed. And I think they're stuck in the mind frame of, "Well, I've got work to do. I don't have time to blog and talk with my peers and talk with my customers, and find out other ideas, better ideas, clarify my own thinking and keep us moving forward. I don't have time for that. I've got work to do."

And honestly, I think that's the silliest thing. There is nothing more important than to either talk with your employees or talk with your customers. Now granted, you've got things to do. I've got to finish some reports this weekend. But on a day-to-day basis, there's nothing more important than talking with customers, influentials, thought leaders, and employees, and they all overlap. I mean our employees are thought leaders. Thought leaders are our customers. And the extent to which I can engage with them in a discussion about what's important to them will help me find a solution for them to be pleased about.

And I go back again—I've got great people. They're overqualified. We pay them more than the narrowly defined position requires. But that means when somebody calls, they get very top talent talking to them and handling their problems. And somebody who's smart and creative, and can communicate in full sentences and write clearly, who can think outside the box every time, and who's confident and mature enough to talk with them like an adult. And know how to treat them personally and yet professionally every phone call, every email, and know where the limits are on both.

Q. *Any advice for CEOs or founders of companies as to how to approach blogging?*

A. You know, I've talked about this with Debbie Weil and a couple other people. Just do it. There's no other way to learn it than doing it. If you want to have the confidence from a coach or a consultant from the initial day, be up and running and maybe learning some of the functions of a blog, go for it. But honestly, what you get from an investment in a blog is so great and so valuable that you should start today.

Q: Anything I should have covered?

A: No, I can't think of anything. You know I can talk all day about this, because I love it. I think it's just fantastic. It's been a boon for our company. We would be dead without this resource at this time in our history.

Tales of a Glass Maker

When is the last time you saw a small glass—suitable as a cup, candleholder, or vase—that did not have "Made in China" stamped on its base? Probably a long, long time ago, unless you've become part of the Glassybaby trend-ette. Glassybaby is a small firm of 25 employees that designs, manufactures, and sells small glasses, all of the same shape but in a huge range of colors. Sales are from both its Seattle, Washington, store and online. Nicola Hewitt does inside sales, outside sales, washes windows, and runs Glassybaby Tales (`http://blog.glassybaby.com`), the firm's TypePad blog, shown in Figure 7-5.

Figure 7-5. *Glassybaby Tales blog*

I asked Nicola a few questions:

Q. *What do your customers who read your blog think?*

A. Interesting question. I wish that I had more insight on this. Our blog gets a fair amount of hits, mostly from web shoppers. I have only had three comments posted by readers. A few people in the store have said, "Hey aren't you the blogger?" It rests there. So, I am hoping to cultivate more interaction with readers to get a sense of what they think.

Q. *What do you most like and most hate about blogging?*

A. I love the MacGyver aspect or the Sherlock nature of it, if you will. I read our web orders for comments to use. In the store, I am constantly interacting with customers. Their stories astound me. The range of emotion people attach to our product is profound—joy, celebration, healing, even grieving. I try to weave it all into the blog.

I would prefer more feedback from readers. I think that greater exchange would create a more dynamic blog.

Q. *Why did you decide to start a blog?*

A. We have read so much about blogs—their potency to both connect with customers and market in a more interesting way. This really appealed to us.

Q. *Is blogging fun for you?*

A. Absolutely. It is definitely a creative outlet. I enjoy writing.

Want a Game of Pool with That Trackback?

Pool halls, like soda fountains, gas station attendants, and enjoyable airline travel, seem to be an idea that has faded from the public scene. So what do you do when you want to start a smoke-free billiards hall and coffee bar in the heart of downtown Bellingham, Washington?

You start blogging.

Brian Rollo is the owner of Kendrick's Billiards and blogger-in-chief of Kendrick's Billiards Blog (`http://kendricks.wordpress.com/`), shown in Figure 7-6. There, you'll find posts on happenings at Kendrick's, photos of customers courtesy of Flickr, and when and how it's time to fire a customer.

Figure 7-6. *Kendrick's Billiards Blog*

I began by asking Brian about that last one:

Q. *Why blog about firing your customers?*

A. I'm really not afraid of driving off prospective customers with opinionated posts. I think the vast majority of people can relate to dealing with people like those described in the post and would find it amusing. I always try to keep people anonymous when dealing with negative situations. I do try to minimize the number of negative posts, as I don't want the business to be thought of in a negative light.

Q. *What has been the reaction of customers to the blog?*

A. The guys described in the post, "The Posse" (`http://kendricks.wordpress.com/2006/08/11/the-posse/`) were pretty excited to hear that we had written about them. Because they are an unusual group of guys and because we want to keep them as customers, we tried to describe them without passing any judgment.

Q. *Has the blog attracted new customers in its first three months?*

A. Very few so far. The one post that has probably brought in a few new customers is one of our first, "Bellingham's Best Coffee" (`http://kendricks.wordpress.com/2006/07/26/bellinghams-best-coffee/`). Pretty regularly, our stats show search engine terms like "best coffee in Bellingham" finding us.

Q. *What has been the reaction of your employees to your blog postings?*

A. They love the postings. They're pretty good about correcting me if I make any mistakes. I've invited them to contribute posts, and a few employees probably will at some point.

Q. *Is it a good idea for small retail establishments to blog?*

A. Absolutely. I do think that certain types of retail shops can benefit more than others. I don't think that Kendrick's will gain a ton of business from the blog, but I really think that our neighbor, a new contemporary furniture shop, could really benefit from having one. I've actually been encouraging the owner, an interior decorator, to start a blog because I think it would help establish her as a top-notch local interior decorator. I think it would help search engines find her, and I think it would help her reputation. Anyone who writes about their craft is viewed as a bit of an expert by the general public.

Blogging the Unbloggable

One thing you hear time and again from people who don't spend most of their days on the Internet is that there are some things you just can't sell online, like jewelry or wine. Let's take a closer look at that assumption as it applies to a custom jeweler—a small business, but a business to be sure.

Sharla Oliveri is the owner, founder, and sole employee of Sharma Designs, a San Jose, California, online jewelry shop. Her blog is at `www.sharmadesigns.typepad.com`, shown in Figure 7-7.

Figure 7-7. *Sharma Designs blog*

Here's how Sharla answered my questions about her blog:

Q. *Has your blog helped or hurt your business?*

A. It has definitely helped. I think that people feel a little more comfortable buying online if they feel like they know the person. In my blog, my customers can get to know me a little better. They can also learn more about the time that's put into the jewelry and the design process.

Q. *Has your blogging increased sales?*

A. Yes, I have had a few sales from people who Googled something and they landed on my blog. I also announce on my blog when new jewelry is on the site, so that gets the customers to come check things out when they may not have thought to do so otherwise.

Q. *Are you enjoying blogging?*

A. Oh yes, I love it. Sometimes it's challenging coming up with enough topics to post about, and some weeks are just too busy to post as many times as I would like, but I love that my customers get to know me better. I have made some great friends.

Q. Have you gotten any ideas for designs from people who have commented on your blog or sent email to you because of your blog?

A. Yes. A few months ago, I put up a poll about what color people would like to see more of (purple). So I made more purple pieces. If customers really like a certain style of necklace that I posted, I try to make more necklaces like that. It's great feedback. I also have had people tell me that they wish they could see the necklaces on a real person, so I added that to the site as well. I get a lot of website feedback. That's great, because I don't shop at my own site, so it helps to know if others find it easy to use.

Q. Should other people who create and sell jewelry blog?

A. I think so. Again, the more the customer feels like they know you, the better. Plus, with jewelry, you can talk about your design process, materials, and inspirations with the pieces. People love jewelry with a story. Handmade jewelry tends to be more expensive than pieces you would buy in your local mall. I did a whole post explaining the time that goes into creating a piece of jewelry, and a lot of my customers responded very well to it! I also add tips about how to wear jewelry and how to flatter your face shape. You don't want your website to be too cluttered with information, and with a blog, you can still get the information to the customer.

Q. Any surprises along the way as you've been blogging?

A. How much time I put into it! I never realized when I began blogging how much of my time it would take! Another surprise is that people are so shy about commenting. People will often email me instead of commenting.

Lastly, there are some people who still don't know what a blog is! I have had people ask me what a "blob" is.

Micro-ISV Blogging

Finally, we take a look at a type of company that's springing up more and more on the Internet, and that some say is the wave of the future when it comes to software: the micro-ISV.

ISV stands for independent (of Microsoft) software vendor. Micro-ISVs are fewer-than-five-person, self-funded software companies existing entirely on the Internet. If you check your PC or Mac, you may be surprised at how many of the programs you've bought and use are micro-ISV products.

By way of example, consider Itzy Sabo's Claritude Software, which sells the highly useful SpeedFiler Microsoft Outlook add-in.[8] Based in Israel, Claritude sells SpeedFiler worldwide via its website (www.claritude.com) and blog (http://itzy.wordpress.com), shown in Figure 7-8.

---

8. I highly recommend SpeedFiler ($19.95)! With it, you can file incoming and outgoing email extremely quickly, reducing inbox bloat and improving productivity.

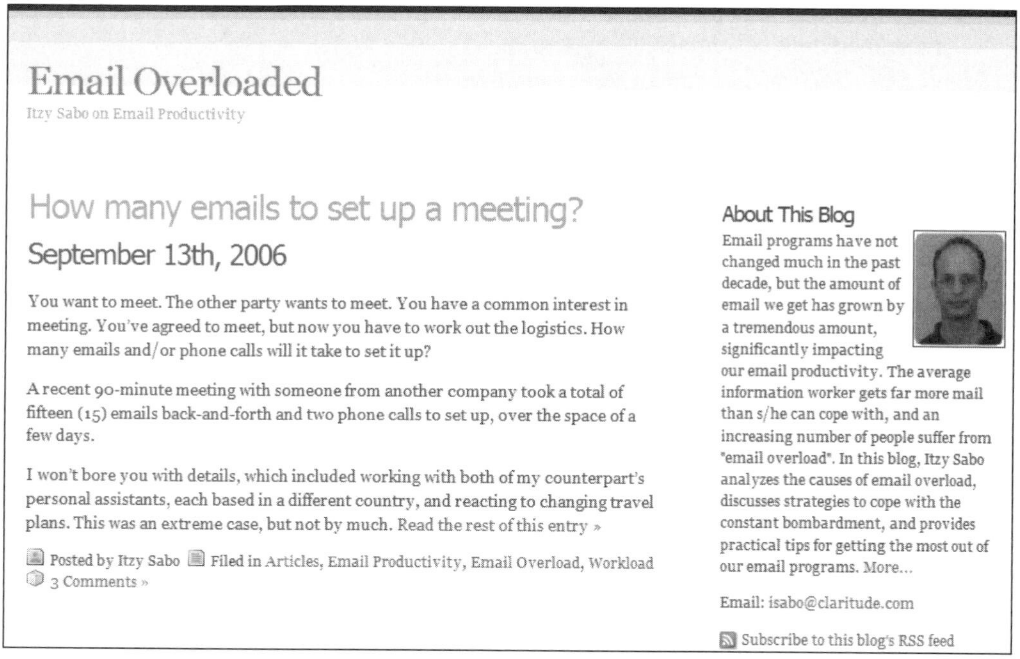

Email Overloaded
Itzy Sabo on Email Productivity

How many emails to set up a meeting?
September 13th, 2006

You want to meet. The other party wants to meet. You have a common interest in meeting. You've agreed to meet, but now you have to work out the logistics. How many emails and/or phone calls will it take to set it up?

A recent 90-minute meeting with someone from another company took a total of fifteen (15) emails back-and-forth and two phone calls to set up, over the space of a few days.

I won't bore you with details, which included working with both of my counterpart's personal assistants, each based in a different country, and reacting to changing travel plans. This was an extreme case, but not by much. Read the rest of this entry »

Posted by Itzy Sabo Filed in Articles, Email Productivity, Email Overload, Workload
3 Comments »

About This Blog

Email programs have not changed much in the past decade, but the amount of email we get has grown by a tremendous amount, significantly impacting our email productivity. The average information worker gets far more mail than s/he can cope with, and an increasing number of people suffer from "email overload". In this blog, Itzy Sabo analyzes the causes of email overload, discusses strategies to cope with the constant bombardment, and provides practical tips for getting the most out of our email programs. More...

Email: isabo@claritude.com

Subscribe to this blog's RSS feed

Figure 7-8. *Claritude Software's blog*

I asked Itzy some questions about his blog.

Q. *How has your blog affected sales?*

A. The blog itself accounts directly for only a small portion of sales. However, it was a crucial tool to get the message out when I launched my first product, SpeedFiler. The blog is indirectly responsible for a much larger percentage of sales. It has drawn the attention of other bloggers to SpeedFiler and seeded numerous posts, which, apart from linking back to the blog, also link to my commercial website and bring me customers.

Q. *Where does blogging fit in your overall marketing approach?*

A. The blog is a major part of my marketing approach. Being a micro-ISV, I have to divide my time very carefully between marketing existing products and developing future products, and I also have a rather limited marketing budget.

Writing a blog gives incredible return on investment in a number of areas. Take visibility, for instance. Claritude Software is in the email productivity software business. The way search engines work, in order to rank highly for terms such as "email productivity" and "email overload," apart from using SEO [search engine optimization] techniques in the website, I need links from high-ranking sites. These are difficult to obtain and take a lot of time. It's much easier to get a blog to rank highly for these terms. It can naturally have much richer content than a product-focused website (richer in good keywords for SEO and also in quality subject matter for the readers), and it's much easier to get other bloggers to link to the various posts. Both of these qualities have a crucial impact on the rankings. My blog appears consistently "above the fold" on the first page of Google results for "email productivity" and "email overload." Once people come to the blog, the challenge is then to convert them into customers.

Another area in which the blog helps is credibility. I have a passion for improving all aspects of email, and the blog allows me to showcase this. The blog paints a picture of who is behind Claritude Software and what motivates him. In addition, I publish my photograph and email address on my blog. I don't believe in hiding behind a corporate veil. I hope that all of this lends an aura of credibility to the product itself.

Thirdly, blogging allows me to keep very much in touch with the market. I treat blogging as a conversation, and I try to attract as many comments and opinions as possible. I learn a lot from my readers about the problems they experience with email, how concerned they are about these problems, and how they go about dealing with them. This is very valuable information when making decisions about new products or features.

Q. *Have you ever made a large-volume sale because of your blog?*

A. It's difficult to say whether any particular sale was because of the blog. As I said before, only a small percentage of sales originate from the blog, but it definitely plays a part in many sales. The commercial website links to the blog, and many potential customers subscribe to it before deciding to purchase. If someone is considering a large purchase and they're the type who does their homework, I hope the blog will leave a lasting positive impression with them.

Q. *How do you manage to find the time to blog?*

A. I try to devote about 30 minutes each day to blogging and developing ideas for future posts, but it's a constant battle. Because I try to write original material, the most difficult periods are when I'm channeling my creative energy into developing a new product or feature, and there's very little left for developing new blog material. So it's not just a matter of finding the time—I've got to have the right kind of energy as well.

Q. *Do you have a blog plan, and if so, what is it?*

A. I don't have a long-term master plan. However, when I started the blog, I wanted to give it a decent backbone, so I picked a number of topics and invested significant effort in researching them and writing them up, creating a series of posts with a common thread. Since then, I've worked on a couple of other series, but these generally come about because of an idea I had rather than as part of a master plan. I like to work on a number of posts in parallel, and every day I spend a few minutes moving each one forward until it's ready. Occasionally, I'll get an idea for a quick post and write it on the spot, but this is not the usual case.

Companies and Blogs: Recap

A decade ago, companies large and small were faced with a choice: build themselves websites with homepages and get on the Internet. A few brave souls took the plunge, and now a few billion lines of HTML later, very few businesses of any size lack a website.

Today, whether you are looking at the Nissans and Edelman corporations of the world or tiny one-man companies like Claritude Software, you're seeing the same small wave of early adopters being joined by the mainstream.

Blogging poses its risks and challenges for a business. But the risks and costs of *not blogging*, as Richard Edelman says, are rising steadily and perhaps inexorably. Perhaps it's time for your company to take the Red pill.

Your Action Tasks

Here are a few steps for getting started with your company blog:

Start small. Blogs are always a work in progress. As such, it pays to start small, and find the right focus and the right people within your company to blog. You can expand from there, if your company's size warrants it.

Blogs are not done by committee. A distant, bland blog run through the marketing department is an abomination and will do you more harm than good. Blogs are not regurgitated press releases. In fact, the best company blogs seldom brag about the company.

Know why your company is blogging. If blogging about your company's products and services is boring, what should you blog about? Your customers. The problems your product or services address. Your industry—good and bad. Most of all, blog about your people.

Blogs are a conversation. You should respond to every comment, especially negative comments, honestly. Blog readers and commenters expect and want conversation, not a monologue. This does not mean accept abuse, but it does mean addressing your customers face to face on your blog.

And then you can continue with these steps:

In-house or out-sourced? Unless your IT department is ready, willing, and able to handle the technical challenges of maintaining a blog, strongly consider using an outside service such as Six Apart's TypePad or WordPress.org's `WordPress.com` for your blogging platform. Don't have an IT department? You have your answer.

Stay on the side of the angels. Ignore entreaties from people within and outside your company who implore you to go the "pay-for-play" approach and attempt to buy favorable coverage in the blogosphere. Whatever its morality, sooner or later, it will come out and do much more harm than good.

Trust your people. In too many companies, the first reaction to the idea of a company blog is fear. What if the bloggers divulge company secrets? Get real. If you can't trust your employees to blog, you can't trust them period.

Connect to others. The blogosphere is powered by conversation and links that make it easy to follow that conversation. Posts need those links to be relevant and timely. Don't do what some companies do and treat links as losses because your readers might leave your blog. They might, but they'll be back if what you have to say is interesting, well written, and above all, passionate.

PART 3

■■■

Secrets of Influential Bloggers

If only it were so! Unfortunately, there's no digital secret sauce that can turn a good blog into a blog hundreds of thousands of people read every day, or for that matter, turn a bad blog into a good blog. The "secret" is putting in the effort to make your blog more valuable, more interesting, and more available to more people. The next six chapters cover a range of ways to do that—and make a little (or perhaps a lot) of money along the way.

CHAPTER 8

Power Tools for Bloggers

In this chapter, we're going to cover several of what I call the power tools of blogging. These are the tools and services bloggers who want to reach a wide audience use to add value to their posts. Unlike the late-night television ads for power car-washer wands and home gym equipment, you won't need to make six easy payments of $99 each. Most of these tools are free, and the others are available for trifling amounts.

The two main power tools we're going to look at in this chapter are Technorati and FeedBurner. These are two very different tools, doing very different things, but both of those things are very important to people who want to make a splash in the blogosphere.

Technorati

I've talked about Technorati, shown in Figure 8-1, elsewhere in this book. In Chapter 2, you learned how to use Technorati to find interesting blogs. Now, as a blogger highly interested in making your mark, it's time to look at Technorati again.

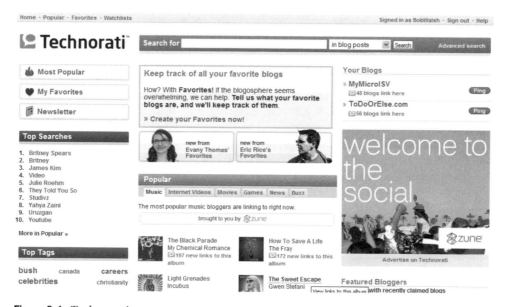

Figure 8-1. *Technorati*

Technorati has been around since November 2002, and it is the oldest blog-centric search engine. As such, its developers had the time and momentum to build a site and a service rich with goodies for bloggers who want to be noticed in the blogosphere.

AN INTERVIEW WITH DAVID SIFRY, FOUNDER AND CEO, TECHNORATI, INC.

David Sifry, founder and CEO of Technorati, is one those serial high-tech entrepreneurs who, as the saying goes, has been there, done that, and has a closet full of tee shirts to prove it.

Q. *So when you started Technorati, how many blogs were there?*

A. We started in November 2002. At that time, we were tracking about 40,000 blogs total. What we are tracking now [December 2005] is 23.6 million blogs. We're seeing the blogosphere is doubling in size every five and a half months, for the past 40 months in a row.[1]

I am flabbergasted every time I go back to these statistics. We know that they can't stay that way forever—there are only so many human beings on the planet—but I think what this tells you is just how the blogosphere has been doubling in its option rate about every six months. And the other thing it's telling you is just how far there is to go. Even though there are a lot of people now who know what the blogosphere is, and what a blog is, and what Technorati is all about, there's still a huge number of people out there who don't know.

As of December 2005, we are tracking between 70 [thousand] and 80 thousand new weblogs being created every single day.[2]

Detecting Spam Blogs

Q. *And these are real, live blogs, not just spam blogs or fake blogs?*

A. We pull out all the spam. If you included spam, those numbers could be anywhere from double to triple. But we actually aggressively quarantine and eliminate spam blogs [sblogs] from all of our indexes and from all of our statistics. It doesn't mean we catch every single thing. So, for instance, you could do a Technorati search for mortgage or refinance or penis enlargement, and I'm not going to tell you [you] are going to find zero spam in our index, but the fact is there are a lot of fake and spam blogs that get created that we are able to eliminate way before they get to our index. And once blogs go into our index, we pretty aggressively monitor and track and then destroy as many of these spam blogs as we can possibly find.

Q. *So do you have a page somewhere at Technorati where people can denounce spam and fake blogs?*

A. Actually we don't. Some sites do, like Blogger.com or Flickr.com. But what actually happens is that people end up using those things as a way to negatively game the system. You end up getting people who are vindictive to another person who then will report their blog as spam.

Q. *That's the problem with denouncement systems. Whether you're talking about the Salem witch trials or the Red Scare in the 1950s, people will game the system.*

A. Yep. So what we do is we try to follow a large set of variables that help us determine whether a blog is spam or not. The good news here is that we actually understand not only what's being said, and what the hyperlink structure is, but at Technorati, we understand two fundamental pieces of metadata that no one else out there really tracks.

---

1. As of November 2006, Technorati tracked 57 million blogs, and 55 percent of those had at least one new post in the past three months (http://technorati.com/weblog/2006/11/161.html). The speed at which the blogosphere doubles has slowed somewhat, from five and a half months to just under eight months.
2. As of November 2006, about 100,000 new blogs were being created each day and indexed by Technorati. This number does not include spam blogs that Technorati excludes.

The first is the concept of time. Not just what was said, and what are the links, but when was it said.

Q. *You mean human time vs. machine time?*

A. Well, it's human time and machine time. So here's a person writing a hundred posts in a minute—that's spam. Or when we start looking at the linking structure inside of these posts, or you look at the information and keywords in these posts. Clearly this is a link farm, because here are 10,000 blogs, all with similar names, with the same pattern, and they were all created within ten minutes, and they all link to the same site.

Because we understand the concept of time [when it comes to searching the Internet], we can actually pull this kind of stuff out before it gets into our index for more than 10 or 20 minutes.

Q. *What's the other metadata?*

A. The other metadata we understand is the concept of a person. This is actually really important. Part of this comes down to a difference in world view between Technorati and say Google or Yahoo. Now don't get me wrong, I use Google and Yahoo every single day. They're fantastic search engines. But it comes down to a difference in world view.

In 1995, '96, '97, where were most of the digitalized documents in the world? In general, they were in universities—in general, in the libraries. That's where all this digitalization stuff started getting a hold. So when you look at these search engines, the fundamental metaphor most of these search engines use today is the metaphor of the library.

So you have Yahoo that makes a directory of everything on the Internet. So you could say I'm looking for a Cadillac, and I would go to Automotive, and then from there to American, and then from there to Cadillac, and that would show me all the sites about Cadillacs. They would be the card catalog of the Internet.

And then you had the Google guys come out and say, "No, no, no, it's not just about being the card catalog, it's really about the bibliographic citation index. What [Google] page rank is all about is understanding the citations between all of these different documents. So we [Google] will essentially be the reference desk."

These are fantastic ways of being able to search though enormous amounts of information.

Q. *So what's Technorati's take?*

A. So the problem is there's no fundamental understanding in the Google or the Yahoo view of the world of how new documents become created and who creates them. It's almost like every morning, the librarian comes into work, and there are 80,000 new books sitting on the floor. They are really good at shelving the book, or helping people find it, but they have no idea how that book got there.

What happens when you start thinking about the Web as a monstrous conversation stream, or what my techies would call an event stream? Documents don't come into existence willy-nilly. Documents are the exhaust of a person's attention as expressed over time.

Q. *That almost sounds like a mathematical formula.*

A. It is! You know, I'm a techie, what do you want? It's the old Charlton Heston line, "It's people, it's people!"[3] You realize, wait a minute, the Web is people! It's not documents. All the sudden you can look at a weblog in an entirely different way. You don't have to look at a weblog as simply a reverse chronologically ordered website full of hyperlinks, comments, and trackbacks. But instead, you can actually look at a weblog and say, "You know what, a weblog is actually the store expression of a person's attention over time."

Q. *That sounds like a much deeper tenet than just a way to keep the spam at bay.*

A. Absolutely.

---

3. A memorable quote from the techie favorite movie, *Soylent Green* (www.imdb.com/title/tt0070723/quotes).

Technorati's Role

Q. *So maybe that rolls into my next question. What do you see as the role of Technorati in the blogosphere?*

A. The short answer is we help you make sense of all this. The slightly longer answer is, Technorati's role here is helping to understand who are the most interesting people. What are they hearing? What are they saying about you and the things that you care about? What's actually going on about your topic, your company, your interest?

When you stop thinking about the Web as being about documents, and think about it being a whole lot of people talking about stuff in real time, one of the things we can do is help be the glue to help you understand conversations. The reason I started Technorati in the first place was, to be frank, I was a weblog author and I became a total stats fiend, and I was really, really interested in knowing if what I was doing was having an impact. There was this part of me that said, enough about everyone else, I just want to know who's talking about me, and the things that I like, and the things that I care about.

And I realized that if I went to Google or Yahoo or one of these big search engines, that inherently, they are time-prejudiced. It takes anywhere from two weeks to six weeks to get your stuff incorporated into the Google or Yahoo index. At best, they're only going to be able to tell you what's being said as of 24 hours ago.

There's a couple of important things to keep in mind when you look at this model. The first is every single one of those steps [crawling and indexing sites] has to happen sequentially. You can't score the index before you do the crawl. The second thing is every single one of those steps has to take time. Doing a crawl takes time. Scoring the index takes time. By definition, the way Google works, you still have to poll.

Q. *So instead, you rely on people raising their hand?*

A. That's right, or even better, people poking us on the shoulder.

Q. *How?*

A. We had built into every single content manager this thing called the ping. Whether you are using WordPress or MSN Spaces or LiveJournal or TypePad, or you name it—any one of the top 30 or so major weblogging engines—it all starts with a ping. What this means is that we can actually go out there and index your content the second that you publish.

Q. *Because you are dealing with events like publishing, not polling all the Web on a regular schedule?*

A. You got it.

Q. *Crass question for a moment. How does Technorati make any money?*

A. Great question. What we've done is built an advertising and sponsorship network that makes us quite a bit of money, because there are a lot of people who want to be able to track "what are people saying about me, or my company, or the things I'm interested in."

When you start to understand the world in terms of time and people, you can do some very interesting things we call discovery, like "What are the most authoritative political bloggers talking about today?" That, in essence, creates a new type of media product that people want to advertise on. We get a lot of attention that way. We syndicate that information out, working with mainstream media sites.

Q. *Besides monetizing where people's attention is aggregating, do you have custom alerts watching for particular topics to be blogged? For instance, if tomorrow cold fusion became a really hot topic, are there people out there paying Technorati to keep an eye on that?*

A. We actually give that away for free. You can create a Watchlist on Technorati, and if you haven't, I highly recommend you do. It's an easy way to keep track of what you are interested in and what people are saying about it, in real time.

Where Is Blogging Going?

Q. *So, do you think blogging is going to change the whole process of how companies and customers relate to each other?*

A. Let me put it this way: Has email fundamentally changed how business and people relate to each other?

Q. *It's made customer service worse, but that's just my opinion.*

A. The answer is yes and no. The answer is yes, because it's easier for me to have contact with people at companies. The answer is no, because I get spammed, and in some cases, customer service has gotten worse. So my perspective on this is no technical tool is going to revolutionize anything. It's how people use the tool that makes the revolution happen. It's the cultural change that accompanies the "frictionless-ness" that the tool brings.

The one interesting thing blogging has done is that it has made posting your thoughts to the Internet as easy as writing an email. That means that the people formerly known as your audience now have the power to talk back, and even more importantly, they can talk to each other.

Q. *What about the effect blogging is having on business?*

A. First of all, there are a lot more businesses getting involved. The reality is that you've got people unrelated to the business that are actually having an effect on the business and its brand. One of the biggest ideas here is the whole idea of who controls the brand goes out the window. The people who you had to message to, they now control your brand. You, at best, have the opportunity to shepherd it a little. The reality is blogging has created a much more friction-free marketplace for ideas. And that means you don't have to have a million dollars to own a printing press in order for other people to hear your ideas.

Q. *So do you think blogging's impact is on the same magnitude as say PCs and the Internet?*

A. I don't know. I've been through four technology revolutions in my lifetime as an entrepreneur, and each one is significant in its way, but you know what? None of them [has] solved hunger in Africa. So I think we all need to take a moment and step back from the hype machine and recognize, is this a good thing? Yes, absolutely. Is this going to change things? Yes, absolutely! Is this walking on water? Come on! Let's all be careful here.

Q. *Last question. If you had a friend who was going to start blogging, what advice would you give?*

A. First off, be human. Don't worry about being perfect. Don't worry about writing the "right" thing. Just write and be yourself. Number two would be link prolifically. This one is for people who want to have some measure of authority. By linking, you're actually doing your readers a tremendous favor: You're saving them time.

And the other interesting byproduct of this is that hyperlinks in this world of people and time start to take on a new meaning. Hyperlinks are now not just nodes of attention; they're actually a new form of social gesture. They're a way of tapping someone on the shoulder and saying, "Hey, I'm paying you some respect." It's a wonderful, wonderful way not only to give your readers more value, but to get more involved with the conversations around you, if that's what you want to do.

David Sifry, CEO of Technorati, suggested five things every blogger should take advantage of at Technorati.

Using Watchlists

First on Dave's list were Technorati Watchlists, as shown in Figure 8-2. Creating a Watchlist is easy: Just enter the keyword or URL you want to watch for and save it to your free Technorati account. For example, David said, "Let's say you see an interesting article in the *New York Times* online. You can enter the URL of the article and see who's writing about it, what the commentary is."

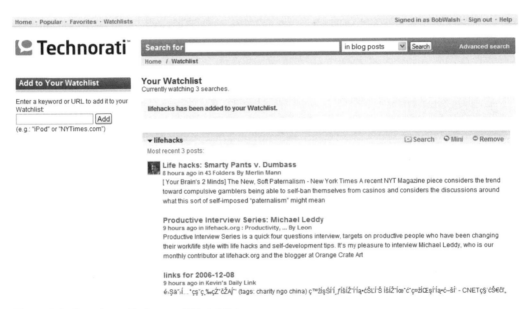

Figure 8-2. *Creating a Technorati Watchlist*

Using Bookmarklets

Next for bloggers is the Technorati Anywhere Bookmarklet, available when you set up a free Technorati account. To start using this bookmark-like object, you drag it from the Technorati page onto the bookmarks or favorites toolbar of your web browser. When you are reading a blog, news article, or any web page, and you want to see what people have blogged about it, just click the Anywhere Bookmarklet, and Technorati will run the search for you.

Creating Tags

The third thing David recommends is to get familiar with tagging. Tagging is something we explored from the reader's perspective in Chapter 2. Now we're talking about how to create and define tags.

"Tagging is just a simple way of allowing an author to be able to give some brief categories or topic keywords about his post," he said. "It's built into many of the modern blogging platforms right now."

"A tag is just a hyperlink with a very special little attribute. It's a way to state there's a relationship between the page you're on and where the hyperlink goes," David explained. Tags let bloggers decided how their posts should be categorized, just by adding one or more links back to Technorati.

David points out two benefits of tagging: Technorati and other search engines use tags to improve their results, and also your post can be found by anyone who searches for that tag at Technorati and elsewhere. Your content will show up in Technorati Tags pages like the one shown in Figure 8-3. "Imagine what you're doing now, when you publish with this tag," David said. "Now your post will show up on this page. Now people interested in Apress stuff will now more easily find your post. And you might not have actually written the word Apress inside your post."

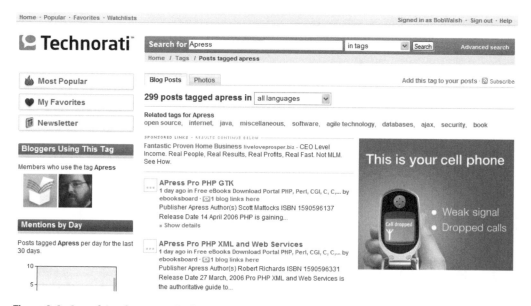

Figure 8-3. *Searching by tag at Technorati*

There's much more to tagging, as you'll see in Chapter 9, but it's worth noting that Technorati not only shows posts when people search for a tagged phrase, but also includes Flickr and Buzznet pictures, links from del.icio.us and furl, and all sorts of good stuff. "We just want to be the best, most interesting, most helpful place to be able to find stuff that's tagged. We don't care if it's a blog post, or it's a picture, or it's a hyperlink that's tagged on del.icio.us. We index it all," David added.

Claiming Your Blog

Number four on David's list is to claim your blog at Technorati, which gives people some more information about your blog and about you. "People are more likely to understand and click on those links," David said. "If you've done some Technorati searches, you've seen that some results have people's pictures next to them. That clearly draws the eye."

Claiming your blog on Technorati is a relatively simple process, especially if you're using one of the major blog publishing engines like Blogger or TypePad. Just click Quick Claim when you see the screen shown in Figure 8-4; then enter your login name and password for your blog.

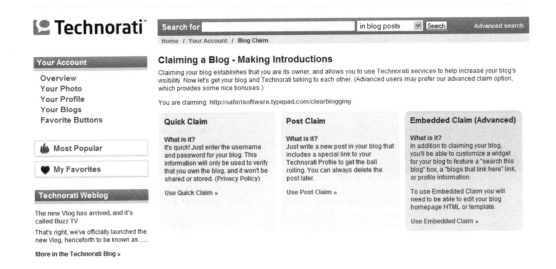

Figure 8-4. *Claiming your blog at Technorati*

Technorati logs on to your blog to validate that it's yours. After a few minutes, you should see the screen shown in Figure 8-5.

Enter a short description (250 characters), your primary language, and up to 20 tags you've used on various posts, as shown in Figure 8-6. Keep in mind that people may use various terms to look for the same thing, such as blog, blogging, posts, blogosphere, and so on.

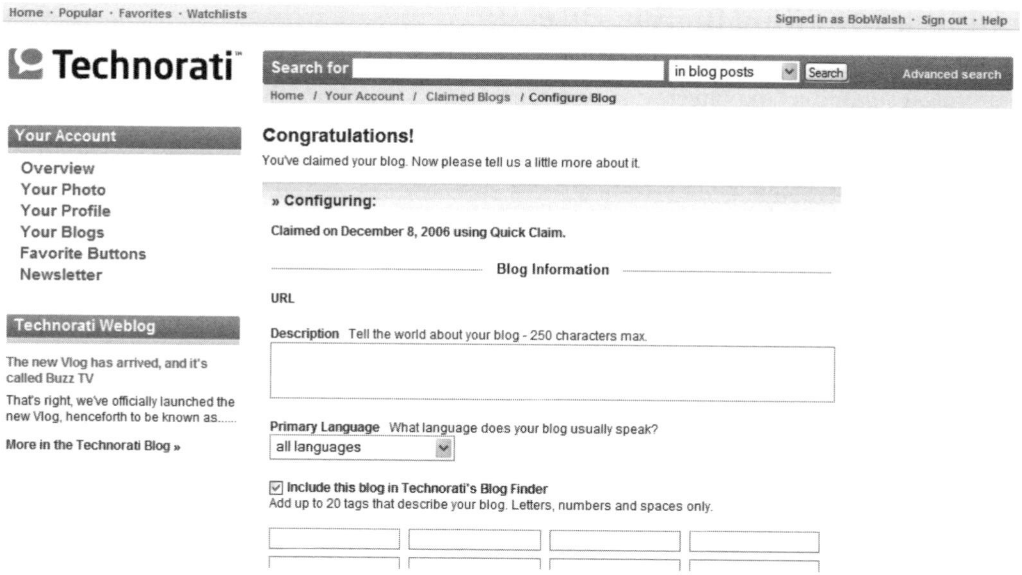

Figure 8-5. *Technorati validates your claimed blog.*

Figure 8-6. *Describing your claimed blog*

Adding Your Blog to Blog Directory

Last but not least on David's list is remembering to add your blog to Technorati's Blog Directory after claiming it. Blog Directory is, according to David, the Web's largest blog directory. "As of this moment, we have over 788,000 blogs that have claimed themselves. And then what they can do is add tags that say, 'this is what my blog is about.' And that's different than saying, 'this is what my post is about.'"

As shown in Figure 8-7, for my oldest blog, ToDoOrElse.com, I've searched for GTD, a tag I use on a lot of posts. I can see blogs by authority or freshness, and I can see handy related tags for GTD as well.

Figure 8-7. *The Technorati Blog Directory*

To make sure that your blog is in the Blog Directory, when you are configuring your claimed blog (or later if you miss it), check the Include This Blog in Technorati's Blog Finder option (see Figure 8-6).

FeedBurner

In Chapter 2, we looked at RSS from the point of view of reading blogs. You learned how RSS lets you automatically compile and collate RSS feeds from blogs you want to read into a single place convenient to you—a desktop application, Microsoft Outlook, or a website you sign on to regularly.

All of the blog publishing services, such as Blogger and TypePad, handle the mechanics of making a basic feed available from your blog. And some of those services keep track of the number of people who are coming to visit your blog each day. But none, as of this writing, provides statistics about who is reading your blog's RSS feed. And each site supports one, two, or three of the not-quite-the-same major RSS formats out there.

Furthermore, making your feed available is not the same thing as making it easy and comfortable for people to subscribe to your feed. Each blog publishing service does things just a little differently than the next and assumes a different level of technical expertise than the other.

Enter FeedBurner.

FeedBurner's goal is to make it as easy as possible for people to take advantage of your feed and for you to get the most benefit from your feed in a variety of ways. Most of those ways are free. For a few of the higher-end services, you pay anywhere from $4.99 USD a month, to handle three of your feeds, to $15.99 USD a month, if you happen to have more than ten different blogs going.

Signing Up with FeedBurner

The first step is to sign up for your free FeedBurner account so FeedBurner can optimize, publicize, analyze, and if you desire, monetize your feed for you.

Figure 8-8 shows where you start with FeedBurner (`www.feedburner.com`). Just enter your blog's URL and click the next button and FeedBurner will take you to screen-by-screen, step-by-step, excellent instructions for configuring your blogging service or publishing application to work with and through FeedBurner.

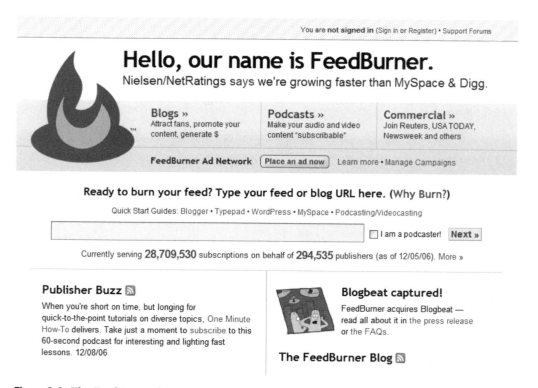

Figure 8-8. *The FeedBurner homepage*

Once you enter the URL of your blog, you'll see a screen like the one shown in Figure 8-9, where you supply your name and a password for your account.

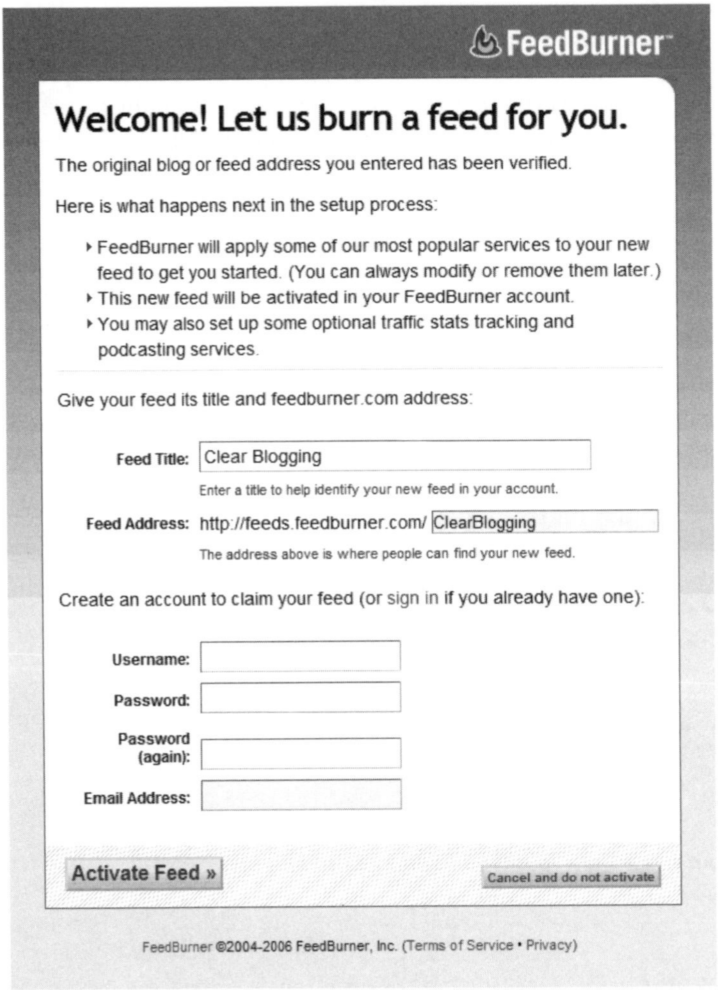

Figure 8-9. *Signing up with FeedBurner*

Once you click Activate Feed, you'll get to the screen shown in Figure 8-10, letting you know that FeedBurner is ready to make it easier for people to subscribe to your feed and for you to know who is getting your feed. Now you can be sure that your feed is as compatible as possible with all the RSS reader programs and websites your readers might want to use.

Figure 8-10. *Activating FeedBurner for your blog*

At this point, you've done some good things for your blog and for your readers, for free. Free is good. Free might be all you need. But if you're doing a business, professional, or especially a product blog, I think it's worth shelling out the 1.2 cappuccinos ($4.99) to get these "Pro" features:

- Statistics not just about your blog's feed, but about how popular each item is or is not with your readers, as shown in Figure 8-11.

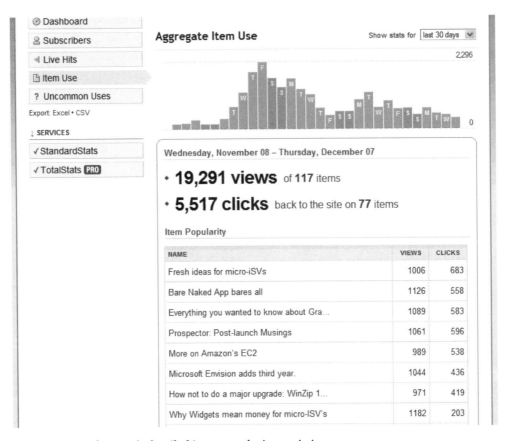

Figure 8-11. *FeedBurner's detailed item popularity statistics*

- Information about exactly how people found your posting: either by clicking it in your FeedBurner feed in their RSS reader or by clicking a link to it from someone else's blog or website, as shown in Figure 8-12.

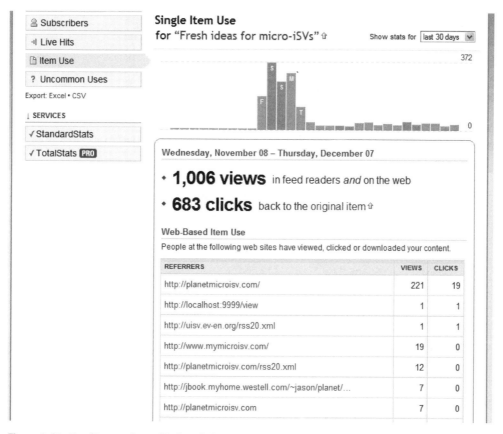

Figure 8-12. *FeedBurner's traffic breakdown*

Connecting Your Blog to FeedBurner

At this point, whether you have signed up with FeedBurner for free or paid for extra services, you have a bit of work to do to connect you blog to FeedBurner. Basically, you need to do just two things:

- Add a Subscribe link on your blog that points to your FeedBurner feed instead of whatever default simple feed your blog service would normally offer.

- Edit a bit of HTML in your blog's main template to direct RSS readers that auto-detect feeds when surfing to blogs to your FeedBurner feed.

The details are a little different depending on whether you're using Blogger, TypePad, Movable Type, WordPress, Vox, or whatever blogging service is the rage when you're reading this book. If you're not using one of the more common blog services, refer to the instructions FeedBurner spells out for you or check its technical support forum. Just to give you a flavor of it, have a gander at Figure 8-13.

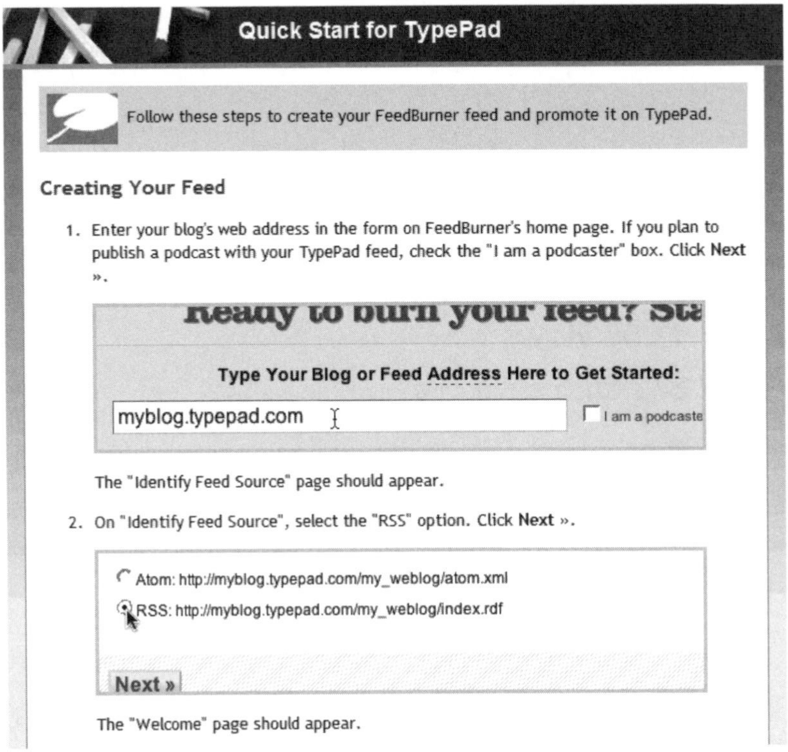

Figure 8-13. *FeedBurner TypePad setup information*

Once that is done (it takes about five minutes at most), you and FeedBurner are in business. Now you can improve, publicize, analyze, and even make money with your feed. You've already made it much easier for your readers to subscribe to your feed. Before, if they clicked the Subscribe button at your blog, your readers would have gotten a page full of raw XML code, something like this:

```
<rss version="2.0">
<channel>
<title>FeedForAll Sample Feed</title>
<description>
RSS is a fascinating technology. The uses for RSS are expanding daily.
</description>
<link>http://www.feedforall.com/industry-solutions.htm</link>
<category domain="www.dmoz.com">
Computers/Software/Internet/Site Management/Content Management
</category>
<copyright>Copyright 2004 NotePage, Inc.</copyright>
<docs>http://blogs.law.harvard.edu/tech/rss</docs>
<language>en-us</language>
<lastBuildDate>Tue, 19 Oct 2004 13:39:14 -0400</lastBuildDate>
<managingEditor>marketing@feedforall.com</managingEditor>
```

```
<pubDate>Tue, 19 Oct 2004 13:38:55 -0400</pubDate>
<webMaster>webmaster@feedforall.com</webMaster>
<generator>FeedForAll Beta1 (0.0.1.8)</generator>
<image>
<url>http://www.feedforall.com/ffalogo48x48.gif</url>
<title>FeedForAll Sample Feed</title>
<link>http://www.feedforall.com/industry-solutions.htm</link>
<description>FeedForAll Sample Feed</description>
<width>48</width>
<height>48</height>
</image>
```

And on and on and on . . . blah!

Instead, when your readers click your new FeedBurner-enabled Subscribe me link, they get a page like the one shown in Figure 8-14. Which do you find easier to understand?

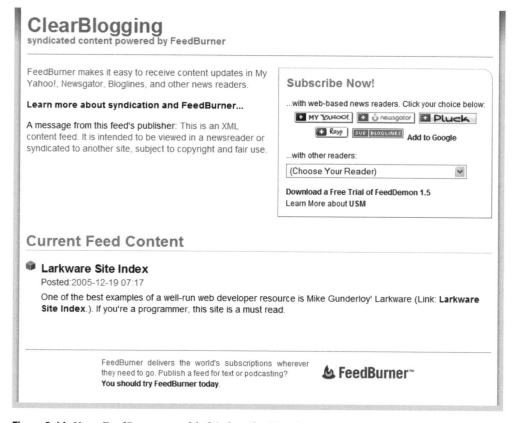

Figure 8-14. *Your FeedBurner-enabled Subscribe Now box*

As a nice feature, FeedBurner will remember each reader's preferred RSS service or major RSS reader application.

AN INTERVIEW WITH STEVE OLECHOWSKI, FOUNDER AND COO, FEEDBURNER, INC.

Steve Olechowski is the Chief Operating Officer and a cofounder of FeedBurner, Inc. Back in the glory days of the dot-com boom, Steve, along with Dick Costolo, Eric Lunt, and Matt Shobe, built an SMS text notification service called Spyonit. They sold that service in September 2000, as the four online entrepreneurs moved onto the next technological development: RSS feeds.

Q. *So what are you trying to accomplish with FeedBurner?*

A. Well, we're trying to make it really easy for publishers to do a number of things with their feeds. Number one is we're trying to make it easy for bloggers to make their content subscribable. We think the model is going to change over the next year or so. In the past, content was reached primarily through search results or bookmarks. We think in the future there's going to be a third component to that: people subscribing to content in many different ways. The whole reason we started FeedBurner is that we thought that content delivery would evolve through the subscription channel via RSS.

Once your content is subscribable, you have to start to build awareness around the content so people know that your feed is there. As people start to get your feed, either from your website or blog or repackaged by someone else, you want to start tracking who is getting your feed. FeedBurner makes it easy for publishers to track their subscribers, analyze their reader preferences, and figure out exactly how people are getting to their content.

The fourth thing that FeedBurner does is one of those things that became apparent to us as we were providing these other publishing services: Publishers were going to want to monetize this delivery channel. Depending on the model the publisher is using, it may make sense to monetize their feed through advertising, because if they are consuming content via the feed, a logical conclusion is that they won't be coming back to the site as often.

Advertising in RSS

Q. *Are you finding that the consumers of feeds are accepting or hostile to having advertising in their feed?*

A. I can tell you in general we see subscribership continuing to increase across the board as publishers start to put advertising in their feeds. A part of what goes along with that is that it's done the right way. It's done in a way that's not intrusive. It's value-added to the content; it's not done in an obnoxious way. We've found a way to marry content to advertising in a very nonintrusive way. Currently, we are putting it at the end of the content. By doing so, we've found that the response has been very good.

Q. *So it doesn't trigger the immune system most people have when it comes to advertising?*

A. No more than any other form of advertising.

Q. *There are the screaming car ads on television and then there are the Google AdSense ads that maybe you care, maybe you don't—they don't yell in your face. They're pretty innocuous. So you're looking to do the same thing with RSS feeds?*

A. Yeah, but we always leave that decision [to advertise] up to the publisher; we just provide the tools.

Q. *Is there some rough yardstick of if I have X subscribers, I'll make Y a month if I advertise?*

A. I don't think we have that kind of statistic available yet. It's still the early days and it varies all over the place.

Q. *Can you give me some idea for the people who are interested in making money from their blogs what kind of money we are talking about?*

A. We think that the way we are doing advertising is roughly equivalent to other online channels as well. We look at it from a CPM [cost per thousand ad impressions] of $7 to $10, but it's changing all the time. It's the early days, and it's a rapidly evolving market.

Q. *Are the ads derived from one of the big online ad networks, like Google AdSense?*

A. We let publishers choose from all sorts of different sources of where the ads come from. One of the important things to realize about RSS advertising is that it's not search marketing. In search advertising, the ads are meant to perform when there's a search, and it's delivering the results, and people are in that mode of searching, buying, doing something. RSS reading is a much different mode. These are long-term readers of your content. These are people seeing your content every day, and they're not arriving via search. So instead of looking to buy something at the point they are reading this—though they may if it your content is a product review—what we're finding is that the types of campaigns that are working much better right now are brand-awareness and brand-marketing campaigns, because they are targeted to the demographics of the people reading the feeds.

The important metric here is we can tell an advertiser that this ad will get in front of this many eyeballs in a day, because the publisher has this number of subscribers, and they publish this many items a day.

Q. *Let's say you had a feed for general contractors who build houses. Would you see ads from companies who sell plumbing fixtures? In other words, brand awareness within appropriate content?*

A. That's a good example, I guess.

What Bloggers and Podcasters Want

Q. *What are you finding is the most popular service you offer, as far as bloggers?*

A. For people using Blogger.com—we have a lot of Blogger.com users—on the Optimize tab [of our site], there are a few things I'd like to mention. Our most popular service is BrowserFriendly. What this does is it puts a style sheet on your feed, so when someone comes across the orange subscribe icon, and they click on it, it doesn't give you raw XML. We found when publishers implement this, their subscriptions start to increase dramatically.

One of the things that's specific to Blogger.com is they only publish their feeds in a format called Atom.[4] But there are actually nine different standards of RSS and two different standards of Atom. Of the 2,000 different RSS readers and aggregators we see out there, a number of these things don't necessary process all nine formats of RSS and many don't support Atom. So one of the things a publisher can do at our service is activate Smart-Feed, which will automatically make their feed compatible with every RSS reader and aggregator out there.

Q. *So this is a way to get everybody speaking the same feed language?*

A. Yes. There are actually over 2,000 different readers and aggregators we see, and the number is growing every day.

Q. *What else do you offer specifically to bloggers and podcasters?*

A. I'd say the service that is most popular with our podcasters is the SmartCast service. What this service does is it allows you to use the existing blogging tools out there, like Blogger, and even though they don't natively support podcasting, by running their feed through our service, we do allow them to be able to deliver a podcast. As long as they are putting links in their content, and running it through our SmartCast service, we'll make the feed compatible with the different podcast points out there like iTunes.

---

4. As of December 2006, Blogger has a new version in public beta that supports RSS 2.0 as well as Atom 1.0 (`http://help.blogger.com/bin/answer.py?answer=42659&query=RSS&topic=&type=f`).

Podcasts Made Easy

Q. *So basically what you're doing there is you're making a whole bunch of plumbing go away.*

A. Exactly. You, as a podcaster, don't have to worry about how to configure your feed template or your blogging engine. It's another thing we've made very easy. Another thing we do along with that is that the different podcasting directories, they want different information passed to them, along with the feed. For instance, the iTunes directory wants to know where it should show up in their catalog, and other specialized things that some of the other podcasting clients don't necessarily care about or use. So one of the things we do is we'll help you, the publisher, put the necessary information in to make it compatible with iTunes, add it to Yahoo Search, and include Media RSS information, and some other things that are coming down the pike will start appearing here [the SmartCast tab at FeedBurner] as well.

There are going to be more and more of these proprietary extensions, because face it, these media companies are competitors and don't want to use each other's standards.

More on the Way

Q. *What would be the next thing you offer that would improve the value for those reading blogs via RSS readers?*

A. The thing we are most excited about, that is probably our fastest growing thing, is our FeedFlare service on the Optimize tab. And we just launched this a few weeks ago. It allows you to publish a number of actions along with your feed. So typically today, reading RSS has been a very passive experience. What we are trying to do is turn it into a more active experience. So when your reader base is reading your feed on a daily basis, you want to allow them to interact with your content and do other things, such as post it to del.icio.us, or email it to a friend, or blog this. So those are some of the things we are enabling with this FeedFlare service. It allows the reader to act on the content beyond just reading it and going away.

One of the things we are going to be doing in the next few months is really opening up the API [Application Programming Interface] around this so that the developer community can create a number of extensions for the FeedFlare service.

Q. *What do you see people doing with these actions?*

We see how you can contact via email the author immediately. We see things like Skype[5] being a part of this—just other ways of making that conversation more active. We have a whole laundry list of ideas we haven't necessarily released yet, but we can't imagine all the ways it's going to be used, so that's why we're opening up the APIs to developers.

FeedBurner for Business Bloggers

Q. *We've been talking about individual bloggers and podcasters. What can FeedBurner do for a business that wants to blog?*

A. It's using all the tools we've talked about already to build their business.

---

5. Skype (http://skype.com) is an Internet telephone and video service that lets two or more members of the service talk and see each other for free, and converse with their non-Skype international friends for rates far lower than conventional international telephone rates.

Q. *Do you recommend they set up a different feed for each of the channels (like technical support, sales, etc.) they want to be talking to?*

A. If the site is small, it doesn't make sense to have ten different channels. But there's certainly the case that if you have different audiences, say new people you're trying to attract versus customer support-type thing, then it makes sense to separate those. But we try to steer publishers today towards fewer channels, more content, than towards more channels, less content. But it certainly makes sense to separate your content if people are unsubscribing because they're not interested.

Q. *Let's say you had a company with three different products and they were blogging about X on Mondays, Y on Wednesdays, and Z on Fridays. Can you set FeedBurner up in a way that routes the right post to the right feed?*

A. It might sound like a cop out, but it depends. You might want to cross-sell those products; there's an argument to be made for meshing those posts. If you sell guns and butter, you might want to keep them apart. However, if you want to sell butter to those people who have guns, you might want to start moving pieces of content from one place to the other.

I think one of the things we'll see over the next year is the ability to more easily do that with feeds, so say publish two separate feeds or publish to a combined feed. But that's going to take a little evolution of the feed model and the consumption model.

Q. *Any advice for bloggers regarding feeds in general?*

A. They should be an important part of any blogger's strategy. I think bloggers will be especially surprised by how many people are subscribing to their feeds, once they use FeedBurner to get very detailed statistics on that.

Recapping Technorati and FeedBurner

While it's still the early days of blogging, two online services have emerged as the indispensable tools for anyone who wants to create a successful public blog. Technorati is the place to strut yourself and make clear what your blog is about. FeedBurner is all about making it easy for your readers to keep up with your blog on their terms.

Your Action Tasks

Here are a few steps for getting started in the blogosphere:

Claim your blog at Technorati. Claiming your blog with Technorati is free, relatively easy, and indispensable.

Activate a free FeedBurner account. Make it easy to know who is getting your blog's RSS feed, easy for your readers who want your posts emailed to them, and easy for your readers to use your RSS feed the way they desire.

Set up free Technorati Watchlists. Blogging is only half about what you say, and you need a range of tools to track the topics and conversations of interest to you. Watchlists are one excellent tool for doing that.

Add the Anywhere Bookmarklet to your browser. The bookmarklet is another free Technorati tool for finding out what others are saying about your blog and the blogs you visit.

Show your FeedBurner Subscribe button. Make it easier for your readers to subscribe to your blog's FeedBurner feed by adding the orange button to your blog's sidebar.

And then you can continue with these steps:

Go Pro. For a few dollars a month, you can track readership of not just your blog as a whole, but post by post by buying a FeedBurner Pro Account. There's simply no better way to know which posts are most interesting to your readers and which ones, despite all the time you may have put into them, are going unread.

Build a Technorati profile. Spend the time to write a short, but engaging profile of you and your blog and add it to Technorati once you've claimed your blog. Others will see this profile when they come across your blog. And yes, do include a photo!

CHAPTER 9

Successful Blogging

"The Medium is the Message" because it is the medium that shapes and controls the search and form of human associations and action.

—Marshall McLuhan, twentieth-century media theorist

Marshall McLuhan might well have been talking about blogging instead of traditional media. The medium called blogging profoundly shapes what you say and how you say it, what you talk about in blog posts, and how others can discover what you've written. This chapter addresses three questions that every blogger needs to have answered to be successful:

- How do I find things to blog about?

- How do I write my blog so others want to read it?

- How do I help other people find my blog?

Along the way, we're going to shoot some arrows into some of the leading rationales people find to avoid blogging:

- It's impossible to keep up with everything in the blogosphere, so why try?

- You have to be a good writer to blog.

- No one is ever going to read my blog, so why bother?

Here's a quick preview of what we'll be looking at in this chapter:

- How to build your own Blogosphere Radar Screen so you can find things to write about

- How to write posts well, **easily**, day in and day out

- Useful tools for improving your writing

- Connecting your blog, post by post, to the blogosphere at large, so hundreds, thousands, and **even millions of people can find it**

Now, if this chapter's introduction seems a bit different than those in the other chapters in this book, that's because it's a lot more like a blog post than a chapter introduction. It's designed to get some blood flowing, start some juices going, and get you involved with this chapter. Later in the chapter, we'll come back to why bullet points, bold text, terse writing, and short sentences are a blogger's best friends. Let's begin with a look at three major techniques for finding things to post about.

Finding Your Posts

The first step to finding what to blog about—whether you're going to do a personal, professional, or business blog—is to pick at least an initial set of topics that you are interested in and passionate about. Blogging takes time and effort, so you want to focus on the people, things, and subjects in which you have a deep, abiding interest. And you want to stick to subjects not just interesting to you in an academic, detached way, but subjects you really care about.

Pick Your Beats

One of the more useful ideas of mainstream journalism is the idea of *beats*.[1] This concept came over from days when cops walked a beat and knew every merchant, kid in trouble, and apple stand on it. For reporters, there are the city hall beat, the cop beat, the science beat, and more.

Bloggers—especially influential, well-read bloggers—have beats they cover as well. For example, Steve Rubel's Micro Persuasion blog (www.micropersuasion.com) covers social networks, social media, Wikipedia, and more.[2] Guy Kawasaki's blog at http://blog.guykawasaki.com covers entrepreneurship, marketing, venture capital, and tech evangelism. Seth Godin's blog at http://sethgodin.typepad.com covers marketing, viral ideas, and the New Economy.

Nor is it just A-Listers who have beats. At my three blogs, I cover Getting Things Done online, the micro-ISV beat, and the whys and wherefores of clear blogging. Knowing what you want your blog to be about clears a lot of mental underbrush away so you can focus your writing and your reading on what matters.

So what do you, Mr. or Ms. Cub Reporter Blogger, want to cover? Here's a form to help you get started defining your beats:

Your top three: Name up to three beats you are interested in and passionate about.

1.

2.

3.

Subtopics for beat 1: Get more specific about topic 1. For example, if you said "the law," do you mean contract, patent, tort, civil, or criminal law; litigation; or the law profession?

1.

2.

3..

---

1. Of course, there are also the mainstream journalism principles of writing the truth as best you know it and checking your facts.
2. Steve talks about how he finds things to blog about at www.micropersuasion.com/2006/09/how_to_create_a.html.

Subtopics for beat 2: Same deal—which parts of topic 2 do you want to read about, or interview influential people about, or disagree violently with?

1.

2.

3.

Subtopics for beat 3: You guessed it—get specific with topic 3. The more specific you can be, the easier it is to find things to blog about.

1.

2.

3.

Extra credit: Another way to ask this is to name the top three blogs you read and follow. What is it about them you like? What do they cover?

1.

2.

3.

Keep in mind that your blog and the beats you cover on it will change as time goes on. All you're looking for now is a starting point you find interesting and can be passionate about. With your three subjects firmed up, you're ready to build what I call your Blogosphere Radar Screen.

Build Your Blogosphere Radar Screen

So you know what you want to cover, now what? Now you need to build an easy means to spot postings, news stories, and happenings in your areas of interest. You need to build a gizmo so you can find just the things you want to blog about and on. Ideally, you want something that has these qualities:

- Is automatic once it's running.

- Takes as little time to operate as possible.

- Is available everywhere, and in both Microsoft Internet Explorer and Mozilla Firefox.

- Is free—free is good!

The Blogosphere Radar Screen is an idea I gleefully borrowed from Steve Rubel (Micro Persuasion). It's how he keeps up on the multitude of happenings he covers for his blog. Here's how you can build your own version in about 15 minutes.

1. **Get a Google homepage and add a Radar tab to it.**

   If you're not using Google's personalized homepage as your homepage already, visit `www.google.com/ig` to create one, and then in your browser's preferences, set `http://www.google.com/ig` as your homepage. As of about mid 2006, Google homepage started supporting adding tabs so you could better group Google Gadgets[3] and RSS feeds. Add a tab, and name it Radar, as shown in Figure 9-1.

   Figure 9-1. *Your Google homepage and Radar tab*

2. **With your Radar tab active, click Add More to This Page.**

   This will take you to the Google Homepage Content Directory, where you'll find all kinds of Google Gadgets that you can add to your homepage, custom RSS feeds from numerous news and tech organizations, and more. For now, resist the urge to digress and go to the next step.

3. **Click the Add by URL link next to the Google search button.**

   One neat, underexplained feature of the Google homepage is the ability to add any RSS feed, including feeds created by searching for specific topics in Google Blog Search and Google News, to name two sources. The link itself is easy to miss at first glance. Take a quick look at Figure 9-2 to get your bearings. Figure 9-3 shows what should appear after you click this link.

   Figure 9-2. *Note the Add by URL link.*

---

3. Google Gadgets are small applets that run within Google's homepage or within Google's Desktop Search sidebar. They can do anything from bringing you personalized weather reports or sports scores to tracking your fitness.

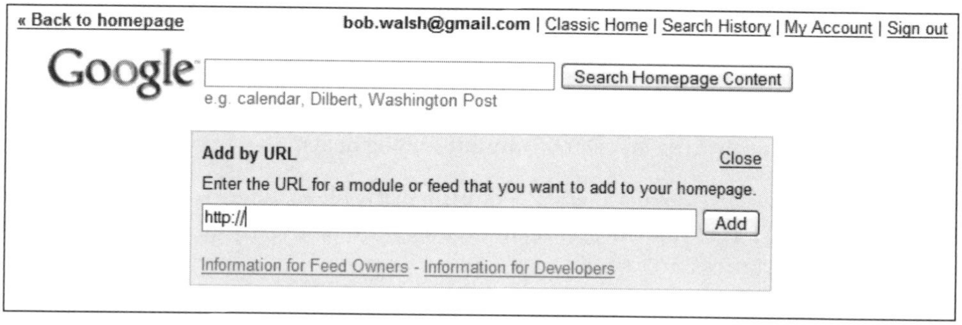

Figure 9-3. *The Add by URL box*

4. **In a new Firefox or Internet Explorer tab or window, open Google Blog Search at** `http://blogsearch.google.com.`

   For now, you're going to make your Radar Screen an all-Google affair. You could just as easily do the following steps from any search engine or service that creates a custom RSS feed for a search. As of this writing, Yahoo, IceRocket, and numerous Web 2.0 sites offer this feature.

5. **Create a search for your first blog beat.**

   You can create a simple search (such as "Time Management"), but you'll probably get better results if you build a more complex search (such as "Getting Things Done" OR "David Allen" OR "Time Management"). Creating more powerful Google searches is a topic for an entire book. Here are three recommendations:

- *Google Pocket Guide* by Tara Calishain et al. (O'Reilly, 2003). My personal favorite—short and sweet.

- *Google Hacks: Tips & Tools for Finding and Using the World's Information* by Rael Dornfest and Tara Calishain (O'Reilly, 2006). All sorts of things you can do with Google. More technical.

- *Google: The Missing Manual* by Sarah Milstein and Rael Dornfest (O'Reilly, 2006). Reputed to be a good read for nonprogrammers.

   When Google returns its search results, you can fine-tune your search by how old each post is. Key point: The more results you get back, the more active the topic, the more restricted your search should be. Here's why: Your Blogosphere Radar Screen's primary job is to alert you to *active blog conversations you can join*. If your area of interest is relatively narrow, such as "Getting Things Done," you might get about ten new search hits a day, which is a manageable number. On the other hand, "copyright law" returned 223 new hits a day, which are too many to track, and a good reason to dial down to, say, results in the last hour.

6. **Click the RSS Feed button, copy the URL you got, and paste it into the Add by URL field back on your Radar tab. Click Add.**

   Congratulations! You've just built the first part of your Blogosphere Radar Screen. Now repeat the process for each of your other blog beats.

   Of course, just looking at what's going on in the blogosphere is a little one-sided. Repeat this process of searching and adding to your Radar tab from at least a few of the following sources:

   - Google News (http://news.google.com)

   - Technorati's Discover area (http://technorati.com/discover), where you'll find custom general RSS feeds for entertainment, life, sports, business, technology, and more

   - Original Signal (www.originalsignal.com), which covers topics like Web 2.0, technology, business, general news, and entertainment

   - Bloggers you read and want to track (add their RSS feeds)

   - FeedMiner (www.feedminer.com), where you can find feeds on topics you're interested in, and then add them selectively to your Radar tab

7. **Click the Back to Homepage link, and then rearrange your search results to suit your preferences.**

   Besides arranging your feeds on your Radar tab, you can set how many items you want to see for each feed. Each time you return to your homepage Radar tab, it will do another sweep.

   Figure 9-4 shows my Blogosphere Radar Screen. With it, I can track my blog beats, my commercial products, and mentions of the books I've written. When I see something interesting, I can pop it open in another tab, blog about it, add a comment, or squirrel it away as something I might post about one day.

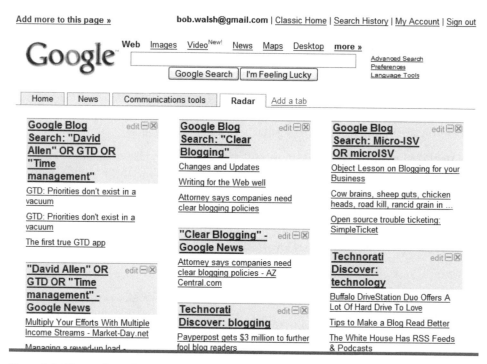

Figure 9-4. *The Radar tab in action*

Tips for Finding Post Topics

While your Radar tab makes it easy to track topics, it shouldn't be the only arrow in your arsenal. Googling "find blog topics," "blog tips," "ideas for blog posts," and the like will lead you to more good tricks and tips for sparking your blog fire than you can shake a stick at.

What follows is my personal list of ideas, tricks, and techniques I use to keep the posts flowing.

Theme Your Blog

Just as newspapers have beats to make it easier for reporters to know what to cover, they have specific sections on the same day each week: a food section on Thursdays, opinion on Sundays, and so on. Do the same for your blog.

For each day you plan to regularly blog, have a set direction you will tend to go. Frequency and regularity are important to your readers.[4] This approach also makes it easier to plan how much time you need for blogging and gives you a fallback answer to the question, "What am I going to blog about today?"

How detailed, flexible, and even recognizable your themes are is entirely up to you. If you're already blogging, take a look at your old posts and especially your FeedBurner or TypePad statistics to see what commonalities your most popular posts have. If you're just starting up your blog, your blog beats make for good themes.

---

4. And so is infrequently dropping in something unexpected, just to liven things up!

I've ended up with one blog apiece for the three beats I'm most interested in, rather than one blog with too little focus.

Here's my theme plan for ToDoOrElse.com:

- **Applied Mondays:** Usually a shorter post on ways I've found to apply or implement or use one Getting Things Done component.

- **Online Tuesdays:** This is a longer look at usually one Web 2.0 site I've found useful, with a focus on streamlining or improving one part of life online.

- **Big Deal Wednesdays:** This is the most in-depth post of the week, or an interview with someone who has something useful to say about Getting Things Done (online or off). These posts take the most time to research and write, so I work on them in stages over the week.

- **Weekly Link Thursdays:** Here's where my ToDoOrElse.com del.icio.us annotated bookmarks post weekly (see the "A Tasty Bit of Del.icio.us" section near the end of this chapter).

For MyMicroISV.com, I've come up with this theme plan:

- **Business Mondays:** Post about some micro-ISV–related business, as opposed to technical, topic.

- **Technical Tuesdays:** Post about some micro-ISV–related techie topic.

- **Guest Post Wednesdays:** These are guest posts or interviews of interest to micro-ISVs.

- **Theory into Practice Thursdays:** These posts tend to be how to apply one good idea to some aspect of running a micro-ISV.

- **Fridays:** Weekly links.

And here's the theme plan for ClearBlogging.com:

- **Mondays:** Clear Blogging tip of the week.

- **Tuesdays:** Clear Blogging interview of the week.

- **Resource Wednesdays:** A set of three techniques, tools, or tricks with TypePad or WordPress.

- **Thursdays:** Weekly links.

Maintain a Story List

Here's another technique newspaper managing editors have used for a hundred years or so to fill their papers: Maintain a list of ideas you want to blog about. Keep a blog story list on paper, your computer, a wiki, or whatever way best works for you.

Blogging story lists are naturally tightly tied to what's happening online, so there are really two components for each item on your list: the idea, point, or observation you want to make and links to other things online that are relevant and valuable to your readers.

Over the years, I've used paper lists, Excel files, outlining applications, and my own commercial products. Here are four quick tricks for getting the most value out of a blog story list:

Make just enough of an entry. A line or two to capture the idea and your approach is enough. Keep your entries short.

Review your list regularly and weed as needed. Last week's brainstorm is this week's puddle. Use your list to marinate your big posts.[5]

Keep your corresponding links in your browser. One easy way to do this is to number your entries in your blog story list, and then create a matching folder in Firefox, Internet Explorer, or your favorite social bookmarking website. That way, when you go back to blog idea 23, you can easily find folder 23 in, say, Firefox.

Use your story list as a log. When you've posted on an item on your list, enter the date and mark it off, but don't delete it. You want the ability to go back and see what you've already covered and how long ago. It's easy to forget and painful to remember too late.

Share Your Knowledge

Whatever your interests and whatever you blog about, sharing what you know and what you know how to do are surefire ways of getting readers. Keep in mind that new people are always coming to every part of the blogosphere, and it never hurts to recap topics you might think everyone knows about. Trust me, they don't, or they forgot and could use a quick refresher.

Do Reviews

Whether it's the latest programming library, power saw, or scalpel, your blog readers appreciate a good product or service review. In fact, many a well-known blog consists of just product reviews and announcements; two examples are Gizmodo (`www.gizmodo.com`) and Engadget (`www.engadget.com`).

Here are some common-sense pointers about doing blog reviews:

Back up your opinions. If you hate a product, explain why. If you love a new release, share why with your readers.

Be up-front with your readers. Just exactly how did you get that item? Did you buy it, rent it, or get if from the manufacturer? Your credibility is at stake, and your readers will want to know.

Write for your readers, not the vendors. If you do review products, you'll quickly find everyone who makes a product or service will want you to tell their story their way. Don't go that way. People who read your blog want your opinion, not a regurgitation of marketing hype.

Show and tell. Product reviews are much more interesting and, frankly, easier to do with a healthy helping of images. Haul out your digital camera, grab a good screenshot application like TechSmith's SnagIt, and start making pictures worth a thousand-word post.

---

5. See `http://lifedev.net/2006/08/blog-post-marinate-forming-great-ideas` for a great post on this idea.

Take the Inverted Pyramid Approach

One more idea worth "liberating" from mainstream media: the inverted pyramid approach to writing. Start with the punch line, rather than ending with it. Put your strongest points first, because your readers may not have the time or the inclination to read your entire missive.

Accessorize Longer Posts

Even if you're the next Hemingway, your longer posts are going to need some help getting across to your blog's readers. A big mass of gray type is as unappetizing as day-old cat food to most people. If your post is going long—say, more than six paragraphs—start finding ways to break up the text with relevant images, bullet points, subheadings, pullout quotations, or anything that gives your readers a break. They will thank you for it.

ELEVEN IDEAS TO MAKE OR BREAK YOUR BLOG, BY RAJESH SETTY

Two particularly good lists of tips to keep your blog healthy come with permission from Rajesh Setty, a Silicon Valley entrepreneur and respected blogger. Rajesh's excellent blog, Life Beyond Code, can be found at `http://blog.lifebeyondcode.com`.

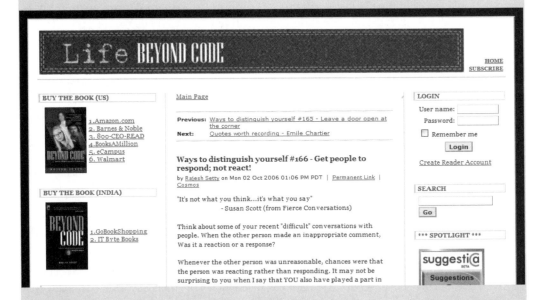

Eleven Ideas to Maintain Your Blog

You get to hear reports about thousands of new blogs getting created almost on a daily basis. Unfortunately, we don't hear much about the number of blogs that get abandoned before their anniversary is up.

So, the burning questions are as follows:

- Why do so many blogs get abandoned?

- What could we do to ensure that we are able to maintain a successful blog?

I thought about this topic for a while and also talked to many successful bloggers who have maintained blogs for more than a year now. I have come up with a few ideas for you to consider:

1. **Make a long-term commitment.**

   Don't start a blog because one of your friends started one. Like many things in life, starting a blog is way easier than maintaining it. You need long-term commitment to make it successful.

2. **Write what you are passionate about.**

   One easy option to start a successful blog is to imitate someone else. That will yield short-term results. You can't imitate someone for a long time. Best is to find your own voice. If you are writing about something that you are passionate about, you may not run out of ideas to blog. Find your own voice and stick to it.

3. **Pick your audience.**

   Unless you are extremely accomplished or a celebrity, attempting to write something that is applicable to everyone may be futile. How about picking an audience to whom you can add the highest value?

4. **Respect your audience.**

   Anyone who reads your blog is investing their most precious asset—their time. If you focus on ROII (return on investment for an interaction) for every visitor to your blog, chances are that they will come back for more. If you don't, there are so many choices that are out there as an alternative to reading your blog.

5. **Observe and listen.**

   The more you observe and listen, the better your writing will be. There is always a lot of focus on "doing" things that sometimes we forget to think, observe, and listen.

6. **Participate in a conversation.**

   The blogosphere is the biggest conversation marketplace. It's like a big party going on all the time. You need to be willing to participate in an ongoing conversation or start your own.

7. **Check your ego.**

   Blogging many times is a spontaneous expression of your ideas, thoughts, or insights. It is possible that you will make a mistake, and it is also possible that somebody will roast you for that mistake. Rather than trying to defend it endlessly, try to admit your mistake and go on. Ego won't help you get far, at least in the blogosphere.

8. **Ask.**

   Sports people have been working with coaches for years, and we know that works very well for them. Coaching works in other areas, too. If you are getting stuck somewhere, go ahead and ask someone who might offer you some help. I have always believed that there is more help than we will ever need in this universe. It is the asking that is lacking. The important point is to remember that while you might get something for free, not everything is available for free. You should be willing to pay the price to win the prize.

9. **Build on a theme.**

When I started blogging about 11 months ago, I created a series based on a theme called "Ways to Distinguish Yourself." Of course, I blog on topics other than this, but having a theme helped me structure my thoughts over the long run. In 11 months, I have only 87 entries in this series, but in the back of my mind, I am always thinking, observing, and discussing ideas that can contribute to this series. You can pick your own theme or series, and the beauty of this approach is that you can later enhance and reuse the content for something else.

10. **It's not the quantity but the quality.**

Many people tell me that they don't want to start blogging because there is no way they will have time every day to dedicate to blogging. There seems to be some misconception. There is no rule anybody has set that requires you to blog every day. However, it will be unlikely that you will get a lot of visitors if you blog once a quarter. Pick a frequency that will let you blog without diluting the quality of the blog. Ultimately, it's not the quantity but the quality that matters.

11. **Keep growing.**

This is something that is outside your blog. One of the ways you can get more attention to your blog is from what you do outside your blog, really! You can get famous through your blog, but it's easier the other way around—meaning you can get famous outside, and then it's easier to get your blog to become famous.

Eleven Ideas to Kill Your Blog

If one of the main reasons you started blogging is because it's easy to start one, by now you already know that it is a lot of hard work to maintain one. The availability of blogging technologies makes it easy to start a professional-looking blog in a few minutes. My friend Dave Taylor [at www.intuitive.com/blog] says that *a blog is nothing but a personal content management system*. A good content management system provides excellent support to manage content.

A blog is only as good as the content within it. While it takes time and effort to build a great blog, it does not take a lot of effort to kill one. Here are some ways:

1. **Focus too much on the form and not the content.**

Blogging engines are very sophisticated now. You can customize and enhance the look and feel of your blog endlessly, even when you don't have a programming background. In other words, you can get carried away with the form and not focus on the content. Having a great format is like having an attractive store in a mall. You can get people to walk in, but if the goods inside the store are not attractive, no one will buy anything.

2. **Have too many ads.**

Of course, making money may be one of your motives. However, there are very few people who are making a ton of money on ads on the blogs. You can try to be one of them, or you can focus on other kinds of leverage from your blog. Now, on a lighter note: Think about it for a second. The way you make money on an ad is when a person clicks on the ad and goes away from your blog. Do you want to take money to send people away from your blog? Of course, ads in moderation may be a good idea. Excessive ads are also a distraction. You don't want your audience to search for your content among the ads.

3. **Steal content.**

Stealing is probably a strong word, but if you pick up content from another place and post it on your blog without proper attribution, technically it is stealing. Sooner than later, people will figure that out. Stealing may be more harmful than helpful.

4. **Lack focus.**

Unless you are a celebrity or a recognized thought leader, you may not get a license to just dish out opinions on everything under the sun. The best would be to focus on a subject where you are an authority or on the way to becoming an authority. This will help you to focus your message to an audience and build credibility among them. On the other hand, once you lose focus, you will start losing your audience too.

5. **Don't respect your readers.**

John Maxwell said it brilliantly: "People don't care how much you know until they know how much you care." The key reason your blog exists is because there are some readers reading it. If you don't want readers, you might as well write your thoughts in a diary. Assume that your readers are intelligent and engage with them in a conversation or risk losing them forever.

6. **Don't build enough credibility to back up whatever you are saying.**

You can say whatever you want on your blog (and say that it is your right of speech). However, if you don't have the credibility and qualification to say whatever you said, very soon people will start losing respect for you as a person. After a while, the blog won't matter anymore. Maintaining a blog is hard not because writing is hard. It is hard because you have to be constantly growing outside your writing for your blog to have a meaning.

7. **Have a bad attitude.**

Did you know that you can get angry on your blog? You can. But should you? Your attitude shows up on your blog. If your intention is anything less than genuinely helping your audience with their concerns, you need to revisit your blog objectives. Bad attitude is bad on or off the blog. That's the fastest way to alienate yourself.

8. **Lack relevance.**

You can have a great focus but not be relevant to your audience. My favorite metric is ROII (return on investment for an interaction). Does your blog provide the right return on the investment of their time in reading it? If not, remember that your audience can run away from your blog in a heartbeat. They can substitute your blog with some other blog that provides a better ROII.

9. **Attack someone needlessly.**

Blogs provide you a lot of power only until you misuse it. You've got to pick your battles in your blog (and in your life). You can attack someone. If the person counterattacks, you enter into a battle. Do you have the luxury of time to engage in this battle? Is that the best use of your time? Why do you think your audience would want to be spectators in this game between you and someone else? When the personal gain from the blog far exceeds the gain by your audience, there will be a problem. Actually, a *big* problem.

10. **Create controversy without basis.**

They say that if you want to appear intelligent, you should keep making controversial or contradictory statements. The keyword here is "appear" and not "be." You can catch someone's attention by creating baseless controversy, but you can't hold on to that attention. If you do this more than once, you will get an entry into the "Cry Wolf Club," and no one will bother to listen, even when you have something substantial to share.

11. **Engage in excessive self-promotion.**

Self-promotion, a bit here and a bit there, should be OK. If you make this your personal achievement newsletter, people will get ticked off. Nobody has time to read about someone endlessly talking about what they have done in their life. Creating a blog that provides great value will lead to enhancement of your brand, which I think is better than self-promotion.

Owning Your Words

Owning your own words covers a lot of ground in the blogosphere. It means being responsible for what you post and for comments. But the first step to owning your own blogging words is making them worth owning. That means finding the right words to get your ideas across with some zip and dash, and properly making use (at least nearly all the time) of punctuation, grammar, and spelling.

Now before you fall completely asleep at the thought of dangling participles, piercing pains of punctuation, and the tepid joys of manual spell-checking, hang on. This is the blogosphere, and we are not going to go there! Not that the mechanics of good writing aren't important—they are. But there are better, more Internet-style ways of doing things than pounding a copy of Strunk and White's *The Elements of Style* into your left ear. Here, we'll look are three easy Internet ways of writing better posts.

> *Progress isn't made by early risers. It's made by lazy men trying to find easier ways to do something.*
>
> —Robert Heinlein, *Time Enough for Love*

The Its/It's Bookmarklet

I guess I skipped out of elementary school the day Mrs. Kincaide drove home with a ruler–hand slap the difference between the possessive form of it and the contraction of it is, because it has never really stuck. If fact, it has often come unstuck when I'm firing off a quick post.

Fortunately, fellow blogger and blogging book author[6] Andy Wibbels has created an its/it's bookmarklet. It looks like a bookmark or favorite in your web browser's toolbar, but when clicked, it runs a tiny JavaScript applet to remind you of the differences between these two words, as shown in Figure 9-5.

Figure 9-5. *Its/it's bookmarklet*

Installing this bookmark is a snap: Just drag it from `http://andywibbels.com/post/1217` onto your browser's bookmark or favorites toolbar.

Firefox 2.0 Spell Checks

If for some reason you have not yet upgraded to Mozilla Firefox 2.0 (or later), or still use that other web browser, here's one must-have feature: Microsoft Word–like spell-checking built in for any and all text fields. So whether you're writing a post in Blogger or leaving a comment, Firefox 2.0 and later will at least make it easy to catch the spelling goofs.

This is one of those blindingly obvious-in-retrospect features you won't want to part with after five minutes' use.

In case you're wondering, Firefox can be downloaded for free from `www.mozilla.com/firefox`.

Writing Happiness with WhiteSmoke

Up until a week ago, if you had told me there was software out there that could actually improve your writing, not just fix the misspellings and tidy the grammar, I would have said "No way!"

Yes way! It's called WhiteSmoke (`www.whitesmoke.com`), available for between $59.95 and $99.95 USD in a number of versions both online and off, and it works.

Let's say you're writing a post online (you could also be using Microsoft Word, Outlook, or virtually any other program), and you decide to improve what you're writing with WhiteSmoke. You hit F2, and the WhiteSmoke window pops up with your text (or you can copy and paste text into it), as shown in Figure 9-6.

WhiteSmoke handles your spelling and trickier grammar well, but where it shines is helping you improve your word choice (the words highlighted in blue). In the example in Figure 9-6, after I fix the *a* that should be *an*, I see replacement words and relevant adjectives or adverbs for the word *example*. Two clicks later, WhiteSmoke has replaced *example* with *practical illustration*, as shown in Figure 9-7.

---

6. Andy's *BlogWild! A Guide for Small Business Blogging* (Portfolio, 2006) is an excellent how-to book for bloggers and highly recommended (after you finish *this* book, of course).

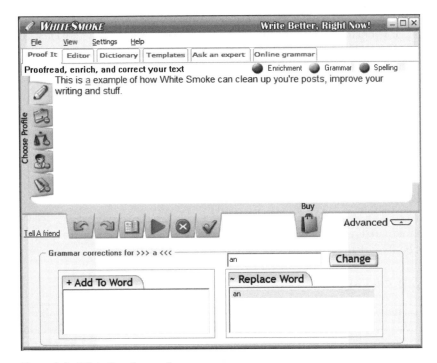

Figure 9-6. *WhiteSmoke marks errors.*

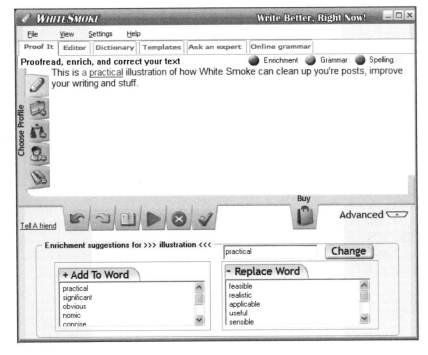

Figure 9-7. *WhiteSmoke makes changes.*

The magic behind WhiteSmoke, according to Elan Nahari, WhiteSmoke's Sales Director, is an artificial intelligence (AI) system that drives both a context-sensitive thesaurus (replacement words) and "enriches" your text with a list of relevant adverbs and adjectives. So it can help you make better word choices, as well as correct your spelling and grammar.

There are a few things to note about WhiteSmoke. One is that the application sends your text automatically to the WhiteSmoke's AI system, so if you happen to be blogging behind the federal firewall at the National Security Council on the next National Intelligence Estimate, this is not software you should use. Secondly, for the same reason, you need to be connected to the Internet while using WhiteSmoke. Lastly, as keen readers will have noticed, WhiteSmoke missed a couple errors in my example in Figure 9-6: a *you're* that should have been *your* and *White Smoke* as two words. You still need to proofread what you write to catch the occasional leak.

Since "enriching" your word choices depends heavily on context, there are no less than eight different versions of the software: basic, business, legal, medical, creative writing, executive, and the intriguing dating versions, plus a comprehensive license.

WhiteSmoke has several other features: various template libraries, the ability to hook up with a live online writing tutor through the application, and an unfinished as of version 1.0 quick online proofreading service.

If you're just not comfortable with the whole writing end of blogging, WhiteSmoke is definitely worth a look.

HOW TO WRITE COMPELLING BLOG POSTS, BY B.L. OCHMAN

Blogger, social media strategy consultant to Fortune 500 companies, and sought-after corporate speaker B.L. Ochman (www.whatsnextblog.com) has a knack for creating posts that get mentioned far and wide in the blogosphere. Here, from one of her posts at http://marketingprofs.com (reprinted with permission), is how she does it.

Blog Style Guidelines

Writing blog posts and comments on blogs is actually very simple. The basic guidelines: keep your copy lively, factual, tight, clear, short, and search-engine optimized.

Here are basic blog style guidelines to follow:

- **Adopt a direct style.** Declarative sentences are good. Web readers demand them.

- **Link like crazy.** One thing that distinguishes blog posts from dead-tree journalism is that bloggers link prodigiously. Link to any other blog or website you mention. Link to articles, books, products, bios, explanatory materials on other sites, and anything you mention in your blog. Always link to information that clarifies or gives background on information and opinions in your post.

- **Write less.** Omit all unnecessary words. The best advice I ever got about writing was from my first boss, the late "press agent" Leo Miller, who taught me a game to play with sentences. He'd keep taking out words until removing one more word destroyed the meaning of the sentence. Aim at keeping your posts at about 250 words.

- **Write good headlines.** Most people use a news feeder like NewsGator to scan blog headlines. They decide after seeing the headline to click into the post. Tell as much of the story as you can in the headline:

  Before: Pakistan: NA body on S&T meets [Huh? Who's NA? What's S&T?]

  After: Pakistan National Assembly Calls Water Resource Problems the Nation's Major Issue

  Before: The B. B. King Book

  After: I'm Writing The B. B. King Biography

- **Keep sentences and paragraphs short.**

- **Don't take yourself too seriously.** Blogging isn't brain surgery. Don't get pompous or dictatorial.

- **Never lose your sense of humor.**

- **Write like it counts.** "No matter what your audience size, you ought to write as if your readership consisted of paid subscribers whose subscriptions were perpetually about to expire. There's no need to pander. Compel them to re-subscribe," said Dennis Mahoney on A List Apart.

- **White space is your friend.** It makes reading from the screen easier. Nothing is harder to read than a solid block of copy on a computer screen.

- **Use the simplest possible word and sentence structure.**

- **Read your post out loud** and make sure you don't get stuck on complex construction. If you trip on a word in the midst of reading a sentence aloud, rewrite the sentence.

- **Forget what you learned about business writing in school if you graduated before 1990.** Go ahead! Start sentences with "and" or "but." Don't be afraid to break archaic rules. But, jeez, follow all grammatical rules that provide clarity to your content.

- **Cardinal Sin:** Say "This is about *me*," never "This is about myself." Same with "you" and "yourself." Stiff, formal writing is only for lawyers. And you know what Shakespeare said about *them*.

- **Use bulleted points whenever you can.**

- **Use subheads** every few paragraphs, even in a 300-word post.

- **Use bold text and italics for emphasis on words and phrases.**

- **Make sure your posts are easy to scan.**

- **Choose your voice and keep it consistent.**

- **Don't be afraid to voice opinions.**

- **Ask these questions to yourself before hitting Publish:**

  Is the topic clear to someone who reads only the headline?

  Does the lead paragraph tell who and what the story is about and why the reader should care about it?

  Is the angle you've used likely to seem newsworthy?

  Would someone who knows absolutely nothing about this topic understand this post?

Is the post free of jargon?

Is it written in journalistic style and does it make an effort to be objective?

Have you peppered the headline and the post with keywords and phrases that will be attractive to search engines?

How to Write Comments on Blogs

Some blogs are more influential than others, and many are trolled by journalists and your potential clients who are seeking ideas, trends, and sources. Commenting intelligently on blogs, even if you don't have a blog of your own, can be a very good way to build a reputation as an expert in a field.

The key is to provide useful, factual information so that over time it becomes clear to other readers of the blogs to which you post that you know what you are talking about. In general, it is a good idea to keep your posts short and on point.

Since blogs are archived online, anything you write in a comment will be there until forever. So think before you write; and edit, edit, edit before you hit Submit.

Blog Comment Guidelines

It is necessary for you to sign your comments. In most cases, anonymous messages will not be published. You're also generally asked for your email address and your URL.

A signature that looks like an ad will simply be cut. Stick to the facts about what you do. The quality of your comments will prove your expertise.

Because of comment spam, many bloggers ask you to register or to have a TypePad key.

If you have a business connection to a product or service mentioned in the blog post, this should be clear to anyone reading your comment.

Comment only when you feel you can offer something of value that is relevant to the types of issues that are discussed.

Size constraints make space limited, and bloggers may shorten your comments. Better to simply write shorter.

Bloggers are free to reject inappropriate posts, including overt solicitations and personal attacks.

When quoting material, strive for accuracy and note where you have omitted copy; provide attribution for the quote, including source and URL (if available).

Tagging Your Ideas

Tags are half of a global navigation system that drives the blogosphere, and if you don't understand how tags work and how to use them judiciously, you're going to regret it. The concept is simple: You, or your blogging platform, need to add a handful of descriptive words or short phrases to each post that serve as links to other, similarly tagged posts.

Why? Because like any huge collection of information, the blogosphere needs some sort of classification system to make it possible to find things by subject. And since no one is going to do it for you, you're elected to the job.

There are actually two kinds of tagging out there in blogland: tagging your own posts, and tagging posts and websites of other people you find interesting and useful. We'll look at each in turn, and how to conjoin the two to raise your blog's prominence.

All Roads Lead to Technorati

We talked at length about Technorati in the previous chapter, and here it is again. The truth of the matter is that when it comes to tagging your ideas, it's all about creating links to Technorati.

When you write a post and tag it, either you or your blogging software create links (like `http://Technorati.com/tag/GTD rel="tag"`) to Technorati's index engine, as shown in Figures 9-8 and 9-9.

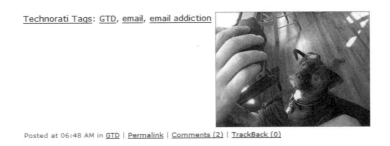

Figure 9-8. *Technorati tags in a post*

Figure 9-9. *Tags lead back to Technorati's index.*

Tag Support

In the bad old days of blogging (say, 2005), if you wanted to add tags to your post, you would need to write your own HTML to create tags. Increasingly, blogging systems have automated the process for you. Here's the tagging situation (as of this writing) for some of the major blogging platforms out there:

Blogger: Like a lot of advanced features, built-in support for tagging is not provided by Blogger, but there are ways around that:

- Use Ken Dyck's XBlogThis! (`www.kendyck.com/2005/08/xblogthis-extended-blogthis-button.php`) to add tags.

- Download Microsoft's free Windows Live Writer from `http://windowslivewriter.spaces.live.com`, which you can use to post to Blogger.

- Get Frank La Vigne's free Windows Live Writer Technorati Tag Plug-in (`http://franksworld.com/blog/archive/2006/09/19/4225.aspx`).

WordPress: WordPress's categories are automatically used by both the hosted and self-hosted versions of this popular blogging software, making it a matter of a few clicks to properly tag a post. For more on this, see Tom Raftery's post "WordPress Categories, Technorati Tags and Search Engine Optimisation" (`www.tomrafteryit.net/wordpress-categories-technorati-tags-and-search-engine-optimisation`).

TypePad: In August 2006, TypePad made it a snap to add Technorati tags to each and every post, but you need to customize your Compose screen in TypePad to enable this feature. Check the TypePad Knowledge Base (search for "technorati" and the "Using Technorati in TypePad" article) or just click the "Customize the display of this page" link at the bottom of the Compose page.

Vox: Tagging support is built in. Just enter your tags in the Tags field.

If your blogging software hasn't automated the process of creating tags, here are a few websites that, for one reason or another (marketing their services, making a political statement, and so on), will create the code for you:

- Fintan Darragh's Technorati Tag Generator (`www.marketwest.co.uk/tools/index.php`) is quick and easy to use.

- Free Tag Generator & Social Bookmark Link Creator (`www.evilgeniusmarketing.com/ice/tag-generator.cfm`) is a tool I've used often, but it can get overwhelmed by would-be users.

- Life in Bush's America Technorati Tag Maker (`www.speciousreasoning.com/tags`) has a definite political point of view, along with an easy-to-use tag-generator form.

Keep in mind these kinds of sites come and go. Googling "generate technorati tags" will probably help you find new and better sites.

Tagging Guidelines

Here are a few suggestions for adding tags:

Double-check your spelling. Tags, unlike search engines, are unforgiving when it comes to misspelling. For example, the tag `micrsoft` leads to all of 18 posts; `microsoft` finds more than 61,000.

Short is better. Tags should be one or two words.

Test your important tags. Odds are you'll end up with a handful of tags you use over and over. Take the time to try out these tags at Technorati and check out alternative tags Technorati shows as related. Take another look at Figure 9-9 to see what I mean.

Multiple tags are good. Categorizing a post with multiple tags improves the chances of your tag being found.

Tag baiting is bad. Tag baiting—using popular tags like `sex`, `free`, and `Britney Spears`—is a sure way to drive all your blog's readers far, far away. Your tags must be relevant.

Tagging Other People's Blogs

Another kind of tagging commonly happens in the blogosphere: tagging blogs, posts, and websites you think are particularly good and that you want to share with others. This is the kind of tagging that drives highly popular sites like del.icio.us, Digg, reddit, and a few hundred other Web 2.0 sites.

Having your blog or website show up on the front page of any one these social bookmarking sites will bring anywhere from hundreds to tens of thousands of new readers to your blog. And, of course, there's nothing that says you can't nominate your absolute best posts to these sites as well.

A Tasty Bit of Del.icio.us

One of the oldest and possibly the best known of the social bookmarking sites is `http://del.icio.us`, now owned by Yahoo (`www.techcrunch.com/2005/12/09/yahoo-acquires-delicious`). By using del.icio.us's handy browser tools, it's easy to tag a post you like to your del.icio.us account, where it's automatically shared.

Del.icio.us has made it easy to add a bit of code to your posts so others can add you to their del.icio.us bookmarks or network of favored users. After getting your free del.icio.us account, have a look at its Settings section for more information on Network Badges, link rolls, tag rolls, and daily blog posting.[7] This last item, daily blog posting, is a very valuable blogger tool. Using it, you can have del.icio.us generate a post for you of what you've bookmarked and why, like the post at Steve Rubel (Micro Persuasion) shown in Figure 9-10.

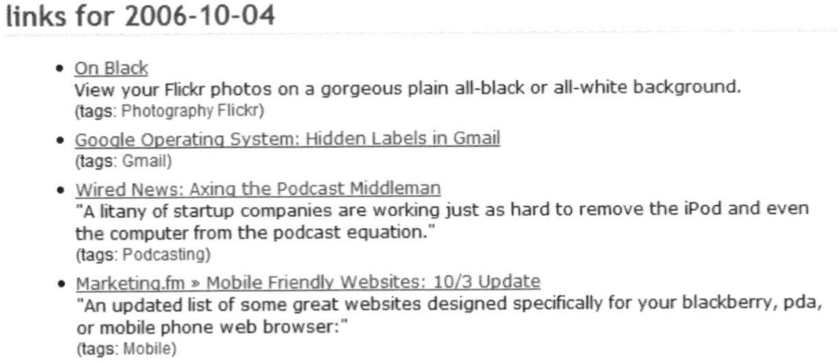

links for 2006-10-04

- On Black
  View your Flickr photos on a gorgeous plain all-black or all-white background.
  (tags: Photography Flickr)
- Google Operating System: Hidden Labels in Gmail
  (tags: Gmail)
- Wired News: Axing the Podcast Middleman
  "A litany of startup companies are working just as hard to remove the iPod and even the computer from the podcast equation."
  (tags: Podcasting)
- Marketing.fm » Mobile Friendly Websites: 10/3 Update
  "An updated list of some great websites designed specifically for your blackberry, pda, or mobile phone web browser:"
  (tags: Mobile)

Figure 9-10. *Links posting from del.icio.us*

Depending on how you want to run your blog, you can create your bookmark posts in two ways:

- Let del.icio.us create these posts daily as you add bookmarks.

- Take the time to first bookmark interesting sites within your web browser, then work through them in a batch and post them as a group to del.icio.us to generate a regular feature for your blog.

---

7. You can also find an excellent step-by-step post about setting up del.icio.us tagging written by Lee LeFever at `www.commoncraft.com/archives/001028.html`.

Using Digg and reddit

Another way of raising your hand in the blogosphere is adding Digg and reddit "badges" to your posts so users of those two popular sites can vote with one click for your post. My online friend Dharmesh Shah at `http://onstartups.com` has used this and other techniques he talks about to build a considerable readership, as shown in Figure 9-11.

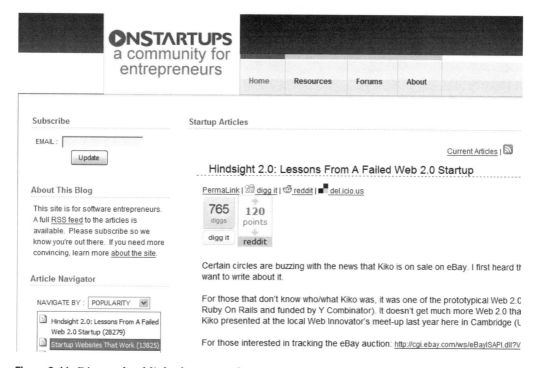

Figure 9-11. *Digg and reddit badges at work*

The drill is essentially the same for both sites: open a free account, and then visit `http://digg.com/tools/integrate` and `http://reddit.com/buttons`.

Socializing Your Blog

As you may have noticed as you've visited blogs, "socializing" blogs can run from making it easy to tag your post at one or two sites to hundreds of different sites. There's a definite trade-off between making it easy to get noticed and making your blog ugly. And there's the time factor—while users of, for example, WordPress can use any one of a number of plug-ins to make this happen automatically (such as shown in Figure 9-12), it can be a real pain to do manually if that's what your blogging software requires.

Where there's pain in the blogosphere, there's someone taking it away. If you want to socialize your blog to the max but don't want dozens of little links littering each post, have a look at Socialize-it (`www.socialize-it.com`). You add one small attractive badge, and when clicked, your readers can add your blog to any and all of the social bookmarking sites shown in Figure 9-13.

Figure 9-12. *Automatically socializing a post*

Figure 9-13. *Socialize-it.com condenses all these bookmark links into one.*

Being a Successful Blogger

Succeeding as a blogger is a lot like succeeding at most things in life: It will take time, it will take effort, and it may even take a little luck. But by structuring your blogs, taking the advice of the bloggers mentioned here, and tapping the power of social networks, you can stack the deck heavily in your favor.

One of the questions most often posted by new bloggers is, "How often should I blog?" You can find all sorts of subjective answers to this, from whenever you have something to say to very formalistic approaches. In November 2006, David Sifry, CEO of Technorati, found something like an objective answer to this question: The most influential bloggers on average post nearly twice a day, and have been doing so for months, if not years (http://technorati.com/weblog/2006/11/161.html).

HOW TO WRITE A BLOG POST, BY SETH GODIN

Here's a November 2006 post by Internet marketing guru Seth Godin, where he spells out his recommended way of how to write a great post (reprinted with permission):

Do it like this: Joel on Software [`www.joelonsoftware.com/items/2006/11/21.html`].

An appropriate illustration,

A useful topic, easily broadened to be useful to a large number of readers,

Simple language with no useless jargon,

Not too long,

Focusing on something that people have previously taken for granted,

That initially creates emotional resistance,

Then causes a light bulb to go off

And finally,

Causes the reader to look at the world differently all day long.

Your Action Tasks

Here are a few steps for blogging successfully:

What's the beat? What is your blog about? Or put another way, what things rock you, get your attention, and move you to write? The sooner you define your core beats, the less chance you'll alienate some of your readers before you find your focus.

Set up your blog radar. Whether you use your Google homepage, Pageflakes (`www.pageflakes.com`), or Protopage (`www.protopage.com`), you want to build something that lets you track your beats on a daily basis.

Theme your blog. Structuring your blog moves it from the realm of walking a tightrope above the alligator pit to integrating blogging into your professional life in at least a somewhat predictable way.

Read for results. One of the best ways of learning how to write well is to read well. Find posts that make you think, "I wish I'd written that!" and try to figure out why that post rang your bell.

Once you've taken those first steps, it's time to crank up the volume:

Listen to your FeedBurner feedback. FeedBurner has been covered in detail elsewhere. The point here is that you need to regularly review which of your posts have the most impact and readers, and why.

Get social. Making it easy for your readers to add your posts to their social bookmarking picks is only the start. After surveying all the social bookmark sites out there (you can find a very long list at `www.socialize-it.com`), decide in which ones you want to be active and get known.

■ ■ ■

CHAPTER 10

The New Fourth Estate

Burke said there were Three Estates in Parliament; but, in the Reporters' Gallery yonder, there sat a Fourth Estate more important than they all . . . . Whoever can speak, speaking now to the whole nation, becomes a power, a branch of government, with inalienable weight in law-making, in all acts of authority. It matters not what rank he has, what revenues or garnitures: the requisite thing is that he have a tongue which others will listen to; this and nothing more is requisite.

—Thomas Carlyle, Scottish essayist and historian

Badges? We ain't got no badges. We don't need no badges. I don't have to show you any stinking badges!

—Gold Hat (Alfonso Bedoya), in *The Treasure of the Sierra Madre* (1948)

If you've been wondering when the mainstream media were going to show up in this book about blogging, they've just entered from stage right. In this chapter, we're going to whip through these topics:

- Why some reporters are firing their newspapers and blogging for a living

- How bloggers are stepping in and covering local news

- How reporters and bloggers are working together

- How you—yes you!—can make it onto CNN

- How blogging determined who controlled the US Congress after the 2006 midterm elections

But before we get to all the exciting stuff going on in the blogosphere, we need to pay a visit to some very unhappy people: newspaper and television reporters.

The Incredible Shrinking Newsroom

The big problem for mainstream newspapers and television networks right now is twofold. Declining ad revenue and declining circulation/viewers are sucking the air and jobs out of newsrooms from coast to coast. 2006 was not a kind year to professional journalists, with layoffs and buyouts chopping down reporters right and left. A quick scan of Google News during the first weekend of December 2006 read like a casualty report from a losing war: up to 30 percent of the newsroom at *Philadelphia Inquirer*, 85 people at the *Toronto Star*, 21 people at the *St. Paul Pioneer Press*, and 6 people at the *Wall Street Journal*.[1]

Newspaper circulation in the US continues to go down. The Audit Bureau of Circulations, a trade organization that audits member newspapers, reported that weekday circulation dropped 2.6 percent in the second and third quarters of 2005. That's on average; the *San Francisco Chronicle* dropped 16.4 percent. Nor was 2006 any better for newspapers. For the six-month period ending in March 2006, the Audit Bureau reported daily newspaper circulation dropped another 2.5 percent and Sunday fell by 3.1 percent.[2]

According to SaveJournalism.org, a site set up by the Newspaper Guild–CWA (see Figure 10-1), 44,000 news industry employees lost their jobs since 2000; 34,000 at newspapers alone. Considering that in 2004 there were approximately 183,000 reporters and editors in the US (per the US Bureau of Labor Statistics, `http://online.onetcenter.org/link/summary/27-3022.00` and `http://online.onetcenter.org/link/summary/27-3041.00`), it's not surprising the morale of reporters cycles between dread and gallows humor.

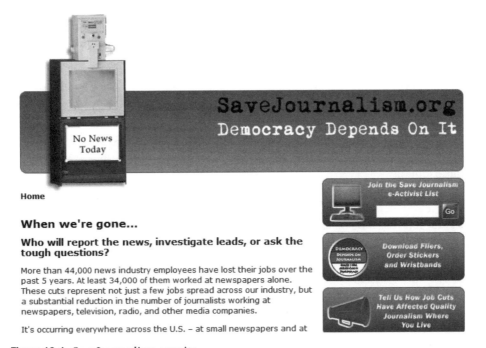

Figure 10-1. *SaveJournalism.org site*

1. You can read these reports at `www.sacbee.com/110/story/86173.html`, `http://www.freerepublic.com/focus/f-news/1756425/posts`, `minnesota.publicradio.org/display/web/2006/11/30/pipress/`, and `www.editorandpublisher.com/eandp/news/article_display.jsp?vnu_content_id=1003467473`.

2. You can read these reports at `www.csmonitor.com/2005/1109/p02s02-ussc.html` and `http://blogs.mediapost.com/spin/?p=929`.

Man Bites Dog; Reporters Fire Newspapers

While traditional reporters are getting to play a particularly grim version of musical chairs, some reporters are turning the tables—laying off the mainstream media and effectively becoming bloggers for a living.

Journalists Online

One of the first mainstream reporters to go over the wire was Mike Magee. Mike was one of the original founders of *The Register* (www.theregister.co.uk) in 1994. He left in 2001 to start another online news publication that mixed IT news with gossip in typical, and entertaining, British tabloid fashion, *The Inquirer* (www.theinquirer.net), as shown in Figure 10-2.

Figure 10-2. *The Inquirer*

I asked Mike for his insights on what it's like running an online news publication:

Q. *You're one of the first online journalists. Why go online?*

A. I launched my first magazine in the early 1970s. Putting together the components for a book was incredibly time-consuming, and so was printing and distribution. Online just cuts through the entire chain and is an incredibly cheap and effective way to communicate.

Q. *How's business?*

A. Good. *The INQ* [*Inquirer*] made a profit every year it existed. Earlier this year, I sold it to VNU. The model works.

Q. *Earlier this year, you were one of the first journalists to report about Sony's battery woes. How did you get the story and why were you able to get the story before so many mainstream media journalists?*

A. The story came from one of our regular readers who just happened to be at a conference in Japan where the Dell machine burst into flames. We have a generally very good relationship with our readers and have built up good contacts in the industry, short-circuiting the usual PR and marketing chain.

Q. *Over the years since you jumped online, has it become easier or harder to be an online journalist?*

A. It has become a lot easier to become one, because the tech is now much cheaper and reliable. But, on the other hand, it's more crowded. There's always room for the new, though.

Q. *What's your typical workday look like?*

A. It's fragmented. I'm usually up at 5 or 6 AM to catch the Asian readers, and keep plugging away until midday to catch European and American readers. Then there's a lull in the British afternoon, although in the evening there's another spike. There aren't weekends, holidays, or office hours. Online hackery cuts across those boundaries as well.

Q. *Any advice to journalists working for downsizing newspapers and media organizations?*

A. If you're a journo and have a good idea, it's worth making the jump. Many media orgs still haven't got their head around just how disruptive the tech is. My son is 19. He's very literate, but books and printed newspapers are not major elements of his reading; the Web is. For old guys like me, there's a sentimental attachment to books, newspapers, and magazines. But he has had a computer since day zero.

OPEN SOURCING MY TECHCRUNCH WORK FLOW, MARSHALL KIRKPATRICK

As the lead blogger for TechCrunch (www.techcrunch.com)—*a newsblog covering the emerging Web 2.0— during 2006, Marshall Kirkpatrick profiled startup web companies, covered breaking industry news, and reviewed new web applications. As Marshall was leaving TechCrunch in late November 2006 to pursue other interests, he blogged at* http://marshallk.com *about how he covered his online newsbeat. With Marshall's permission, the following is a reprint of that discussion.*

One of the things I'm most excited about regarding this transition is that the research methods I used to train people in are no longer a trade secret. Those tactics, specifically ways to use RSS, were what got me the job at TechCrunch and were a big part of my everyday work flow there. Though many of the stories I wrote came from press releases and TechCrunch contacts, I live in Portland, Oregon (not San Francisco), and had to come up with the vast majority of my stories on my own.

The following is a description of my feed reading methodology. It's how I break stories, if not in the first place, then into the larger blogosphere. It's a work flow that I believe can be applied in almost any sector. I'm looking forward to helping a variety of people learn to use these tools so they can be put to use for more than just bloggers blogging about the blogosphere. This is a big picture of what I know now, and I know that a week from now, I'll have more to offer. I haven't included any discussion about small things like filtering feeds, scraping feeds or using RSS and email together, but there's a lot more that can be done with RSS for research than I feel like writing about this morning. My plan for consulting is to offer customized training in the use of these tools, other related practices, and whatever else I learn about in the future.

How to Read Feeds and Rock the Blogosphere

RSS feeds make it possible to consume far more information at a faster pace than would otherwise be possible for the human brain. That said, many people experience a new level of information overload once they begin reading feeds. Here's an overview of how I read thousands of RSS feeds without breaking a sweat.

Using a Startpage

I've recently added the use of a startpage or single page aggregator to my workflow to complement my regular feed reading. I've dragged the link to OriginalSignal [www.`originalsignal.com`] and now Pageflakes [www.`pageflakes.com`] onto my toolbar, and I give it a click a couple of times an hour. It provides a quick and easy way to see if my competitors have written anything new since the last time I looked. Almost anything can be read by RSS feed, so you can display almost anything on a startpage. These services fulfill a very specific function for a person working on the web—they provide a one-click view of updates from various sources, inside the browser and distinct from the more heavy-duty environment of a feed reader.

Organizing a Feed Reader

I use NewsGator's desktop feed reader for Macs, NetNewsWire [www.`newsgator.com/NetNewsWire.aspx`], to subscribe to RSS feeds. It's the fastest and most reliable RSS reading tool I've found yet. It's nice to be able to read my feeds when I'm not online, too.

I am subscribed to thousands of RSS feeds and currently have thousands of unread items in my feed reader—that suits me just fine. The secret is to organize those feeds so that the most important information is easy to access. I have several folders that include feeds from the blogs of companies I wrote about at TechCrunch, news search feeds for those companies, and other high-priority topics. I refresh and check those folders frequently throughout the day. I keep everything else in low-priority folders that I only check if I find the time. That way I end up reading 100% of what's most important and probably 10% of what's unimportant enough to miss.

Finding the right feeds is a whole topic in and of itself that I'll save for another time, but I will say that it is very helpful to subscribe to feeds without a moment's hesitation. As long as they are well organized, even a list of feeds that you almost never read will be more likely to catch your attention than something you didn't subscribe to in the first place. I also subscribe to a lot of news, blog, and web searches that never have any results—but that I will want to see right away in the event that those searches do result in something.

High-Priority Sources

The single most helpful tool for me in my efforts to blog about news events first has been an RSS to IM/SMS notification tool. I use ZapTXT [http://`zaptxt.com`] to subscribe to very high-priority feeds. It sends me an IM and SMS whenever a high-profile company blog is updated and in a number of other circumstances. There are quite a few services that offer this functionality now and it's invaluable. A big part of taking a prominent position in the blogosphere is writing first on a topic. That's a large part of what got me the job at TechCrunch, and it's something that an increasing number of people are clearly trying to do.

In sectors where people are already using tools like the above, I expect further developments to emerge that differentiate writers' handling of the huge amount of information available. New tools and new practices. It's a very exciting time to be someone who works with information.

Those practices described above are relatively simple but they worked well for me to get and do my job at TechCrunch. In six months of writing the majority of the posts there, I helped the site grow from 75,000 subscribers to almost twice that number at its peak last Tuesday. Over the last six months the blog has gone from the ninth most linked to blog on the web to now the sixth most linked to.

Journalists Start Blogs

Mike McGee was among the first journalists to go online, but not the first to actually adopt blogging as the specific means of doing his stuff. That honor goes to Tom Foremski, late of the international business newspaper the *Financial Times*. Tim chucked it all and started his blog at www.siliconvalleywatcher.com, as shown in Figure 10-3.

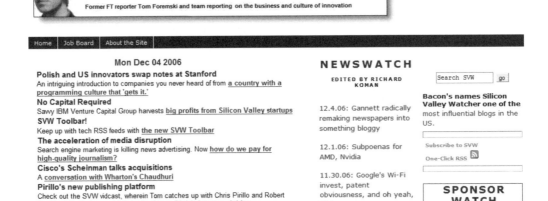

Figure 10-3. *Silicon Valley Watcher blog*

In his blog's About section, Tom explains why he fired his newspaper and started Silicon Valley Watcher:

In May 2004 I became the first journalist from a leading newspaper to resign and become a full-time blogger. I had one of the top jobs in journalism and I had never blogged. Yet I knew in my gut that the timing was right, and that the business of online journalism would continue to improve while the print business model would continue to worsen.

Silicon Valley Watcher is now one of the most read and respected publications covering the IT industry, with a Technorati ranking of 2,052 (2,105 links from 814 blogs) as of November 2006.

I caught up with Tom in late November 2006 to ask him more about his break with mainstream media.

Q. *How did you come to decide to do Silicon Valley Watcher?*

A. It was about two and a half years ago . . . about three years ago. I started looking around and seeing what was happening in the media, and quite clearly there was a little disruption going on. And from where I was sitting at the desk of a major global newspaper, it didn't look like it was going to get any better soon; if anything, it was going to be getting worse.

My management seemed oblivious to that fact, and blogging was something that friends of mine were doing, and getting a lot of attention. I didn't think much of blogging myself. I never really read blogs, but I could see that it was a really robust publishing platform. And I could see that, for example, publishing platforms of a newspaper, like my newspaper, were extremely expensive, extremely difficult to support and fund. It was costing them millions of dollars. And here [for blogs], we had these systems like Movable Type and so on. They cost hardly anything to run, were really robust, and didn't require an entire IT department to support and maintain. And so things like that made me realize, well, I can probably create pretty much the same kind of quality that the FT [the *Financial Times*] is producing with my columns, and do it in a way that gives me a chance to play on the other side of the disruption that is going on.

So, I decided to leave the FT and try to make a living as a journalist blogger. It has taken me a bit longer than I expected, about two plus years on. And certainly it has only come true, but it's still going to continue and be a lot more common.

Q. *When you go after a story and you're talking to sources, and you tell them, "Hi, I'm an online journalist," do you find that that's a problem ever?*

A. No, people pretty much know who I am. I don't have to explain who I am to anybody. Really, I had the benefit of 25 years in the industry. I had a byline that was pretty much well known to most people in Silicon Valley, so the transition . . . there really wasn't a transition. I was still getting pitched with the same high-level access and so on as I was at the *Financial Times.* But I do sometimes come across people who look at my business card and say, "Oh, so this is just online?" And I tell them, "Well, I can print it out for you."

I try to make the distinction that it's not the distribution mechanism that counts. It's the value of the news source. The newspaper is not a news *paper*; it's a news *organization* that uses paper to distribute its column.

Q. *As a journalist who has sort of fired his newspaper, other than the other way around, how are you liking it? Are you finding that you are being able to be more the reporter you want to be?*

A. I love it. I love it. It doesn't feel like work most of the time, except when it's late at night and so on. I'm still the same employee I was before. I'm still writing pretty much the same things, but also able to write in a broader style, different formats, and also pick topics and quickly get them out there. That would have taken much longer before, so I really enjoy it.

I didn't realize I would be the first industry journalist to leave a big paper and do this. That was surprising to me.

Q. *As you look from where you are now, online, back toward mainstream media, do you see any sort of acceleration toward more and more reporters going online as fewer and fewer mainstream jobs are left?*

A. Well, what's happening is that the reporters [who] are staying in their jobs are not very happy about things, and having to write more online for their bosses. Now, I was telling them two years ago or more, start your own blogs—that they'll be grandfathered in. Because otherwise, you'll be blogging for your boss and working harder, and not really enjoying it, and building their brand. But hardly any of them listened to me.

Q. *Well, much to their detriment.*

A. But I'm surprised several people haven't done what I've done.

Q. *I'm wondering if you were to appear in front of your typical school of journalism class, advising students who wanted to be reporters, what would you say to them about online journalism?*

A. I would say that online journalism is the same as any other kind of journalism. It's journalism. And the quality of your work is judged in the same way, whether it is in the paper, online, or if it's on the radio or TV. The distribution mechanism is not what defines the quality of the journalism.

Q. *Do you think that they could jump right into being online reporters, or should they work their way through a regular newspaper or media organization first?*

A. Well, it's always great to work with people who are better than you. I learned a tremendous amount working at the *Financial Times*, working with world-class reporters, editors, and so on. And jumping into online journalism, yeah, you can do it, but if you have some training, some background—everything like that counts. And it can be at an online news site; it doesn't have to be online or offline. I keep stressing that point.

Q. *One question that some of the reporters that I know are going to want me to ask: Are you making more or less money than you used to as a regular journalist?*

A. My revenue is higher than my salary back at the *Financial Times*, but I'm pumping it back into the business. Right now, I'm pretty much reinvesting almost everything that I get back into the business. But I could just keep it in my pocket.

Q. *How can readers of blogs know what type of quality they are getting from online reporters and from the mainstream media? What can they do about that?*

A. Readers are pretty smart. They question everything they read, whether it's from the *New York Times* or from the local newspaper or from the local blog. And the way they make judgments about the quality of what they read is through trust, the trusted relationship. That somebody—a reporter, or an online publication, or an offline publication—consistently produces great stories, new stories, features, and so on. That's how media brands are built. If you look at something out of context, you're going to be very suspicious of it. And that's the way it is, and readers aren't stupid. It's about consistent production of quality journalism.

Q. *What do you make of some of the mainstream media efforts to include blogging and bloggers in their coverage—for instance CNN? And you have the CBS Evening News bloggers, and you have various other bloggers sort of being either adopted or reached out to by mainstream media.*

A. I think it's a good move. Because it's all part of what I call the *mediasphere*, rather than the blogosphere or mainstream media. And these are distribution platforms, CNN and so on, so it makes sense for them to feature other content, especially since they are not paying for that content. They don't have to pay a journalist to write that stuff—they are just grabbing it off the air, but that's fine. You might think, well, they should be paying for that content. Well, at some point they probably will. But right now, for a lot of online journalists, bloggers, including myself, I see it as a distribution platform. Somebody wants to copy my stuff and use it and so on, let them do it. As long as they keep my name on it, and my links, I don't mind. So I think it's all a good thing.

Q. *Great, anything else I should ask? Let me ask a different way. Any advice you would give to some of your non-online reporter friends—jump or not?*

A. I would say that this is the most exciting time to be a journalist, because there is a tremendous amount of construction going on in our industry. And whenever you see that kind of construction going on, that's known as a chance to make a name for yourself, to move out ahead of the old guard, which is still trying to figure out what's going on. They are always going to be a couple of steps behind, so let's say that at no point in our careers as media professionals will we have such a great opportunity.

Journalism Gets It, Somewhat

Mainstream media, for all of its supposed cluelessness according to both liberal and conservative bloggers, does realize something is going on, and a few news organizations are trying fitfully to Do Something! All three traditional news networks in the US have summarily drafted their reporters into the blogosphere and started reporter blogs at `www.cbsnews.com`, `http://abcnews.blogs.com`, and `http://dailynightly.msnbc.com`. In fact, it was at MSNBC's the Daily Nightly blog (see Figure 10-4) that news anchor Brian Williams announced that the "NBC Nightly News" was going to be trying something new and refreshing: going to a single sponsor with two short commercials, in a bid to make the television show more engaging.

In newspaperland, one chain hopes it has found a way to stem the tide of readers and revenue: convert its newspaper websites to newsblogs and go "hyper-local." During the second half of 2006, the Gannett Company—the single largest newspaper publisher in the US and publisher of *USA Today*—began testing the idea of converting 11 of its newspapers to "Information Centers." This is where reporters and photographers post continuously throughout the day; where it's the Web first, the newspaper second; and where a fleet of mobile journalists, or "mojos," roam the countryside looking for news, street by street, to post to their hyper-local news to "micro-sites" (see Figure 10-5).

Figure 10-4. *The Daily Nightly blog*

Figure 10-5. *The Cape Coral micro-site wants you.*

Gannett is as serious as a heart attack about turning newsrooms upside down and hyper-local. Gannett CEO Craig A. Dubow described Information Centers in an internal memo:

> *What is it? The Information Center is a way to gather and disseminate news and information across all platforms, 24/7. The Information Center will let us gather the very local news and information that customers want, then distribute it when, where and how our customers seek it. It is the essence of our Vision and Mission and a key element of our Strategic Plan.*

The Information Center, frankly, is the newsroom of the future. It will fulfill today's needs for a more flexible, broader-based approach to the information gathering process. And it will be platform agnostic: News and information will be delivered to the right media—be it newspapers, online, mobile, video or ones not yet invented—at the right time. Our customers will decide which they prefer.

Will becoming newsblogs save Gannett's newspapers? It's way too soon to tell, but at one test site, the *Fort Myers News-Press* (www.news-press.com), traffic had grown from an average of 58,000 unique visitors per week in 2002 to 140,000 per week in late 2006, and traffic to the paper's community micro-sites in August–October 2006 was up 106 percent over 2005.

AN INTERVIEW WITH FABRICE FLORIN, EXECUTIVE DIRECTOR, NEWSTRUST

One of the big problems for journalism—both professional and blogger—is trust. And trust of the media is very low. A January 2006 CBS/*New York Times* poll (www.cbsnews.com/htdocs/pdf/020306POLL.pdf) found only 15 percent of those surveyed had a great deal of faith the mainstream media were telling the truth; 36 percent had very little or no confidence in the news media. Blogs, and blogs dedicated to reporting news (newsblogs) have even less of the public's trust according to a ten-nation poll done for the BBC by GlobeScan: 38 percent of those polled trusted newsblogs, and only 25 percent trusted blogs in general (www.globescan.com/news_archives/bbcreut.html).

Enter NewsTrust (http://beta.newstrust.net), a nonprofit Web 2.0 site where members can rank news media and newsblog stories based on their journalistic quality, fairness, and trustworthiness, rather than their popularity. NewsTrust launched its public beta November 28, 2006.

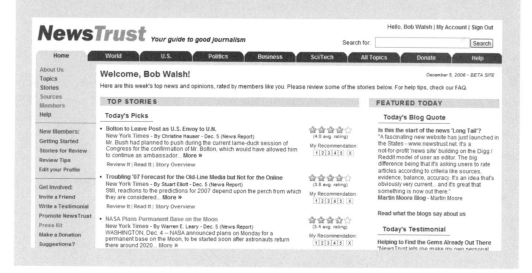

I caught up with Fabrice Florin, the executive director of NewsTrust and a 25-year veteran of both the high-tech and media industries, two days later.

Q. *Why is NewsTrust necessary?*

A. There is a confluence of events that are all taking place simultaneously that are making it harder for regular citizens to access quality journalism. On one hand, you've got the consolidation of big media, which is leading to some cutbacks in newsrooms, and it is also encouraging journalists to give people what they want rather than what they need.

On the opposite side of the spectrum, you have got a lot of newcomers who are starting to access journalism and don't necessarily have all the training that's required to do good journalism. So whether it is a blogger or an online publication, you are getting a lot of novices who are just getting started. It's wonderful to get everybody empowered to get their own voice, but journalism is the practice that requires discipline, training, and just like being a good doctor, a cop, it takes experience to get to a point where you can really serve the public.

So you have got the tsunami of information that is descending on the average consumer. You can now get so many different bits of news, and how do you assess whether the information that is being sent to you is credible or not? In the old days, you can say, well, I trust Walter Cronkite or I trust the *New York Times*.

That was fine, but nowadays, the information is coming from millions of different sources, and you don't really have a quick way to assess what people are doing. You can do it the hard way, which is to basically take every article you read and spend a couple of hours researching it. However, people don't really have that kind of time to do this routinely.

Q. *So what does NewsTrust do about this?*

A. What we created is a way for people to aggregate that kind of work and that kind of evaluation, so that you can evaluate a story pretty thoroughly and others will get the benefit of that evaluation. The way that we evaluate the stories is by looking at their journalistic quality. Does this story have factual evidence? Is it balanced? Does it offer diverse viewpoints? Is it fair and respectful to the subject matter? Does it give the big picture in the context that people need to put this in context?

All of these qualities are necessary for citizens to make an informed decision based on the article that they have just read. If these qualities are missing, it is harder for the citizen to make an informed decision without doing a lot of extra work.

So that's the general premise in a nutshell. We offer both a quality newsfeed—which has been vetted by other citizens like you who have used our review tools to assess the piece based on its journalistic quality, not just its popularity—and second, we offer media literacy tools to help citizens collectively arrive at a fair evaluation of the work of journalists. So it is both media literacy and a quality newsfeed.

Q. *Well, the site as a whole is a media literacy tool?*

A. Yes.

Q. *OK, so basically for people to use this, they need to either pick up the feed or visit the site and see what has been rated and what looks good to them.*

A. Yeah.

Q. *I'm curious—do you have any plans for doing this as far as blogs are concerned?*

A. We are already reviewing blogs. If you go to the homepage of the site, you will see there are some blogs that appear in our listings. If you look on the right side, the right column, we list all of the sources that track. Not only do we review the individual stories, we also keep track of the quality ratings for each publication—whether it is a blog, a newspaper, or a TV station. We keep track of their quality ratings over time. We aggregate reputation of that source. Even if someone does not have time to review a story from a particular publication, at least you can right away go to the source page for that publication and find out what kind of ratings it is getting overall.

So already we have a lot of prominent blogs that are climbing to the top, that are doing well: Global Voices [www.globalvoicesonline.org], FireDogLake [www.firedoglake.com], and Informed Comment [www.juancole.com], which are thoughtful works of journalism. Time and time again, these bloggers do quality work according to our members.

Q. *Would you say it's a fair statement that both people on the left and on the right in the United States are extremely dissatisfied with where, let's call it "mainstream media," has gone?*

A. Absolutely. I've reached out to both sides of the political aisle because this is a general problem. This is a problem for the entire nation, for all citizens of the world, actually. How do citizens make more informed decisions based on journalism? Without journalism, you can't figure it out by yourself unless you spend an enormous amount of time at research. You've got to have good journalism or there's no democracy.

It's absolutely true that both the left and the right feel that's an issue. We feel privileged that we have a member of MoveOn.org and the Heritage Foundation on our advisory board, and they've both made significant contributions to keep us honest.

Q. *Can blogs produce news? Are they ever going to be in the same league as traditional newspapers and other media?*

A. Absolutely. There are some fantastic blogs that are doing great journalism. Now, not all bloggers are journalists, and I'd say the majority of bloggers are more opinion writers than they are news reporters. But we also review opinions. We think opinions are also very important to help you make informed decisions. What we look for in an opinion is to see if the opinion is logically constructed, whether it presents both sides of the argument, and whether it treats the opposing views respectfully. Fairness and diversity are also important in an opinion piece.

Even if you're presenting your opinion as the primary point you're making, it's important for you to acknowledge the other points of view in the course of making your argument. From that standpoint, we're able to review a lot of blogs. Where we have difficulty is sometimes a blog is primarily a link to a mainstream media piece with a short note next to it. Those blog posts we're having a bit of difficulty evaluating because often they evaluate just a single sentence.

Q. *What has surprised you about things as you put this together?*

A. The biggest surprise for me was that I thought that what we were doing initially was a quality news piece, and that was our primary purpose. Basically, you help pull out the good stuff from all the noise out there. But it turned out what we're providing beyond the news feed is this media literacy tool. If you look at the testimonials on our site from current members, they're saying that what they appreciate about news most is the ability to come in and really evaluate the story on its own merits, and what it helps them do is go past their initial gut reaction.

We're all human. When we read a story, our reptilian brain kicks in, and for survival reasons, we have to immediately form an opinion about that story. The opinion we form is typically influenced by whether or not we trust the source, and secondly, whether or not the view presented in this article tends to reinforce our preexisting view.

That's a really interesting discovery, but if you ask yourself a couple of more questions about the story, you can go past your initial gut instincts and you could start forming a judgment on that story that is based on its actual merits. For example, is the story fair? Does it offer factual information? Does it provide the context that I need to understand it? When you answer for yourself these extra two or three questions, you start viewing the story differently, and you often find that your initial gut reaction may not have been the right one.

Q. *How many members do you have so far? Do you have a sense of it? I realize it is still early.*

A. We were just launched a couple of days ago. We have already 1,600 reviewers who have at least visited the site and viewed some stories. In terms of active reviewers, you are probably talking about 500 or 600. It's a bit early to throw numbers at this because we are really two days old. Stay tuned, we are going to find out in coming days and weeks just how big this is going to be. I would encourage you to try reviewing a story or two on the site if you haven't already.

The Blog As Small-Town Newspaper

While professional journalists are struggling to adapt to a world gone Internet mad, some people are just getting out there and doing it for the fun of it.

That's what Lisa Williams is doing. She's the publisher, editor, and chief comment-washer of H2otown.info—a Watertown, Massachusetts, homegrown, hometown newsblog (see Figure 10-6)—which she started in 2003.

Figure 10-6. *H2otown*

Lisa was kind enough to take a few minutes to answer the questions I emailed her about the newsblog.

Q. *Small-town newspapers have been folding or being bought up by media corporations for years. Can and should blogs like H2otown take their place?*

A. No, I frequently tell people that H2otown is not a substitute for a local newspaper and that it would be a bad thing for the community if the newspaper disappeared. What I think will happen, and is happening already, is newspapers wrapping H2otown-like communities around their traditional media product.

Q. *How are you supporting the blog? Is it profitable?*

A. H2otown breaks even, largely because it's very cheap to run. My total out-of-pocket cost for the site is about $40. While the tools to create an online community have fallen to free or extremely cheap, the cost of acquiring advertisers has not changed. Online ads mesh poorly with local sites, since ads are keyword-driven and not location-driven. When that changes, local sites will become much more profitable than they are today.

Q. *What has been the reaction of the "movers and shakers" of the town?*

A. As for people in prominent political positions in town, it's hard to say. Three or four of our nine town councilors have blogs at H2otown, as does our state representative, and many representatives of town boards and public/private organizations like Watertown Community Housing maintain blogs on H2otown that they use to get news out about their initiatives and organizations. The former town council president as well as a columnist for the local newspaper who writes about politics are frequent bloggers on the site. The response by people who use it has been positive.

It's hard to say what people who don't contribute to it but read it—lurkers—think about it. Do they see it as a good or bad thing? Hard to say. I had a long talk with one controversial town councilor who felt that comments on posts containing video of her at Town Council meetings were unfair.

I work very hard to separate fact from assertion in my own writings on H2otown. When I write about my own opinions, it's clear to readers that it's my opinions. As for other contributors to the site, I ask them to think about three principles: Truthfulness, Transparency, and Tactful.

People can be very blunt on H2otown, but I moderate comments that contain attacks based on things like ethnicity or personal appearance, and I'd moderate out derogatory comments about ethnicity, race, or sexual preference if they ever happened, but they haven't. But you shouldn't get the idea that I have to do that a lot, because it's relatively rare.

Q. *Any advice to bloggers who want to start their own newsblog?*

A. Be willing to do it on your own indefinitely. The strategy that Tom Sawyer used to get others to whitewash the fence won't work in community media. When people do participate, spend time thinking about community values. That's more than rules, but what participants get out of it. Do they get information from the site? Contact and conversation with their neighbors? A placeblog has just as much in common with an Elks Club as it does a newspaper. Think about the social aspects of your site.

Respond to every comment with one exception: if a comment gets you hot under the collar, wait 24 hours to respond. Thank your users with signs of affiliation. H2otown members who participate in things that we encourage on the site, like contributing to an annual charity drive for a food pantry or voting, get online "buttons" that display next to their comments showing that they're community superstars.

One very important thing: if you have a day job or a family at home, your ability to do it consistently—3 to 5 posts a day—will hinge on your efficiency as a blogger. Efficiency in blogging is about what happens before you write up your entry. Gathering items to blog about via RSS and RSS search feeds, Flickr, YouTube, local media sources, and local bloggers is vital. Get an RSS reader and subscribe to all local bloggers you know, as well as feeds from the local newspaper and any other source you can find. Get proficient with tools like Flickr and YouTube. Sites that are all text are boring.

Use humor. If it's not fun, you're not doing it right. Using humor, especially self-deprecating humor, in your work gets more people to interact with you. If your pieces read like traditional news articles, it may not occur to readers that you want to talk to them because the tone isn't conversational and may be intimidating.

Citizen Journalism, Crowdsourcing, and You

If you look up the definition of *citizen journalism* on Wikipedia, you'll find that it's "the act of citizens playing an active role in the process of collecting, reporting, analyzing, and disseminating news and information." That sounds pretty tame for what has been going on.

While citizen journalism has had its proponents before blogging,[3] it wasn't until blogging started to ramp up that citizen journalism in the US started to look less like a lofty ideal and more like a going concern. Sites like the Philly Future (www.phillyfuture.org) in Philadelphia, Pennsylvania; the Muncie Free Press in Indiana (www.munciefreepress.com); the Canadian Orato site (www.orato.com), with its mix of professional and amateur first-person new stories; and the previously mentioned H2otown.info are springing up all over the Web, most as a form of blogs.

Citizen Journalism Resources

If you're thinking about starting your own online newsblog, here are few sites you should visit:

- **The Online Journalism Review:** This site (www.ojr.org) has several excellent articles on reporting, shooting video, editing, earning revenue, and ethics. Look for the links on the sidebar. Also check out its current and archived articles.

- **Backfence:** Want to start a newsblog in your town, but don't care about running a content management system or ad revenues? Backfence (http://backfence.com) is instant citizen journalism. The organization provides the structure and format and manages advertising. You provide the posts, free classified ads, and photos.

- **The 11 Layers of Citizen Journalism:** You'll find a great overview of 11 ways of doing citizen journalism by Steve Outing at www.poynter.org/content/content_view. asp?id=83126.

- **I, Reporter blog:** By content/media professional Amy Gahran and former journalist Adam Glenn, this blog (www.ireporter.org/) keeps track of the citizen journalism scene.

- **Reporter's Guide to Citizen Journalism:** This UK guide (www.pressgazette.co.uk/ resources/pdfs/reportersguide_citizenjournalism.pdf) by the *Press Gazette*, the magazine dedicated to the UK, was part of the kickoff for the Nokia Citizen Journalism Awards (www.citizenjournalismawards.co.uk).

Open-Source Reporting

What if you want to do citizen journalism but are more drawn to the research side of reporting? You might decide it's time to join an online crowd, such as the ones described here.

---

3. A notable early proponent is Dan Gillmor, a former *San Jose Mercury News* technology columnist and author of *We the Media: Grassroots Journalism by the People, for the People* (O'Reilly Media, 2006), who started the Center for Citizen Media (http://citmedia.org).

Sunlight Foundation

Formed in January 2006, the Sunlight Foundation (www.sunlightfoundation.com) is one of a growing trend of online sites dedicated to bringing some much-needed light to the governance process. For example, in October 2006, the Sunlight Foundation put together a project to determine just how many members of the US Congress had relatives on the public payroll. By December, the Sunlight Foundation reported (as shown in Figure 10-7), "Citizen Muckrakers have investigated 438 members of Congress, and tentatively found 19 spouses who were paid by a member's campaign committee—totaling some $636,876 since January 1, 2005."

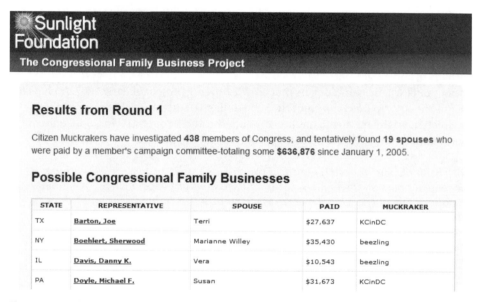

Results from Round 1

Citizen Muckrakers have investigated **438** members of Congress, and tentatively found **19 spouses** who were paid by a member's campaign committee-totaling some **$636,876** since January 1, 2005.

Possible Congressional Family Businesses

STATE	REPRESENTATIVE	SPOUSE	PAID	MUCKRAKER
TX	Barton, Joe	Terri	$27,637	KCinDC
NY	Boehlert, Sherwood	Marianne Willey	$35,430	beezling
IL	Davis, Danny K.	Vera	$10,543	beezling
PA	Doyle, Michael F.	Susan	$31,673	KCinDC

Figure 10-7. *The Congressional Family Business project*

I asked Sunlight Foundation Senior Fellow Bill Allison,[4] "What is driving citizen journalism?" He responded as follows:

> *First of all, I think the same things that are driving bloggers. One is a disaffection with media and just a sense that reporters aren't quite answering the questions that they want answered, or that there's more information that they want to know, or they really want to get in the belly of the beast. Newspapers are written for a general audience, and I think of a lot of bloggers as being high-end users. What they're interested in is getting more detail, more information, and how does this really work. When you read in the newspaper that somebody put an earmark in, they want to know how did they do that, why did they do that, who asked for it, and what else is behind it. I think that's one thing that's driving it.*

---

4. Bill Allison is a veteran investigative journalist and editor. He has worked for the Center for Public Integrity and coauthored *The Cheating of America* (William Morrow, 2001) with Charles Lewis. Bill was also senior editor of *The Buying of the President 2000* (Harper Perennial, 2000), and coeditor of the *New York Times* best seller *The Buying of the President 2004* (HarperCollins, 2004).

Second, and probably as important, at least for us with our mission, or more important, is disaffection in Congress. It remains to be seen, with the 2006 elections, how much that's going to change. My suspicion is that it won't change that much.

NewAssignment.net

The idea of *crowdsourcing*—inviting bloggers and other online people to collaborate on, investigate, and research projects basically for the fun of it—will be meeting up with citizen journalism in a big way in 2007, if the backers of NewAssignment.net are successful. NewAssignment.net describes itself as "a nonprofit site that tries to spark innovation in journalism by showing that open collaboration over the Internet among reporters, editors, and large groups of users can produce high-quality work that serves the public interest, holds up under scrutiny, and builds trust."

Launched by Jay Rosen, a New York University journalism professor, long-time advocate for citizen journalism, and blogger (at http://journalism.nyu.edu/pubzone/weblogs/pressthink/), NewAssignment.net will be launching its first crowdsourcing project in early 2007. It plans to combine a full-time *Wired Magazine* reporter with online volunteers to do the type of journalism for which mainstream media has lost the appetite and budget. David Cohn, editor of NewAssignment.net's blog, filled me in on the goal behind the project:

The idea behind open-sourced reporting is you can tap into a social network—groups of people who are passionate about, say, the environment or people who are passionate about political openness. A lot of them are being journalists individually, publishing to their blogs. But if you can harness the power of the Internet to get them to focus on one issue all together, each contributing little parts of the story, you can eventually get a type of investigation that no single professional journalist, or citizen journalist, could do by themselves.

My favorite example right now is what the Sunlight Foundation did. It would take a single reporter 435 phone calls to find that out in order to do that story. Honest phone calls. You can look it up online, but you would have to do it 435 separate times. I would guess that would take a reporter, a journalist, two weeks to do.

But the Sunlight Foundation did an open call. They said, "Hey, this is a really interesting question. Why don't you guys all find out and report on your local congressman?" They put up the call on Friday, and by Sunday, it had been finished. They got all the information.

While David applauded the Sunlight Foundation's project, NewAssignment.net wants to go further:

You can get the information but it doesn't give it context, because there are probably valid reasons why some of those spouses were hired. I'm sure that if Hillary Clinton hired her husband, he probably has the qualifications. Those databases aren't really the story, you know, that's a database. That's important. That's part of open-source journalism is creating those databases. But the real trick to open-source journalism is allowing the reporting process to be open. Anybody can contribute. But there are different models of doing this. Right now, NewAssignment.net is going to focus on pairing that with professionals. We call it Pro Am. Pro Am is an acronym for professional and amateur collaboration.

NowPublic

If there ever was a line between citizen journalists, bloggers, and online amateurs who want a say in what gets called news, that line is fast being erased by Web 2.0 sites like Vancouver, B.C.–based NowPublic (www.nowpublic.com), shown in Figure 10-8. Here's how NowPublic described itself:

> *NowPublic is a participatory news network which mobilizes an army of reporters to cover the events that define our world. In twelve short months, the company has become one of the fastest growing news organizations with over 31,000 reporters in 130 countries. During Hurricane Katrina, NowPublic had more reporters in the affected area than most news organizations have on their entire staff.*

Figure 10-8. *NowPublic blog*

NowPublic citizen reporters can do several things:

- Contribute and rank mainstream news stories, blog posts, and photos, while adding their own comments and visuals via a cool Firefox bookmarklet button

- Post to NowPublic as well as up to five of their own blogs

- Either control their story or open it up to other citizen reporters for contributions

All this happens under the steady eye of NowPublic's Managing Editor Mark Schneider, a Canadian journalist with 30-plus years' experience, who can bump up stories to NowPublic's front page, regardless of ranking.

Bloggers As Stringers

It used to be if you wanted to get your 30 seconds of reporting fame on television, you could (a) be unfortunate enough to be the victim of some horrible tragedy, (b) be lucky enough to win the hyper-slippery pole climb to be hired to be in front of the camera, or (c) be patient enough to be a "stringer" for a media organization in some obscure place where news, might—just might—happen.

Back in the early 1980s, I was one such stringer. I was making $50 a six-paragraph story whenever I could convince the desk editor at United Press International in San Francisco something newsworthy had happened across the San Francisco Bay in Berkeley.

Now the entire blogosphere has, in effect, become stringers for the mainstream media, who from the top of the news pyramid to your local weekly throwaway, pick up newsworthy posts—sometimes attributing them and sometimes not. More and more newspaper, radio, and television websites implore you to post, not just your comments about their news, but your reports and photos of news you eyewitness. Here are a few examples:

- BBC staff can now issue payments for footage from cell phones or digital cameras. Similarly, Britain's Channel Five announced in 2006 it would start paying 100 pounds for each cell phone video it aired. (See www.editorsweblog.org/news/2006/11/bbc_will_pay_for_citizen_journalism.php.)

- In a deal with Reuters wire service, Yahoo—the largest news website in the US—has started You Witness News at news.yahoo.com/page/youwitnessnews, as shown in Figure 10-9. Here, people formerly known as the audience can submit photos and video for Yahoo News. Just like the work of professional news photographers, submissions are reviewed by Reuters and Yahoo editors. Reuters plans to initially use selected visuals on its site, and then sell to its media customers (selected submitters will get paid something). Yahoo, on the other hand, wants to build up a network of citizen journalists reporting local news. (See www.nytimes.com/2006/12/04/technology/04yahoo.htm.)

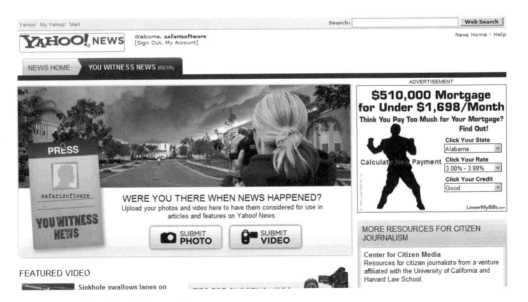

Figure 10-9. *Yahoo You Witness News*

- CNN has added a new section to its US and international websites, I-Reports (www.cnn.com/exchange), as shown in Figure 10-10. Here, viewers can submit stories, video, audio, and photos as unpaid stringers.

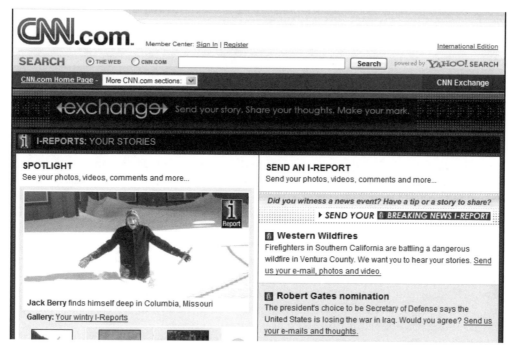

Figure 10-10. *CNN's I-Reports*

GARY WALTERN, GETTING ON CNN, HURRICANE WILMA

In mid-October 2005, Hurricane Wilma caused at least 63 deaths and over $28.8 billion in property damage as it hit the Yucatán Peninsula of Mexico, Cuba, and Florida. As the most intense hurricane ever recorded in the Atlantic Basin careened from landfall to landfall, CNN supplemented its coverage with live reports, video feeds, and postings from bloggers in the path of the storm.

Several weeks later, Gary Waltern, one of CNN's main citizen reporters from Cancun, Mexico, explained what it was like going from blogger to news source.

Q. *What's it like being effectively a reporter during a hurricane?*

A. It's a thrill and challenging to think on your feet and be accurate, informative, interesting with good verbal imagery, and not stutter. Hindsight is always 20/20 regarding what you could have said to really nail it, so a mental rehearsal before you go on is key.

Q. *How did you connect to CNN? Did they contact you or the other way around?*

A. I contacted them from an email address on the CNN website for the Situation Room [CNN show].

> **Q.** *Any advice to other people who find themselves being journalists?*
> **A.** If you are in weather conditions, put your still/video camera in an underwater housing. I used an 8 megapixel still camera with video capability because it is small. Make sure the memory card is big enough (1GB is OK). Turn off the camera screen when you don't need it to save the battery. Shoot small vid clips less than 10MB so you can email them as an attachment without much editing, if locations dictate that. I used a Yahoo email account.
>
> Don't be afraid to hang it out there to get the dramatic images, but don't get yourself injured in the process. Communicate quickly with your news contact person, or you won't make the show.

Blogs and Politics

Anyone who spends more than 15 minutes browsing blogs at random will soon find that blogs have become part and parcel of politics, especially in the US. From Instapundit (www.instapundit.com) to FireDogLake (www.firedoglake.com), from The Huffington Post (www.huffingtonpost.com) to the Captain's Quarters (www.captainsquartersblog.com/mt/), the political blogosphere ranges from thoughtful commentary to vicious slander on both sides of the American political divide.

One of the first times bloggers made international news was at the height of the 2004 US Presidential election. On September 8, veteran news anchor and reporter Dan Rather reported on "60 Minutes" about the discovery of documents written by President George Bush's Texas Air National Guard commander critical of his service during the 1970s. Within 12 days, criticism and fact-checking efforts in the blogosphere[5] had spilled over into the mainstream media, causing CBS News to, in effect, repudiate the story, leading to Dan Rather's early retirement in 2005 (see http://en.wikipedia.org/wiki/Rathergate).

In 2006, two stories that began online and in blogs were the last straw (in my opinion) for an electorate profoundly dissatisfied with the Iraq war and cost Republicans their majority and control of the US House of Representatives and Senate:

- Rep. Mark Foley's underage congressional page sex scandal

- Senator George Allen's calling a rival campaign volunteer who was taping him at a public event "macaca," and that tape making it to YouTube

In September 2006, Rep. Mark Foley's (R-Florida) practice of sending sexually suggestive email to former congressional pages became public. This sparked cries of outrage from both sides of the political divide, and cries of cover-up by Republican House Speaker Dennis Hastert and others.

Rumors of Foley's possible sexual predator behavior and email were brought to the attention of at least 13 Republican Congressmen or congressional staffers in the years before the scandal broke. Investigations had been conducted by two newspapers and a national television news show (the *St. Petersburg Times*, the *Miami Herald*, and "ABC News"). But it was not until two weeks after a then-two-month-old blog, Stop Sex Predators (http://stopsexpredators.blogspot.com), posted several of those email messages (see Figure 10-11) that the story became an item on "ABC News." Foley subsequently resigned from Congress, but the taint of scandal and possible cover-up cast a pall over many Republicans running for reelection.

---

5. Notable in these efforts were two conservative blogs: Little Green Footballs (http://littlegreenfootballs.com) and Power Line (www.powerlineblog.com).

(See http://en.wikipedia.org/wiki/Mark_Foley_scandal and www.time.com/time/nation/article/0,8599,1542405,00.html.)

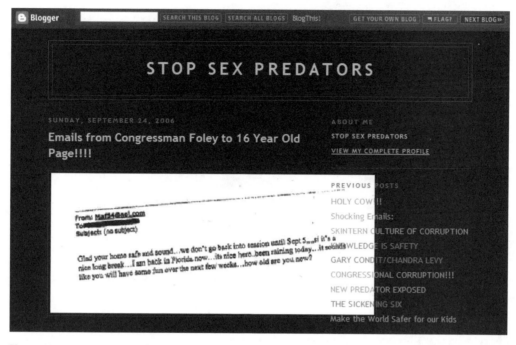

Figure 10-11. *Stop Sex Predators blog*

Considered unbeatable at the beginning of the 2006 election cycle, Sen. George Allen stumbled—stumbled badly—when on August 11, 2006, at a campaign event, he mocked, berated, and repeatedly insulted an operative from his competitor's campaign as being a macaca. A *macaca* is monkey native to Asia. The man, S. R. Sidarth, a native of Virginia and second-generation Indian American, described his surprise at Allen's remarks (www.washingtonpost.com/wp-dyn/content/article/2006/11/10/AR2006111001381.html):

> *Allen's actions that day stood out because they were not representative of how I was treated while traveling around the state. Everywhere I went, though I was identifiably working on behalf of Allen's opponent, people treated me with dignity, respect, and kindness. I cannot recall one event where food was served and I was not invited to join in the meal. In southwest Virginia, hospitality toward me was at a high point.*

Within hours of the video being posted at YouTube (see Figure 10-12), the blogosphere was abuzz with commentary on Allen's remarks.[6] Allen lost his seat by 7,231 votes (2,338,111 were officially cast).

---

6. As of this writing, Technorati shows there are 10,163 blog postings with the keywords of "macaca" and "Allen."

Figure 10-12. *Former Sen. George Allen's "macaca" moment*

The New Fourth Estate Recap

From tiny one-person operations like Lisa Williams at H2otown.info, to citizen journalism sites like NowPublic, to political blogs read by millions each day, bloggers—as political commentators and citizen journalists—have, in effect, become the new fourth estate.

Once upon a time, the mainstream media was the fourth estate. Sometimes this was in fiction, like the Humphrey Bogart classic movie *Deadline, U.S.A.* (www.imdb.com/title/tt0044533/); sometimes in reality, like murdered investigative journalist Don Bolles (http://en.wikipedia.org/wiki/Don_Bolles, http://www.azcentral.com/specials/special01/articles/weisz.html, and http://jeff.scott.tripod.com/donbolles.html); and sometimes both, such as the Watergate scandal (http://en.wikipedia.org/wiki/Watergate).

But starting in the 1980s and accelerating to this day, muckraking—the fine art of pinning hypocritical leaders, corrupt officials, lying politicians, and the like in the bright glare of public attention and outrage—became a casualty of tightening newsroom budgets and corporate media profit projections.

But a funny thing happened on the way to the ultimate talking heads, ten-second-soundbite-election mainstream media world. The people formerly known as the audience found out that, as A. J. Liebling (a famous twentieth century American reporter) once said, freedom of the press belongs to the people who own the press—or in this case, the blogging software. And that freedom is heady stuff.

Here's a case in point. As I finished this chapter on December 6, 2006, the Iraq Study Group released its recommendations on "The Way Forward" for the US in the Iraq war. In the course of ten hours, Technorati recorded 1,654 blog postings about it: 318 by blogs, each with more than 400 linking blogs.

The fourth estate was hard at work.

Your Action Tasks

Whether you decide to stick your toe into citizen journalism or go whole hog and start a news-blog and/or political blog, here are some starting steps toward earning your blogosphere new reporter ID:

Pick up some tips. Both CNN and Yahoo News have good, short tutorials on how to take video and digital shots suitable for the Web at their sites, www.cnn.com/exchange and news.yahoo.com/page/youwitnessnews.

Read the eHow-to. eHow has a nice article on how to be an online reporter at www.ehow.com/how_246_become-online-reporter.html.

Go tell it to the media mountain. Every media organization hoping to get through this decade is begging for comments on its stories. Accommodate them by pointing out where they go right, left, and way off. Don't forget to post about it at your blog with links to their sites.

Start following these two blogs. I recommend Jay Rosen's PressThink at http://journalism.nyu.edu/pubzone/weblogs/pressthink/, which covers citizen journalism like no other blog. I also recommend Poynter Online ("Everything you need to be a better journalist") at www.poynter.org.

If the journalism bug takes, here are a few ways to get into deeper trouble:

Join NewsTrust. Start sharpening your journalistic sensitivities by practicing them at NewsTrust.com.

Start asking questions. Ask at your local city council meeting, your school board, your local newspaper's website. And start blogging the answers you get and what you think of them.

Push your local paper around. Start posting comments at your local newspaper's website, no matter how lame that site is. Ask them why they aren't covering the things you see in your life and neighborhood that they should be covering. Don't be surprised if they want to deputize you. Feel free to remind them you don't need no stinking badge.

Start a newsblog. Whether you do it on your own blog or as part of a larger network, start acting like a reporter in your part of the online or real world. You'll find a great read on how Lisa Williams did this at http://journalism.nyu.edu/pubzone/weblogs/pressthink/2005/11/14/lw_h2tn.html. While there's a tiny chance of making real money, there's a huge chance you'll like more the person you now see in the mirror.

CHAPTER 11

Adding Podcasting to Your Blog

Up to now, this book has been all about text, text, and more text. But the Internet-fueled revolution in publishing is not just about text. It's also about audio and video, and the ability for your words to reach millions of people for next to no cost. Welcome to podcasting!

Podcasting is to traditional broadcasting what blogging is to traditional newspapers. The rules of the game just got a big fat set of exceptions, and people are doing what they aren't supposed to be doing: recording and broadcasting completely outside the nicely ordered world of radio and television conglomerates, bureaucratic rules, and the primacy of advertising.

Of course, these recordings, or podcasts, tend to be anything but broad. Looking for a passionate interview on the superiority of one breed of dog over another? You got it. Want to know more about hand bells? That's here, too. Want to listen to an organic master gardener on how to be clothed, healed, fed, and soothed by plants? Tune right in. Need a new fix of mountain biking fun and mayhem? Look no further.

In this chapter, we're going to cover the ins and outs of audio podcasting, and the whys and wherefores as well. And even if you've never been bitten by the radio bug, never hankered to interview someone you think is interesting, read on. As we all move further into the world of media everywhere, podcasts are a great channel for information, entertainment, and new things you can use.

The Big (Audio) Picture

If you thought blogs were fresh, new, and up-and-coming, podcasts almost make them look like yesterday's news. Seriously, the things running around the Internet called podcasts were really only named in September 2004, when Dave Slusher asked on his Evil Genius Chronicles blog if anyone knew about Podcast.net and wondered if audioblogs were about to get popularized as podcasts. They were. We'll talk about Podcast.net and other podcast directories in a moment, but first we need to attend to an anti-marketing message of some import:

Note As much as Apple Computer might wish otherwise, in no way, shape, or form do you need an Apple iPod or any other MP3 player to listen to podcasts. And, what's more, as with most things on PCs, podcasts can be created, edited, and heard on Microsoft Windows desktop PCs, laptops, and other mobile devices just fine. And before the Linux community starts sticking pins in voodoo dolls of me, you can absolutely, positively create/listen to podcasts on that operating system as well. As the saying goes, it's all good.

In a lot of ways, what happened in 2005 to geek-produced audioblogs when they became podcasts was the same as what happened to geek-produced weblogs when they became blogs: Power to the People, rapid adoption, rampant commercialization, and a whole lot of people (perhaps like you) wondering what all the racket was about.

A podcast is nothing more than a computer file in the MPEG-1 Audio Layer 3 format, the same way a blog is nothing more than a web page. It's all about how people get, discover, and use those files that make a blog a blog and a podcast a podcast:

- Just like blogs, you can subscribe to podcasts via RSS and get the content you want delivered to your computer automatically.

- Just like blogs, podcasts are more about passion, enthusiasm, and shared interests, and less about professional standards required by mainstream media.

- Just like blogs, anyone can start podcasting for next to nothing.

- Almost like blogs, you can find podcasts you want to hear, but it's not quite as easy.

This last point—it's harder to find a podcast you want to hear than it is to find a blog or web page you want to read—is podcasting's weakness. And while numerous search engine companies are working on this, there's no single Google out there when it comes to finding podcasts, not even Google.

Now that you know what a podcast is in theory, it's time to take a break from reading and listen to one so that you really get what a podcast is. So make a note of this URL: http:// podcast.net. That's the Podcast Directory, shown in Figure 11-1, with a wide variety of podcasts. Go indulge yourself, pick out something interesting, click the green Play button, let your web browser sort out how to play it, and audition yourself a podcast.

SEARCH:
Title & Description ▾   [   ]   SEARCH

Browse Tags: A B C D E F G H I J K L M N O P Q R S T U V W X Y Z 1 2 3 4 5 6 7 8 9 0 _ TOP

Top 10 Tags

1. music (2064)
2. comedy (943)
3. podcast (813)
4. news (791)
5. radio (689)
6. rock (647)
7. technology (556)
8. politics (522)
9. christian (428)
10. indie (423)
[more]

Entertainment (6640)
Music, Celebrities, Comedy...

Business & Money (932)
Career, Investment, Marketing...

Arts (1898)
Poetry, Storytelling...

Computers & Internet (1823)
Hardware, Software, Podcasting...

Science & Nature (818)
Technology, Animals, Environment...

Home & Lifestyle (1095)
Relationships, Health, Pets...

Hobbies & Recreation (1052)
Games, Autos, Travel...

Learning & Instruction (1382)
Biographies, How To, Education...

News & Media (1662)
World News, Newspapers...

Politics & Government (1023)
Crime & Law, World Politics...

Religion & Philosophy (1722)
Ethics, Christianity, Philosophy...

Society & Culture (2010)
History, Fashion, Parties...

Sports (764)
Basketball, Olympics, Tennis...

Soliloquies (604)
Rants, Personal Journals...

Local & Regional (1661)
Africa, Canada...

Shopping & Commercial (80)
Companies, Classifieds...

International Podcasts (1090)
Italian, French, German, Other...

Kids & Teens (443)
School, Hobbies...

MOST RECENTLY ADDED PODCASTS...

Luke's Lost Podcast

Alert! Podcasts

WHAT'S NEW

Suggest A Category
We want to know what you think! Want to see a **NEW CATEGORY** created for your specific interest? Now you can suggest a catagory to be submitted for review. Just click on the orange "suggest a category" in small letters inside the category lists.

Podcast.net...now with TAGS!
Tags are an exciting way to organize content on the web. Other sites have used tags to organize weblinks and photos. Now at **Podcast.net** you can find podcasts on your favorite topics via tags as well. You can navigate our tags via the "Browse Tags" feature

Figure 11-1. *Pick something interesting.*

Back now? Good. Here are a few things you might have noticed about your audio selection:

- In the vast majority of podcasts, you're listening to an earnest amateur, not a seasoned radio professional with a "radio voice." Put another way, you can sound like yourself on your podcasts.

- Nearly all podcasts start and end with some kind of music. Where did they get that music and how did they get the rights to it? We'll cover that in the "The Sound of Music" section later in this chapter.

- The podcast probably had some sort of structure and rhythm to it, whether it was just the podcaster talking, an interview, or a conversation. Knowing what your podcast is going to be about is a requirement for recording a good podcast and something we will talk about in the next section.

- The audio quality ranged from pretty bad to near professional quality. Podcasts haven't had 80 plus years to get sound levels, balance, transmission, and all the rest right, as radio has. You are going to hear some pain here. Later in this chapter, in the "Fun with Postproduction" section, we'll cover some basic techniques to make your podcasts not painful to the ears of your listeners.

Well, enough of the big picture. If you think podcasting is for you, it's time to start working through the steps to getting your first and future podcasts recorded.

Recording Your Podcast

The first step to making your podcast is deciding what your series of podcasts—your radio channel, if you will—is going to be about. For purposes of this book, let's assume you're interested in podcasting about the same subjects you blog about.

Next, there's the question of what you're going to do differently in your podcast than in your blog. One big difference is that you can interview people who have interesting things to say and interesting ways of saying it.

A good blog is first-person. It's about your experiences, your passions, your company. It's a lot about you. Radio—or podcasting—doesn't work that way, with the possible exceptions of comedians and politicians (some say they're the same thing). When it comes to listening, by and large, people are more interested in conversations than monologues, regardless of the subject.

Let's say I blogged about Time Management and the Getting Things Done (GTD) productivity methods of David Allen, which I do at my To Do or Else blog. And then let's say I wanted to start podcasting, which I will have done by the time you read this. I could bore my audience to tears covering the same ground I've blogged about, or I could go out and interview productivity coaches, professional organizers, my fellow bloggers, or maybe even David Allen himself. Which would you find more interesting? Right.

Defining Your Podcast's Format

So, once you've decided on your podcast's theme, it's time to work up a format. In radio, the format dictates what is going to happen when, minute by minute. For example KCBS in San Francisco does traffic and weather at :08, :18, :28, :38, :48, and :58, a feed from national CBS news during the first 7.5 minutes of the hour, sports at 15 and 45 minutes after the hour, and so on—hour after hour, day after day, year after year.

Your podcast needs a format too, although it can be what you want.

Here's an early cut of the format I plan to use for the To Do or Else podcast:

Length	What/Why
10 seconds	Intro music. Let people know the show is about to start.
20 seconds	Introduce the To Do or Else podcast, episode *X*, with your host, Bob Walsh. Explain why I'm doing this podcast, what our theme is, and what the listener will get out of it. Important: Tell listeners the `http://ToDoOrElse.com` URL, where they can find other shows, the blog, and more.
10 seconds	Mention our sponsor, assuming we have one that week.
15 seconds	Cover what's in this episode: an interview with *X* on *Y*, our blog of the week, our one-minute GTD pointer.
1.5 minutes	Talk about our recommended blog/website for the week—one URL that will help them be more productive doing *X*.
1 minute	The one-minute GTD pointer: How to do one particular part of the GTD methodology, with pointers and advice.
20 seconds	Introduce the main guest and transition.
10 minutes	The main interview.
30 seconds	Recap the interview, the interviewee's main points, mention their URL again, and thank them!
2 minutes	Read/play a couple of GTD questions from listeners, thank the listeners, highlight some coming interviews, and wrap up.
15 seconds	Outro music.

Total time: 16 minutes, 30 seconds. And that illustrates another point: *Keep it short!*

Few people today are going to pour themselves an adult beverage, settle into their favorite chair, and hang onto every word of your long, rambling podcast. Keep it tight. Your listeners are in a hurry, and they will thank you for keeping it short.

So you've got a theme, and you've got a format. Next, assuming you're not doing a monologue, is how to interview.

The Hidden Mysteries of Interviewing

Actually, the mysteries of good interviewing aren't mysteries, and they're not hidden. Preparation (or as they say in the radio business, preproduction) is the key.

Interviewing Tips

Here are a few tried-and-true pointers for preparing for and conducting interviews:

Research your interviewee. There's no faster way to crash and burn interviewing than not knowing your interviewees. Take the time to find out what they have been working on. Know their most recent accomplishments, writings, presentations, and even failures. Visit their website, blog, podcast, and, if they are in the news, Google News.

Write down your questions. Start with a few easy ones to get the ball rolling, then get to the good stuff. Short, simple questions are the way to go. Leave multipart, convoluted questions with two follow-ups to the White House Press Corps. One of the absolute best questions to ask is "Why?"

Listen to their answers. Remember that you're trying to have a conversation here, not score points. Absolutely let the conversation go off script—that material tends to be the most interesting.

Layer your questions. There are two types of questions: those you really want to ask and those that would be nice to ask. As you write up your questions, make sure to format them differently so you know at a glance which questions can be skipped.

Flip the mic. Ask the interviewee what question you should have asked, but did not.

Be nice. Thank your interviewee at the start and the end of the interview. And if you have any doubts about your guest's correct title, affiliation, or name spelling, ask.

Successfully Lining Up Interviews

So you have your questions and you've done your research. How do you get people to agree to be interviewed? You ask them nicely. And you point out exactly what you would like to ask them, and you let them know that, since they are doing you the favor, you'll be happy to work around their schedule.

For example, here's the text of the email message I sent to request an interview with Dr. Ned Hallowell, a leading expert on coping with Attention Deficit Disorder (ADD) and its productivity-destroying cousin, Attention Deficit Trait (ADT):

To: Melissa Orlov, <morlov@HallowellConnections.com>

From: Bob Walsh, <bobw@safarisoftware.com>

Subject: Interviewing Dr. Hallowell for The To Do or Else Podcast

Hi Melissa,

After the news.com interview with Dr. Hallowell, I wonder if we can set up a 10 minute interview on what is ADT, ADT's symptoms and what you can do if you think you have ADT at my podcast, To Do or Else. We can do it via telephone or Skype, at the Doctor's convenience, and will be more than happy to discuss his new book, CrazyBuzy, as well as provide links to it and the book's site at http://todoorelse.com.

The To Do or Else podcast focuses on David Allen's Getting Things Done methodology, time management and online, desktop and real life productivity, and is available via Apple iTunes and several other podcasting directories. Dr. Hallowell's work with ADD and ADT is a natural fit.

Can we set a time in say the next few weeks for the interview?

Regards,

Bob Walsh

Blogger/Podcaster, http://ToDoOrElse.com

Here are a few things worth pointing out about this interview request:

Know who to ask. According to Dr. Hallowell's CrazyBusyLife.com site, Melissa is Dr. Hallowell's press contact. Guess what? You're a member of the press!

What's in it for them? Dr. Hallowell has a new book out, and believe me, authors will happily do podcasts until the cows come home and hell freezes over, with any and all takers!

Make it easy for them. You're asking a favor. Making it easy for them to say yes is always appreciated. And make it clear you only need a few minutes of their time.

Be relevant. Shoot for interviews with people relevant to your podcast's theme. How do you know they are relevant and you are relevant to them? Do your research.

Ask for the interview in a reasonable period of time. Two days is too short. Two months is someday/maybe. Two weeks is reasonable, and reasonable is what you want to be.

The Sound of Music

Theme, format, interviewing, and interviewees—those are the basic building blocks of a great podcast. Now it's time to turn to the mechanics of podcasting. But first, a word from the friendly people at the Recording Industry Association of America (RIAA):

If you use copyrighted music in your stinking podcast without paying, we are going to send our pack of snarling, blood-crazy lawyers after you to haul your sorry ass through the federal court system for the next decade. Have a nice day.

Actually, they said no such thing! The RIAA makes sure artists (and record companies) are each fairly compensated for their creative work, regardless of whether we are talking about counterfeit CDs, music file sharing, or podcasts. The RIAA does this by building public awareness of this important issue, working with Congress to ensure there are up-to-date statutes on the books and by periodically suing by the plane-load copyright infringers.[1]

If your podcast is just not going to be complete without using "real" (read "commercial") music, you can pay for that music and make sure you're on the right side of the law. In that case, you'll need a high level of detail and expertise, which is aptly covered in *Podcast Solutions: The Complete Guide to Podcasting* by Michael W. Geoghegan and Dan Klass (friends of ED, 2005). In fact, *Podcast Solutions* is a great resource for taking your podcast to new heights after getting it off the ground.

So what do you do for intro and outro music? Visit Creative Commons at `http://creativecommons.org/audio/`, shown in Figure 11-2.

Figure 11-2. *Creative Commons*

---

1. For an example, see the article "RIAA Announces New Round Of Music Theft Lawsuits," dated February 28, 2006, at `www.riaa.com/news/newsletter/022806_2.asp`.

The Creative Commons license makes it easy to for content creators of all stripes to grant, in advance, specific permission to use their works. In this case, look for music and sound effects with a Creative Commons Sampling or Share Music license at places like Jamendo (`www.jamendo.com/en/`), Freesound (`http://freesound.iua.upf.edu/`), and SectionZ (`www.sectionz.com`).

AN INTERVIEW WITH JOSH MCADAMS, PERLCAST

Working since 1997 as a computer programmer, mostly with the Perl language, Josh McAdams started Perlcast in early 2005 because he wanted to do a programmer-to-programmer podcast. "I really love Perl, and I started listening to podcasts because I jog a lot and needed something else besides music to listen to," he said in a Skype call recorded with Skylook (see this chapter's "Now for the Technical Bits" section). "I found that most of the podcasts I was listening to were very shallow-tech, and I wanted something deeper, and at the time there weren't a lot out there, so I saw an opportunity to make Perlcast. That's how it all started in a library in Conway, Arkansas—me and a microphone."

Perlcast
PODCASTING PERL

Learning Perl is easy	EDI Experts
when you take classes from the authors of bestseller Learning Perl	EDI Consulting and Training 20 years of EDI Experience

[HOME]   [MAILING LIST]   [PODCAST RSS]   [EPISODES]

[Make a Donation]

- LATEST PODCASTS -

Audrey Tang
brian d foy
Tom Limoncelli
Chris Pine
Chad Fowler
brian d foy
Chris Nandor
Jason Stajich
Peter Wainwright
Richard Foley

Save $5!
Coupon Code: TBFIVE
Restrictions Apply

- PERLCAST LINKS -

Interview with Audrey Tang

Perlcast is back in action with an interview with Audrey Tang, the creator of the Pugs project, maintainer of numerous CPAN modules, and general contributor to open source. In this interview we discuss Pugs, what it is and where it is going.

O'Reilly is also giving away ten editions of the upcoming book "Perl Hacks" through their new Rough Cuts system. To be entered in a drawing for "Rough Cuts", just send an email to perlcast+perlhacks at yapcchicago.org.

- Interview Audio
- Audrey's Blog
- Pugs
- Perl Hacks

- SPONSORS -

Platinum Sponsor

Stonehenge

- AFFILIATIONS -

Vote at Podcast Alley

MacMall
Starting at
$574!

Q. *How many listeners do you have now?*

A. Usually, within the first three weeks of any show coming out, I have about 2,000 or more downloads. And they continue. Typically, whenever anyone comes to the show, they listen to the current one and then download the past ten.

Q. *It looks like your Perlcast site (`http://perlcast.com`) is a WordPress blog. Do you blog as well as podcast?*

A. I do mostly just podcasting. That takes up enough of my time that I don't blog a whole lot.

Q. *So your podcast is for Perl programmers, or at least programmers?*

A. Yes. I definitely went into this not knowing who my audience would be, expecting them to be Perl programmers that I knew, and that's grown. There's the hardcore Perl community—I know a lot of those guys listen. And then a lot of Perl newbies come on, so I get a lot of beginning Perl questions.

Q. *I notice you've got a couple of ads on your blog, and a PayPal make a donation button. Have they made you any money?*

A. A little. Almost $100 on the make a donation button, about $25 on Google ads, and about $50 or so on affiliate marketing. Very small money. If anybody knows how to make money on podcasting, it's not me. It's such a niche podcast, I get most of my personal benefit through a kind of a trade system, through barter. I've been sent to conferences, gotten free tickets, books all the time, and things like that. I don't get a monetary reward from the podcast, but there are a whole lot of physical items and access that I would not normally get, that I do get with the podcast.

Q. *How often do you podcast?*

A. Early on, it was every week. Recently, every other week. I originally did a lot of monologue-type shows, so those are really easy—I say it, I put it out, that's about it. But I've moved to a full interview format now, and workload as far as postproduction quadruples whenever you interview, because you are trying to make sure the conversation flows smoothly.

Q. *Is there a length you try for?*

A. I don't try at all for a length. As long as a person is willing to talk and stays interesting. I don't like to go over 40, 45 minutes. I feel you lose a lot of attention, honestly, after 10 or 15 minutes.

Q. *Let's say it's a 30-minute podcast. How much time do you need to get that 30-minute podcast done?*

A. Depending on the quality of the audio, from 5 to 10 minutes for every minute of podcast. I probably overedit my podcasts. I listen to it once all the way through, taking out "uhs" and pauses and things like that. And you are actually making two passes. You edit and go back, edit and go back. So a show can easily take several hours to edit.

Q. *What equipment do you use?*

A. I'm on a Mac PowerBook G4. I take that out to an Inspire 1394—that's just an external sound card/ mixer. It has two mic jacks on the front and two RCA jacks on the back. And then for microphones, I use MXL M.A.R.K [Mobile Audio Recording Kit] mics. MXL makes a good condenser mic. I got the M.A.R.K. because I like going to conferences and recording on the road, and these little microphones have onboard phantom power[2] and little stands and cases, and are normally about $100 apiece. You can probably find a decent MXL condenser mic for $60 or so and be fine. I do have a mixer for those times I have more than two people that the Inspire can handle.

Q. *So did you have any audio training before you started podcasting?*

A. None at all.

Q. *So how do people find Perlcast?*

A. I get a few people through Google, but I've associated myself with `http://techpodcasts.com`, and that is a group of podcasts that are very tech-focused. If you're looking for technical podcasts, you're more likely to find techpodcasts.com than my podcast, but I happen to be listed there.

---

2. With phantom power, no batteries, which can die in the middle of an interview, are required.

There's one thing that's worked even better than that. The one thing that's been amazingly valuable has been networking at conferences. I'll go out to these and meet people, and they'll learn that I do a podcast, and they will share it with their friends. And there are also trade journals. The *Perl Review* is the only print publication for Perl, and so I became really good friends with the editor. We do a little cross-promotion, where I'll ring him every time he does an issue and talk about him in the show, and in return, I get ads in his magazine.

Q. *So what do you use to edit your podcasts?*

A. I started originally using Audacity for editing, and because I became so used to using Audacity, I had trouble going to anything more advanced than that. Definitely Audacity—it's a free option and it works beautifully.

Q. *What do you use to tag your audio files?*

A. Typically, I stick with Audacity, which has the ID3 tags, and so I'll put the comments and the name of the podcast and the link and everything like that in the ID3.

Q. *Where do you list Perlcast?*

A. Podcaster Alley. I'm now also listed in iTunes. I think what happened is Apple came along and slurped everything listed at Podcaster Alley into iTunes when they included podcasts. So I magically appeared one day on iTunes, and I didn't know I did. But I'm glad I did!

Q. *Besides the access and the physical access, what have you enjoyed about podcasting?*

A. Since one year ago, I've learned more about the subject area I podcast on than I would have ever imagined I would know. It's kind of like what I've always heard: If you want to learn something well, teach it. Well, I'm not teaching it, but I realize now that I'm not passively taking in information; that I'm actively parsing it so I can spit it back out to people. And so I think in the last year I've become a far better programmer than I was in the six or seven years that I coded before starting the podcast.

Q. *This is not your day job. Do you work for a company? Are you your own company?*

A. I actually work for a company here in Chicago. Actually, I got this job because of my podcast. I had just moved from Arkansas to Chicago, and some guys at the company knew me through the podcast, and we started talking, I found out they had positions open, and the next thing you knew, I had a new job.

Q. *Any advice to people just starting their podcasts?*

A. First off, just do it. That was the hardest thing for me. I sat there for hours and hours for my first little short show because I was so nervous and so scared to hear my own voice and actually send that out. So do it. People are interested—it's amazing. People are just dying to hear things they are interested in. They want to hear you talk about it, and you'll meet new friends.

Now for the Technical Bits

With the thorny and litigious issue of music out of the way, let's get to the hardware and software you'll need to start podcasting.

Basically, all the hardware you need to get going for monologue podcasts is your PC or Mac and a decent condenser microphone, available for between $60 and $100 USD. As for software, Audacity (http://audacity.sourceforge.net) is a great application and may be all you'll ever need. Audacity, shown in Figure 11-3, is a cross-platform, open source, and free sound editor.

What about interviews? If you plan to interview people "in the wild" at conferences, trade shows, events, or their workplaces, you'll need something else. You need something to plug your two or more microphones into and to plug into your Mac or PC to provide those two separate channels to Audacity. That something is a combination audio card/mixer, like PreSonus Audio Electronics Inspire 1394, which will cost you about $200 USD.

Want to do interviews for your podcast and not leave the comfort of your own desk? You can go with the traditional technology known as a telephone and combine that with a small digital recorder connected to your phone line.[3] That will work, but be forewarned: Telephone audio quality is terrible, and batteries die at the exact wrong moment.

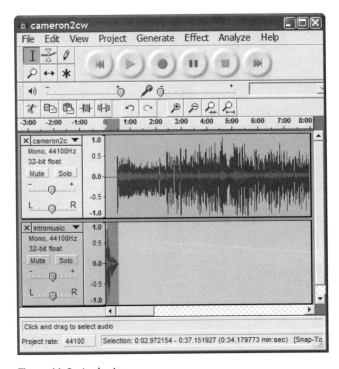

Figure 11-3. *Audacity*

Or you can *get with the times* and download Skype (`http://skype.com`). Skype is a free broadband Internet telephony service and software package, as shown in Figure 11-4. It lets millions of Skype users talk, audio conference, and even video conference for free. And it allows users to call out of the Skype system to traditional telephone users for a fraction of what telephone company long-distance rates run.

---

3. As of this writing, an Olympus VN-120PC digital voice recorder will cost you about $40 US and a RadioShack Smart Phone Recorder Control costs around $30.

Figure 11-4. *Skype, an eBay company*

What's more, for about $40 USD, you can buy Skylook (`www.skylook.biz`), a Skype add-in that can automatically record your Skype calls with excellent audio quality. How excellent? With my Logitech QuickCam Fusion web camera's ($60 USD) built-in microphone, I interviewed Melbourne, Australia-based podcast publisher Cameron Reilly via Skype. We talked for about an hour, for free! If I had telephoned Cameron, on a business day without a special rate plan, my phone company would have charged me $7.22 *a minute*. Enough said.

AN INTERVIEW WITH CAMERON REILLY, THE PODCASTER NETWORK

Cameron Reilly started the first Australian podcast, G'day World, and the first Australian podcasting network, The Podcast Network, in November 2004. Currently, with 55 podcasts, The Podcast Network bills itself as the world's biggest publisher of independent podcast content, giving advertisers one company to do business with, associated podcasters technical and production support, and listeners a one-stop shop for professionally produced podcasts on a range of subjects from jazz to Tablet PCs.

Formerly with Microsoft Australia, Cameron and his partner Mick Stanic are based in Sydney, Australia.

Q. *I guess the place to start with is tell me about the podcast network and how this first Australian podcast directory and the first Australian podcast got started?*

A. Well, the first Australian podcast, which was G'Day World, started in November 2004. There was a chap called Phil Torrone, who back then was doing the Engadget podcast. I started listening to Phil's podcast, and Phil really inspired me. And he was always urging his listeners to stand up and fight for their rights. Anyway, I remember listening to Phil and just getting really excited, because it was the first time I'd ever heard anyone that sounded like me. Phil was intelligent, he was angry, he was a geek, he was passionate, he was a revolutionary, he was a rebel, and I thought, "Wow, that sounds like me! I could do that!" That's how I sound to myself inside my head.

I also thought that we could easily see how—I think at the time there were already a couple thousand podcasts in the world—we could easily see a day where there would be 500,000 podcasts. And I remember thinking that it was difficult already to find the blogs that I wanted to read, and how it would be increasingly difficult to find the podcasts that I wanted to listen to in a directory-style world. So we had this idea that we could create a network that only consisted of high-quality shows that we produced and had some management control over, that would hopefully become a destination site for podcast audiences.

And the third idea that we had was that advertisers, once they caught on to what was happening with podcasts, wouldn't want to deal with thousands of individual podcasters to put ads on their inventory. They'd want to deal with some sort of central buying process, acquisition process.

So with those three things in mind, we started The Podcast Network [TPN] in January of 2004, and we launched it on 14 February 2005. And at the time, it was the first podcasting business. So I guess we surprised a lot of people when we launched TPN. In a lot of ways, most people still hadn't heard of podcasting, and yet we'd seen a commercial opportunity and decided to throw ourselves into it and build a commercial model around podcasting. So that was how it began, man!

Q. *Is The Podcast Network making money?*

A. Yeah. It's not making a lot of money, but we've been making money for seven or eight months now. We run at a very low-cost structure, so it's not hard to make money, but we've had advertising on our shows now for at least six months, well, some of our shows. So, yeah, it's profitable.

Q. *So do you have other people besides the two of you who are the producers or the interviewees for each of these approximately 60 different shows or channels that you do, or do you guys do all those every week?*

A. No, all of the hosts that we have under TPN—we have about 55 hosts now—are the hosts and the producers, typically, of the show. I take the role, really, of executive producer. So we decide what shows we are going to let into the network. We get the people who are applying to the show to first do a pilot. We keep an eye on the quality of the show, both in terms of the content and quality and the technical quality. We set the guidelines and those sorts of things. But we have a range of people around the world now that are contracted to us to produce weekly shows on subjects that range from science to sports, lifestyle and health, and music and entertainment, religion . . . you name it.

Q. *How about the actual recording side of the business? In other words, any recommendations you'd have there for people who would want to start doing good-sounding podcasts?*

A. My recommendation to all of our people is to start light and start inexpensively—with a decent headset and microphone. By decent, I mean something that costs between $25 and $50. You can get a reasonable-quality recording these days. There are two, actually there are probably three, kinds of different scenarios that most of our shows are produced under. The most prominent, certainly in my case, is recording Skype calls. Most of my shows involve a cohost or a guest, and they usually are in a different part of the world from me. So we do them all over Skype. And there's a piece of software that I use called Skylook. It's produced by a small Australian firm. The URL is `http://skylook.biz`.

Q. *Really? Good, it's the one I'm using, as a matter of fact, right now.*

A. Well, there you go. It's produced by a couple of Melbourne boys, Paul and Jeremy. And when they came out with Skylook, it really made the whole process of recording a Skype call, for the first time, really easy and really smooth, and something that anybody could do. So we record under Skylook, and then I tend to post-produce in Adobe Audition.

The other piece of software that we recommend to Windows users is Audacity, which is a freeware audio-recording and editing tool. For Mac users there is, well, I think most Mac users use GarageBand [`www.apple.com/ilife/garageband`] these days. GarageBand has some pretty sophisticated podcast recording setups in it.

Q. *Well, that's the technical side of it. I guess a lot of people are going to wonder how do you find things to talk about? How do you find people to interview?*

A. That's sort of the easiest part of the job. My show—I do a number of shows on TPN—my main one, G'Day World, which is where most of the interviews go, has always been a show about things that I'm interested in and people I'm interested in. And I guess I meet people all the time in my daily life or on email. People introduce themselves to me through the course of running my business or running my life. I'm always meeting people that have very interesting views or experience in certain domains, and that's where a lot of my interviews come from. People will introduce them to me. I get emails all the time from people who say, "Hey, you should get this guy on the show." Or, "I know this guy who would be really good for you to talk to." And occasionally, I will deliberately reach out to people. Last year, I had Noam Chomsky as a guest on the show and Ray Kurzweil.

And those really came to me from me just reaching out and saying, "Would you be available to be interviewed on our show?" I just shoot them an email. I find that a lot of people are happy to come and be interviewed on a podcast. There's a growing awareness about what podcasting is out there today.

Q. *Where do you see the future of podcasting going?*

A. We are now in an era where there are really no barriers of entry for people to set up their own media business or to set up their own radio show or their own television show. We're now doing a number of video podcasts on TPN. It's relatively simple now to shoot an hour-long show and put it up on the Web for global distribution. Now it's very hard for us to understand the consequences of this. I fully expect that by the end of this decade, there will be a million shows, audio and/or video, that I can freely download onto my portable media player.

Q. *The problem I see is that with a million shows out there, how will anyone ever find what they are looking for? How will they even begin?*

A. Google! Today, if you jump into Google and you type what your favorite hobby is and the word "podcast," there's a good chance you're going to find a podcast about it. Now, hopefully you're going to find that podcast on TPN, but if you don't, you'll find it somewhere else. That's the best place to start, and I think that as mainstream audiences wake up to the idea of podcasting, as they get educated and they get advice, etc., Google will be one place to start. The big open directories. iTunes will be another place to start. Also, TPN will hopefully be another place to start. Once they want a place that only has high-quality shows, they'll start looking for destinations, lots of publishers like TPN. But Google is a great place to get started.

Q. *Do you think that we are going to see advertisements in podcasts as a way that these things will get funded, and people will make money? Or are they going to stay, hopefully, advertising-free?*

A. Well, we've already been running ads in our shows for six months, and I actually believe that most of us don't mind advertising as long as the advertising is relevant to the things that we're interested in. I'll give you an example: one of the shows on podcasting that we launched yesterday, the Digital Photography Show. If you're subscribing and listening to the Digital Photography Show, chances are that you are interested in digital photography. Now, if there are ads in that show that are promoting the latest digital cameras or the latest digital photography-editing software, or ads for books that are going to make you a better digital photographer, as long as those ads are short and sparse enough throughout the show, I don't think people are going to mind that.

Q. *It sounds like if you were going to give some advice to a new podcaster, passionate would be the first word you would say. Am I wrong in thinking that?*

A. No, you're not wrong at all. That has always been my criterion. This thing we are doing now we refer to as *citizen media*, and to me, the big differentiator between citizen media and traditional radio is the fact that the people that produce citizen media shows are people that are passionate about a subject and they're communicating that passion. Traditional media—your radio disk jockey or host—they may cover a range of subjects, but usually they are doing it as a journalist or as a professional commentator. They aren't the man in the street who's passionately excited about trains or llama breeding or whatever it is. To me, the passionate enthusiast is much more interesting to listen to than the professional commentator. I've always encouraged our hosts on TPN to conduct their shows like they're sitting down having a beer or having a coffee with a friend and discussing their favorite subject, because I've always really enjoyed listening to people who are really knowledgeable or passionate about a subject. Explain it to me; that's how I learn.

Fun with Postproduction

Congratulations! After a bit of practice and preparation, you've recorded the raw content for your first podcast. Now comes the un-fun part: postproduction.

Postproduction is a multistep process with the goal of creating a good sounding, well-playing podcast without spending the next two months of your life trying for the perfect audio production.

The most important point about postproduction, in my view, is that there are two big black holes that can suck up all the time you are willing to give them, with little to show for your extra efforts. Mark these hazards well:

- While you'll need to edit out all the pauses, uhs, and the like, you can go nuts trying to cut to the exact split second and agonizing over whether a pause in the conversation should be 2 seconds, 1.9 seconds, or 2.1 seconds.

- Once you have trimmed your content, you'll in all likelihood want to improve the audio quality and the sonic characteristics of your podcast to make for a clear, distinct, easy-to-listen-to podcast. The problem is you can descend into the world of equalization, noise gates, audio filters, normalization, and the rest and never be seen again. A little audio engineering will markedly improve your podcast; a lot will improve it only slightly more.

Before starting to edit your podcast, I suggest making a set of empty folders for each step in the process, then copying this set of folders as you need for a specific podcast. At each step, do a Save As to the next folder in line.

Each of the following steps is just a brief outline of what needs to be done. If podcasting turns out to be your thing, rest assured, you will be learning a lot more about postproduction as you continue down that road.

Edit down content. Removing pauses, uhs, and off-topic content makes for a better podcast. It's select-and-cut time in whatever audio-editing program you use (for example, Audacity or GarageBand). Hint: Cut from silence to silence, and remove any "dead air" longer than 3 seconds.

Clean up your audio. This is where you get into fun and time-consuming topics like notch filters and ambient noise reduction—or not. If you minimized background noise when you recorded, you got the input sound levels right. You can use your audio-editing application or a specialty program such as SoundSoap from Bias Inc. (www.bias-inc.com).

Add your music. Plug in your music tracks. Intro and outro music are fairly standard. You might also want to use music to transition to standard parts of your show, such as playing listener audio comments. Music "brands" your podcast, giving it a tone and pace. Your audio-editing program should support multiple tracks that later will be merged together into a single file. Hint: Keep a master file of your clean (both audio quality and copyright) standard audio tracks.

Master the MP3 file. At this point, the goal is to merge your tracks into one, adjust the volume of the podcast as a whole, and create the MP3 file. Hint: While MP3 can be produced at a wide range of sampling and bit rates, podcasts have standardized on stereo, with a sample rate of 22.050Hz and a bit rate of 64Kbps.

Tag and name your MP3 file. This is where you add text information describing your podcast, this particular episode, who you are, and all the rest, in the form of what's known as ID3 tags. You also give the file a podcast-friendly filename. If your audio-editing program does not support this, Apple iTunes (www.apple.com/itunes), a free download, can do it for you. Hint: Short entries fit better on MP3 players like an Apple iPod. Define and stick to a filenaming convention, such as podcast initials with date.

By now, you've got your first podcast "in the can" as the professionals would say. Next comes getting that podcast file out to the world.

Hosting Your Podcast

Before getting to how to get your podcast to the ears of the entire world, there's the matter of where your podcast files are going to reside. Podcast files are large—typically 1MB for every 2 minutes of airtime. Also, typically, the Internet service providers (ISPs) that host blogs and websites set a limit to how many megabytes your blog or website can transfer in the form of page views and podcast downloads per month. For example, Six Apart's TypePad Pro account ($14.95 a month) sets a limit of 10GB per month; after that, expect to be throttled back or have to pay more.

Now 10GB, 100GB, or 500GB sounds like a lot, and it is. But if your podcast becomes popular, and downloads or plays of each of your podcasts start climbing into the thousands, you may find yourself in trouble. Or suppose that one of your old podcasts that had maybe 100 downloads somehow gets to the front page of Digg, Slashdot, or one of the other social networks, and 10,000 people download it today. Then your bandwidth will vaporize.

If you've decided to have more of a permanent relationship than a fling with podcasting, start researching your alternatives and consider two possibilities for hosting your Podcasts: a podcasting-friendly ISP like Liberated Syndication (`http://libsyn.com`) or the Ourmedia project (`www.ourmedia.org`), shown in Figure 11-5. An outgrowth of the Internet Archive, which seeks to preserve digital artifacts such as websites for future generations, the Ourmedia project promises to store and serve your podcasts forever, if you agree to let others use your content to some degree, via a Creative Commons or similar license.

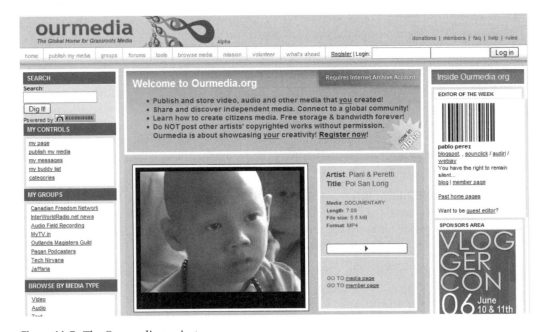

Figure 11-5. *The Ourmedia project*

Publicizing Your Podcast

Publicizing your podcast is very similar to how you get your blog known (covered in earlier chapters), with a couple of twists all its own. While you can rely on Google and the like to find and index your blog, podcasts, being audio files, tend to need a bit more of a push to get them out on the main street of the Internet.

At least right now, the better-known podcasting directories, like Podcasting Alley (www.podcastalley.com), Yahoo Podcasts (http://podcasts.yahoo.com), and Apple iTunes (http://apple.com/itunes), are eager for new podcasts, and they make it easy to submit your podcast to be listed. For example, Figure 11-6 shows the Apple iTunes podcast submission page.

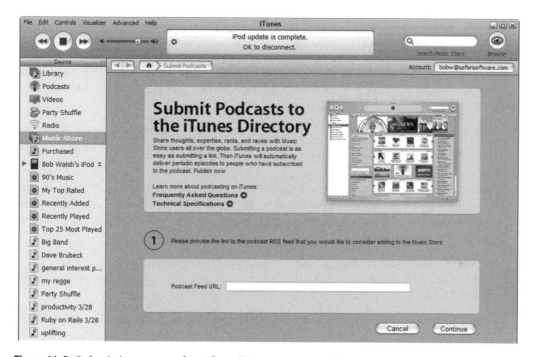

Figure 11-6. *Submitting your podcast from iTunes on your desktop*

In addition, one of the best ways to publicize your podcast is to blog about it. Nearly all good podcasts are part of blogs. Create a post for each episode and mention Internet addresses, production notes, interviewee biographies, or other items of interest.

That's a Wrap!

Well, that's our whirlwind tour of the mechanics and structure of podcasting. There's only one last point to cover: Did I mention that doing podcasts is a hell of a lot of fun? It is! That's why more and more people are turning from the "talking heads" of professional and commercial radio and television to listen to (and watch) the nonprofessionals who are excited about sharing their passions with the world.

Never underestimate the power of passion.

—Eve Sawyer, American journalist

Your Action Tasks

Here are a few steps for getting comfortable with podcasts:

Are podcasts for you? Download and install free Apple iTunes (`http://apple.com/itunes`) or just visit Yahoo Podcasts (`http://podcasts.yahoo.com`), search for something you are interested in, and listen to a few podcasts. If you can see (or hear) yourself doing the same thing about the subjects you blog on, keep going.

Accessorize. The bare minimum you need for a you-only podcast is your computer, Audacity (`http://audacity.sourceforge.net`), and a decent microphone like the Samson C01U USB Studio Condenser Mic (about $70 USD). If you are going to cohost a show or do interviews, get Skype (`http://skype.com`, free) and Skylook (`www.skylook.biz`, $24.95 to $49.95 USD) or a similar product.

What do you want to talk about? Make a list of the specific topics and the people you've read about, heard, or know who you want to interview. Look for topics that get you excited and interviewees who you would want to hear.

How do you want to talk about your topic? Put on your executive producer hat and start thinking about format, tone, and pace. Do you want to keep things loose and easy or march to a professional beat? Is your podcast fun and frolic or serious people being serious? It's your show, so you get to decide!

Get comfortable with yourself. Before anyone else knows, practice a bit with your new toys and get used to talking clearly, projecting your voice, asking questions, and generally the whole podcasting process.

Populate your green room. Start contacting the people who you want to interview. Until you've got a few dozen shows under your belt, aim midway down your list of interviewees, not for the stars. Being polite, keeping upbeat, and knowing what you want to talk about will win you those interviews.

Quiet on the set. Do a sound check just before you start recording your first podcast. Air conditioner or heater off: check. Phone ringer off: check. Cat has fresh food and water, and is sound asleep: check.

Have a conversation. Have your questions in hand, but have your attention focused on your guest. Don't be afraid to pull the conversation back to those questions, but sometimes the most interesting material is the tangents you take. Give and take, back and forth—those are what make for a good conversation and a good podcast.

Go postproduction lite. When you are putting together your podcast, cut what needs to be cut, mix in your legally clean music, do a bit of audio cleanup, adjust the volume, and stop there. Then have a friend listen to your podcast on her computer. Does it sound okay? If all lights are green, launch!

And here's where you get serious about having fun with podcasts.

Learn from others. Start listening to podcasts with an ear toward how they structure their shows. Then visit the blog or website home of these shows, and ask "How did you do that?" nicely. Most podcasters are happy to share their knowledge.

Make podcast checklists. Take the time to create and maintain three checklists—preshow, show, and postproduction—that cover all the large and small tasks you need to perform. They will make it much easier to concentrate on your content, questions, and guests.

Prepare for hard disk death. What happens if your computer's hard drive dies today? Do you have backup copies of your shows, music, working files, email, and all the rest? Or are you out of business?

Get the best mic you can afford. While you can do a lot in postproduction, nothing beats a really good microphone for improving sound quality. Of course, what's the best choice changes from day to day—time to do some research.

Interview the interviewers. Do what the talking heads do—interview other podcasters!

Create transcripts. Regularly creating a transcript for your podcast will do wonders for its findability on the Internet, your Google AdSense revenues, and your overall professionalism. You can type them yourself; figure at least 5 minutes of typing for every minute of show time. Or you can get with the times and use one of the podcasting transcription services like CastingWords (http://castingwords.com, 42 cents per minute) to make the pain go away.

Don't forget the links! Each time you blog about a new episode in your podcast, make it a point to include all URLs mentioned in the show. Don't forget to include products, books, and music mentioned (a good opportunity to make a little money via Amazon Associates, which we'll cover in the next chapter).

■■■

CHAPTER 12

Monetizing Your Blog for Fun and Profit

No man but a blockhead ever wrote, except for money.

—Samuel Johnson, English literary figure and author

One of the truly beautiful things about blogging is that you can make money with it—not pie in the sky, Nigerian email scam money, but honest, real money you take to the bank, except it has already been deposited there for you.

Thousands of people today make five- and even six-figure incomes from their blogs. Steve Pavlina's Personal Development for Smart People is one (www.stevepavlina.com/blog/2006/05/how-to-make-money-from-your-blog/), and Darren Rowse at ProBlogger is another (www.problogger.net/archives/2005/09/01/im-a-six-figure-blogger/). And more than a few of the Technorati top 100 blogs—like engadget.com, gizmodo.com, dailykos.com, and michellemalkin.com—have millions of readers and are full-scale businesses.

What percentage of bloggers make this kind of money? Damn few. One study (www.problogger.net/archives/2005/09/16/4-of-bloggers-generated-100000-in-12-month-period-study/) pegs the number at 4 percent, which sounds about right, especially since so many online trends follow a Long Tail[1] distribution curve. But—and pay attention, this is a key point—while only a small percentage of bloggers make "real" money blogging, *most* can make significant to respectful to nice money, depending on how popular and interesting their blogs are. It's all a matter of how many people read your blog, how much effort you put into your blog, and whether your readers feel you've given them value and they're prepared to reciprocate the favor.

In other words, if you were reading this chapter to find the secret incantation that will make a big wad of cash appear magically in your lap—sorry, no luck. But if you want to find ways to generate revenue proportionate to how much effort you put into making your blog interesting, popular, and respected, you are definitely in luck.

---

1. Back in October 2004, *Wired* magazine's editor in chief Chris Anderson wrote about the Long Tail—the idea that the Internet made it practical and *more profitable* to do commerce focused on all the non-blockbuster products rather than focusing on just the top few products. His book, *The Long Tail: Why the Future of Business Is Selling Less of More* (Hyperion, 2006), expands on the idea, and the Long Tail concept has been applied by many people to describe why and how certain online activities succeed. Get Chris's book, or see http://en.wikipedia.org/wiki/Long_Tail, for more information about this important concept.

In the pages ahead, we are going to cover a lot of different ways of monetizing your blog, divided into the following categories:

- **Sure things:** These are the few ways of making money with your blog that are so well-proven, so easy to do, and so open to bloggers of all sizes that they percolate to the top of the monetize your blog list every time: Google AdSense and Amazon Affiliates.

- **Affiliates:** Besides getting paid for when your readers click an advertisement, there is the revenue model of getting paid when someone actually buys something through you.

- **Advertising networks:** When your readership numbers get to a certain point, several hundred different companies besides Google want to put their ads on your blog.

- **Multiple streams:** Besides advertising in general, there are several other ways you can create multiple streams, or at least trickles of revenue heading your way.

- **Not a chance:** There is nothing like the lure of easy money to bring out scams, con artists, and the ethically challenged. There are some ways of monetizing your blog that, in my opinion, you should avoid like the avian flu.

Some Quick Thoughts and Jargon

Before we dive into ways to monetize your blog, here are four quick thoughts that apply to the rest of this chapter:

- There are plenty of very good reasons *not* to monetize your blog. Depending on what you blog about and how you blog, monetizing your blog could be a total mistake. For example, if you're blogging about your own business or services, having advertising about other people's products and services makes no sense whatsoever.

- In disagreement with Samuel Johnson's quote at the beginning of this chapter, there are other reasons to write than money. If money is not part of what makes you passionate about blogging, more power to you. We live in a world where every flat surface, including more than a few people's foreheads, is used to flog some product or another, and blogs without advertising tend to be more credible than blogs with too much advertising. Keep up the good work!

- While most of the methods described in this chapter will generate money even if you have ten readers, unless you want to be counting your quarterly revenue in pennies, your blog needs readers first, monetizing second. In my totally arbitrary judgment, put off reading this chapter until your site statistics and FeedBurner tell you your blog gets a thousand page views a month. In fact, ten thousand is a more realistic number for most advertisers, given the amount of overhead and work involved if you want to deal with pay-the-rent instead of buy-a-cappuccino type money.

- If the blogosphere evolves and changes quickly, the day-to-day realities of monetizing your blog start at that speed and then go faster. Between the time I wrote this chapter and the time you read it, new ways will have evolved, old players may have declined, and as the saying goes, your mileage may vary.

When you enter the world of blog advertising, the following are some terms[2] you need to know:

Page views: A single page viewed by one person.

Impression: A single ad served to a user's browser from your blog.

Clickthrough: Both the action of clicking an ad and the raw number of people who click a given advertisement during a given period.

Clickthrough rate (CTR): The number of clickthroughs divided by the number of impressions, multiplied by a hundred and expressed as a percentage. The typical CTR for banner ads according to Google is 0.05 percent; for text ads, it is 3.0 percent.

Conversion rate: The number of people who actually buy a product or service divided by all the times that ad was shown.

Cost-per-1000-impressions (CPM): What an advertiser pays to have a given ad seen by one thousand people, online or off. Numbers vary wildly, but in one comparison (`http://answers.google.com/answers/threadview?id=445860`), a half-page, black-and-white newspaper ad cost $23.32 CPM, compared to $0.98 CPM for a four-week-long online ad.[3]

Sure Bets

The undisputed top-dog, sure-bet way of monetizing your blog is Google AdSense. The other works-nearly-every-time way of monetizing your blog is Amazon Associates. In this section, we'll take a look at both from the point of view making them part of your blog.

Google AdSense

From single lines of text to full-classified-ad-like displays, Google ads are by far the most popular way to make money with your blog. Take a look at three typical Google AdSense ads in Figures 12-1, 12-2, and 12-3.

Figure 12-1. *Google AdSense above the Engadget masthead*

---

2. You'll find an excellent e-commerce glossary at `www.elearners.com/resources/advertising-glossary.asp` and another at `www.google.com/ads/glossary.html`.
3. Hence why newspaper revenue and newspapers in general are in such economic trouble.

Ads by Goooooogle
Photoshop Elements 5.0
$65.99, Premier Elements 3 - $55.99 Get both for $99.99 after rebates.
www.pcsoftware4u.com
SolutionSet
Internet Consulting Design, Development, Strategy
www.solutionset.com

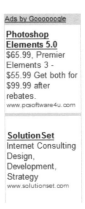

Figure 12-2. *Google ads in a blog's sidebar*

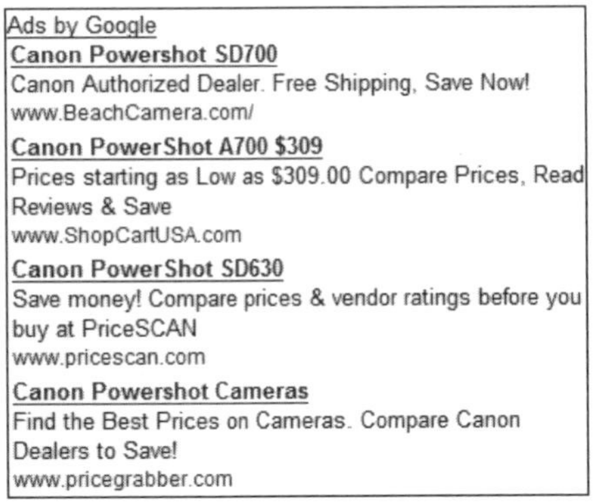

Ads by Google
Canon Powershot SD700
Canon Authorized Dealer. Free Shipping, Save Now!
www.BeachCamera.com/
Canon PowerShot A700 $309
Prices starting as Low as $309.00 Compare Prices, Read Reviews & Save
www.ShopCartUSA.com
Canon PowerShot SD630
Save money! Compare prices & vendor ratings before you buy at PriceSCAN
www.pricescan.com
Canon Powershot Cameras
Find the Best Prices on Cameras. Compare Canon Dealers to Save!
www.pricegrabber.com

Figure 12-3. *Google ads inserted beween posts*

How It Works

Google AdSense's large competitive advantage is that, like ads in the Google search results, ads relevant to the contents of your blog are served. If you happen to be posting about, say, what you can use your new Canon SD800 IS for at work, ads like those in Figure 12-3 are likely to appear.

Furthermore, Google maintains fairly strict editorial control over ads, ensuring your blog about family hiking doesn't get sex ads, for example. You can block ads from competing products and services, and customize the appearance of ads to match your site.

How to Get It

To get Google AdSense, you just need to complete a short application at `https://www.google.com/adsense/`. Google reviews and approves your blog. You insert HTML code that feeds in the ads, and you're in business.

Tips and Resources

Here are some ideas to help you succeed with Google AdSense:

Start with the Google AdSense Help Center. Google does an excellent job of explaining the ins, outs, and tricks of good AdSense inclusion on its help pages, starting at `https://www.google.com/adsense/support`.

Read Graywolf. Graywolf's blog on search engine optimization has a great post on AdSense at `www.wolf-howl.com/22/google-adsense-tips-tricks-and-secrets/`.

Visit the online collection of AdSense tips and tools. This site, at `www.quickonlinetips.com/archives/2006/07/google-adsense-tips-and-tools-collection`, has one of the most comprehensive lists of AdSense tips and suggestions on the Web. Be prepared to spend some time.

Get acquainted with others. One of the best AdSense-related forums I've found is `www.adsensechat.com`. I especially like the twin subtopics of good examples of AdSense use and requests from the community for site reviews.

Curl up with a good book. I recommend three very good books for people who want to do the full Monty with Google AdSense:

- *Make Easy Money with Google: Using the AdSense Advertising Program* by Eric Giguere (Peachpit Press, 2005) is a good introductory text. Skip it if you've digested the Google AdSense Help Center.

- I hope Brad Hill updates his *Building Your Business with Google for Dummies* (For Dummies, 2004). It's an excellent introduction to both AdSense and AdWords, but is beginning to show its age.

- Don't be put off by the "Da Vinci Code"–like cover or the "Make Money Now!" tone of *The AdSense Code: What Google Never Told You About Making Money with AdSense* (Morgan James, 2006) by Joel Comm. This is an extremely useful book for anyone who wants to really understand how to make AdSense, and blog ad monetization, work for you. Also see Joel's site at `www.joelcomm.com`.

Use Google (or another search engine). Like a lot of the online world, blogs and sites abound with ever-new information. Do both a blog and a website search for "Google AdSense tips" to find the latest techniques.

Amazon Associates

The concept of Amazon Associates is simple. People see something that Amazon sells on your blog. They click the text link, display ad, mini-Amazon store, or Ajax pop-out listing. They decide to buy that product or another. You make somewhere between 4 percent and 8.5 percent of the sales price.[4]

---

4. As of this writing, Amazon actually has two different referral commission plans going: Classic and Performance Plan. Go to `http://affiliate-program.amazon.com` and click Help, then Referral Fees for details.

On one hand, you can offer any number of Amazon's products. On the other hand, your readers can do business with a trusted online retailer.

How It Works

Amazon Associates works very well, as I can say from personal experience! Consider Figure 12-4.

Figure 12-4. *A typical Amazon Associates ad*

With ads like this,[5] I generated about $500 in referral fees in 2006 from my first book—not bad for incidental money.

Amazon Associates is a referral commission system, which means that you get paid only if someone buys. I personally think these links work best when your blog explains what the value of a given item is to your readers, then offers the opportunity to buy it from Amazon. In a way, your readers can reward your hard and comprehensive reviewing efforts by clicking the Amazon link.

How to Get It

Sign up at `http://affiliate-program.amazon.com`, where you'll be issued an Amazon Affiliates ID. The ID is the bit of data embedded in text and image links that accumulates your referral fees.

Once you've signed up, there are several ways to create both inline and display-like Amazon links. You can create ads like the one in Figure 12-4 in a variety of shapes and styles within the Amazon Associates portal. One new way of building Amazon Associates links I particularly like is the product preview, like that shown in Figure 12-5. As your reader's mouse moves over the link, the window pops up, and the user can order the item. It uses very little space on the page, since it's a text link, and feels like you are helping the reader.

---

5. My friend and fellow blogger Brian Plexico ran this ad at his `http://microisv.com` site. I prefer text ads, but I wanted to show a more typical Amazon ad placement.

Figure 12-5. *A sample product preview ad*

Tips and Resources

Here's some further advice for using Amazon Associates:

Experiment. Different Amazon Associate ads will mesh with your blog's layout and tone better than others, but you need to experiment a bit to find this out.

Don't overdo it. No one wants to read an overly commercialized blog. Err on the side of caution here.

Leverage the rest of Amazon. Let's say you've come up with a list of 12 gardening tools every gardener needs for your blog. Besides posting about it, you might decide to create a Amazon list of these products and add an Amazon aStore (essentially, a customized portal to Amazon where everything has your Amazon Associates tag built in) to your blog.

Use built-in tools to create links. TypePad, Vox, and WordPress have built-in tools that make it easy to build Amazon Associate links. Vox is especially good.

Use Amazoner. Programmer Roy Osherove offers Amazoner, a free Windows tool for creating Amazon Associate-enabled links on the fly. I've used it for several years now to build my links. Find it at `http://amazoner.osherove.com`.

AN INTERVIEW WITH DARREN ROWSE, PROBLOGGER

The good news is that Australian Darren Rowse has found the "magic mix" to making over $100,000 USD a year blogging, and wants to tell you how you can to at `http://Problogger.net` (note the `.net` domain; `.com` is *not* ProBlogger). The bad news is that it's going to take an enormous amount of hard work, perseverance, time measured in years not days, and perhaps a bit of luck to hit that magic number.

I caught up with Darren in his native Melbourne, Australia, via Skype and posed to him the following questions.

Q. *I guess the place to start is a little bit of background about yourself and how you started ProBlogger.*

A. I started blogging four years ago. Really, it was a personal blog, my first blog. We were starting a new church actually, and we were wanting to find information about how to do that and connect with others who were doing it around the world. And a friend put me on to a blog of a guy, a New Zealander who was living in Prague, who was writing a blog on the same topic. So I discovered this blog and got hooked right into the conversation—got hooked into the people, and the whole medium as well—and within a few hours had started my own blog.

Q. *That was back in 2002?*

A. Yeah, 2002. I think it was November 2002.

Q. *That makes you probably one of the first thousand bloggers out there.*

A. It was a much smaller medium back then. I guess I was impressed by the fact that there were quite a few people talking on that topic, which isn't really a mainstream topic. Blogging was at the beginning. I just started a cheap Blogspot blog straight away, and swapped out of that a few months later when I discovered some of the limitations of using that system, and set up a Movable Type blog with the help of a friend.

Q. *At that point, what were you doing for a living?*

A. I was a minister at a church . . . completely different.

Q. *Very different. What denomination?*

A. Baptist.

Q. *So that was 2002, and if I characterized where you were today as a full-time blogger who has stated several times that you're making income in excess of $100,000 a year American, would I be wrong?*

A. No, that's correct. Still above that figure.

Q. *Well, here's the simple, short question, but complex I guess: How did you go from there to here?*

A. It was a slow process. That personal blog, I had no intention of it ever earning income, but the job I was doing . . . I had a grant, and so I was employed part time and decreasingly so. The whole object of that job was to work myself out of a job, and so I was looking for other work at the time, and I accidentally started a blog one day on digital cameras.

It wasn't my intention for it to be a camera review site. It was more about the photos I was taking, but no one was interested in the photos; people were interested in the camera I was using. And so I began to review cameras and watch what was going on around the Web with cameras. And around that time, I discovered Google's AdSense program, which is their contextual advertising program.

And on a whim, I put that on that site one day, hoping it would cover my Internet costs and maybe replace my computer one day. And over the next few months, it kind of met those goals. I guess my entrepreneurial spirit came through, and I began to wonder what would happen if I had numerous sites and if I put more and more time into it, and it was a very gradual process. It probably took me a couple of years to get to a point where I thought it was time to go full time on it.

Q. *Sounds like there's definitely an accelerating curve here.*

A. Yes, there was an exponential sort of thing. The first six months, virtually it didn't seem like there was any increase. But there was 10 percent to 20 percent growth per month, which, when you're only earning $4 or $5 a month, it's not much. But once you get past that curve, it takes off.

Q. *How many blogs do you have presently?*

A. I actively write these days on about five. At my peak, I had about twenty. My strategy was to start picking different topics and to pick the ones that really took off and worked, and to concentrate on those.

Q. *Can you give a one-sentence summary of each of those five blogs you have now? I'm familiar with ProBlogger, but not the others.*

A. ProBlogger is a blog on how we bloggers make money. My digital photography blog [at www. livingroom.org.au/photolog/] is a blog on cameras and reviews and industry news. Digital photography school is another blog, which is more on tips for cameras, so it relates to the other one, but is basically for beginners just starting out with their cameras, and that's what I'm putting a lot of my time into at the moment. Then I have another couple of blogs that I've got someone else writing for me: one on camera phones and one on printers. And then I'm also involved in a network of blogs called b5media [at www.b5media.com], which has 150 blogs. I don't write on them.

Q. *What's your involvement with b5 and how did that come about?*

A. Officially, we launched a year ago. A few months before that, five of us just began talking one day by email about how we could blog together and how we could support one another, and the conversation led us to start a network of blogs. We started with three of us actually taking up the offer: Duncan Riley from Western Australia, Jeremy Wright from Canada, and myself. And a few months later, Shai Coggins, who is also an Australian, brought her network of blogs about weblogs into the network, and we merged them together. So it was again a fairly slow, but a bit quicker process than my previous experience with blogging. It has gradually grown over the last little while, and we have just taken on some funding, some investment from Canada.

ProBlogger—Early Days

Q. *How did ProBlogger get started?*

A. On my first-ever personal blog, I did write from time to time about blogging. And as I learned how to make money from it, I was increasingly writing on that. Unfortunately, that blog was also on spirituality, and my personal life, and all kinds of things, and my readers began to complain that I was mixing up too many topics. So I thought it was probably best to move all that content across onto a blog that was specifically about making money from blogging, and ProBlogger was born. I think it was about two years ago.

Q. *Well, I guess two things come to mind. First off, how many people in a month read ProBlogger according to your RSS stats and your web stats?*

A. My RSS stats, I'm just looking at it now, says 8,541 readers.

Q. *How about web traffic?*

A. Web traffic is averaging on my site slightly under 7,000 a day at unique readers. I think last month it was about 120,000 readers.

Q. *Wow! I guess the other thing that I sort of pull out from what you said a moment ago was that as your audience grows, you found that it made sense to specialize blogs into sort of one blog for this, one blog for that. Do you think that is one of the absolute things that a full-time blogger really needs to do?*

A. I think you can make it work with a blog that has multiple topics. But if you analyze the blogs that are most successful, and particularly ones obviously on doing this as a profession for an income, if you are wanting to make an income, it makes a lot of sense to specialize for a number of reasons. Firstly, it is easier to monetize traffic that is all looking for one particular topic. Advertisers are much more willing to put an ad on your site if it is only about what they are advertising. It also helps you with search engine optimization and getting ranked in the search engines.

I found the more topics I wrote about on my personal blog, the fewer people I found who shared my exact interests. I had plenty of people who were interested in one of the things I was writing about, but very few who were interested in the ten things I was writing about on my site. And so, it kind of made sense. Also there were a few people who complained when I split it up into a number of blogs, but the majority went, "Great—at last."

Q. *When you go from no ads to some ads in your blog, what should you do as far as alerting your readership that that's going on, so that they don't take umbrage at it? How do you avoid outraging your readership if you decide to monetize your blog?*

A. I have done a couple of things. On my blog, I announced it and explained that I needed to do it to support the ongoing work of that blog, and people responded quite well to that. On another blog, I just did it and didn't announce it, and had no comments. I think it probably depends on your audience—how cynical, how tech-savvy they are, how politically minded. It probably depends a little bit on your readership and you know whether there is a possibility of a backlash from doing it.

I wouldn't do anything in a big way all of a sudden. I would want to increase it slowly. Another way is to do it when you do a design change of your blog, so you are making changes anyway. People are excited about the changes, and there is also an ad in that change, and so that might be a good time to do it as well.

The Secret to His Success

Q. *OK, this is an unfair question, but what's the secret of your success?*

A. I would say I am lucky. That is part of it. I was in the right place at the right time. It was easier when I started to, I guess, get a foothold. But having said that, it has been something that I really stuck at, and in those early days, I didn't really see much of a rise in traffic or income. But I guess I took a real long-term view of it. It's been four years of blogging every day. I had a goal at one point of writing 20 or 30 posts a day. So it was a lot of work. It wasn't something quick and easy. I would say working hard and working long.

Q. *So when you say full-time job, you mean full-time job?*

A. Oh yeah, for sure. I'm working much longer hours than I ever worked before.

Q. *What happens if you want to take a vacation?*

A. I have done a number of things on my vacations. Occasionally, I take the blogs with me and have done a little work at Internet cafes. Generally these days, I find a guest blogger for some of my blogs, and others I will write seven posts for the week and set them to go off at midnight every day.

Q. *What would you say would be the three things that a blogger who has a, let's say, 500 FeedBurner stat? Where do they start with monetizing a blog today?*

A. It depends on the topic. You really need to be careful about the type of advertising or the type of affiliate program that you run on a blog. I've got my product-based blog, say, my digital camera blog. I find that that monetizes very well with a program called Chitika, and they have an ad unit called eMiniMalls. And it converts very well, because their ads are very much product-related ads. Chitika doesn't work at all on ProBlogger because ProBlogger is not about products. So you really want to be thinking about what's a logical extension. What would people click on? What would people be interested in buying that's related to the topic I am writing on? So it is about matching your blog, your topic, with an appropriate monetization strategy. So that would be the first thing.

In terms of pricing your ads, one of the biggest mistakes I see people doing is putting their ads below the fold, or putting them below that line where you can't see anything below it when you first come to a site. So it's like any advertising. If you want to have success with a billboard, you don't put it on a back road that goes nowhere. You put it on a highway. And so you want to place the ads on your site where people will look naturally, and that it is above the fold.

Generally we are finding these days that if you put ads near or in your content, that works a lot better than having them, say, over on the sidebar where no one looks. It's about experimenting, too, I guess, and seeing what works. A lot of the advertising programs like AdSense and Chitika allow you to track which ads on your site are working and which ones aren't.

So you really want to look at those statistics and track what works, and then tweak things as you go. There are a lot of little things about how you design your ads to make them blend into your site. That seems to work better than having big, loud ads that flash or are bright red. You don't want to go for that. You want to go for something that is a lot more blended into your site as well.

Q. *I know this is another one of those unfair questions. Let's say you have 500 readers pulling down FeedBurner's RSS just kind of as a general indication of how you are doing. Let's say approximately the same number of people or same number of unique visitors a day. If you do things right with Google AdSense or perhaps with Chitika eMiniMalls, if you were running more of a product blog, what sort of money could you actually be making sort of as a beginner monetizer?*

A. It is a bit of a cop-out to say, but it varies so much between blogs. For instance, on ProBlogger, if I had the same amount of traffic on that as the digital camera site, my digital camera site would make a lot more, again, because it is product-related. There are things that people could buy, and advertisers are willing to pay more for those ads. So with AdSense, the topic that you are advertising, different clicks pay different amounts of money. So I am kind of hesitant to answer the question because it could be anything from $2 a day up to $30 a day if it were a high-paying ad.

Q. *But if you were trying to explain this to, well let's say your brother-in-law, and he said, "Are we talking about pencil money? Are we talking about Ferrari money?" What should they reasonably expect so they have some sense if they are doing very well or not well at all?*

A. I find it hard to come up with an answer there. I would think with 500 unique visitors to your blog every day, you probably would not be earning much more than coffee money. Which is all that a lot of people want. Again, if you've got a good specialized topic, you might actually be at more like $20 or $30 a day. I know of one blog that is on a very specialized topic. I am not allowed to even say what it is because the blogger doesn't want competition. He's on about 400 visitors a day. He is earning $30 a day. He has designed his site in such a way that the ads work well. He hasn't given his readers anything else to click on that site at all. It's just ads and good-quality content.

Advice to Bloggers

Q. *What are the three mistakes that people often make that you've seen when it comes to monetizing or trying to monetize their blog?*

A. Irrelevant ads. I see a lot of people putting up ads for iPods on their political blogs or their religious blogs. I don't see why anyone would click on those ads. I'm sure people are interested in iPods or plasma televisions, but the chances of someone clicking on that ad are pretty low. If you have a religious blog, put up some books that relate to your topic. If you have a political blog, try to find some books or a newspaper or something like that that might relate to your topic—relevancy.

Again, the position of your ads. I don't know why people think the bottom of page is the best spot for their ad. Sure sometimes people do scroll down that far, but if you have a choice between the bottom and the top, put it up on top.

And probably the other one would be just the design. I think the blending of ads is what people are using quite successfully. It has been proven that blended ads work better. These days, people are moving to integrated ads, so they are actually starting to integrate the ads into the design of the site using borders and using pictures. It is hard to describe what they are doing, but they are putting borders around their AdSense ads and making them blend and integrate right into the design of their site, which is something that I've started seeing Google accepting more and more. You have to be a bit careful about it. They have got some rules about what you can and can't do with the ads. That's what we will see over the next six months or so is people integrating their ads a little bit more.

Q. *What do you see as the future of blogging?*

A. I think what we are seeing at the moment is some interesting experimentation around blogging with media with video, audio—more of a multimedia-type experience. There have been a few reasonably high-profile bloggers who are moving into that space. So that would be interesting to watch.

The increase of people coming to blog networks. I know at b5, we have just been inundated with people wanting to join the network. I guess that is part of the realization that it is a cluttered space now. There are something like 15 million blogs out there, so how do you raise yourself up above that in terms of finding traffic? One of the things people are doing increasingly is clustering together to support one another in that. That's happening in formal ways, but also as well in informal ways such as a blog network. I suspect we will see more and more of that type of people banding together in collectives and networks to work with one another. I guess also there are lots of possibilities, once you do that, to repackage that content in an interesting way in matching that content up as well. And I think we will see people doing that more and more over the next probably 12 to 18 months.

Q. *I see. OK, I think that does it for me. Thank you so much.*

A. No problem.

Affiliate Networks

The next major zone of monetization for blogs is affiliate networks. The basics of affiliate networks for blogs are simple. Find a network that you like and sign up. Pick the products the network sells that you want to embed in your blog. Collect commissions when and if your readers become their buyers. Amazon Associates is an affiliate network.

As more and more companies realize that the Internet abounds with "amateur salespeople," that the Internet can automate the entire process (post, measure, and pay affiliates), and that paying anywhere from 10 percent to 70 percent commission on a sale is more efficient than shoveling money down the mainstream media advertising rathole, expect to see more affiliate networks and more kinds of goods and services enter this channel.

Beyond the basics, you're going to need to either plan to spend considerable time "shopping" for the right affiliated products to carry or let the network decide what's going on your site.

Before we have a quick look at three leading affiliate networks, here are a few pointers to keep in mind:

Relevance is the key. Let's say that you have a blog where you review Windows desktop software for small business. Setting up shop as an affiliate with Digital River's oneNetwork—a network for software products—makes sense. That's the first level of relevance. Let's also say you happen to have switched to Webroot Spy Sweeper—a popular Windows anti-spyware program—and you want to blog about your experience. It just so happens that Webroot is a member of Digital River's oneNetwork, and if that company accepts your site, it is prepared to pay you up to 50 percent of each sale initiated from your blog.

Too much is too much. As with all forms of advertising, adding too many affiliate network product links will erode your credibility with your readers. As with every form of media—mainstream or Internet—you need to find the right balance between content and advertising.

Beware of make-money-now networks. For every reputable, legitimate, trustworthy, and professional affiliate network out there, you'll find at least ten "networks" that are somewhere between shady and outright criminal. Do your due diligence! At the very least, Google any affiliate network (both for websites and blog search results) before signing up.

Digital River's OneNetwork

Digital River's oneNetwork is a well-respected affiliate program for software vendors who typically sell their products online through Digital River e-commerce services (see Figure 12-6).

While I have not used oneNetwork, Digital River has a very good reputation among micro-ISVs (small software startups), and I would recommend it to anyone whose blog focuses more on the online than offline world.

Figure 12-6. *Digital River's oneNetwork*

How It Works

Once you sign up with oneNetwork, you pick the "campaigns" in which you wish to participate. A campaign could be a single product offered by a company or everything that company sells. Joining most campaigns on oneNetwork requires that the advertiser approve your site. As of this writing, oneNetwork listed 41 campaigns, with more being added weekly. Commissions ranged from 12 percent to 70 percent. Certain campaigns also paid for clicks and leads as well.

After you successfully join one or more campaigns, you can cede a part of your blog to a rotating banner that will cycle through each of your selected campaigns as readers visit, or you can, on a campaign-by-campaign basis, select HTML that will display the advertiser's advertising.

How to Get It

Go to https://affiliates.digitalriver.com/partners/ and apply to join oneNetwork.

Tips and Resources

Here are some tips for using oneNetwork:

- **Offer your advertiser's coupons.** About half of oneNetwork's advertisers offer coupons you can run on your blog. Everyone likes to save a little money.

- **Track your stats.** Put aside time to use oneNetwork's tracking and customizing tools, which let you test and measure which advertisers' ads work best on your blog.

- **Don't go overboard.** Remember that every time a reader sees an affiliate ad on your site, you are, in effect, recommending that product. Be selective.

Commission Junction

Commission Junction (CJ) is probably the largest single affiliate network on the Net today, and that's both its strength and weakness. On one hand, you can find all sorts of products and services that are relevant or at least complementary to your blog. On the other hand, more than a few bloggers I respect have complained that searching for the right product and getting approved by the advertiser to sell it can be painfully slow.

How It Works

Once you've completed the automated application process, you can search through the CJ Marketplace of CJ's many advertisers by subject, kind of commission program, or name. For example, under Computers ➤ Software, there were 92 different advertising programs available as of this writing.

Once you find advertisers, you're likely to have to wait some number of days—sometimes weeks—for them to review and approve your site before you can start running their text, banner, or image ads on your blog.

How to Get It

After completing a form at `https://signup.cj.com/member/publisherSignUp.do`, you'll be emailed your login information and a tax form to sign and send back. Once you log in, you can start browsing available affiliate programs that range from cosmetics to watersports and just about everything in between.

Tips and Resources

Once you've opened your CJ account, you can get access to CJU Online, as shown in Figure 12-7. This is a nicely done set of Flash tutorials covering both the basics and more advanced ins and outs of selling with CJ. Look for the link to CJU Online in the upper-right area of each screen.

Figure 12-7. *CJU Online*

More Affiliate Networks

Commission Junction, oneNetwork, and Amazon Affiliates are only three of the thousands[6] of affiliate networks out there. Here's a quick rundown of several others that at least a few bloggers swear by:

- Performics (http://performics.com), part of the DoubleClick family of companies, offers excellent commissions if your blog makes the cut.

- ClickBank (www.clickbank.com) sells all sorts of digital products, and has gems among a clutter of "make money now" ebooks.

- LinkShare (www.linkshare.com) has been in business since 1996, and was acquired by the Japanese e-commerce portal Rakuten in 2005.

Advertising Networks

While Google AdSense reigns supreme, it is by no means the only advertising network of interest to bloggers who want to make money.

---

6. AffiliateDirectory.com (www.associateprograms.com/directory/) lists no less than 9,139 affiliate programs as of this writing.

From a blogger's point of view, advertising networks fall into two categories: those you can join, and those who decide whether your blog is interesting enough, professional enough, and above all else, popular enough to be a good outlet for their ads. We'll go though a quick rundown of some of the former first, then turn to how you might be able to get the attention of one or more of the premium ad networks.

Chitika eMiniMalls

Going beyond static ads, Chitika eMiniMalls are interactive selling kiosks that live within your blog, selling your choice of products, as shown in Figure 12-8. Chitika's other advertising pipeline is Chitika ShopLincs, which lets you build full-page online stores of your choice of products. For obvious reasons, Chitika eMiniMalls and ShopLines work best for bloggers who are talking about, well, products. Again, relevancy is king when it comes to monetizing your blog.

Figure 12-8. *A Chitika eMiniMall*

How It Works

Chitika automatically scans your blog page where its eMiniMall resides to serve up relevant ads that you can limit by country or category. This combination of Chitika doing the hard work of finding relevant ads and you deciding what kinds of things you want to sell is powerfully attracting to bloggers. But keep in mind that Chitika will review your blog and is presently interested in English-language blogs with more than 10,000 page views.

How to Get It

Apply at `https://chitika.com/mm_overview.php`. Once you're accepted, pick from the 15 different formats, select your categories, specify countries to include, and you're off to the races.

Tips and Resources

Darren Rowse has a wealth of excellent posts on Chitika at ProBlogger. Start at `www.problogger.net/archives/category/chitika-eminimalls/` and go from there.

Text Link Ads

Text Link Ads (TLA) is essentially an ad broker. It signs up bloggers who commit to making space available on their blog and advertisers who want to place text link ads in that space. TLA keeps half of what advertisers pay for the space; you get the rest.

Several things make TLA an attractive monetizing choice for bloggers:

- You can approve or deny any ad from running on your blog.

- TLA makes it extremely easy for advertisers to find relevant blogs for their ads—doing a lot of the work for you, the blogger.

- TLA ads can happily coexist with other contextual ad systems, such as Google AdSense, because TLA ads aren't contextual. You're selling space, not keywords.[7]

- TLA has a very cool link-worth calculator at `www.text-link-ads.com/link_calculator.php`, as shown in Figure 12-9. It gives you a good idea of what space on your blog is worth, at least to TLA.

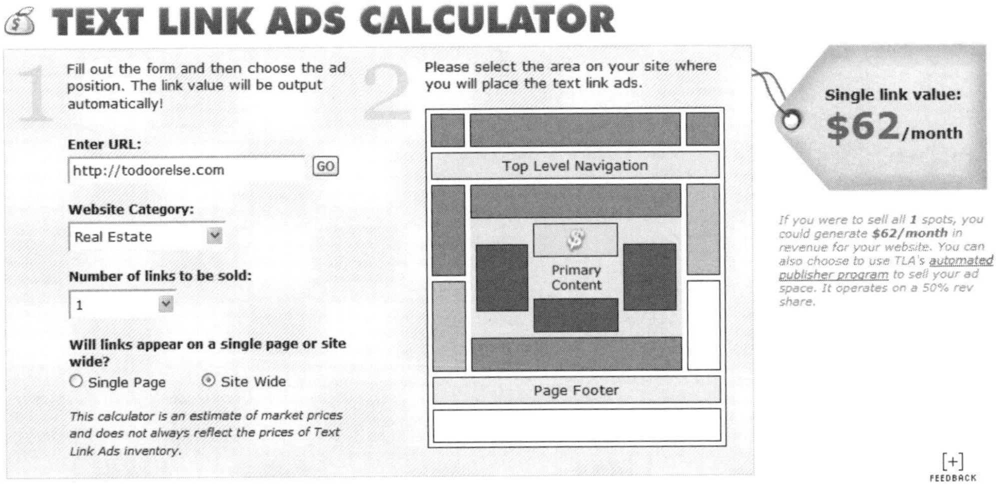

Figure 12-9. *TLA's calculator*

How It Works

Advertisers visit TLA, shop for blogs by category, and buy ads. As a TLA publisher, you approve or reject new ads. TLA handles both sides of the accounting. It pays on the first of every month via PayPal or check (minimum payout, $25 USD).

How to Get It

Submit your site to TLA to become a publisher at `https://www.text-link-ads.com/publisher_signup.php`. Activate your account when you get the TLA email confirmation. Then design your link code, as shown in Figure 12-10, and insert your code into your blog.[8] You can then either let TLA approve ads for you or have TLA email you, giving you 24 hours to blackball an ad.

---

7. At least according to TLA. See `www.text-link-ads.com/publisher_program.php`.
8. TLA supports a wide variety of blogging engines that you install on a server you control, including WordPress, Movable Type, Drupal, and Ruby on Rails However, it does *not support* TypePad, the hosted version of WordPress, Blogger, or other hosted blog sites as of this writing.

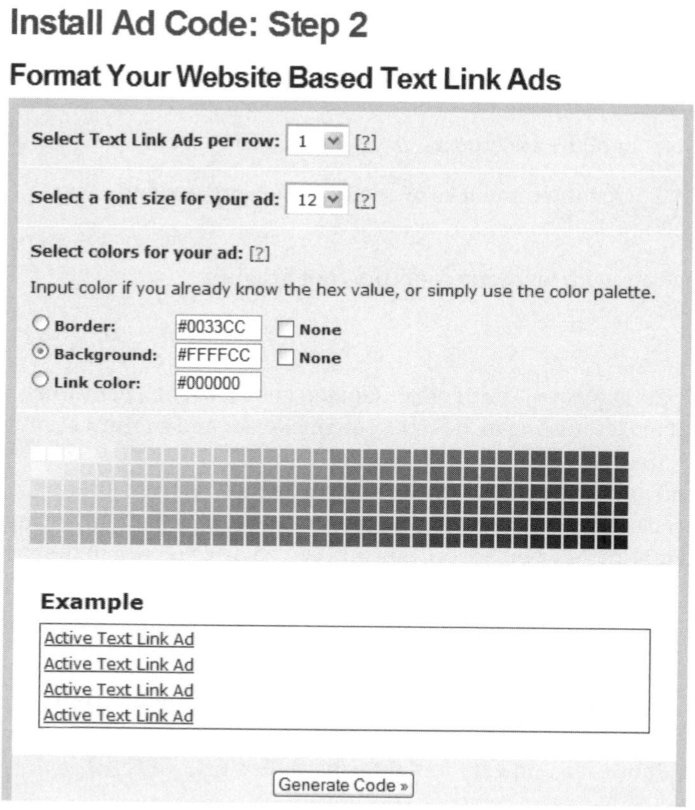

Install Ad Code: Step 2

Format Your Website Based Text Link Ads

Figure 12-10. *Designing your TLA space*

Tips and Resources

Here are some tips for using TLA:

- **Get to know TLA's categories.** Be sure to take a look at TLA from an advertiser's point of view. Look for blogs similar to yours, and get a sense of your competition.

- **Pay attention to how other advertisers describe their blogs.** For example, which do you think will attract more advertiser attention and therefore dollars: "Site-wide link on a fast-growing blog devoted to home-based business" or "A blog about home-based business"?

- **Alexa rank matters.** A key metric used by TLA advertisers is your Alexa rank. A quick Google search using "improve Alexa rankings" will get you a lot of information about this topic, and a lot of links to unscrupulous services and outright scams.

Performancing Partners

Performancing Partners is an offshoot of Nick Wilson, Patrick Gaven (cofounder of TLA), and Chris Garrett's Performancing (an online community for and of professional bloggers).

How It Works

Performancing Partners works much like TLA, with advertisers buying space in your blog, with three twists:

- Blog publishers get 70 percent of the advertisers' payments for ads.

- Blog publishers can earn 5 percent referral fees by recruiting advertisers and other publishers.

- Advertisements are image ads with JavaScript pop-ups, not text links.

How to Get It

Join Performancing at `http://performancing.com`. Performancing has excellent, spam-free forums, a Firefox extension that makes posting to most blog engines easy, and a robust metrics tool for measuring your page views and more.

Then list your blog in the ad network, specifying how many ad spaces you are offering. Insert the provided HTML code near the top of your blog. Set a price per ad, or let Performancing do it for you. Approve or reject ads if and when advertisers find your blog attractive in the Performancing ad directory.

Tips and Resources

A central part of Performancing, the forums are an excellent way to learn the ins and outs of Performancing Partners. You'll also find great tips and techniques on all blogging topics from bloggers who have been there, done that, and got more than just a tee shirt.

RSS Ads

As RSS feeds become more popular, more than a few companies are capitalizing on the opportunity to offer feeds adulterated with advertising. The jury is still very much out whether this brand-new advertising medium will be accepted or go the way of toilet paper display ads.[9]

If you decide to go this route, three companies are currently doing good and fair business in this space:

- FeedBurner gives you your choice of types of ads to include: Google AdSense (if you are already doing that), Amazon Associates, or if you have more than 500 FeedBurner subscribers, FeedBurner ads. Ad revenue is presently split 65/35 (65 percent to you and 35 percent to FeedBurner).

- Feedvertising is an extension of TLA text link ads into RSS. Revenue is split 50/50, but is currently available only to WordPress bloggers.

- Pheedo has the distinction of being the oldest of the RSS advertising networks. It splits revenue with you 65/35. It works with TypePad (Pro subscription) and other blogging engines.

---

9. "After all, we'll have a captive audience!" advertisers cried. If it sounds like I'm one of those pseudo-intellectual anarchist types who somehow disbelieve in the sacred right of advertisers to adorn every surface found on earth with their commercial messages, you're right.

How It Works

Each of these services creates or modifies an RSS feed from your blog, inserting their advertising. When and if readers click ads in their RSS readers, you make money.

How to Get It

Apply at each site:

- FeedBurner at `www.feedburner.com`

- TLA's Feedvertising at `www.text-link-ads.com/feedvertising`

- Pheedo at `www.pheedo.com/publishers`

Tips and Resources

Here are two tips and three online resources for using RSS ads:

- **Take your review responsibilities seriously.** As with other ad networks, it's up to you to keep inappropriate/low-paying ads out of your feed and off your blog's pages. This means you will be spending time, an investment you may be losing money on.

- **Keep in mind that many of your RSS readers *hate* ads.** One of the two reasons most people use RSS feeds is to avoid being advertised to death. (The other is convenience.) Think long and hard as to whether squeezing the last drop of revenue from your blog is really worth it.

- **Consider RSS from a marketing perspective.** Clickz Network's Heidi Cohen has a good summary article of what RSS looks like from a general online marketing perspective at `www.clickz.com/showPage.html?page=3623776`.

- **Check in with ProBlogger.** Darren Rowse has a good roundup of RSS advertising as of October 2006 at `www.problogger.net/archives/2006/10/21/rss-advertising-options`.

- **Read what the advertisers are reading.** Pheedo (`www.pheedo.com`) handles placing ads in the RSS feeds of over 8,000 blogs and websites. The Pheedo folks know a thing or two about it and share their info at their blog, `www.pheedo.info`.

Other Ad Networks

Like affiliates networks, a lot of ad networks are out there. Here are three more worth a look:

- AdBrite (`www.adbrite.com/mb/publisher_landing_page.php`) sells both text image and pop-up inline ads to advertisers.

- Yahoo Publisher Network (`http://publisher.yahoo.com`) is a late arrival to Google's AdSense party.

- Microsoft AdCenter (`https://adcenter.microsoft.com`) currently is all about selling ads in Windows Live Search results today, but maybe it will be soliciting bloggers someday soon.

- BlogHerAds (`http://blogherads.com`) is an ad network of women bloggers and advertisers seeking to target women blog readers. It's among the first targeted blogging ad networks, but unlikely to be the last.

By Invitation Only

As I said earlier in this chapter, there are blog ad networks you can apply to and join in minutes, and then there are ad networks who pick and choose who they want in. These networks tend to go after the heavy-hitters in the blogosphere. To get their attention, your blog needs to be read by a lot of people each month—500,000 page views is a good starting point.

How you get into these invitation-only networks is a little like asking how you get a loan from a bank—be in a position where you don't need a loan from a bank. In other words, these ad networks will more than likely find you if you've transcended to the upper reaches of the blogosphere and risen far above where this one book can take you.

That said, it doesn't hurt to know who some of the players are and how to get in touch with them.

- Blogads (www.blogads.com/publisher_html) is one of the oldest and most successful ad networks, and claims its participating bloggers average $50 a month, with some making $5,000 a month. How to get in: Be sponsored by a Blogads member or make your pitch at sellers@blogads.com.

- Federated Media (www.federatedmedia.net), begun by John Battelle, founder of *Wired* magazine, boasts a bevy of major bloggers arrayed into "federations" like boingboing.com. How to get in: Make your pitch at www.federatedmedia.net/authors/mores or wait for the phone to ring.

- Glam (www.glam.com) claims 7 million visitors a month to its retinue of fashion and style blogs. If your blog lives in this world and is getting known, stop by www.glam.com/g/p/48513427/48674213/77/48674213/.

- Gorilla Nation Media (www.gorillanation.com) exclusively represents 250 or so influential, well-read bloggers, primarily writing on film, television, DVD, comic books, and games. If you want to go this route, and you're getting more than 500,000 page views a month, throw your hat in their ring at www.gorillanation.com/solutions_pub_signingup.htm.

Multiple Streams

In case you're wondering if ad and affiliate networks are the be-all and end-all of making money from your blog, here's a potpourri of other ways to legitimately monetize your blog:

Get ads yourself. Direct advertising sponsorship is an excellent way of monetizing your blog by cutting out the middlemen. This could work if you have the time, diligence, and knack for directly soliciting ads from businesses and companies that complement your blogger interests and readership.

Start selling your own goods. Got a catchy tagline, a good logo, and passionate readers? Help them accessorize with custom tee shirts, hats, and coffee cups. The best-known company online for this is CafePress.com, with its 2.5 million members and its ability to produce custom items from your choice of more than 80 products.

Ask for donations. Be it TypePad's Tip Jar (see TypePad's Knowledge Base), PayPal Donations (`www.paypal.com/cgi-bin/webscr?cmd=p/xcl/rec/donate-intro-outside`), or Amazon's Honor System (`http://zme.amazon.com/exec/varzea/subst/fx/home.html`), consider asking your readers for donations, especially if you are not running ads.

Get sponsored by mainstream media. Some newspapers, television stations, and other traditional media outlets are taking the "if you can't beat them, hire them" approach to bloggers. If you think your blog will interest big-name media outlets, contact them. For example, you can try to get on the *Washington Post*'s blogroll by applying at `http://blogroll.adify.com/Apply.aspx`.

Join a blog network. Blog networks are just that—a group of bloggers who join together, cross-promote, share advertising revenue, and expand their influence. I'll have a lot more to say about blog networks in the next chapter. For now, consider that as of this writing, `www.blognetworklist.com/`, a compendium that tracks blog networks, lists 80 networks consisting of 1,823 blogs.

Not a Chance!

When it comes to making money online, besides all the decent, honest, upright, and legitimate means, you'll find a plague of indecent, dishonest, and illegitimate scams, cons, and tricks out there. Don't be fooled, and don't fool with your readers. Here are some tips to help you separate the gold from the fool's gold when it comes to monetizing your blog:

- **There are no secrets.** You read about this expert or that expert who has, through mysterious means, discovered the hidden secret to mega-energizing your Google AdSense earnings, advertising revenue, or attractiveness to the opposite or same sex, and that secret can be yours for a mere $197.50 or $1,990.95. Take a big breath, hide your credit card, and consider: If they know this alleged secret, why would they sell it?

- **There are people you can learn from.** Be they stodgy book writers like yours truly, reputable experts like Darren Rowse and Danny Sullivan, or your fellow bloggers, there are people who can and will help you make real money via your blog. But be prepared to spend some time, invest some effort, and keep a skeptical attitude.

- **If it sounds too good to be true, it probably is.** It used to be said, "Trust, but verify." Nowadays, that saying should read "Trust, but Google." Online dirt lasts a very long time. Before doing business with someone you are trusting with at least part of the fate of your blog, check them out online.

- **The only way to double your money.** Is to fold it in half and put it back in your pocket. Scammers and con artists are experts all right—at disconnecting your credibility and rational thought. Before jumping into some grand new venture, look twice, pause, let it sit for a day (or a week or a month), and then reconsider.

Your Action Tasks

Here are some steps for getting started monetizing your blog:

Pick and choose. As you've seen in this chapter, there are plenty of ways of monetizing your blog. Consider carefully before picking text link, contextual, image, or product-specific advertising to add to your mix. Take a look at other blogs like yours. Consider what has worked for them and which went one ad too far. The right advertising strategy delivers at worst inoffensive and at best useful ads to your blog's readers. Take your time and consider all alternatives.

Align ads with content, *not* **the reverse.** Your readers will smell a rat a mile away if your blog's content begins to come across like an "advertorial." They've had plenty of practice sniffing this out as mainstream media consumers. Don't go there.

Build readership, then monetize. This has been the process for every monetarily successful blogger I've interviewed or know. Focus first on building your audience, then when you inevitably redesign your blog's layout, gradually monetize if you are going to run ads.

Keep an eye on your return on investment. Monetizing your blog takes time, and time is money. If you're spending more time than you're making money, and the prospects are for more of the same, it's time to readjust your blogging strategy.

And then you can continue with these steps:

Read ProBlogger. I really do think `http://problogger.net` needs to be on your daily must-read list if you're going to make more than casual money with your blog. The dynamics of this process change all the time, and it makes sense to let Darren Rowse finds the news you need.

Join Performancing. Regularly reading and participating in the forums at `http://performancing.com` will give you a continuing education in how to make money with your blog.

Invest in layout. Once you start including more than one simple ad, strongly consider investing some time and money in improving your blog's layout. Whether you do it yourself, work with a web designer, or contract someone to make the pain go away, the goal is the same: an easy-to-read format that reflects what your blog is about and, at the same time, appropriately monetizes your blog.

Focus on content. This point is worth repeating. People read your blog because of your blog's content, not its advertising. Keep writing a great blog front and center, and your readership will keep growing.

■ ■ ■

CHAPTER 13

Building Readership

The difficulty of literature is not to write, but to write what you mean; not to affect your reader, but to affect him precisely as you wish.

—Robert Louis Stevenson

When I interviewed Seth Godin, the noted marketing expert and CEO of Squidoo, for this chapter, he boiled the intricate, mysterious riddle of how to build readership into five words:

Voice plus reputation equals readership.

For good or ill, it's going to take me a few thousand times that many words to lightly cover some of the things you can do to build readership of your public blog. But hang in there—those five words are the beacon to guide you as you climb the influence hill in your part of the blogosphere.

First a disclaimer: Like most things in life, your mileage from these techniques will vary. Some are right for you; some are not. It's up to you to decide. And if you're looking for a single magic bullet, software, or writing technique that will do it all for you, please let me know when and where you find it! Building readership takes time and a good deal of effort; magic bullets work only in the movies.

Before we delve into the four main techniques I recommend you use to you find your blogging voice and build your blog's reputation, let's look at some of the many tools out there that will let you know just how many people you're influencing.

Tracking Your Readership and Influence

If you're interested in boosting the readership of your blog, you're going to want to know how many people are already reading your blog, and get a sense of which of the methods from this chapter (and elsewhere) are working for you. And that means knowing your stats.

Like a lot of things on the Net in general and the blogosphere specifically, you can spend anywhere from a little time a week to more than you can possibly afford on acquiring and analyzing readership stats. Before you dive right in and spend the next two workdays pulling in stats to crunch, a word of caution: Don't go overboard. You will get the most benefit from your first few consistent ways of tracking membership and less value from mastering every intricacy available to you.

Page Stats

The first place to look to get a sense of how many people are reading your blog is your blog's software. If your blog is hosted at TypePad, you're two clicks away from seeing your stats and your referrers,[1] as shown in Figure 13-1.

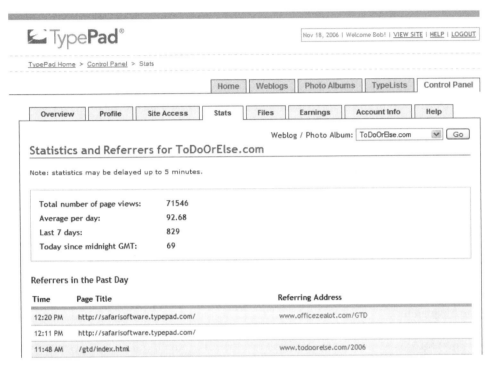

Figure 13-1. *Checking your TypePad stats*

WordPress has similar features, as do most major blogging services, except Blogger.[2] You'll need to resort to either a free or paid service if you want to track your Blogger blog. Here are three such services, which offer free and paid versions of their site-tracking software (just copy the enabling code to your blogger template):

- Google Analytics (www.google.com/analytics/) is a free service, primarily intended for AdWords advertisers but open to all.

- Site Meter (http://sitemeter.com) has been around for years, providing both free basic and paid ($6.95 USD per month) website statistics for websites and blogs.

- Free Stats (http://freestats.com) has more reports than Site Meter, but wants ad space on your blog in exchange for tracking visitors, or $8.33 USD per month for the ad-free, more robust version.

---

1. Referrer addresses show where people out on the Net are clicking to arrive at your blog.
2. For WordPress stats, see http://wordpress.com/features/stats/. As of this writing, Vox had adding readership stats on its Known Issues List page, at http://help.vox.com/cgi-bin/blogs_us.cfg/php/enduser/std_adp.php?p_faqid=217.

If you are running your blog on your own server, or more likely, hosting your domain with a web-hosting service, you have access to what are called *server logs*. These logs contain raw statistical information that is recorded each and every time your web server responds to a request for a given page, like the post you did last week on furry kittens on your blog. Both the WordPress online community and Movable Type community have created plug-ins to track and report this kind of data for you.[3]

RSS Stats

As useful as this data is to get a sense of how "big" your blog is, page-view counts and referral logs are only the first third of the story. While only a small percentage of computer users know about and use RSS, both Microsoft and Apple have baked RSS into their latest operating systems, and Microsoft Internet Explorer 7, Outlook 2007, and Mozilla Firefox have support for RSS subscription and management. Who is getting your RSS feed is the second part of the readership equation.

Again, while your blogging software takes care of providing an RSS feed for your blog, FeedBurner both makes this feed more usable and reports back to you the statistics you need. I covered FeedBurner in detail in Chapter 8. Suffice it to say here that if you're serious about knowing what your readership is and increasing it, you should have, at a bare minimum, a free FeedBurner account so you can track your RSS stats, like those shown in Figure 13-2.

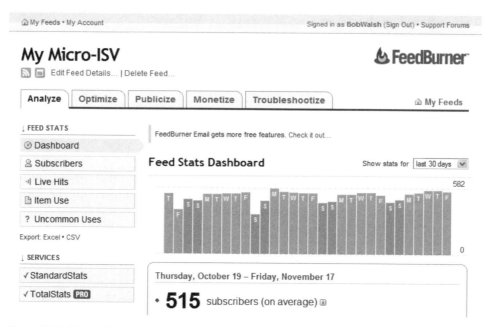

Figure 13-2. *Your RSS stats at FeedBurner*

---

3. For WordPress, see the plug-ins listed at http://wp-plugins.net/ under Stats. For Movable Type, sample the buffet at www.eatdrinksleepmovabletype.com/tutorials/monitoring_site_statistics/.

Link Measurements

The final part of knowing what level of influence you blog has reached is how many and how often other blogs and websites link to your posts. This is more art than science. Search engine optimizers, online marketers, and online advertisers have their own take on exactly how important a link is to your blog versus a link to a post, and a few dozen other ways of measuring imprecise terms like *traffic*, *reach*, and *influence*.

Measurement Tools

As mushy as link measurement is, it is by far the most important of way of knowing how you are doing. Here are three measurement tools to help you gauge your blog:

> **Your Technorati rank:** Simply go to www.technorati.com, search for your blog, and you'll see some ranking numbers. As shown in the example in Figure 13-3, you'll see the number of links to your blog in the past 180 days (95); the number of distinct blogs linking to your blog in the past 180 days (50); your rank, defined as how many blogs have as many blogs linking to them as yours (64,114); and the number of links to your blog ever recorded by Technorati (216).

Figure 13-3. *Technorati ranking*

> **Blog Juice Calculator:** While blog link counts are good, what about links from websites, and how likely people will find your blog if they search for a given subject? Enter the Blog Juice Calculator, offered by Text Link Ads. Originally designed to support Text Link Ads valuation of your blog for its ads (see Chapter 12), this handy tool can be found at www.text-link-ads.com/blog_juice. It returns a simple numerical score and HTML you can add to your blog to post your score if you are so inclined, as shown in Figure 13-4.

> **Bloginfluence:** Another useful way of comparing your blog's influence to that of other blogs is at www.bloginfluence.net. This site is useful in three ways: it breaks down your various rankings via Google, Yahoo, and Bloglines; provides links to show your blogs popularity charts on IceRocket, BlogPulse, TouchGraph, and Alexa; and lines up eight searches including your Technorati ranking.[4] Figure 13-5 shows an example of a Bloginfluence score.

---

4. For Bloginfluence to work correctly, you need to enter both the URL of your blog, and, if you've registered your blog with http://www.bloglines.com, your Bloglines site ID. The easiest way to get your site ID is to look at your blog's feed within Bloglines.

Figure 13-4. *Blog Juice rating*

Figure 13-5. *Bloginfluence rating*

More Measures

While we're in a measuring mood, I'd like to share with you three more ways to measure your blog. These measurements are a little more out there, but they are invaluable as you start applying the techniques in this chapter.

Page Strength: How relatively hard or easy it is to find your blog via search engines is an important thing to know. SEOmoz is a Seattle-based search engine optimization company that offers a tool for estimating this called Page Strength (`www.seomoz.org/tools/page-strength.php`). For example, my MyMicroISV blog recently got a 3 out of 10 score and this commentary: "Although not a considerable presence, your site/page is making inroads online. Visitor traffic and search engine visibility is within your grasp."

Conversational Index: Stowe Boyd, at his blog `www.stoweboyd.com/message`, came up with this in February 2006: Want to measure the health and likely success of your blog? Divide the number of comments and trackbacks you've gotten by the number of posts. This is your Conversational Index (CI).[5] If your CI is less than 1.0, it is more monologue than blog. The higher the CI, the more likely, in Stowe's opinion (and others, including mine), your blog is going in the right direction. As Stowe said in his follow-up blog:

> So, to put back into context: The Conversational Index is intended as a leading indicator of present and future blog viability and vitality. I don't know whether an index of 3 would be twice as good as an index of 1.5. Perhaps there is some sort of reverse log scale involved, where 3 only indicates a slightly more engaged and active community than 1.5. But I do know, empirically, that those with subpar CI, where there are way more posts [than] comments or trackbacks, are unlikely to be successful in the long run.

Socialmeter: Social networks permeate the blogosphere, but is your blog on their radar? The socialmeter (`www.socialmeter.com`) measures your presence in eight ways, as shown in Figure 13-6.

---

5. Actually it's a modification of Stowe's original formula (posts/comments+trackbacks) he proposed in his post at `www.stoweboyd.com/message/2006/02/the_social_scal.html`, suggested by Don Dodge and adopted by Stowe in his follow-up post at `www.stoweboyd.com/message/2006/02/the_conversatio.html`, if you really, really wanted to know.

socialmeter score: 825

Report for: `http://mymicroisv.com/`   [check]

Ⓑ	**Bloglines links**	▆▆▆▆▆▆▆▆▆	173
▰	**Delicious links**	▆▆▆▆	67
▦	**Digg score**		0
Ⓖ	**Google Links**	▆▆▆▆▆▆▆▆▆▆▆▆▆	328
Ⓡ	**Rojo links**		0
♋	**Shadows links**		0
Ⓒ	**Technorati Links**	▆▆▆▆▆▆▆▆▆▆	216
Ⓨ	**Yahoo! links**	▆▆▆	41

Home - Bookmarklet - Feedback - Sponsor

Figure 13-6. *Socialmeter score*

Four Ways to Build Your Readership

Now that we've dealt with measuring your readership and influence, let's talk about how to build it. We'll focus on four major ways of increasing your blog's readership and influence.

Network Formally and Informally

The Internet is all about the power of networks, but it's up to you to harness the power of your informal network of fellow bloggers and to join more formal networks of blogs. Let's look at how to tap your informal blogging network first.

Who's in your informal blogging network? Every blogger you've ever chatted with via your blog, their blog, or email. Every blogger who has mentioned one of your posts and you've had the courtesy and common sense to send a thank-you message. Every blogger who has been mentioned in the same post as one of your posts. That's a lot of people.

There are plenty of books and blog postings out there on how to build your own network, but here are a few pointers to remember vis-à-vis your blog:

Be thankful. When you find that someone has referred to one of your posts and start seeing traffic from that link, drop them a thank you email. For example, I recently blogged about a post at Pamela Slim's excellent blog, Escape from Cubicle Nation (`www.escapefromcubiclenation.com`), and got an email from Pamela that read in part, "I just wanted to say thank you for the kind link to my post today. I have gotten many new visitors from your site as a result, and I appreciate each and every one of them. I wish you much luck, happiness, and adventure in all your endeavors." You can bet I would bend over backwards to do Pamela a favor in the future.

Be interested. Show an interest in the people who are writing about your blog. Make the effort to read some of their recent posts and contribute a comment or two of value. Just as you notice who posts comments to your blog, they will, too.

Be respectful. Give credit when someone else's post sparks your creativity. Respect the hard work someone has put into a particular post by not quoting all of it and instead sending your readers to it. Include other blogger's referral links.

Be helpful. If you see a wanton typo or broken link on a post, drop the blogger a short, friendly email pointing it out. I definitely appreciate people who've helped me as I blog, as long as it's in a kindly way. Don't trash those who made mistakes on your blog—we all live in glass houses.

Be organized. It's easy to lose contact with people in the blogosphere. Make the effort to keep their contact information handy and to keep in touch with them. Networking services like LinkedIn (www.linkedin.com) are great for this, but even a simple email folder called My Network will work, if you put the effort into it.

In addition to your informal blogging network, you can find hundreds of formal blogging networks, blog carnivals, and blogging centers that might want you to join them. Let's look at examples of each.

9rules Blogging Network

Blogging networks are all about implied quality. If readers are familiar with the network, they assume someone, somewhere has done the hard work of vetting the blog they are now reading. One of the best at this is 9rules, which started in 2003 and, as of this writing, had some 32 communities of between 4 and 25 member blogs. Run by Paul "Scrivs" Scrivens, Mike Rundle, and Tyme White, 9rules bloggers sport a network badge (see Figure 13-7), get featured at the 9rules website, and help each other.

Figure 13-7. *Guy Kawasaki's 9rules member badge at blog.guykawasaki.com*

Unlike some networks, 9rules periodically has open calls for prospective new members. In response to their last such call while this book was being written, 1,190 bloggers applied (http://9rules.com/blog/2006/10/9rules-round-5-analysis). The 9rules list of what it looks for in prospective blogger members pretty much applies to most networks: passion, good-quality writing, consistent posting, relevant topics, and a well-designed blog.

Blog Carnivals

Blog carnivals are a form of ad hoc blog networks. One or several bloggers start the carnival, picking a topic, defining what kinds of posts they want, and setting submission dates. Then other bloggers who have heard about the carnival and posted about the topic submit posts for inclusion in the next roundup "edition" posting.

Readers like carnivals because it gives them a single high-value posting with numerous excellent posts on a subject they care about. Bloggers appreciate the extra attention and readership a carnival generates.

You can kick off a blog carnival, complete with managed submission forms, or find carnivals you're interested in at `http://blogcarnival.com`, as shown in Figure 13-8. Of course, you can organize a blog carnival manually, as well.

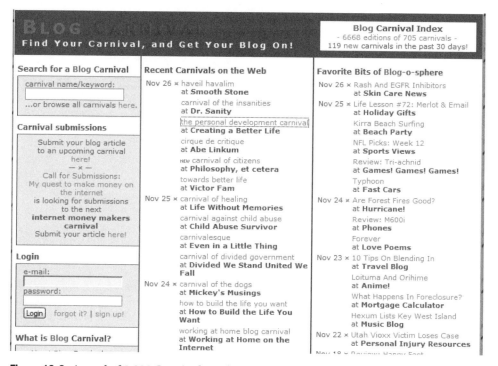

Figure 13-8. *A total of 6,668 Carnivals and counting at blogcarnival.com*

MyBlogLog Blogging Center

MyBlogLog (`http://MyBlogLog.com`) is something of a hybrid. On one hand, it's a social network for blog readers. On the other hand, it provides member blogs with detailed demographic information for free, as shown in Figure 13-9 (and even more information is available for $3 USD per month).

Member bloggers can show a badge on their site with pictures of the most recent MyBlogLog members to visit. They can also see on their MyBlogLog profile page what's hot in other blogs in their MyBlogLog communities.

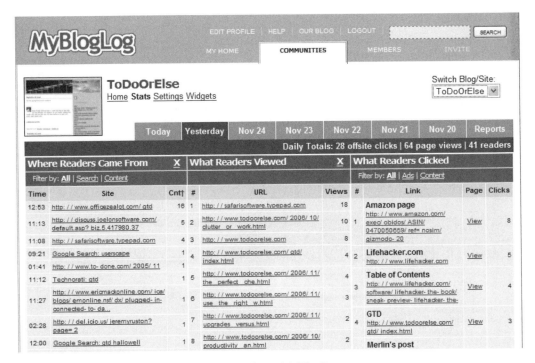

Figure 13-9. *Excellent free stats and community at MyBlogLog*

Eric Marcoullier, CEO of MyBlogLog, explains the MyBlogLog proposition this way:

MyBlogLog is all about helping you connect with your blog readers. When you sign up with us, you empower your readers to develop a closer relationship with you and with each other. After all, who better to promote your business than other satisfied customers?

Who would be a part of your community? Anyone who has a real interest in what your business is about and feels a connection with what you say in your blog. MyBlogLog offers your readers a way to become a more active person in the conversation, with you and with each other.

Additionally, MyBlogLog is the only service of its kind that lets you know what your readers are doing on your site and elsewhere. With our integrated stats reporting, you get key actionable data about how your readers get to your site and where they go to leave, plus you get insight into what they do elsewhere on the Web.

Formal Networking Tips

Blogging groups and networks, with the exception of MyBlogLog, tend to be selective about who they let join. Additionally, some of these networks share not only links and branding, but advertising revenue, and people get considerably more picky about who they are doing business with when money's involved. Here are some common-sense suggestions about getting into formal blogging networks:

Be relevant. Either you fit in a blog network's scheme of things or you don't. That means that you should take the time to get to know the network you want to join first and apply second.

Be selective. Blog networks are not like Boy Scout merit badges—the more you collect the better. In fact, some networks demand exclusivity. Again, canvass the blog networks before rushing out to join one or more.

Know who to ask. Every blog network has someone somewhere to ask to be let in. Find that person, or at least the online submission form.

Endorsements definitely help. Want to greatly increase your chances of getting in? Get to know a blogger already in that network and ask him when it's appropriate to endorse your membership bid. Mercenary campaigns along these lines rarely work. You are best off looking at and contacting your informal blog network for this.

One key to getting into a network is to find the right network. Take a look at the networks listed at www.blognetworklist.com/networklist.php and www.blogherald.com/2005/09/21/list-of-blog-networks-v3-september for some possible networks to peruse.

Create Good Linkbait

Linkbaiting refers to creating a post specifically designed to draw traffic. This practice has been called everything from savvy marketing to devil worship at one time or another in the blogosphere. Matt Cutts thinks that if linkbaiting is done right, it's a good thing, and I agree. Matt Cutts, by the way is the GoogleGuy—a Google employee well known for *almost* explaining how Google actually works under the server hood. Trust me, when Matt Cutts talks at his blog, Matt Cutts: Gadgets, Google, and SEO, online people listen. Here's his advice on linkbaiting (www.mattcutts.com/blog/seo-advice-linkbait-and-linkbaiting):

> On a meta-level, I think of "linkbait" as something interesting enough to catch people's attention, and that doesn't have to be a bad thing. There are a lot of ways to do that, including putting in sweat-of-the-brow work to generate data or insights, or it can be as simple as being creative. You can also say something controversial to generate discussion (this last one gets tired if you overuse it, though). Sometimes even a little bit of work can generate a reason for people to link to you.

The basic idea behind successful linkbaiting is coming up with a really linkable post, and then promoting it far and wide, including on social bookmarking networks (see the next section).

You can find numerous suggestions on how to linkbait. Darren Rowse at ProBlogger has a list of 20 linkbaiting techniques at www.problogger.net/archives/2006/09/21/20-linkbaiting-techniqes, and Nick Wilson at Performancing has five suggestions on how to put the hook into your linkbait at http://performancing.com/node/38. Here are five tried-and-true ways of creating good linkbait:

The big resource list: This is a favorite on Digg and other networks. Take the time to build a big, useful online resource list about the topics you really know about.

The definitive *X* tutorial: Whether it's building an aardvark nursery or installing a WordPress theme, the right tutorial will attract readers and links, especially if it's a video that you can post to YouTube.

The 20 bloggers who know the most about *X*: If you know who's blogging about the topics you follow closely, create a blog-centric linkbait list of who are really the top bloggers in your given area and email each and every one of them.

An online tool: Admittedly, you need to know how to program for this one, or know a cooperative programmer who can code your brainstorm, but online tools are very high on the linkbait list of star players. For example, Dane Carlson at the Business Opportunities Weblog (www.business-opportunities.biz) built a little Web 2.0 mashup using Technorati's API that gives you a cash value based on your blog's popularity, as shown in Figure 13-10. According to Google, the post "How Much Is My Blog Worth?" has over *30,000* links to it. That is serious linkbaiting.

Figure 13-10. *Your blog's comparative worth*

Breaking news about *X*: Everyone and anyone can be a reporter.[6] If there's a niche—large, small, or micro—in which you know what's happening before most people do, news link-baits work.

Do the Social Network Thing

Social bookmarking networks, like Digg, del.icio.us, Furl, and reddit (shown in Figure 13-11), can be a powerful drug for boosting your blog's readership, as well as worthwhile experiences in and of themselves. A lot of social networks exist; Wikipedia lists about 74 as of December 2006 (en.wikipedia.org/wiki/List_of_social_networking_websites).

---

6. Amendment I, U.S. Constitution: "Congress shall make no law . . . abridging the freedom of speech, or of the press." So there!

Figure 13-11. *reddit's homepage*

Social bookmarking sites tend to work in the same general way. Something—a website, a news article, a post to your blog, and so on—is added by network members to alert other network members that it is of interest. The more of these votes that one of your posts gets, the higher it is at that moment in that social network's homepage.

While each social networking site has its own values, community, and following, there are basically five key concepts to getting a social network's attention:

Understand the network. Each social bookmarking site has its own way of doing things, its own set of favorite topics, and its own way of looking at the blogosphere. Take the time to research and understand what makes them tick now.[7]

Make it as easy as possible. We covered this in detail in Chapter 9, but it bears repeating again here: Make it as easy as possible for members of the social networks that are important to you to vote for a given post.

Be selective. Not every post you write is a candidate for every social network—not by a long shot. If one in twenty posts is really good, you are doing well. Don't be hesitant to join selected social networks and very selectively promote your very best posts and the very best posts you encounter elsewhere.

Be patient. There's no accounting for taste or the vagrancies of what's hot and what's not in a given social network at a given time. Be prepared to wait for lightning to strike.

---

7. One really good resource is Jeff Clark's www.neoformix.com. His analytical posts on the characteristics of top reddit posts and Digg topic popularity (www.neoformix.com/2006/RedditAnalysis.html and www.neoformix.com/2006/DiggAnalysis1.html, respectively) are very good.

Be prepared. If the gods of the Internet—or a handful of active members who are responsible for a large chunk of what goes on the front page of a particular social network[8]—favor you, you had better be prepared. That means keeping an eye on your referral logs, having a few really good posts ready to go to entrain people who come to your site, and having a very clear conversation with your web host company's tech support people in advance about what their traffic surge policies and procedures are. Nothing is more discouraging than clicking a cool item on Digg's front page only to find that blog's server is crashed from the overload.

DHARMESH SHAH, ON SOCIAL BOOKMARKING NETWORKS

Dharmesh Shah's blog OnStartups (`http://onstartups.com`) is one of the best known in the relatively small micro-ISV online community.

Dharmesh has seen firsthand what it's like when a post makes it to the front page of both reddit and Digg, so I asked him what his take is on increasing your blog's readership via social bookmarking communities. Here's his reply:

Most bloggers at some level are looking to increase the traffic on their sites. This is either for financial reasons, ego reasons, or altruistic reasons. In any of these cases, social news sites like Digg and reddit can be an important factor in getting a new blog off the ground. The reason is very simple. For a blog, traffic ultimately becomes a function of the popularity of the blog. Your traffic eventually is going to be based on how many sites link to you, how you rank on the search engines for specific phrases of interest, and the number of subscribers you have to your blog via RSS or email. But the question is, how do you build traffic in the early days when nobody knows about you? This is where the social sites like Digg and reddit can help a lot.

---

8. See `www.seomoz.org/blogdetail.php?ID=1228` on this fascinating application of the 80/20 principle (and `en.wikipedia.org/wiki/Pareto_principle` and `www.the8020principle.com` if you've somehow gotten to this point in your life without knowing about the 80/20 principle).

First, a quick overview: Social sites like Digg and reddit are basically community-driven, link-sharing sites. Members of the community submit links to articles and content that they find interesting. Hundreds of articles get submitted to these sites every day. Once a link is submitted, the community gets to "vote" on which articles they like or find interesting. If someone posts a link to your blog article on one of these sites and it rises to the front page (because the community liked it), it can mean thousands of visitors to your blog in a single day. The first time this happens, you'll get a big thrill as you watch your traffic numbers.

In January 2006, I had a new blog called OnStartups.com. Like many new blogs, my traffic was primarily driven by friends and family that I had sent emails to ("Hey, check out my new blog!"). I kept plodding along, writing articles on a topic I cared a lot about (software startups). Then, one day, I saw my traffic levels, which had been about 10–50 visitors a day, spike to over 2,000 on a single day. At first, I thought there must be something wrong with my blogging software (which was internally developed), so I checked my referral logs. I discovered that just about all of that traffic was coming from reddit.com. Evidently, someone had submitted one of my articles to reddit, and it had wound up on the reddit homepage. A few months later, I had an article get submitted to Digg and also make the front page, driving over 10,000 visitors on a single day. The point is, for driving traffic to a new blog, the social news sites work.

Of course, it is not easy to get to the front page of these sites. There is a lot of competition. But at least you have a chance. If you are writing really great content on a topic that lots of people care about, you've got a decent chance of driving some traffic through one of the social bookmarking sites. The good news is that you can be a brand-new blogger and still be able to attract a lot of visitors—i.e., it is not completely a function of existing blog popularity (though even on these sites, it helps). For new bloggers, it is also a great way to experiment and begin to discover what works and what doesn't. You realize that some times are better than others to post (11:00 a.m. ET is the best time for me). You realize that article titles have a strong influence on whether you will get voted up or not. You realize that making it easy for your existing readers to submit your articles to the popular sites makes it much more likely to do so (hence the "submit to reddit" link on all my articles).

Like many new initiatives, blogging comes down to a combination of constant experimentation and determination. You have to try a lot of things to figure out what works. And you have to stick with it long enough to give it a chance.

Think Outside the Blogbox: Squidoo

Started by Internet trendsetter Seth Godin in late 2005, Squidoo takes a bit of explaining. On one hand, you have one-page how-to get started/going/better guides on subjects ranging from advertising to vintage travel posters and everything in between.[9] On the other hand, you have an ultra-easy way of creating a guide to a topic you blog about, complete with Amazon picks, YouTube videos, your favorite posts, NetFlix rentable DVDs, del.icio.us links, custom RSS feeds, eBay postings, and *New York Time* articles to add to your own commentary in text and images.

Figure 13-12 shows a typical Squidoo lens (`www.squidoo.com/africansafaris`).

---

9. For example, in today's most popular Squidoo lens, you'd find advice and information on one-deal-a-day sites; funky, chic, and cool laptop bags; popular torrent sites; magic tricks; printable coloring pages; wedding speeches; Japanese tattoos; the meaning, symbolism, and psychology of color; free dog sweater patterns; ninjitsu techniques; the best free online video-hosting sites; music of the '70s; what's with the television show *Grey's Anatomy*; guitar tools; selling your home yourself; and Area 51.

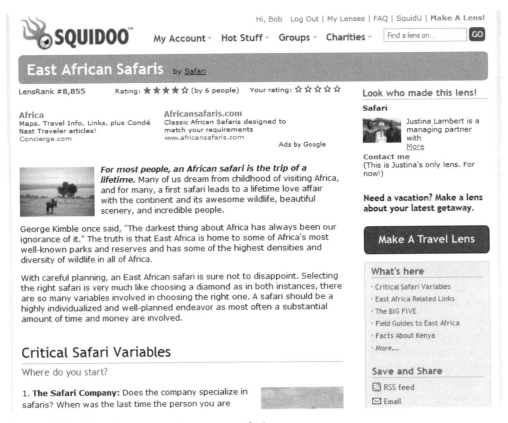

Figure 13-12. *A Squidoo lens on planning a safari*

The beauty of Squidoo lenses is that they are excellent orientation guides to all sorts of human endeavors. For example, if I Googled "East African Safari," I would get back over *3.7 million pages* and be dropped into a vat of bubbling information overload until my brain turned to tapioca. Instead, I can read Justina Lambert's Squidoo lens. Here, she lays out what to look for in safari companies and guides; the pros and cons of traveling in a group; what the Big Five animals are and the best places to see them; recommended field guides; her favorite wildlife parks and reserves; travel guides; photos; weather for Kenya, Uganda, and Tanzania; and the answers to several frequently asked questions about safaris.

Now how does Justina know all this and how good is her information? Well, she's one of the three partners who run Kimbla-Mantana African Safaris, which has been in business since 1959, and her links speak for themselves. The combination of Justina's advice and knowledge, coupled with her links, on top of a bed of relevant Google AdWords ads, makes for a very tasty information meal.

What really makes Squidoo shine is its built-in rating and ranking system. It's one thing to see a supposed expert's Squidoo lens, but when you see other people have rated it highly and that it's popular, you have a lot more faith in what you read.

Squidoo is still in its early days, steadily growing but not making the kind of splash of, say, Digg. One interesting thing about Squidoo is that 5 percent of its post-expense revenue goes to charities, and lensmasters can elect to have some or all of their income go to charity as well.

For bloggers who want to build a reputation, Squidoo is an easy way to climb fast in Google's rankings:

- Roger Jennings, a well-known and respected author and programmer, started a Squidoo lens on the Black Scholar. Google returns that Squidoo lens as its second result (oakleafblog.blogspot.com/2006/09/michael-arrington-badmouths-squidoo.html).

- The Long Tail is a theory about how commerce and attention work on the Internet defined by Chris Anderson, *Wired* magazine Editor-in-Chief and author of "The Long Tail." His Squidoo lens, The Long Tail (www.squidoo.com/longtail) is the fifth result Google returns.

- Margaret Schaut, a lensmaster, says this on the Squidoo blog (www.squidoo.com/blog/?p=113): "I decided to Google my Squidoo topics today and discovered several of them are either on the FIRST page of Google, or the second. I have competitors out there who have been at this for a long time, with a lot of backing, and they're NOT ON GOOGLE'S FIRST PAGE, BUT I AM! It just blows my mind."

- Kimberly Dawn Wells, a prolific lensmaster, added this to the Squidoo blog (www.squidoo.com/custombreastcancermemoryshirts/): "During some researching, I looked up "personalized breast cancer" on Google and my Squidoo lens is the first result! That's pretty impressive considering the number of breast cancer sites out there."

- A TypePad Widget lets you easily connect your TypePad blog to your Squidoo lens (www.sixapart.com/typepad/widgets/content/squidoo.html).

Rajesh Setty (whose blog at blog.lifebeyondcode.com ranked as the 9,061 most linked to blogger by Technorati, at the time of writing) has several Squidoo lenses (www.squidoo.com/lensmasters/rajesh301) and offers this advice to bloggers:

My internal blogging goal is to have 90% of my posts be relevant a few years from now. So I work hard to ensure that there is some "timeless" content on my blog. However, the big problem is that with time, that timeless content gets buried and new readers may never discover it irrespective of the content's relevance. This is where Squidoo comes in. Most of my lenses will have a collection of links to my previous articles in my blog interspersed with other relevant information. As the lens gets popular, I get more traffic to my blog.

However, I have to say that it is a two-way street. My blog gets [a] reasonable amount of traffic and I link to my Squidoo lenses on my blog wherever applicable to ensure that my blog readers discover the lenses. So my blog works to send traffic to my Squidoo lenses, and my Squidoo lenses in turn work to send traffic to my blog.

Not to forget the power of social bookmarking. Some of my Squidoo lenses have been bookmarked by many social bookmarking sites [which] has led to more traffic to my lenses leading to more traffic to my blog.

AN INTERVIEW WITH SETH GODIN, CEO, SQUIDOO

With ten Internet-marketing related books out, Seth Godin has become the one-man think tank of the Internet marketing revolution. Seth's ideas, thoughts, rants, and posts have shaped much of what has become conventional online wisdom.

Wikipedia's entry for Seth does a very good job of summarizing his enduring message (http://en.wikipedia.org/wiki/Seth_Godin):

Godin's ideology combines three elements. First, the end of the TV-Industrial complex means that marketers no longer have the power to command the attention of anyone they choose, whenever they choose. Second, in a marketplace in which consumers have more power, marketers must show more respect; this means no spam, no deceit and a bias for keeping promises. Finally, Godin asserts that the only way to spread the word about an idea is for that idea to earn the buzz by being remarkable. Godin refers to those who spread these ideas as "Sneezers," and to the ideas so spread as "IdeaViruses." He calls a remarkable product or service a purple cow.

What Wikipedia doesn't explain about Seth is that since he started getting his message out there back in the twentieth century, he's been proven right by the success of countless online businesses that have adopted his view of marketing. His blog, sethgodin.typepad.com, ranks as number 32 (as of this writing) at Technorati.

Seth's latest venture is Squidoo.com.

Q. *I guess the place to start is, if you are blogging, why should you take a look at Squidoo?*

A. I'm going to start with the big conceptual reason, and then I'll go into two practical reasons. The big conceptual reason is that, because anyone can have a blog, just the fact that you can publish your ideas online doesn't mean very much. As far as the reader is concerned, you might be an idiot.

What happens over time is that people develop a voice, and they develop a reputation, and when those two things meet, they get a readership. If you have a reputation of having insight on a particular topic, and you can deliver that insight in a unique way, then people have an incentive to come back and read more of what you have to say. So Squidoo can't help you develop a voice, but what it can do is help you develop a reputation.

The way that people tend to develop reputations is by saying things that their readers, or the people who are listening to them, believe are true. Meaning that if I say five things, and three of them resonate with you as things that you already believe, you are more likely to believe the other two. What Squidoo does is provide a platform that allows anybody to build a page, which we call a lens, about something they are passionate about. That page can include links to products; it can include little mini essays; it can include links to websites, Google Maps, YouTube videos, Flickr pictures, a collection of ideas from all around the Web. And if your lens is a good one, if you have done a great job of capturing the essence of your area of expertise, then people are more likely to believe your opinions, because it shows you know what you are talking about.

Q. *So that's the big conceptual reason. That makes a lot of sense to me. What about the practical reasons?*

A. Well, the two practical reasons are this: first of all, as a blogger, I was frustrated because I would post something three months ago, something I was really fond of, and because blogs push ideas down as you add new ones, it would essentially disappear; and if you don't see it, it's like it doesn't exist, like I never wrote it. What a lens lets you do is highlight your best blog posts.

So let's say you have a blog about antique cameras. Let's say you restore antique cameras, you collect antique cameras, and now you have a blog about them. If you built a lens about antique cameras on Squidoo, you could include in it three websites that have lots of data and pricing on antique cameras, you could include pointers to auctions on eBay about antique cameras, and you could include pointers to your five best blog posts of "Things You Should Know Before You Buy an Antique Camera." Well, if I see all that in context, I am way more likely to go and start becoming a regular reader of your blog, which never would have happened if you hadn't built the lens on Squidoo to amplify the blog you're building in the first place.

Q. *So it's a way of building reputation. It's a way of amplifying that reputation by basically creating another way that people can find you. It's a way, also, to monetize some of the things you're doing with your blog. I'm curious, how is that working out now that we're about a year on from your launch?*

A. We went out of beta in March. It's about eight months. We hit about 30,000 people yesterday, who have more than 50,000 pages. Some of those people are making well over $100 a month. Some of those people are making way more than $100 a month. And the best part is that more than 40 percent of the people are giving their royalties to charity, and that is why we built the site in the first place. Because the fact is, nobody is going to be able to retire on the money they make from Squidoo. But if 30,000 people end up giving their nickels, pennies, and dimes, all at the same time to charity, we ought to be able to make a significant difference to some of the world's problems.

Let me just go back for a minute to the point about people finding you. Back to the guy with the antique camera page. If you built a blog about antique cameras, and someone types in "antique camera" in Google, they may or may not find your blog. But if you have a blog about it and a lens about it, you dramatically increase the chances that somebody is going to find you via Google. The reason is that your lens is easier for somebody else on the Web to link to, because it doesn't change so often. I've been writing my blog for almost four years, and when you do a Google search on, say, "marketing chocolate," I come up in one of the top three posts or top three matches, for something I wrote two and a half years ago. So my blog is a moving target, whereas my lens is more stable, and it is sort of the filter, and it is the place you want people to start. So I think they work together. Both the tools are free, or close to free, but in the case of Squidoo, free, and you can look at it as just built-in SEO [search engine optimization] for your blog.

Q. *I would like to get your perspective, if you feel in the mood to pontificate a bit here, on where you see the blogosphere going in the next few years?*

A. I think that feeds are the key. I think that Digg did an interesting thing, which is Digg turned the entire Internet into one giant current-events blog. So when you go to Digg.com, it's a constantly refreshed page that grabs everything from all over. So an individual blog is not as important because Digg aggregates them all.

So there are only two kinds of blogs in the world: the blogs I read today in my reader, or because they are linked to those blogs, and the ones I don't. So when everyone has a blog, and I think soon everyone will have a blog or something like a blog, having people who subscribe will become the critical asset. And it is going to be a land grab, because the fact is, if I subscribe to your blog about antique cameras, I am probably not going to subscribe to somebody else's, because I don't need to know that much about antique cameras. So that's another reason to start fast: you have the opportunity now to build subscribers.

Q. *I guess you'd call it a land grab for attention more than anything else.*

A. Exactly.

Building Readership Recap

There's an old adage in the business world: If you want to improve something, you first have to measure it, whether it's the number of widgets coming off an assembly line or the number of readers your blog delights. While it is a little tricky to do so, given your readers could be visiting your blog via their web browser or reading your blog's RSS feed via their preferred RSS feed reader, it is still doable.

If you're going to get serious about increasing your audience, you need to get from the "how many read me" to the "what do they like" data, and that's going to mean going from free tools like Site Meter and a free FeedBurner account to programs like Google Analytics and a paid FeedBurner account.

Once you know your numbers, you can improve them in any number of ways:

- Join blog networks where appropriate and informally network with as many bloggers as you can.

- Do guest posts for other bloggers and invite other bloggers to post at your blog.

- Take the time to research, write, and present really valuable posts for the people who read your blog and others like them.

- Take the time to participate, share, and engage with social bookmarking networks, both by making it easier for those networks to notice your posts and by contributing to the network in general.

- Step beyond the confines of your blog to provide value on the topics you blog about, be it via Squidoo, through newsgroups, or by contributing to Wikipedia.

As I said at the beginning of this chapter, there are no magic bullets when it comes to building readership. However, consistency is a key component. Keep doing what works, add in a few readership-building efforts, and you will see your audience increase.

Your Action Tasks

Having covered how you measure your readership and influence, and four major ways to build your readership, here's a longer than usual list of small but useful things you can do to build your blog. We'll start with some basic, cover-your-bases stuff and move on from there to more advanced techniques.

Know your stats. At a bare minimum, you need to know where to find your stats in your blogging software and/or have a Site Meter badge. As RSS continues to ramp up, get that free or paid FeedBurner account!

Who are you? Don't be coy about your About page and profile if you want to garner readers. Even if you are blogging anonymously, give your readers something.

Master basic social skills. Whether you love or hate social bookmarking sites like Digg and del.icio.us, at least some of your readers love them, so make it easy to vote for your posts. There's a multitude of ways of doing this, but the simplest is Socializer, a free automatic bookmarking tool by Pierre Far (http://ekstreme.com/socializer). Check it out.

RSS above the fold. For blogs, "above the fold" means before you need to scroll, and that's where you want your RSS stuff—standard, FeedBurner, or specific RSS reader badges—to reside. Making it as easy as possible for readers to subscribe to your blog and save clicks pays off.

Get listed. Multitudes of blog directories are out there. Three you should make the effort to check out and get listed in are Blogwise (www.blogwise.com), Globe of Blogs (www.globeofblogs.com), and Blogarama (www.blogarama.com). Looking for more blog directories? See RSSTop55 (www.masternewmedia.org/rss/top55) for an excellent list.

Get listed, part 2. Don't forget website directories that accept blogs, such as Yahoo Directory (`http://dir.yahoo.com`, paid), the Open Directory Project (`www.dmoz.org`, free), and specialty directories in your industry or geographic locale.

Respond to comments. At the risk of boring you, let me say it again: Blogs are a conversation, and that means you absolutely should respond to comments. Doing so will turn first-time visitors into loyal readers.

Be contrarian—post on weekends. Conventional blogging wisdom is you shouldn't post on weekends because fewer people read blogs then. By the same token, there are fewer posts competing for attention.

Show your back stock. One way or another, get a list of your best/most popular posts onto the front page of your blog. There's no better way of turning a chance meeting into the start of a lasting relationship with your blog.

Give credit and links where they are due. Simply put, the more links out of your blog, the more people will link to your blog. So even when you can't pin to a specific post, link to that blog or website and give credit where it's due.

Post when your readers expect you to post. When you post creates expectations. If you post twice a day for months then not at all for two weeks, your readership will drift away. Know what your posting goal is and keep to it, and don't be shy sharing that with your readers.

Make use of trackbacks. When you're blogging about some major blogger's post, either positively or negatively, use your blogging software's ability to send a trackback to that blogger. You will be surprised how often the trackback recipient will comment on your posts. This technique works only if you're blogging in earnest, not fishing for links.

All done? Here are more ways to get more readers that take more effort:

Make friends with fellow bloggers. That means follow their blogs, be helpful, get to know them, and comment intelligently. Don't ask for links up front. Don't expect instant acceptance. Don't be irrelevant. And don't nag!

Use photos. The right photo triples the impact of a good post. Take them yourself, find them at Yahoo Flickr already permissioned at `www.flickr.com/creativecommons` (2.7 million and counting), or spend a dollar each at `http://istockphoto.com`.

Post your photos at Flickr. People are interested in seeing themselves and other people. If you take digital photos, post them to Flickr and include a Flickr gallery on your blog (Google "Flickr Gallery" for the right widget for your blogging service).

Participate in newsgroups. While newsgroups have faded in recent years, you'll find at least one very active newsgroups covering just about every topic imaginable. Dive right in. And don't forget to include your blog's URL in your signature line.

Use Squidoo. Build one or more lenses to showcase your best blogs about a given topic, or which together form a great tutorial, or just to establish your reputation as someone who knows a thing or two.

Convert old posts into new ezine articles. What's the difference between a great post you did on a subject six months ago and a free ezine article that drives traffic to your blog? About ten minutes' effort on your part at ezine sites like iSnare (`www.isnare.com`), Ezine Articles (`ezinearticles.com`), and especially the SiteProNews directory of article directories (`www.sitepronews.com/article-directories.html`).

Guest post. This technique worked for me when I started `ToDoOrElse.com`. Offer another (more influential) blogger guest posts to keep the content rolling while that blogger is on vacation, overextended, and so on. This technique presupposes you have some sort of relationship going, that the other blogger has either asked for guest posts or seems ready for the idea, and that you have at least a few posts that would fit the bill.

Provide answers. In just about every area, there are current questions that need answers. Think about the subjects you blog on. What questions could a little non-blog research or data-gathering answer?

PART 4

■■■

Blogging Toward the Future

In this part of the book, we're going to meet some of the bloggers who are posting from war zones, police beats, and Antarctica to get a sense of how blogging in the future can redefine our connections with each other. And I'll make a few predictions about the future of blogging.

CHAPTER 14

■ ■ ■

Blogging from the New Front Lines

What did you want to be when you grew up? I wanted to be a scientist doing research in some distant exotic place. Or a soldier fighting the good fight. Or a cop putting away the bad guys I saw in my world getting away with murder or worse.

Those dreams didn't come true; they were too far removed, too remote a possibility. When you grew up last century in a housing project in Los Angeles, opportunities to connect with and understand the lives of cops, scientists, and military personnel were few and far between. That's not so now.

When you read in this book and elsewhere about the tens of millions of people blogging, it has a nice abstract ring to it. Blogging takes on an entirely different dimension when you realize that people on the boundaries of their societies are blogging about what their daily lives are like.

Today, real people who walk beats, take measurements, and see their friends and buddies fight and sometimes die are blogging. They're blogging from Antarctica, from Iraq, and yes, even Los Angeles. They're sharing the good and sometimes decidedly bad aspects of what their lives are like, and most are only too willing to reply to comments or even questions from nosy authors.

One of the major unnoticed effects of the rise of the blogosphere is the easy access it affords anyone with access to the Internet to learn about, talk about, and connect to people in professions, occupations, and circumstances you could once only read dusty biographies of or watch passively on television unreality shows like *Miami Vice*.

Want to know what it's like to work in Antarctica? Go find a blog and read. What's it like to be a cop in Los Angeles or a copper in the UK? Go find a blog and ask. Want to know what the men and women in the US Armed Forces think of what's happening in Iraq? Go find a blog and ask.

Blogging gives a whole new meaning to the old saying of walking a mile in someone else's shoes. Whether you just happen to have the same three futures in mind as I did when I was growing up, or you want to know what countless other occupations, places, and circumstances are like, there's a new answer, courtesy of the blogosphere: Go find a blog and ask. In this chapter, I've done just that.

On the Beat

A few things stand out about the day-to-day blogs of policemen and policewomen: their management is clueless, the bureaucracy is stifling, and every so often, they make a huge difference in someone's life.

Blogging from Bermuda

First up in our lineup of police bloggers is Dan, whose Little Eye on the World blog (see Figure 14-1) was all of two months old when I interviewed him via email in March 2006.[1]

Figure 14-1. *The Little Eye on the World blog*

---

1. As of this writing, Little Eyes of the World had disappeared from Blogger and from the blogosphere. But I think that Dan's responses are still both interesting and useful to other bloggers.

Dan who? I don't know and didn't ask. Like virtually every cop who blogs, Dan prefers to stay anonymous lest present or future department management decide he is guilty of telling too much truth to the public.[2] Here is how Dan answered my emailed questions about his blog:

Q. *So Dan, are you a police officer, and if so, how long and in which country?*

A. Yep, I'm a cop with ten years' service. Currently serving with Bermuda Police, but previously with a UK service. I actually stopped the blog a few weeks ago after I heard that police services didn't like the idea of their cops blogging. Hence, I'm now extra careful that neither (Bermuda or my UK police service) are mentioned.

Q. *Some of the "stupid criminal" posts are hilarious. Where do you find them?*

A. The stupid criminal posts are collected from all over the Net, and not just from one source. It's purely a lighthearted poke in the eye after the balance seems to have turned in their favor. Occasionally, there's a semi-serious item, but I like to keep it light. Nothing is ever posted from personal experience.

Q. *Are criminals really that stupid?*

A. From my experience, not that stupid! I've encountered some who beggar belief, but that's the minority. Most are aware and careful in what they're doing.

Q. *Well, why start blogging?*

A. I started the blog a few months ago, but I've wiped all the contents at least twice (especially after the police services began to frown upon them). Bermuda Police recruits some of its cops from the UK, although I knew that there wasn't a lot of information available for them. I guess that was the intention of starting it. When I know Bermuda is recruiting, I'll place the email link with an offer to contact me if there are any questions they have.

Q. *Which blogs do you read and how often?*

A. The only blogs I read are the ones linked on the site (Magistrate and two police blogs). There's a new one that I'm reading about a New York cabbie, but I've lost the link at the moment. I think the majority of cops (or any other profession) blog as an opportunity to vent. Me? I guess I've got too much spare time on my hands!

Q. *If all you're doing is "venting," should police blog?*

A. I think police should be allowed to blog if they chose. One blogger named Cayman Cop (also a UK cop) started a blog about the Royal Cayman Police and closed after a few months after he was informed that senior management "wanted words." I've no doubt that if his identity were ever discovered that he'd be on the next flight home. So it's a delicate balancing act. I've tried to put the odds in my favor by not ever mentioning my service. I don't think any police blog is going to change anything.

---

2. Nearly all of the bloggers profiled in this chapter chose to remain anonymous, most fearing reprisals from managers in uniform who might not appreciate their comments.

The Policeman's Blog

David Copperfield (not his real name, in case you skipped reading Dickens) calls his blog, The Policeman's Blog (`www.coppersblog.blogspot.com`), with the subtitle, "a Journey into the mad, mad world of the British underclass and the Public sector, where nothing is too insane for it to be written down and copied in triplicate" (see Figure 14-2). If you are looking for the ever-helpful, ever-cheerful bobby of televisionland, David is not going to be your role model.

Figure 14-2. *The Policeman's Blog*

Here is how David responded to my questions:

Q. *Why did you start* `http://www.coppersblog.blogspot.com`?

A. Policing is a fairly frustrating job, especially in the UK. I thought a blog would be a good way of relaxing and getting over the petty infuriations that seem to make up my working days. I also realized that victims who I met had no idea how their crime would be dealt with. I thought writing a blog would lift the lid in a fairly harmless way.

Q. *How did your fellow officers who knew you were blogging react?*

A. None of my fellow officers know I write (at least I hope they don't). You simply cannot keep a secret in the police, and if I told one person, within days I'm sure they would all know.

Q. *Why should police blog?*

A. Lots of people think they know about the police, but in reality, hardly anyone knows what uniformed police officers do all day. It's the public who pay our wages, so I think they should have at least some idea of where the money goes. This is especially important in the UK, where the public have virtually no say in how their neighborhoods get policed.

Q. *A lot of your posts describe the overwhelming bureaucracy your department puts in the way of actual policing. Is your blog, and other police blogs, just a way of venting or can blogs make change happen?*

A. The one thing I'm certain of is that my blog will have absolutely no effect on anything. Bureaucracy in the police is here to stay and nothing I, or anyone else, can say is going to change that. Despite lots of hype within the mainstream media, blogs really aren't read by that many people.

Q. *But I see from your posts' comments a lot of police constables feel just as frustrated with management/bureaucracy as you do. Do you think more should blog their experiences? If enough do, would things change?*

A. No, ordinary constables will never change anything, especially using the format of a blog (which can safely be ignored). When an ordinary constable writes a book which becomes a bestseller, then things might change.[3] For now though, the public will have to put up with the police service that they have. I would like to see more police blogs. In fact, I'd like to see more blogs by people working at the front line of government, as an antidote to the constant stream of government propaganda saying how good things are.

Q. *Why do you continue blogging?*

A. Although at first it started out as a personal thing, it has now become a focus for many officers unhappy at the direction the service is going. I like to think that I'm providing something for the officers at the bottom who get ignored most of the time.

It's the Law—Johnny Law

Somewhere in the American Southwest, Johnny Law has just started a new career in law enforcement and a blog about it, as shown in Figure 14-3. One thing you'll notice about Johnny's posts at `http://law-chronicles.blogspot.com`: they are extremely well written.

---

3. In fact, David *did* write a book, *Wasting Police Time: The Crazy World of the War on Crime* (Monday Books, 2006), available at Amazon UK (5 stars, 28 reviews) and other fine booksellers.

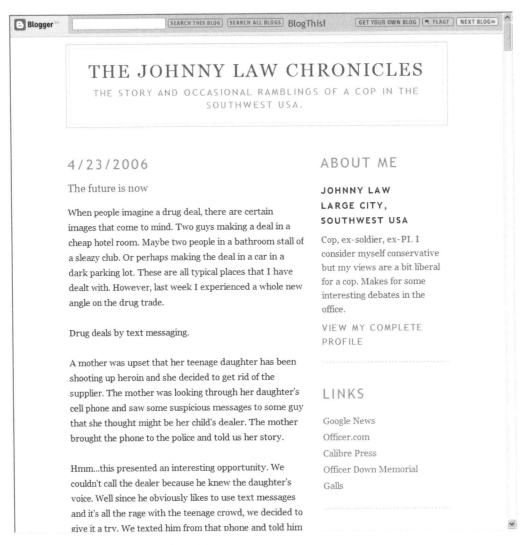

Figure 14-3. *The Johnny Law Chronicles*

I asked Johnny (not his real name, in case you wondered) some questions via email.

Q. *How did you get started blogging, and how are you liking it?*

A. I have always had a desire to write a book about my police experiences once I retire. To help preserve my memories for the book, I figured the best way to do it was to start some kind of journal. I kept putting it off until one day, I was surfing the Internet and came across a police blog (http://texas-music.blogspot.com). This guy really impressed me with his writing, and I started looking at other blogs out there. After reading a few different ones, I started thinking that a blog would be a good way to start my journal and practice my writing skills.

I am really enjoying it so far. It is very therapeutic to be able to put my thoughts in writing. For example, the story I wrote about almost shooting the guy with the cell phone was something that I have been wanting to get off my chest for a long time. Writing about it seemed to be a release of some sort. Now, when something happens at work that I find interesting, I start thinking about how I want to describe it in my blog.

Q. *Do your fellow officers know about your blog?*

A. Two officers who I consider close friends know about the blog. I told them because I trust them and I wanted someone to act as a bullshit meter to prevent me from exaggerating things. They are supportive but constantly warn me to not write things that would get me trouble. Because of that, I am always trying to keep from being too critical about my department or coworkers. However, I don't have a problem complaining about general police problems.

Q. *Your world is unlike anything we've ever seen on television about what cops do. It's jolting to read. Why is there such a disconnect?*

A. I think that Hollywood has given people unrealistic expectations. People expect you to be able to shoot the knife out of a person's hand. Cases should be solved within a few days at the maximum. You should be able to fingerprint anything and come up with a match every time. People don't understand the limits of technology or about how overworked we are. They think we have all this high-tech equipment and can devote all our time on their one crime. I remember my reaction when I saw that the detectives on "CSI: Miami" drove a shiny Hummer 2. LOL—that is such bull. We drive Ford Tauruses with 80K+ miles on them.

Being a cop has ruined most cop movies for me. I can't watch them without complaining about the way they portray things. However, it would be a boring movie if it were 100% realistic. The hero would get in a gunfight that would last a couple of seconds and be chaotic. He would probably miss 75% of his shots and then be on restricted duty for several weeks during the investigation.

Q. *What has surprised you most about writing this blog?*

A. I think the biggest thing is that people are actually reading it! The site recently got over 1,000 hits. That is not that much traffic in the scheme of things, but it is very flattering to know that some people are reading about my experiences and coming back for more. I also always enjoy reading the comments that people leave. It seems that some are cops and others are civilians. I hope that I am able to help a few people see that police are human beings, too, and maybe be a little more understanding when they have to deal with us.

Q. *Do you have anything else you want to say?*

A. I hope to continue blogging for as long as I can. I think it is a great medium, and I read quite a few myself. Where else can you get insight into so many lives? I have come across blogs as varied as military recruiters to nightclub bouncers to strippers. It's like reality TV but with more substance and commentary.

Fear and the Knock at the Door

Being a cop is tough, but it's also tough on the wives, husbands, and significant others of police who must live with the possibility that their loved one might not come home tonight.

LAPD Wife (www.lapdwife.com) is a blog by "Renee" (see Figure 14-4), the wife of a veteran Los Angeles Police Department officer, whom you first met in Chapter 1. Renee posted this at her blog:

> *Life is a little different when you're married to a police officer. Sure, you have the same jobs as the other wives out there, the same household chores, child-rearing and everyday routines. But those little differences keep popping up, making you aware that this marriage isn't your stereotypical one.*

> *. . . the question I hear most of all is, "How do you deal with it? How does it not totally stress you out being married to a police officer?" There's no secret answer. No one thing to do. But it does help to have a network of friends in the same situation as you. Men and women you can turn to for advice, support, laughs and just to listen. Welcome to my life as an LAPD wife.*

RECENT POSTS

Ed Davis Memorial

Ring of Fire

Married to The Badge: Police Wives Unite!

Former LAPD Chief Ed Davis, 89

Married to The Badge: Viewer Statistics

Married to the Badge: Fantasy vs. Reality

Former Chief Ed Davis Update

Married to the Badge: Family Concerns

Married to the Badge: High Priority Issues

National Dispatchers' Week

RECENT COMMENTS

Ed Davis Memorial

The family of Ed Davis, the legendary former Chief of the Los Angeles Police Department and maverick three-term Republican State Senator who died Saturday, after a brief bout with pneumonia have announced a public memorial service to celebrate his life.

The celebration of life will take place on Thursday, May 4th at 2:30 pm at the Los Angeles Police Academy in Elysian Park, 1880 N, Academy Road, Los Angeles.

In lieu of flowers, the family requests that donations be made to The Los Angeles Police Memorial Foundation, which was established to provide assistance to families of police officers who were killed in the line of duty. Checks should be made payable out to the Los Angeles Police Memorial Foundation, 1880 N. Academy Dr., Los Angeles, CA 90012

April 26, 2006 in L.A. Insight | Permalink | Comments (1) | TrackBack (0)

Ring of Fire

ME & MY BLOG

Who Am I?

Want to be a guest writer here?

Email Me

BOOKS I'D RECOMMEND

Click here to purchase these books at Amazon.com. Select "Book Reviews" in the categories section on the left to read all about them.

How to Be the Funniest Kid in the Whole Wide World (or Just in Your Class)

Everyday Italian: 125 Simple and Delicious Recipes

I Love a Cop: What Police Families Need to Know

Figure 14-4. *LAPD Wife blog*

Renee was kind enough to answer my email questions at length.

Q. *Why did you start LAPD Wife?*

A. There were several reasons. Most importantly, to reach out to other spouses of police officers. The singularities of life married to a veteran LAPD narcotics police officer are very unique, and I was craving community and friendship with others who understood and could empathize. This city is so widespread, and people's lives are so hectic these days, this seemed like a good way to start. Second, I've always loved writing, and this blog was a way for me to develop my skills and put them in front the public eye for critique, however it may come. Third, to serve as a journal. So many colleagues always ask me what it's really like being married to an officer. "Is it just like in the movies?" This was my way of sharing.

Q. *What has been the reaction of your husband, friends, and others in the police community?*

A. My husband has always been very supportive. That said, this blog was started only after much careful consideration, mainly about the importance of protecting our identity and our safety. My friends that know about it are also very supportive. And excited—they are learning more about a part of me that they didn't know before. As for the general police community, the reactions have been mixed. I am amazed, actually, at the positive feedback overall I've received from other officers, their wives, and police admin. The *LAPD Blue Line* (the monthly union publication) lets me write columns at will and thanked me for bringing to light something they (as police officers) really hadn't considered much before (that extended family members of officers can often have as many issues to deal with as officers).

Police and their wives from around the nation and the world even have written me in support and admiration for talking about something so common, yet so hidden, that we all have in common. That said, there have been the few (thank goodness, only a very few) who say "shame on me" for talking about the deep, dark secrets of the police world. Or imply that I should just stay in my place and not be out talking about our life like this.

Q. *You recently published the results of a survey on your blog. Can you tell me about how you got the idea for that and what results really stand out to you?*

A. I was chatting once with a coworker of mine about how I wish I could know more about who reads my blog so that I could better write for that audience. She mentioned the website SurveyMonkey.com and how great a survey could help me with that. She was right. I fell in love with the idea immediately. And the feedback was tremendous.

What stood out to me is how amazing it is that wives of officers from around the nation, and even in other countries, have so many similar issues that concern us in our lives. Guns in the house, keeping our children protected from idiotic police stereotypes, worrying about our husbands when they are overdue from work, feelings of being left out from their "world" at work, etc. I started out writing this mainly for LAPD wives. Turns out I'm writing for all law enforcement wives out there. Military ones are starting to check in, too.

Q. *What has been the "official" reaction of the LAPD, if there has been one?*

A. Nothing official. The police union recognized me by letting me write as a columnist in their publication (as I mentioned above). The brass has made no comment, but I don't expect them to. I'm not a police officer. I don't answer to them, though I always strive to respect them and stand as a good example of the department and profession.

Q. *What does your blog accomplish that other forms of communication (the press, informal gatherings, etc.) can't?*

A. Personally, I've made friends through my blog throughout the country and in Europe that I never would have met otherwise. I've been encouraged and supported when I felt like giving it up. I've been inspired to volunteer more in services for police families, as other wives have shared stories of need and heartbreak that touch me. This blog also gave me a voice, one that after two years is respected and taken seriously. Sure, I could have written the occasional op-ed piece for the paper. But that would have only been once or twice a year at the most. This way, I've reached out, through a medium that many detractors of the profession frequent, and shown them a more humanized view of us.

Q. *How much time does your blog take and has it been worth it to you?*

A. A lot, really. I try to write at least three times a week. It has been two years now, and I'm still mostly sticking to that. Some nights I sacrifice an hour or two of sleep to write. And I toss and turn thinking of what to write next. I sometimes resent the blog and the time I'm spending with it instead of my family. (Hence the losing sleep. I write late at night when the kids are asleep, so I don't feel guilty about ignoring them for the computer.) But yes, yes, yes, it has been worth it. It has opened up possibilities for my future to me I never thought of before. And given me a sense of worth and a sense of wonder to help me keep going. I do not regret having this blog and really am grateful for the worlds it has opened up to me.

Blogging from the Ends of the Earth

There's another kind of front line: the frontline of science, where research gets done, theories are tested by facts, and scientists endure horrible conditions for the sake of expanding what we as a species know. It used to be the closest you got to such expeditions was watching old black-and-white movies and the occasional National Geographic special. No more. Blogging has connected scientists to other scientists, but it has also connected scientists to nonscientists in a way more real, immediate, emotional, and valuable than all the television specials. In this section, you'll meet two such blogging scientists working in Antarctica.

This Is Palmer Station, Antarctica

George Westby has a job in heaven or in a frozen hell, depending on your point of view. George is an environmental chemistry student at State University of New York, only he isn't in New York, or even North America; he is working at Palmer Station, Antarctica. His blog is Research in Antarctica (`http://antarcticresearch.blogspot.com`), as shown in Figure 14-5.

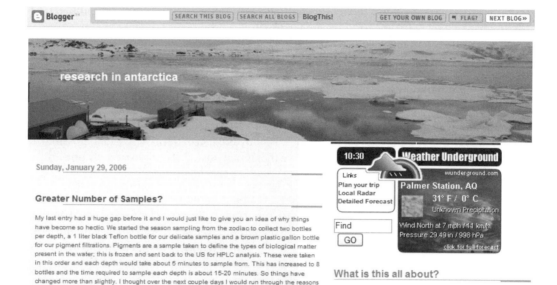

Sunday, January 29, 2006

Greater Number of Samples?

My last entry had a huge gap before it and I would just like to give you an idea of why things have become so hectic. We started the season sampling from the zodiac to collect two bottles per depth, a 1 liter black Teflon bottle for our delicate samples and a brown plastic gallon bottle for our pigment filtrations. Pigments are a sample taken to define the types of biological matter present in the water; this is frozen and sent back to the US for HPLC analysis. These were taken in this order and each depth would take about 5 minutes to sample from. This has increased to 8 bottles and the time required to sample each depth is about 15-20 minutes. So things have changed more than slightly. I thought over the next couple days I would run through the reasons for increasing the amount of samples and explain what these samples are used for.

Back when we were experiencing early growth of a pretty large phytoplankton bloom, we realized that the DMS samples (delicate gas samples) needed to be sampled out on the boat instead of trying to re-pour the samples after getting them home. The reason for this is that the phytoplankton are more apt to create DMS while being disrupted. There is not really any good way to keep from disrupting them while transferring them from the black bottle into a sample vial. This is one of the difficult sampling situations we had decided against back in the beginning of our stay. This is unfavorable for us due to the increased amount of time out in the boat pushing our very full day back and potentially sacrificing our ability to perform well on rough sea days. We fear this from the aspect of seasickness and loss of good sampling technique.

Since we started this type of sampling we have had better reproducibility until the bloom really started to produce. A couple samplings later it became obvious that there was still some DMS production occurring in the samples. Too many of the phytoplankton were getting into the samples so we had to resort to increasing our time out on the boat again. This time the answer was to pass the water through a Nytex mesh screen to remove a large portion of the phytoplankton. Since the transportation of the samples with the phytoplankton still in solution was the cause of extra DMS, this simple screening keeps the DMS levels stable and our analysis more exact.

The next issue...

Weather Underground

10:30

Links
Plan your trip
Local Radar
Detailed Forecast

Find
GO

wunderground.com

Palmer Station, AQ
31° F / 0° C
Unknown Precipitation

Wind North at 7 mph / 11 km/h
Pressure 29.49 in / 998 hPa
click for full forecast

What is this all about?

This blog will cover our group on the Antarctic Peninsula stationed at Palmer Station, a U.S. research installation. Here a team of two SUNY ESF students, I an Environmental Chemist (George Westby) and an Environmental Policy Major (Kerry McElroy) will be gathering data, and leading newcomers, on a project revealing pathways of organic sulfur. In this blog we will talk about our research and will also cover much of the social aspect of being on a lengthy research trip. Please ask any questions.

About Me

Name:George Westby
Location:Upstate NY, United States

I have been given the awesome opportunity to travel the world while finishing a Masters Degree in Chemistry. My family is the best thing on earth. I miss my cocker (quinlan). I am totally stoked to be back in Antarctica.

Figure 14-5. *Research in Antarctica blog*

Here's how George answered my questions about his blog:

Q. *Why did you decide to blog about your Antarctic experience?*

A. It has become more and more difficult to contact all of the important people on my email lists. There are so many people and so little extra time to send them personalized info on how things are going in my life and to show them all the cool things that I am seeing. How come I want people to know what is happening? The research that I am conducting is very important to the status of the global climate, and I think it's fun.

I also have enough going on these days that everything gets overlapped, and I end up forgetting about some of the really cool adventures, and the experimental experiences fade away much quicker. With a blog, I can send out one mass email at the beginning of an event with a link and tell them all what it is about and invite them to "Tune In."

This also allows them to choose whether they care enough to hear about this stuff and let them take their own time to come and check it out. This "check it out on your own time" is so that I am not that guy who sent out a million emails and ended up getting put into the junk mail filter.

Q. *Is Internet connectivity a problem?*

A. Connectivity can be an issue for research events. In Antarctica at Palmer station, we have a satellite Internet connection, which is on all of the time. This is not always the case for field work, so things have been made easier by Blogger. They have made it possible to email a specific account at Blogger to have that email posted. This is extremely powerful—all you need is to send a text email and you have a post.

The importance of this is most field projects include a minimum of two email connections a day to help keep in touch with family and important colleagues. This allows regular postings to your blog. It is also possible to text a post to your blog and even to call your blog and leave a voice posting. These things are way too cool. Thanks to Google, the makers of Blogger.

Q. *What's it like when people comment on one of your posts and you reply to them?*

A. Getting a comment is what blogging is all about. The more interest you inspire in your readers, the more they comment. You know that you are doing a decent job if people take the time to post a comment to your blog. It is not difficult, but nobody wants to give up their precious time to a cause they do not feel strongly about.

To answer your question more fully, seeing a comment pop up is invigorating and inspires good writing and continuous postings.

Blogging from Amundsen-Scott South Pole Station

What's life like in Antarctica? "When I'm not doing the incredibly important job of looking at the sky, spending time writing reports, or adding to the blog, I have a part-time job working in the South Pole Station Store (affectionately known as Pole-Mart)," says Neal Scheibe, who works as a research associate for Raytheon Polar Services Company (RPSC) at Amundsen-Scott South Pole Station, an American research station approximately about 100 meters from the South Pole. His blog is called Nowhere to Go But Up (`http://nowhere-to-go-but-up.blogspot.com`), as shown in Figure 14-6.

Q. *Why did you decide to blog your Antarctic experience?*

A. Originally, this started out as a way to keep in touch with relatives and friends back in the States. I was going to just send out a mass email, but a friend suggested that I start a blog. I felt like a blog was less intrusive than filling up everyone's inbox; people could check the blog at their leisure. Now I get more visits/comments from people that I've never met than from people I know.

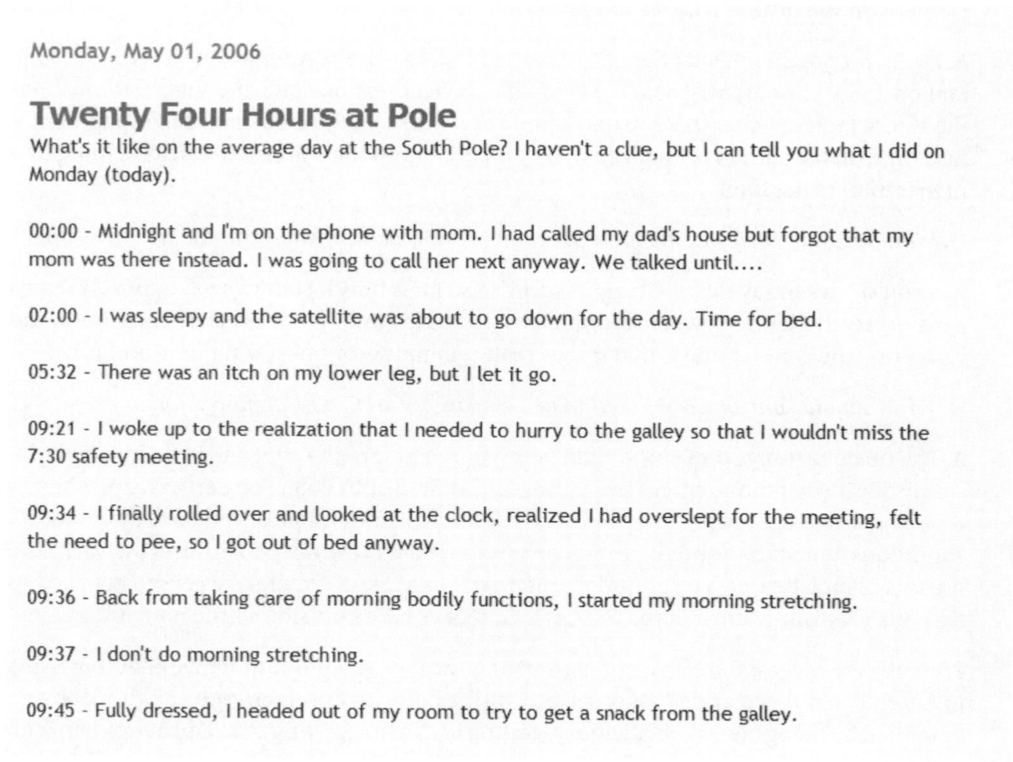

Monday, May 01, 2006

Twenty Four Hours at Pole

What's it like on the average day at the South Pole? I haven't a clue, but I can tell you what I did on Monday (today).

00:00 - Midnight and I'm on the phone with mom. I had called my dad's house but forgot that my mom was there instead. I was going to call her next anyway. We talked until....

02:00 - I was sleepy and the satellite was about to go down for the day. Time for bed.

05:32 - There was an itch on my lower leg, but I let it go.

09:21 - I woke up to the realization that I needed to hurry to the galley so that I wouldn't miss the 7:30 safety meeting.

09:34 - I finally rolled over and looked at the clock, realized I had overslept for the meeting, felt the need to pee, so I got out of bed anyway.

09:36 - Back from taking care of morning bodily functions, I started my morning stretching.

09:37 - I don't do morning stretching.

09:45 - Fully dressed, I headed out of my room to try to get a snack from the galley.

Figure 14-6. *Nowhere to Go But Up blog*

Q. *Is Internet connectivity a problem?*

A. At the South Pole, we have Internet access for about half the day. There are three satellites that fly over on consecutive runs. The time that they are overhead shifts by a few minutes each day, so we can't get online at the same time from day to day. Right now, I can only access the Internet at night, before going to bed. In a few weeks, it will be in the middle of the day, then in the morning, etc.

Q. *What's it like when people comment on one of your posts and you reply to them?*

A. The first time I got comments were from friends and relatives. They tended to be generic comments just letting me know that they were reading my blog. Most of the comments that I get from people I haven't met fall into one of three categories: 1) Are you really at the South Pole or is this a joke? 2) Wow, you're in such an amazing place. What's it like down there? 3) How do you handle/do _____? (Fill in the blank with some normal everyday activity.)

Many of the questions are just naive about Antarctica (Do you see polar bears?). Sometimes I get questions that really stump me or spur me to do a special posting on that topic. I try to answer every comment and visit every site of the commenters. I enjoy reading what they have to say as much as they might enjoy reading my stuff.

Q. *What do you do and who do you do it for?*

A. I work for Raytheon Polar Services Company (RPSC) at the Amundsen-Scott South Pole Station. I am a research associate. My job it to collect seismic data and information about the aurora for researchers back in the States. I also maintain the data-collecting equipment. Everyone on the station is involved in helping maintain the station as well as helping in preparation of the food.

Q. *What has surprised you the most about living and working in Antarctica?*

A. I would have to say that the biggest surprise so far is how fast things have gone. It seems like time really flies here, which is opposite what I expected. That may change as the winter wears on. The general rule is that things really get monotonous during June and July.

Q. *What should someone interested in working in Antarctica be prepared for?*

A. The obvious things that you should be prepared for are the cold and isolation. A warm, sunny day is still many degrees below freezing at the South Pole. You can never just hop in a car and cruise somewhere else either. At different Antarctic sites, you have different conditions, but at the South Pole it is very dry, so there is the need to drink extra water and use lots of moisturizer. The altitude is high, so it can take a couple of weeks to get used to that. It's very windy most of the time, which makes being outside a little more tricky.

Probably the biggest thing to be prepared for is the fact that the cumulative effects of being in Antarctica put you at risk every second you're here. Any problem you can think of is amplified by being here. A small injury, getting lost, a fire, getting sick, and a problem with a coworker are examples of things that are exacerbated by the environment. On a final note, anyone thinking about working in Antarctica should be prepared to go through a life-changing experience.

Greetings from Iraq

If the Vietnam War was the first televised war, the Iraqi war, now entering its fourth year, has become the blogged and podcasted war, with American servicemen and servicewomen making most, but not all, of the Internet coverage.

In the email interviews that follow, I've steered clear of the politics of the situation as much as possible. Not because the bloggers who kindly took the time to respond did—they all have strong political feelings—but because this is a book about blogging, not politics.

An Atheist Soldier

SPC Brian D. Kinser (his real name) of the 7th Battalion, 159th Aviation Regiment (US Army) is not your typical enlisted man in Iraq. He blogs and podcasts, and his wife back in the US blogs, too. His blog at http://godlesskinser.com, as of May 2006, is shown in Figure 14-7.[4]

---

4. As of the end of December 2006, Brian Kinser had returned home from Iraq, left the Army, and archived his blog, An Atheist Soldier. He has started a new blog (www.watchitburn.org/blog) to supplement his podcast.

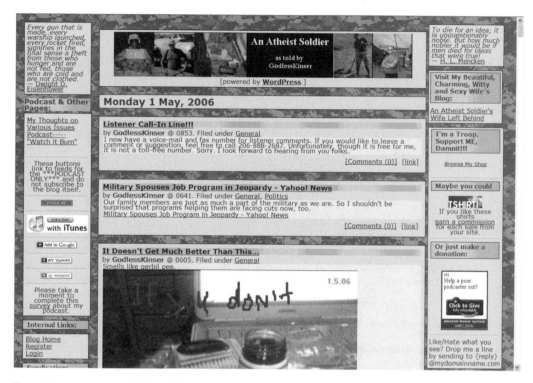

Figure 14-7. *An Atheist Soldier blog*

Q. *Why did you start your blog, An Atheist Soldier (*http://godlesskinser.com*)?*

A. I first started my blog on a free service called tblg.com when I was first in Iraq in 2003. I mostly did it because I was bored, but also partly in response to how much I saw religiosity being conflated with patriotism. I wanted people to know that there were indeed "atheists in foxholes," despite what so many claim. I wanted it to be known that, though we face death, we do not turn to superstition for our courage, but know that it is something all of us have within us. I also wanted to make the bigger point that one can be moral and happy without being motivated to do so by fear of punishment or expectation of reward, which I feel is a shallow and selfish reason for doing what we all know to be right.

Q. *What has been the reaction to it by other soldiers at LSA Anaconda, Iraq?*

A. I don't know how many of the other service members here (we are a mixed post with sailors and marines, as well, but it is primarily an Air Force base, with airmen being the largest population and soldiers the second) are aware of my blog, but the ones in my unit who are seem to be fairly positive about it. Though they don't always agree with my political views, they respect that I am sincere about them and that they come from a good place inside me.

Q. *Do you think your blog, and others like it, helps them understand what you're going through in Iraq, and why?*

A. I'm not sure that mine does, as I don't generally focus on the experience here. My Military Occupational Specialty (MOS) is in short supply here, so I do not get outside the wire, and this base is so large (at least 12 miles in circumference) that we generally don't know what goes on elsewhere on the post.

Because of this, I do not have a very definitive grasp on current local events, unlike my first time here. Our camp then was so small that we heard every mortar or rocket that was launched into or over it, usually directly over my platoon's tents. Because of this, I generally leave the "war correspondent" style to those who are more directly involved in the tactical situation here.

Q. *How does the chain of command feel about milblogs? And how do they feel about your blog?*

A. I don't know how my higher chain-of-command feels about it, but I figure in this case no news is good news, so to speak. I do know my team leader and squad leader seem to enjoy most of what I have to say and have been generally sympathetic, but never negative.

Q. *The positions you take in your blog are very different from what many other milblogs have to say. What's been the reaction of those other milblogs to yours?*

A. I don't read other milblogs, so I can't really say if they have reacted to me at all.

I have been made aware of how different mine is from the vast majority of others by emails and comments I have received from readers. These generally come in the usual form of describing my viewpoint as "refreshing," "breath of fresh air," or "a lone candle in the darkness."

I am also pleased to note that I was asked permission by the Library of Congress to archive my blog (which I have agreed to), was asked to appear on "NewsHour" to discuss milblogging, and was approved by our division's Public Affairs Office (though the taping ultimately was cancelled), and have been favorably mentioned on Daily Kos. I don't like to brag, but those things really were powerful affirmations for me.

My favorite description actually came from a detractor, though. She described me as "the inane bellowings of the old drunk at the end of the bar, who everyone works hard to ignore, though he spoils the party for everyone else." I do not censor my comments beyond removal of commercial spam, so I think the relative lack of negative responses there is a good sign, though my relative obscurity or their unwillingness to make an effort may be more the reason.

Q. *I notice you're considering running for office in your home state of Oregon when your enlistment is up. In one post, you say, "I am a loud opinionated blowhard with a soft-spot for workers, wounded warriors and wetlands and am fully ready and capable of kissing as many hands and shaking as many babies as it takes to get some changes made." Where do you see blogging fitting into politics?*

A. I think that with the current media climate in our nation being so heavily skewed to suit the interests of its corporate owners, the blogosphere will continue to become more important in American politics. I think I will use it, as it already has been, to bring attention to issues and viewpoints the "big-money media" tends to minimize or ignore.

Howard Dean and Dennis Kucinich, and others, whether one agrees with their ideas or not, have shown that the Internet can be an amazing tool to organize and energize the electorate. "Netroots" organizing is now supplementing traditional "grassroots" efforts, and will likely continue to grow in effectiveness and use as its capabilities are more fully explored and refined.

Q. *What would you like nonmilitary readers of your blog to understand about why you blog, and your experience in Iraq?*

A. I would like them to take away an understanding that my blog is meant to show that there is more to an issue than a 30-second sound bite and that the best means to insure healthy democracy is to educate yourself. I would also like them to see that we in uniform are not a monolithic block of identical viewpoints, but that to be patriotic one does not need to agree with everything that comes down from on high. The real face of patriotism is that of the person who asks if there are things wrong with their country and, if they find there are, then works to fix them.

As for my experience in Iraq, I would want them to see that even when soldiers do not agree with policy, they act according to their honor and obey lawful orders, as they have sworn to do. In a situation such as this one, as probably in every military action since even before the Battle of Kadesh, soldiers generally don't fight for ideology once the fighting starts. They fight for each other. It isn't up to us to decide policy; we are just the instruments for carrying it out. In the United States, it is up to the civilian leadership (Congress or the Supreme Court in extreme cases) to decide the legality of the policy.

Q. *Any advice for others in the military who want to blog?*

A. I would say, first and foremost, insure that you maintain Operational Security (OPSEC). Be sure that you are not endangering the lives of your brothers and sisters in uniform. Secondly, be sure your chain-of-command knows of your blog. You don't have to give them a detailed description, just the URL and a basic overview. Third, I would say that if you are going to discuss politics, be familiar with DoD Directive 1334.10 "Political Activities by Members of the Armed Forces," as well as the policy on milblogs. Finally, and most importantly, tell the truth.

Q. *Can I/should I use your actual name, rank?*

A. Go right ahead, and thank you for your interest.

Currently Stationed in the Sandbox

Sure Fire, an MP now stationed in Iraq, is the primary author of the Pass the Brass blog (http://passthebrass.com), shown in Figure 14-8. PasstheBrass.com "is meant to follow Sure Fire throughout his years in service and to catalog his thoughts and most of the events that have affected him."

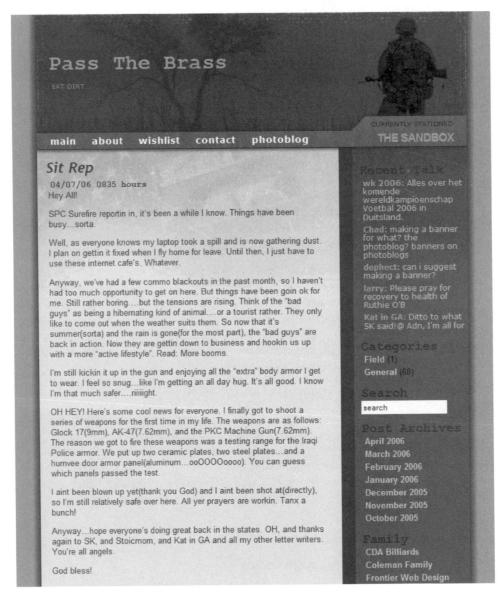

Figure 14-8. *Pass the Brass blog*

Here's how Sure Fire answered my questions:

Q. *Can you tell me how PasstheBrass.com got started?*

A. PasstheBrass.com (PTB) was originally the brainchild of my brother Chad, the owner of PasstheAmmo.com (PTA) [http://passtheammo.com]. The original intent was to simply catalogue my experiences in the military. The reason the name is so similar is because it was also originally designed to be a sister site of PTA. What I didn't know was how regulated the whole thing would turn out to be.

Q. *What do you feel you get out of blogging? What do you think the people who read your blog get?*

A. I never really thought that I would get anything out of blogging except the satisfaction of my family and friends knowing what I was going through. The good times, the bad times, all that nonsense. As it turns out, blogging is one of the best ways to vent any emotions one wants. I use blogging to try to help people see what I see in the military. To sort of go through the motions without actually having to join. And I hope that that is exactly what my readers are getting from my postings.

Q. *What's been the reaction of your fellow troopers to you blogging?*

A. There are two parts to this answer, cuz there are two parts to my "fellow troopers." There are those enlisted and alongside me in the lower enlisted ranks, and then there are those in authority. The former, thinking that what I'm doing is genuinely funny and unique, while the latter sees the security risk as well as the other risks associated with free information. It's all understandable, but kind of a sick irony when you think about it. Goes back to the whole "join to protect free speech, and give it up when you swear in" bit. Just technicalities, I'm afraid. Everyone has got their rules they have to follow.

Q. *Do your commanders know, and if they do/did what would be their reaction?*

A. Oh my command knows for sure. I've been noticed at both of my duty stations I've been assigned to. My previous station saw my site as only a potential risk of Operations Security (OPSEC), whereas my current station actually saw my darker humor as a negative picture of the Army. I've caught some flak for the site.

The command group is only trying to maintain the standards that have been so long in standing with the United States military and I am not one to try to break them down. I just want to be able to show people "how we do" with my personal taste added. It just points back to the quote, "People sleep peacefully at night because rough men stand ready to do great violence on their behalf." —George Orwell

I've actually been blogging since October 2004, which you will see by my first post. I removed a years' worth of blogging, after some hardcore crackdown by the higher-ups. Well, I'm storing it offline at least. I decided to start fresh, and to stick to the rules a bit closer.

Q. *I see more than a few of your commenters are talking to each other as well. Did they know each other before you started blogging?*

A. My blog has become a small hub where a handful of people from around the States enjoy my material and have come to enjoy each other's conversation. The only people on the site who know each other are my friends and family from back home.

Other than that, everyone else has come to meet each other through my site as well as other milblogs. A warm feeling indeed, to be able to help others meet new and interesting people through my writings.

Q. *I see your brother Chad handles the mechanics of keeping your blog going. Good way to go for deployed bloggers?*

A. My brother has a side business building websites, and he does them for a hobby as well. So he enjoys moderating the place, as well as giving it any upgrades or maintenance it might require. But it's nice knowing that if there's a problem with the site, he can get it back in working order. He has a bit of a head start over what most other brothers might bring to the table. Hahaha!

Q. *Any suggestions for other soldiers who want to blog?*

A. First, follow the rules of the road. Anyone and their mother can access the Internet, including our enemies. Try to stay within reason and not give out any secrets, huh? Also, don't bother listing company names and such, as it will usually lead to you getting found out. Haha!

I have also found that brutal honesty and core feelings are a big hit with the public. People like to see how we soldiers really feel sometimes. All they see are our products. The mainstream media never shows them our personalities.

New Front Lines Recap

Television wars and television cop and doctor shows have reduced the toil, suffering, and cost of people who walk the front lines to fit nicely between commercials. Blogging has the potential to take back reality from the hands of clever marketers and reconnect us—the civilians—with the people at the front lines of our streets and battlefields.

If you're one of those people—the doctors who save our lives, the scientists who expand our knowledge, the cops who keep us safe, the troops who didn't ask to go to war, and others in the trenches—blogging is a way to deal with the stress and to explain to the rest of us the anguishes and triumphs of what you do.

If you, like me, are incredibly lucky to live a life where you don't have to make life-and-death decisions every day, blogging is way to understand these brave men and women, and pay a tiny part of what you owe them by giving them your attention, interest, and time. They all deserve it.

Your Action Tasks

If you are on the front lines of your community, your unusual profession, or an actual shooting war, here are a few starter suggestions:

What do I talk about? Anything you want—it's your blog! But keep in mind you probably have two audiences: people like you and people unlike you. The first group will get the lingo you use day to day; the second won't. Decide early on if your blog is for others in your profession or not. If not, make the effort to explain when you write the terms and abbreviations you use.

Be anonymous. Whether you walk a beat or drive a tank, start your blog anonymously. In uniform, the rules—both written and unwritten—are different than other occupations. The Electronic Frontier Foundation (`www.eff.org/Privacy/Anonymity/blog-anonymously.php`) has a great guide to blogging anonymously. Read it before you start.

Be careful what you say. Before you finalize a post, give it a second read-through. Is there anything in your post that could be compromising?

It's all about the conversation. Respond to commenters. They may not agree with you, but the more you respond, the more likely they'll understand your point of view.

And here are a few other blog points to consider:

Don't tolerate spam or insults. This is your blog. Don't hesitate to delete spam or insulting comments.

Prune/fertilize your blogroll. As you build your blog, periodically add/edit your blogroll of similarly minded bloggers.

Who's talking about you? One very good way to expand and improve your blog is to go to sites like IceRocket (`http://blogs.icerocket.com`) and Technorati (`www.technorati.com`), plug in the name of your blog, and see what people are saying about you. Then go talk to them and talk about them on your blog.

CHAPTER 15

■ ■ ■

Welcome to Your Future

Concluding chapters in computer books tend to come in several flavors: the key points about Product X conclusion, the thank god this is the last chapter conclusion, and even the future is so bright you need sunglasses conclusion.

After spending a year researching and interviewing for this book, I don't pretend for a minute to be able to predict what the blogosphere as a whole is going to look like in five months, let alone five years. Still, I would like to go out on a limb here and saw it off after me by making eight predictions about the future of blogging and your future because of blogging. Feel free to laugh uproariously at them or ponder their impact on you as you like.

Blogging Is Still in Its Early Days and Will Continue to Grow Explosively

Okay, this is a safe prediction to make. The number of blogs has been doubling every six months or so, and yet only the really early adopters are blogging.

According to a Pew Internet and American Life study in July 2006 (`www.pewinternet.org/PPF/r/186/report_display.asp`), about 12 million American adults currently blog, but more than four times that many—57 million American adults—read blogs. That 12 million is only 8 percent of all American adults who use the Net. What's clear from previous studies and how blogs work is that the blog reader of today often becomes the blog writer of tomorrow.

Or consider Technorati CEO David Sifry's quarterly "State of the Blogosphere" for October 2006, shown in Figure 15-1.

David Sifry's count of worldwide active bloggers (people who posted in the last three months)—55 percent of 57 million, or 31.5 million—is in line with the numbers stated in the Pew Internet and American Life study.

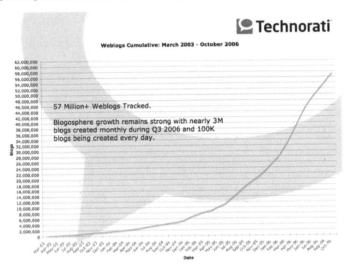

Currently Tracking More than 57 Million Blogs and Counting.

Figure 15-1. *The blog power curve*

Barring disaster, it's a safe bet that by 2008, something approaching *10 percent* of all Americans will be blogging one way or another. Numbers in the UK, Japan, and the rest of Europe will lag by about a year, with other countries each following their own version of this growth curve. Worldwide, I would conservatively bet 50 million people will be actively blogging by 2008, and 100 million by 2010.

The bottom line: When 10 percent of a country does something, that country is going to change. The next seven predictions are based on that.

The Problems with Comments Will Get Solved

If you blog or read blogs, it won't take long for you to realize not everything is happy-happy when it comes to blog comments. Specifically, two problems exist:

How do you know when someone responds to your comment? While several solutions exist for finding who has responded to comments you've made at blogs (Commentful, co.mments, and coComment, as discussed in Chapter 2), this is still a largely broken part of the blogosphere. What's missing is a mechanism for this that's as easy as email and just as universal.

How do you prevent spam comments? Will ever-increasing levels of spam comments and spam blogs degrade blogging in the same way spam has degraded email?[1] While several excellent tools can filter out *most* spam comments—most notably Akismet (http://akismet.com), as shown in Figure 15-2—the problem is getting worse, not better. Again, as the blogosphere scales up, the problem multiplies and the need for solutions grows.

---

1. As of November 2006, 91 percent of all email is now spam according to one email security company, as reported at http://searchsecurity.techtarget.com/originalContent/0,289142,sid14_gci1229172, 00.html.

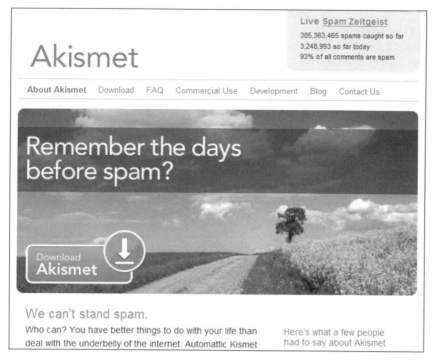

Figure 15-2. *Akismet*

Fortunately, if one thing is clear about how the Internet has evolved, especially over the past decade, it's that problems turn into new, important companies fairly quickly. I'm optimistic that the vision of becoming the next multibillion-dollar Google is going to continue to fuel attempts by companies, large and small, and one or more of them will succeed.

The bottom line: While comment spam and spam blogs will continue to be churned out by the millions by zombified Windows XP PCs all over the world, smart, hungry programmers will find a way to beat this disease, and in the process, build new companies, large and small.[2]

Okay, so much for the safe predictions. Fair warning: The next six predictions are more out there.

In the Global Online Society, Blogging Will Be a Critical Differentiator

As more of the economy—from the things we buy, to the people we work with, to the ways we interact—continues to move online, blogging becomes a critical skill for defining who you are.

Whether it's posting reviews at Amazon or a thousand other online stores, participating in the nascent citizen journalism movement, blogging for friends and family at Vox or Blogger, or having your say on TypePad—all of these forms of blogging are discoverable online. To a large degree online, you are what Google can find about you.

---

2. I also believe Good will triumph over Evil—which, come to think of it, is the same thing.

If you Google "Bob Walsh" (also known as ego-surfing), the first and third entries are my main blogs at ToDoOrElse.com and mymicroisv.com, which is an experience I think most bloggers who have been at it for more than a year would share. And that's fine by me.

Whether you are in a business or profession where you define yourself or you work for a company or organization, blogging can profoundly accelerate your career. Consider Marshall Kirkpatrick, who got noticed because of his blogging skills, or Microsoft's Don Dodge, who had this to say about how blogging has enhanced his career:

> *Blogs are the easiest way to gain a company-wide reputation at Microsoft. Of course, there are more than 3,000 employees blogging, so it takes a lot to get noticed. My blog has been picked up by* BusinessWeek, CNN/Money, Business 2.0, Seattle Post Intelligencer, Fortune, Barron's, *and many others, so my blog has definitely built a reputation inside Microsoft and outside as well. There is no way I could have gained as much visibility in the normal course of my job. Blogging is a great platform to express your views and influence public perception.*
>
> *Blogging is now part of my performance metrics as a technical evangelist and business development executive. It is a critical part of my job.*

The bottom line: Simply put, for those of us lucky enough to be part of the emerging online society and economy, the problem is too much choice. Blogs and blog writing can be the critical factor for deciding who to hire, who to work with, and who to listen to.

In the Global Online Society, Time Is the Ultimate Scarce Resource

Of course, every brave new world has its own brave new problems. At the top of the list of problems for the blogosphere is that there isn't enough attention to go around. I could spend every hour of every day reading great incisive posts by blogging giants across the world, and nothing else. How do you cope with information overload when the overload is exponentially growing?

The short answer is you can't do it alone. No matter how good your computer information skills are, no matter what software gets designed, there is no way to keep up with most of the information flow we increasingly float around in, let alone all of it.

That's where a little help from your online friends and their online friends comes in. I predict one strong trend in blogging will be the growing importance of blogging networks whose goal is to provide above-average information and content.

On one hand, sheer numbers will mean each of us in the blogosphere will need to become highly selective in who we read, listen to, and watch. On the other hand, being able to rely on trusted others who have spent some of their attention creating something becomes a powerful way of leveraging your time.

Visit some of the 9rules network of bloggers, whom you met in Chapter 13. Or have a look at the eighth most linked-to blog Technorati ranked today (74,862 links from 14,217 blogs on December 1, 2006): The Huffington Post (www.huffingtonpost.com). Or take a quick look at a blog network I came across just yesterday, TheGoodBlogs network (www.thegoodblogs.com), as shown in Figure 15-3.

Now it's not just one blog raising its hand and asking for my attention, it is entire networks, which I can choose to pay attention to or ignore.

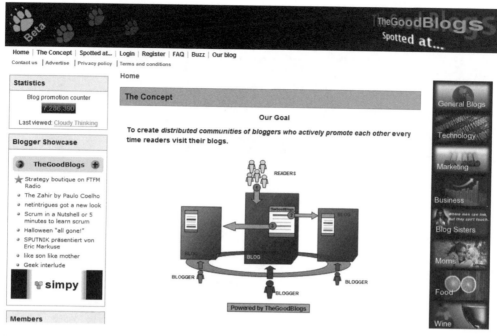

Figure 15-3. *TheGoodBlogs network*

The bottom line: I predict that in the months and years ahead, creating, joining, and meeting the expectations of blogging networks will increasingly determine which public blogs succeed and which ones fail.

Welcome to the Neighborhood, Your Global Blogging Network

Not everyone wants a public blog. The Pew Internet study I cited earlier found that 37 percent of the bloggers surveyed named "my life and experiences" as a primary topic of their blog. Six Apart, arguably one of the most blog-savvy collections of people in the world, is betting heavily on Vox with its blogging for friends and family approach, as shown in Figure 15-4.

Friend and neighbor networks like Vox and MySpace are the flip side of the rising importance of blogging networks (see the previous section) and the world having become a lonely place (see the next section).

As more and more people relate to each other and converse with each other via blogs, it becomes more natural to use blogs as a way of keeping up with your online network of friends and family.

And as much as it pains me to say this, personal blogging is very much a generational thing. Bloggers tend to be young,[3] and socializing via the blogosphere/social networks is easier

---

3. The Pew Internet and American Life study in July 2006 (www.pewinternet.org/PPF/r/186/report_display.asp) found that "The most distinguishing characteristic of bloggers is their youth. More than half (54 percent) of bloggers are under the age of 30."

when you've never lived in a world without computers and the Internet. Old ways of doing things get replaced by new ways of doing things by younger people.

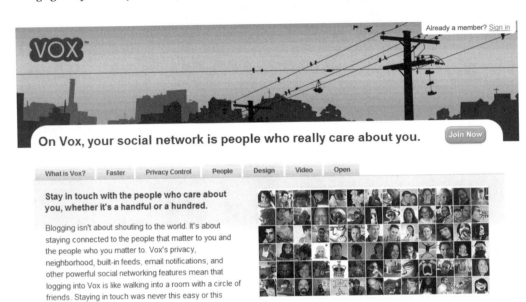

Figure 15-4. *Vox focuses on your social network.*

Consider 30-year-old Canadian television personality and total geek Amber MacArthur, whose blogs at TypePad (see Figure 15-5), MySpace, and Vox (to name three) keep her in touch with her fans and friends.

With regard to the photo in Figure 15-5, Amber posted this (http://ambermac.typepad.com/ambermac/2006/11/and_you_think_w.html):

> *My parents just emailed me this great pic, which is from one of their colleagues (David) who works with them on Rebuild Ampara—a tsunami reconstruction project they run in eastern Sri Lanka. David was driving back to my parents' house in SL* when he snapped this photo.*
>
> *Now like all good tech kids, my brother Jeff and I are making sure that my folks are using all the right web tools to get the word out about rebuilding Ampara.*

I asked Amber, via email, if she found herself increasingly keeping up on her network of friends/acquaintances via their blog/social network posts. "Yes, when I tell stories about what's new in my life, even my mom comments that she read about that on my blog," Amber replied.

The bottom line: Amber MacArthur is in many ways the poster girl for living in the blogosphere. But as you'll see when you blog, your network of online friends turns to your blog to keep in touch.

« How well do you know your Web 2.0? Take the test | Main
| Don't call me, I'm watching YouTube »

November 27, 2006

And you think we have traffic problems...

(Road to Ampara District, Sri Lanka - Nov. 27/06)

My parents just emailed me this great pic, which is from one of
their colleagues (David) who works with them on Rebuild
Ampara - a tsunami reconstruction project they run in eastern
Sri Lanka. David was driving back to my parents' house in SL*
when he snapped this photo.

ABOUT

WHAT I DO

Subscribe to this blog's feed

MY ONLINE LIFE

Amber Mac on
 myspace®
a place for you

CNI VIDS THIS WEEK

Top 10 web videos ever
LonelyGirl15 is a fake
Canadian Idiot?
Modern-day Robin Hood
Death creeps up on us online
SF blogger still in jail
Is Mahir the real Borat?

I SUPPORT

Figure 15-5. *Amber MacArthur's blog*

The World Has Become a Lonely Place; Blogging Can Change That

It used to be that people—prospective customers, clients, friends, and even spouses—learned about you by being plugged into a community and via the network of people knowing people face to face. In the online world, it doesn't work that way, but there's still the need to know who you might be doing business with or might be interested in personally.

Blogs and social networking are filling the vacuum created by the failure of industrial society's institutions and practices to keep up, says futurist and author Alvin Toffler, and I think he's right. Here's what Mr. Toffler told me in part during an interview in August 2006:

Q. *One thing that's happening very quickly online is the creation of these new social networks like MySpace and CyWorld and many others, where people sharing interests, or even not, are coming together completely outside the traditional industrial framework of association. Do you think that these networks are just an outgrowth of the technological toys that are now out there that make it possible, or is something deeper going on there from your point of view?*

A. I would sense that something deeper is going on. I'm not sure I know what that is. I think what we're seeing in one respect is, again, the dehomogenization of our society, and the increasing complexity and diversity of the system. And also one could make a kind of case for the historical reversion to a preindustrial system, but now on a high-technology basis.

For example, it used to be the only people you knew were the people in your village, but you knew everything about them. Nothing was private in the village. Then came the industrial revolution, and we had working-class neighborhoods but it was urban, and people didn't know each other as well, and a lot was written about loneliness and so forth and so on. Now, it's possible to create digital villages in which people know a lot about each other, although they may not know what is true or what is false.

People are doing good things perhaps, but doing them with no longer focusing their identity necessarily on the company they work for, or the bureaucratic organization, or the geographic organization they may be involved with. This may not provide their whole identity, but it could provide a significant piece of their identity.

Q. *Their online identity?*

A. Oh no, their real identity. Their real identity, whatever that is, can be influenced and shaped or reshaped by their activities online.

I know, for example, someone who plays poker online. And theoretically, the function of that is to play poker, but, in fact, the people in the game are getting to know each other, and some have visited one another. So a little social organism is sort of growing up, and to the degree that has happened, it seems to me that a lot of those . . . well, it's like "let me start at a different place." Much of this activity—an enormous amount of it I would say—is a reflection of a single word: loneliness, in our society.

Q. *And I thought that geeks were the only ones who were lonely.*

A. I think there is an enormous amount of loneliness in this society, at not only the young ages—and teenagers are frequently lonely—but adults who were cut loose from a company to which they had devoted their efforts for years. Or people who have moved frequently or into a new community, they find the new community so different from the old. I just think America is steeped in loneliness, and that a lot of going online is a way to assuage that loneliness.

Q. *Is it an American phenomenon of American origin, or is it an industrial breakdown phenomenon? In other words, in your travels, have you seen the same thing in, say, Europe, the UK, Japan?*

A. No, I think that of all those, Japan is going through some big changes along these lines also. But Europe far less, and that's because Europeans have moved less quickly toward a third-wave economy and society. They are studiously examining the books of the past, and year by year continue—that they're going to be the most, the best, the fastest, the quickest, the smartest third-wave economy on the planet—but they do nothing.

So they are not yet at the stage of this transformation that we are, and therefore, it seems they're complacent about their society. They don't know what's going to hit them.

The bottom line: The blogosphere is above all else a network of people connecting to other people, and that connecting is something we as a species and we as a society deeply crave.

Blogging Is Reinventing Journalism

Think back to Chapter 10 on the new fourth estate. The message of that chapter is that blogging has the potential to break up a lot of logjams we've taken for granted for the past several generations.

Note that I said "potential." If you think either traditional politicians or news/entertainment conglomerates are going to peacefully give up their power to shape and control to bloggers, you are very mistaken. They will fight; they will rail against the growing threat to Our Way (their way of doing business, that is); they will be dragged kicking and screaming all the way to the future; but dragged they will be.

But if you are powerful and have a secret in this world, blogs are not the simple-minded unquestioning media you're used to spinning. Be it former US Congressman Mark Foley's first exposure as a sexual-predator-in-waiting, at `stopsexpredators.blogspot.com`, or former US Senator George Allen's revealing racist remarks, shown to the world on YouTube (`www.youtube.com/watch?v=r9Oz0PMnKwI`) and linked to by countless blogs, blogs have not been kind to people in public positions of trust who have something to hide.

Whether it's the next incumbent senator who thinks he can safely say one thing to one audience and something else elsewhere, or it's media networks clinging to the "we make content, you consume it" model, blogging technology and the Internet have the force of the sea, and politicians and mainstream media are in the riptide.

The bottom line: Bloggers and online crowd-sourced muckraking projects are going to put journalism back into the media, much to the consternation of not-so "public servants" across the world and at all levels of government.

The Future of Blogging Is Up to You

Here's my final prediction: What blogging will become is up to you. While hundreds of thousands of blogs up to now have made the blogosphere the wild, entertaining, thought-provoking connected place it is, you and *tens of millions* of your new online friends, business contacts, and acquaintances will make it what it will be. We all make the future one day at a time, and nowhere is that more true than online.

I hope this book on writing your own invitation to the global party called the blogosphere helps you start or improve your blog. Drop me a line at bobw@safarisoftware.com, or stop by my blogs at mymicroisv.com, ToDoOrElse.com, or ClearBlogging.com, and let me know how you're doing. Be seeing you!

-30-

(That's old reporter-speak for "You've come to the end of the story, now get out there and do something!")

Index

Find it faster at http://superindex.apress.com

Find it faster at http://superindex.apress.com

You Need the Companion eBook

Your purchase of this book entitles you to buy the companion PDF-version eBook for only $10. Take the weightless companion with you anywhere.

We believe this Apress title will prove so indispensable that you'll want to carry it with you everywhere, which is why we are offering the companion eBook (in PDF format) for $10 to customers who purchase this book now. Convenient and fully searchable, the PDF version of any content-rich, page-heavy Apress book makes a valuable addition to your programming library. You can easily find and copy code—or perform examples by quickly toggling between instructions and the application. Even simultaneously tackling a donut, diet soda, and complex code becomes simplified with hands-free eBooks!

Once you purchase your book, getting the $10 companion eBook is simple:

➊ Visit **www.apress.com/promo/tendollars/**.

➋ Complete a basic registration form to receive a randomly generated question about this title.

➌ Answer the question correctly in 60 seconds, and you will receive a promotional code to redeem for the $10.00 eBook.

2560 Ninth Street • Suite 219 • Berkeley, CA 94710

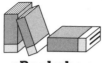

eBookshop

THE EXPERT'S VOICE™

Offer valid through 8/12/07.

FIND IT FAST
with the Apress *SuperIndex*™

Quickly Find Out What the Experts Know

Leading by innovation, Apress now offers you its *SuperIndex*™, a turbocharged companion to the fine index in this book. The Apress *SuperIndex*™ is a keyword and phrase-enabled search tool that lets you search through the entire Apress library. Powered by dtSearch™, it delivers results instantly.

Instead of paging through a book or a PDF, you can electronically access the topic of your choice from a vast array of Apress titles. The Apress *SuperIndex*™ is the perfect tool to find critical snippets of code or an obscure reference. The Apress *SuperIndex*™ enables all users to harness essential information and data from the best minds in technology.

No registration is required, and the Apress *SuperIndex*™ is free to use.

❶ Thorough and comprehensive searches of over 300 titles

❷ No registration required

❸ Instantaneous results

❹ A single destination to find what you need

❺ Engineered for speed and accuracy

❻ Will spare your time, application, and anxiety level

Search now: *http://superindex.apress.com*